MARKETS IN EARLY MEDIEVAL EUROPE

Markets in Early Medieval Europe

Trading and 'Productive' Sites, 650–850

Edited by Tim Pestell and Katharina Ulmschneider

WINDgather PRESS

Markets in Early Medieval Europe

Published by: Windgather Press Ltd, 29 Bishop Road, Bollington, Macclesfield, Cheshire SK10 5NX, UK

Distributed by: Central Books, 99 Wallis Road, London E9 5LN

British Library Cataloguing-in-Publication Data
A catalogue record for this book is available from the British Library

ISBN 0 9538630 7 7 (hardcover)

Typeset and originated by Carnegie Publishing Ltd,
Chatsworth Road, Lancaster
Printed and bound by The Cromwell Press, Trowbridge

Contents

List of Illustrations

Figures

Tables

Contributors

Mark Blackburn *Department of Coins and Medals, Fitzwilliam Museum, Cambridge*

Stuart Brookes *Institute of Archaeology, University College, London*

James Campbell *Worcester College, University of Oxford*

David Griffiths *Kellogg College, University of Oxford*

Lars Jørgensen *Department of Danish Prehistory, National Museum, Copenhagen, Denmark*

Kevin Leahy *North Lincolnshire Museum, Scunthorpe*

Jacques Le Maho *CNRS, Rouen, France*

Michael Metcalf *Department of Coins, Ashmolean Museum, Oxford*

Matthew Moran *School of World Art Studies and Museology, University of East Anglia*

John Newman *Field Team, Archaeological Service, Suffolk County Council*

Ben Palmer *Exeter College, University of Oxford*

Tim Pestell *Department of Archaeology, Norwich Castle Museum*

Julian D. Richards *Department of Archaeology, University of York*

Andrew Rogerson *Finds Identification and Recording Service, Field Archaeology Division, Norfolk County Council*

Peter Sawyer *Trondheim, Norway*

Caroline Tulp *Institute of Archaeology, University of Groningen, The Netherlands*

Astrid Tummuscheit *Department for Prehistoric Archaeology, University of Kiel, Germany*

Katharina Ulmschneider *Worcester College, University of Oxford*

Abbreviations

BM	British Museum
EMC	Early Medieval Coins
SMR	Sites and Monuments Record

Preface

In 1989, a gathering of distinguished archaeologists and numismatists met in Oxford to discuss the growing number of Middle Anglo-Saxon sites, dubbed 'productive', then being revealed by metal-detection. Ten years on, and thousands of metal-detected artefacts later, the two editors of this volume organised another conference on a similar, though somewhat broader, theme, as an update. Fittingly it was again in Oxford that, in December 2000, Worcester College played host to a meeting, this time international, of historians, archaeologists and numismatists, to reconsider the knotty problems of trade and economics in Early Medieval Europe.

The success of this event has owed much to the award of a conference grant by the British Academy and in particular to the generosity of Mr David Newkirk of London. Without their kind support, neither the conference nor this subsequent book would have been possible. We are also very grateful to the Danish National Museum for a generous grant for the publication of the extensive illustrations to accompany Lars Jørgensen's contribution on Lake Tissø.

The essays contained in this volume are essentially those papers as delivered to the Worcester College conference, modified to a greater or lesser extent. Indeed, such has been the enthusiasm for the publication of the conference's proceedings that only one paper delivered is not included. By way of compensation we are very grateful to Stuart Brookes for contributing an article on the economic framework of Middle Anglo-Saxon Kent. It will also be apparent that there is no survey of the continental sources for markets and fairs in the period covered by this volume. Such a contribution was intended, but unfortunately circumstances prevented Prof. Johanek from submitting his paper. In its place the editors would like to draw attention to his two important and still highly relevant surveys on the topic in 1985 and 1987.

Finally, we owe debts to the many people involved at different stages in this project. For his enthusiastic response to our publication proposal, and assistance in the production stages, we would like to thank Richard Purslow of Windgather Press. Thanks are also due to Joy Southam and Fiona Fergusson, and to all the contributors for their prompt and efficient responses to our many requests for clarification. We would like to acknowledge Philip Salmon, Martin Ulmschneider, and the staff of Worcester College for their help in the smooth organisation and running of the conference. Last but not least, we owe a debt of gratitude to Julia and Philip for all their support and tolerance.

CHAPTER I

Introduction: Early Medieval Markets and 'Productive' Sites

Katharina Ulmschneider and Tim Pestell

This book presents the first survey of inland markets and smaller trading sites in Early Medieval Northern Europe between the seventh and ninth centuries. The period is one of considerable interest to social and economic historians, archaeologists and numismatists alike. Not only did it herald the revival of international trade networks after two centuries of disruption and upheavals during the Migration period. It also witnessed the emergence of a large-scale silver coinage, which was to act as a common currency for the kingdoms and peoples of the North Sea littoral. The scale and importance of this economic renewal can be seen most vividly in the sudden emergence of the great *emporia* or *wics*, which sprang up along the coasts of Northern Europe. These extensive international trading stations, such as *Hamwic*, Dorestad and Quentovic, with their large amounts of coinage and foreign goods, have long been at the centre of studies of Early Medieval markets and trade (among others see Jankuhn *et al.* 1973; Hodges and Hobley 1988; Hodges 1989a; Clarke and Ambrosiani 1991; and most recently Hill and Cowie 2001).

However, despite their undoubted importance, it is becoming increasingly clear that the *emporia* were not the only sites acting as markets or actively participating in international and regional trade between the seventh and ninth centuries. An expanding body of archaeological and numismatic evidence, mostly derived through metal-detecting, has not only begun to reveal the existence of many smaller, less well-documented trading places during this period. It has also started to challenge the notion that such rural sites were of little importance to the economic system as a whole (*contra* Hodges and Whitehouse 1983, 92 and 101).

It was with the aim of redressing this longstanding imbalance in research at a European level, and drawing together recent advances made in the study of smaller, more rural, trading sites, that a conference on 'The Archaeology of Inland Markets, Fairs, and "Productive" Sites' was held at Worcester College, Oxford, in December 2000. There were three major objectives.

The first was to survey and assess the current knowledge of the so-called 'productive' sites of Anglo-Saxon England. This term (which remains archaeologically somewhat unsatisfactory) was first used by numismatists during the 1980s, when a boom in metal-detecting activity in England led to the discovery of new types of sites yielding unusually large quantities of coins and sometimes metalwork (for example, Booth and Blowers 1983; Blackburn and Bonser 1986, 65–80). However, as many of the following essays show, a lack of systematic archaeological investigation frequently left the function or interpretation of such places unclear. A first attempt at assessing these sites was made at an important symposium on 'productive' sites organized by Mark Blackburn and Michael Metcalf in Oxford in 1989. Unfortunately, the proceedings of the 1989 meeting were never published (Blackburn, this volume), although some of the important papers delivered then have since been circulated privately (for instance Blackburn, Rogerson and Margeson, unpublished).

The continued recovery of material from known 'productive' sites, the discovery of important new examples, and the opportunities for more detailed archaeological investigations in the intervening eleven years, have provided the chance to revisit the entire question of 'productive' sites and their interpretation. A key objective of the Worcester College conference was therefore to bring together and publish all of the latest evidence for 'productive' sites in England, many for the first time, and to develop and assess new strategies for the study and interpretation of these mainly metal-detected sites. Given some of the recent debates surrounding the term 'productive' site, it should be pointed out that it is used in this volume to refer to 'places, whether excavated or metal-detected, that produce large quantities of coin and metalwork finds' (Ulmschneider 2000b, 62–3).

It is the large scale of the coinage found on 'productive' sites, second only to that of the great *emporia*, which, together with their location along major lines of transport and communication, first led to the suggestion that they represent the places of former markets, fairs and/or settlements involved in trade (Metcalf 1984a, 27 and 41). Despite having been known to exist for some time now, the recognition and acceptance of 'productive' sites in the literature has generally been slow. For instance, their discussion is notably lacking in McCormick's monumental *Origins of the European Economy* (2001), and with the exception of John Moreland's contribution, finds little space in Hansen and Wickham's recent *The Long Eighth Century* (2000).

Much of this problem stems from the unusual circumstances under which these sites have been revealed and the unconventional recovery of their finds. Because most 'productive' sites have been identified by hobby metal-detecting, there has been a general lack of controlled archaeological excavation. As a result, the artefacts recovered not only lack archaeological context, but, perhaps even more unsatisfactorily, they almost always represent only a small proportion of the range of finds that might be expected from such sites. Metal-detectorists generally screen out non-ferrous metalwork in their searches, and not all of them choose to recover other classes of object seen on the surface, such as ceramics. This highly selective recovery strategy, naturally, is at variance with any archaeological research agenda, and has contributed to the tension between some archaeologists and detector users. One of the greatest remaining challenges for archaeologists is to persuade *all* finders to submit their finds for archaeological examination and to provide accurate findspots for their material (Lewis 2002, 332). Often, the disclosure of such data has depended upon the personal initiative of archaeologists who over the years have built up close contacts with local metal-detectorists. It is only since the later 1990s that this process of liaison has become more formalised with the introduction of the Portable Antiquities Scheme in England and Wales, which employs archaeologists to seek out metal-detectorists and convince them of the need to have their finds and sites recorded (Hobbs 2001).*

Even when both finds and findspots become known to archaeologists, the research and discussion of metal-detected sites can still be hampered by the requirement to keep certain find locations secret for fear of being looted by unscrupulous 'nighthawks'.

This unsatisfactory situation has meant that there have been few opportunities to consider the archaeological nature of metal-detected 'productive' sites. While some archaeologists have as a result remained extremely cautious about metal-detectorists and their finds (and others have even seemed to demonise them – see for example the naïve comments of Langford 2002), the vast majority now agree that these finds have an enormous potential for archaeological research, which

* According to the most recent annual report of the Portable Antiquities Scheme, 39,346 objects were recorded in the twelve months from October 1999 to September 2000. However, the 1,788 finders apparently responsible for this material are well short of the estimated 13–30,000 metal-detector enthusiasts in Britain (Hobbs 2001, 25 and n. 1).

has yet to be fully realised and can no longer be ignored (Ulmschneider 2000a, 101; Pestell 2001b, 52; Lewis 2002, 333). This may be seen no more clearly than in the important discussions of Early Medieval trade and economics by James Campbell and Mark Blackburn (both this volume).

It is not only in England, however, that metal-detector finds, excavations, and historical research have begun to challenge fundamentally our understanding of trade and the economy in the Early Medieval period. The second major objective of the Worcester College conference, and its proceedings presented here, has been to compare, for the first time, developments in Britain with those on the Continent and in Scandinavia. By its nature such a survey and comparison cannot be exhaustive and has been based on a selection of recent or ongoing research projects undertaken in six European countries including the Netherlands, Denmark, Germany, France, Italy, and Scandinavia. The aim has been not only to exchange new research, ideas, and methodologies across the North Sea, but to re-ignite the debate on Early Medieval markets and trade on a European basis.

It will be immediately apparent that there are great differences in the research material and approaches between the different countries. For example, the Netherlands and Denmark, like England, have experienced the large-scale impact of metal-detecting. Denmark in particular has been at the forefront of collecting and utilizing the new information thus recovered, with many of the metal-detected sites being followed up with large-scale excavations (Jørgensen, this volume). These are providing archaeologists with crucial evidence about the varying nature and functions of economic sites, and are starting to reveal an hitherto unsuspected complexity and structure to Early Medieval settlements, the economy and society. This work stands in stark contrast to many other European countries, such as Germany, France and Italy, where metal-detecting as a hobby remains largely illegal. Here important discoveries continue to be made through more traditional detailed, and often extensive, excavations and historical research, which allow rare insights into the network, contacts, and seasonality of market and trading sites, and their development over time (for instance Le Maho; Moran, this volume).

Finally, a third objective of the Worcester College conference was to establish a broad, interdisciplinary forum for discussing economic sites comprising archaeologists, numismatists and historians of the period. With the explosion of data available through metal-detector finds, trade and the economy has become one of the fastest moving fields in Early Medieval studies. As the papers in this volume show, its importance cannot be overemphasised. Equally, it is becoming clear that only a multi-disciplinary approach with an integrated research agenda will allow a fuller appreciation of the complex and sophisticated pattern of marketing, exchange, and trading-place hierarchies.

At present archaeologists are only just beginning to understand and utilise the new sources that are becoming available. Central to any advance will be the continued refinement of data on coin-use and circulation. As Blackburn points out (this volume), the popularity of metal-detecting is revolutionising our knowledge of European coinage. His study of coin-loss patterns in England demonstrates a sudden burst in monetary activity around 700 with a volume of currency in circulation unparalleled in England until the thirteenth and early fourteenth centuries. Not only does this pattern appear to reflect wider European trends, on a more specific level it has provided new ways of comparing sites, raising the possibility that future research will be able to understand local and regional economic activity and interactions between sites. Already, the newly-developed statistical approaches of Michael Metcalf (2001 and this volume) are enabling the identification of areas of particular coin-loss and therefore coin-use. These, for example, may not only help to point to the location of mints which currently remain unidentified, but they can also highlight the importance of certain hinterland areas (and their resources) into which coins diffused from a market and mint place. The information from such studies will be of obvious importance to economic, political and social historians. For instance, the identification of more-or-less isolated 'hot-spots' of coin finds, as for example the primary porcupine sceattas in parts of the upper Thames valley, not only raises interesting questions about trade-routes and the way money was transferred into the region, but also potentially indicates the economic importance of the wool trade in the chalklands of the region already by the late seventh century, well in advance of our first documentary evidence of the mid eighth century (Metcalf, this volume).

Another theme which will need to be reassessed in the light of new discoveries is the thorny question of the influence of political power on the economy, and the extent of political control over coinage, markets and trade. This, of course, is a problem already long familiar from the study of the *emporia* (Palmer, this volume). Political power could clearly have a profound effect on the development and fate of a market and settlement. In her discussion of Groß Strömkendorf, Astrid Tummuscheit (this volume) shows how this settlement may be identified with the *emporium* of *Reric*, mentioned *s.a.* 808 in the *Royal Frankish Annals*. Excavations suggest that Groß Strömkendorf's layout was structured in part by a central authority, especially from *c.* 770–90. That the Danish king Godfred came to relocate all the merchants to

Hedeby over 130km away provides an ample demonstration of the importance of controlling economic exchange. An essentially similar phenomenon is expounded by Jacques Le Maho in his analysis of Rouen (this volume). From an organic landscape of ports and small trading places in the Lower Seine, many owned and run by monasteries, the political circumstances of Viking raids and settlement were to induce a profound change. While Rouen itself survived, becoming a refuge from Scandinavian raiders, the shifting balance of power saw the extension of royal control over the city and its development as an urban centre.

But how far did such political control reach? Metcalf draws attention to the eighth-century monetary economy being regionally integrated, but also displaying a free movement of currency between regions and kingdoms, while Blackburn can find no real evidence for political circumstances affecting the pattern of coin loss on three geographically and functionally very different trading sites (both this volume). In some cases attempts at gaining control of trading sites may have involved their relocation to more permanent positions. For instance, Lund's 'Fair of the Three Mounds' was probably transferred from an earlier site at Uppåkra (Sawyer, this volume). However, many other Scandinavian markets and fairs seem to have been based on Lunar cycles and pre-Christian religious festivals, or simply grew up around temporary cult sites. Lars Jørgensen's discussion of the spectacular aristocratic site at Lake Tissø in Denmark provides an important example of how a settlement with workshops and a large market area may have been attracted to a site of former cult activity, in this case based around 'the lake of Tyr'. The monumental halls revealed by excavation at Tissø are not only comparable with the royal settlement of Lejre near Roskilde on Zealand, but possibly represent an extension of royal control and occupation over former religious practice and economic activity.

The extent to which social control by either secular leaders or religious institutions could provide a motor for trade and economic development is another important question raised by the presence of smaller 'productive' and inland trading sites. While the concept of planned *emporia* of Hodges 'Type B' is familiar to Early Medieval economic historians (Hodges 1989a, 51–2), the nature of 'productive' sites at present remains very much open to debate. For many scholars, the crucial role of the Church looms large. At San Vincenzo al Volturno, it was the presence of a monastery that was responsible for the assembly of tile, glass and metalworkers, and the subsequent production of a range of prestige goods such as belt buckles and bridle furniture (Mitchell 1994b; Moran, this volume). Similarly, many

English sites such as Coddenham in Suffolk, Wormegay in Norfolk and that 'near Carisbrooke' on the Isle of Wight have been related to a former ecclesiastical presence (Newman; Rogerson; Ulmschneider, this volume; see also Palmer). A religious component can be clearly demonstrated by the eleventh century at many former 'productive' sites, as is the case in East Anglia (Pestell, this volume) and the role of the Church as a force in economic development in the eighth and ninth centuries is perhaps best championed in the work of John Blair (Blair 1996a and forthcoming).

However, it is becoming apparent that success in trade need not necessarily have been the sole preserve of ecclesiastics. Caroline Tulp's consideration of the *terp* at Wijnaldum (this volume) suggests so far nothing other than a purely secular settlement involved in trade, yet manufacturing and consuming prestige goods. Likewise, Kevin Leahy's analysis of the 'productive' site at Melton Ross found 'most of the main elements of Middle Anglo-Saxon administration, the main omission being the absence of any direct evidence for an ecclesiastical function' (this volume). The difficulty of clearly identifying the religious or secular nature of even well-excavated 'productive' sites is perhaps best reflected in the current English debate over the identification of Brandon in Suffolk and Flixborough in Lincolnshire as 'monasteries', and over the early structures at Northampton and Cheddar as 'royal palaces' (Carr *et al.* 1988; Blair 1992, 261–4 and 1996b; Pestell forthcoming). Indeed, there now seems to be a distinct possibility that sites such as Flixborough may have changed in nature several times during their lifetime (Loveluck 2001, 121). Such detailed archaeological studies unfortunately remain very rare at the moment, but they should alert us to a potentially much greater complexity and structure in Early Medieval settlements and the economy, a theme which has already started to become apparent from the study of metal-detected sites in Denmark (Jørgenson, this volume).

While the impact and involvement of secular and religious elements in the promotion of local and inter-regional markets and trade remains to be elucidated, the overriding importance of good geographical locations and in particular maritime and riverine communication routes for the development of markets cannot be doubted. This seems to hold true not only for virtually all of the Anglo-Saxon 'productive' sites, but also for those rare examples identified in the Celtic West, which, as David Griffiths shows, share many characteristics with their English and European counterparts. As examples, Meols on the Wirral peninsula stands on the conjunction of two river systems facing the Irish Sea, while Glyn, Llanbedrgoch, on the Isle of Anglesey, stands at the centre of the Irish Sea region (Griffiths, this volume). In the east of England the clustering of sites in south-east Suffolk has led Newman to see a 'productive landscape' connected by the Lark/Gipping valley corridor to the equally 'productive' region of West Norfolk, while Le Maho has illustrated the importance of a major navigable river in the development of ports along the Lower Seine. Likewise, Stuart Brookes's analysis of Kent has shown the coastal distribution of high coin-loss areas, consonant with a model of coastal trading with 'gateway communities' providing access to imported goods.

This broad picture is, again, likely to mask a much greater variety and complexity of choices in the location of markets and trading sites, which will provide ample scope for future research. For example, the site of Melton Ross in Lincolnshire lay inland at a junction of regional pathways, while the settlement at Hollingbourne was situated on the cross-roads of routeways linking the territories of East and West Kent (Leahy; Brookes, this volume). Similarly, analysis of the local geography and geology of an inter-regional and perhaps international market site 'near Carisbrooke' on the Isle of Wight, has suggested that easy access to a navigable river seems to have been of secondary importance in the choice of its location, the site instead being situated three kilometres inland, close to a fording point at the junction of three very different ecological zones (Ulmschneider, this volume).

It will only be through more detailed topographical work and a full programme of archaeological excavations that some of the most stubborn elements in the interpretation of many 'productive' sites – their precise nature and the wide variety of places that this term invariably encompasses – will eventually be teased out. One of the main difficulties in assessing these sites at present remains our inability to ascertain accurately the nature and intensity of occupation on any site, and its development over time. It is perfectly conceivable that many 'productive' sites were only temporary fairs. However, it is becoming increasingly clear that some of the recovered assemblages closely reflect those found on more permanent settlements. The excellent communication links which most 'productive' sites had make it unsurprising that they might develop as central places, acting as foci not simply for trade and exchange, but production, consumption and, like Melton Ross in Lincolnshire, administration and justice. The very notion of which elements came first or should take the lead in their interpretation – trading site, administrative centre (such as the *caput* to local landholdings or as a multiple-estate centre) or religious estate – is therefore difficult. In a radical reassessment, based on his fieldwork at Cottam, Julian Richards (1999a and b, and this volume) has suggested that they need not be any or all of these but may simply represent 'normal' settlements which have seen above-average metal-detecting activity. While Richards' argument may be contradicted by the number of 'productive' sites known from elsewhere to have had a visible importance by Domesday, his approach is important in questioning our terms of reference. Just how much material must a site yield to be called 'productive'? And upon what types of artefact must such a definition be made?

There remains a desperate shortage of the sorts of detailed data needed to allow better interpretations of the likely multivariate functions of such economically important sites, and their role within the hierarchy of Early Medieval markets and other settlement types. These problems should not be seen as insurmountable. Important new approaches in the study of settlement and economic hierarchies in England are already beginning to emerge, from large-scale fieldwalking such as John Newman's work for the East Anglian Kingdom Survey and Paul Blinkhorn's detailed study of Ipswich ware (Newman 1992; Blinkhorn 1999). Similarly, Ben Palmer's and Stuart Brookes' studies in this volume act as important signposts as to how detailed temporal and spatial analysis, aided by Geographical Information Systems (GIS) models, can help us to understand the wide variety of, and interactions between, sites involved in the economy and trade, and provide crucial information on their origins and development against the background of the landscape.

With so much of the study of inland markets and 'productive' sites still in its infancy, what might we expect in the future? As this book shows, the vast body of new archaeological and numismatic evidence derived through metal-detecting in countries such as England and Denmark has allowed the identification of an hitherto unsuspected network of inland markets and other sites involved in trade. This is providing archaeologists with an unprecedented opportunity not only to reconsider the complexities of the Early Medieval economy, but also to study its influence on settlement hierarchy and on Early Medieval society at large. Our prime agenda in Britain must now be both to harness successfully the information from these dramatic new datasets, and even more importantly, to lobby for a programme of large-scale excavations of such metal-detected sites, to shed light on key aspects such as their possibly seasonal nature, their varying functions and status, and their development over time. On the present evidence, these questions simply cannot be answered. The need is all the more pressing given the immediacy and scale of destruction occurring on most rural archaeological sites in the United Kingdom through agricultural activity. There is a real danger now that without the excavation of a representative selection of those endangered archaeological sites our chance of fully understanding and assessing the 'productive' site phenomenon will be irretrievably lost.

Equally as important – if not more so – is the need now to view and compare the English findings against the background of developments elsewhere in Northern Europe. As this book shows, the identification of new market and trading sites by metal-detector is not just rife in the United Kingdom, but is also a prominent feature of Danish, Dutch, and, more recently, Swedish archaeology (Hårdh 2000). The systematic excavations on such sites, together with ongoing large-scale research projects on known trading sites and the much greater abundance of Continental written sources, provide a wealth of data from which archaeologists must develop a more integrated and European-wide research agenda for the study of smaller markets and fairs. It is only through such an integrated and multi-disciplinary approach, that we will really begin to appreciate the complex and sophisticated pattern of marketing, trade and exchange in seventh- to ninth-century Europe. Each contributor makes this case in their own fashion, but the broader message of this volume is unequivocal. The study of inland markets and 'productive' sites has begun fundamentally to challenge and rewrite the history of the economy of Early Medieval Europe.

I

History, Numismatics and the Early Medieval Economy

CHAPTER 2

Production and Distribution in Early and Middle Anglo-Saxon England

James Campbell

Difficillima ars nesciendi is the best motto for a Dark Age historian. What can be more necessary than the most difficult art of not knowing, granted that sources are very thin, heavily skewed and, for many important areas of activity, completely absent? Paradoxically, students of 'productive' sites, in adding importantly to the archaeological record, have demonstrated how deficient it is. The Faustian pact which they have (rightly) made with the detectorists has led to the discovery of much, the existence of which had been hardly suspected, let alone known, a commanding reminder of how much there is we cannot know. A guide – *some* guide – to the scale of the unknown, is to follow the advice of Marc Bloch: 'Let the figures speak, they have a brutal eloquence'.

Suppose that the population of the area under English control in the time of Bede was half a million.* What quantity of materials would have been needed to keep them reasonably warm and decent? On a very rough, but restrained, calculation, an Anglo-Saxon man or women could hardly have been provided with clothing made of less than three square yards of cloth (I do not set store by the detail of any of the guesstimates here; except to say that, on any guess, we are dealing with very large quantities). Let us allow two square yards each

* I do not know how to guess the population at the period concerned with even spurious accuracy. The considerations advanced by Esmonde Cleary (1989, 174–5) suggest that half a million could be a modest estimate. If, as Maddicott (1997) shows very possible, bubonic plague raged in the seventh century, then this may have greatly reduced the population. Not to be excluded is that such a reduction (resembling that after the Black Death) could have increased the prosperity of the survivors, whose resulting demand for consumer goods could have contributed to developments evidenced by 'productive' sites.

for children under fourteen and assume them to compose a third of the population. The total amount of cloth being worn at any one time would have been of the order of 1.3 million square yards (1.08 million square metres), no allowance being made for persons owning more than one suit of clothes.* Surely one may safely assume that all the population over toddler age wore footwear; call it at least three quarters of a million shoes in use at one time, most of a kind which would wear out quite easily and would be hard to repair (possibly some kinds of patten were also in use).† How much metalwork did the population as a whole wear? It is possible that in the lower reaches of society the functions of brooches and buckles were performed by thorns, frogs and pieces of rope (buttons were not introduced to western Europe until the thirteenth century). But we can reasonably assume that a large proportion of the population depended for warmth and decency on small metal goods.

The question of how large a proportion is important because the answer affects judgement on the social significance of the commonest grave-goods. If it is assumed that brooches, strap-ends and the like were normal kit then (on the half-million population assumption) something like two million pieces of metal could have been in wear at one time. It will not escape attention that questions implied here are relevant to Martin Biddle's thesis on the availability of metal goods (Biddle *et al.* 1990, 42–74). His argument is that there was a major increase in the supply of these in the tenth century, perhaps not paralleled until the sixteenth. This can be but indirectly relevant to our immediate concerns, yet it leads one to wonder how far there may have been a comparable increase in supply in the Early and/or Middle Anglo-Saxon periods. Biddle and his colleagues demonstrate the importance of the assiduous archaeological recording of what could appear to be inconsiderable trifles. They almost show that the study of numerous fragments can be more revealing than that of objects larger, more complete, and more attractive. Detectorist exploration can hardly lead to minute investigation and recording of Biddle's kind.

* An unknown portion of clothing would have been of leather; the earliest reference to such in England known to me occurs in the *Life and Miracles of St William of Norwich* (Jessopp and James 1896, 15), and relates to the mid-twelfth century, but this must stand for much which went unrecorded before.

† For medieval shoes see Blair and Ramsay 1991, 308–11. The shoe problem is an instance of to how limited an extent important manufactured goods edge into the 'archaeological record'. A relevant question is this. Off what did 'ordinary people' eat and out of what did they drink? If they drank from turned wooden cups, by what economic mechanism did they obtain these? On what did they sit? Not all, one may suppose, with their legs dangling into the pits of sunken-floored buildings.

Nevertheless, his arguments lend importance to minor metal items and fragments found on 'productive' sites; 'odds and ends' can help provide a major means to understanding the economic state and development of society.*

Other figures, somewhat more secure and somewhat more surprising, are those for the physical extent of *emporia*. To take three of the best known: *Hamwic* extended over 100 acres, Ipswich over some 125 acres, while *Lundonwic* seems to have been even more extensive, perhaps 148 acres (Ulmschneider 2000a, 83–5; Russo 1998, 142 and 151). Naturally there are problems in relation to density and continuity of occupation. Nevertheless, these are very large areas and clearly indicative that *emporia* had wide functions, involving many people and/or quite widely distributed articles, imported, exported or manufactured. We also have to bear in mind the strong likelihood that there are other *emporium* sites still to be discovered. A major question here is that of how late the palatalised *-wich* element which, as Ekwall showed (1964, 14–29), seems very specially associated with major commercial sites, was newly applied to appropriate places: for example Greenwich, Harwich, Dunwich, Swanage, Norwich and Woolwich have to fall under consideration. The last case has some special importance. In his place-name dictionary (Ekwall 1960, 533) Ekwall interpreted Woolwich as meaning either 'farm where wool was produced' or 'town where wool was exported'; but in his later work (Ekwall 1964, 17) he chose the second option because of the palatalised form of the suffix. If his case is accepted it is important because it takes evidence for the export of English wool back to at least the tenth century. There is no direct evidence for such export until the early twelfth century, though a powerful case has been made for the eleventh (Sawyer 1965, 162–3).

A warning against assuming the absence of an eighth-century *emporium* site because one has not been found so far is Professor Hodges' distinguished book *Dark Age Economics* in which, arguing from the absence of archaeological evidence, he expressed considerable scepticism about the existence of *emporia* at either London or York, notwithstanding the plain words of the literary evidence (Hodges 1989a, 70 and 73). The great extent of *emporia*, implying involvement with large quantities of relatively low-value goods, has to imply a hierarchy of lesser places involved in distribution and collection.

Not the least interesting of the palatalised 'wich' names is Droitwich.

---

* The significance of the metal finds on some 'productive' sites provokes speculation. Could such bits have been used as currency? For the notion that pins might have been used in this way see Ross (1991, 452).

Mawer and Stenton interpreted this place-name as follows: *-wic*, they say, 'is simply descriptive of a settlement' (1927, 285–6). Ekwall has shown that this can hardly be true of the palatalised form. The 'droit' element they take to mean 'muddy' or 'dirty'. The possibility of derivation with Old English *dryhten* with the archaic meaning of ruler or lord is touched upon but dismissed. However, Droitwich (*Salinae*) had been a major source of salt in Roman times and appears in a comparable role as soon as we have charters to tell us about it. The early references or alleged references to Droitwich are revealing as forms corresponding to 'Droitwich' do not appear until the fourteenth century. In earlier sources the 'droit' does not appear. Thus in a charter (judged spurious) of 716 it is called *Wiccium emptorium*; in another of 716×717, better regarded, it is *Wico emtorio salis quem nos saltwich vocamus*; in an imperfectly recorded grant of 716×757 we have *in vico emptorio salis* (Sawyer 1968, Nos 83, 97 and 1824). These texts are not such as to inspire general confidence, but it is notable how each combines *wiccium*, *wico* or *vico* (it being unclear whether the word is being used as a proper noun or not) with *emptorium* (which I take to be the same word as *emporium*).

Interest attaches also to the name of a nearly place, Wychbold (Mawer and Stenton 1927, 285). The suffix can have a meaning varying from an ordinary house to a manor house (Mawer 1924, 7–8). Of note in this context it has been argued, with reference to continental evidence, that it can indicate a fortified place of importance (Morris 1973, 192 and 472–3). That Wychbold was significant is shown by its having been a meeting place for ninth-century Mercian councils (Cubitt 1995, 219 and 222). Thus the *emptorium* of Droitwich resembles others with a different economic basis, in being near to a centre of royal power; notwithstanding the authority of Stenton and Mawer, one must incline to suppose that the first element in the name had to do not with mud, but with early power.

Consideration of Droitwich brings one naturally to salt. Those of us who generally only see salt as a tiny mound in the corner of a plate can easily forget the vast quantities of salt earlier societies needed to preserve their food. Consider how much salt is needed to preserve one herring. Sources from the eighteenth century and later give a highest estimate of 1.7oz (48g) per fish and a lowest of 0.6oz (17g) (Bridbury 1955, 3; Young 1813, 230). Suppose the hypothetical half-million inhabitants of the Anglo-Saxon lands in early England ate the salted equivalent of ten herrings annually and that it took an ounce of salt (28g) to preserve one herring, then the total of salt required would have been nearly 14 tons (14,225kg). Yet ten 'herring units' per head is likely to have been vastly less than the true Early Anglo-Saxon consumption of salted food. One can see the great economic importance of *emptorium salis* and reflect on the significance of the possible continuity of Droitwich salt production from Roman times (Hurst 1998). Salt was boiled out in lead vessels, so one may wonder also about the continuity of lead production.

Consideration of 'productive' sites inevitably forces us to peer, if in relative ignorance, then in hopeful ignorance, at the whole economic system of Anglo-Saxon England. All I can offer is a handful of guesses, easily open to correction or amplification.

A starting point for one such guess is the recent reinterpretation by Steven Plunkett of discoveries made so long ago as 1953 at Pakenham, Suffolk (Plunkett 1999). He shows that at this site there was a weaving establishment, probably of the sixth century, containing two or more looms. A reconstructed version of one of these has been made for the Ipswich Museum. The original loom was certainly 8ft (2.4m) wide and was probably the same high. This machine and its companion (there may have been more than one such) are argued to 'indicate organised production workshops making large textiles of standardised quality and character probably for commercial as well as domestic purposes' (*ibid.*, 295).

Let us put texts beside this archaeological evidence. It is well known, from a letter of Charlemagne (796), that in negotiation with Offa he objected that cloaks being shipped from England were too short. This passage is complemented, most interestingly, by another in the account of Charlemagne by Notker, a monk of St Gall writing 884–7. Notker describes the ruler's testy concern with the excessive brevity of a new style of riding cloak:

> 'What is the use of these little napkins?' he asked. 'I can't cover myself with them in bed. When I am on horseback I can't protect myself from the winds and the rain. When I go off to empty my bowels I catch cold because my backside is frozen.' (Thorpe 1969, 133).

Notker writes of these cloaks as supplied by Frisians, but the link between his account and what appears in Charlemagne's letter is strong enough to support the possibility that these cloaks were woven in England but exported by Frisians. Furthermore, the importance of cloaks from England is emphasised by references in the eighth-century letters of Boniface and Lul. One letter refers to a gift of two woollen cloaks from Æthelbert II, king of Kent, to St Boniface; their value is suggested by the fact that the other part of the gift was a silver cup, lined with gold, and weighing three and a half pounds (Tangl 1916, No. 105). The second letter is from Alhred, king of Northumbria, sending twelve cloaks and a gold ring to Bishop Lul (*ibid.*, No. 121; Whitelock 1955, No. 187). Important store was set by the cloaks of great men: thus Theodulf mentions the 'double cloak' of Charlemagne's son Charles (Raby 1934, 190).

Let us set beside these references another, from Bede's *Ecclesiastical History*. Here is described how King Æthelwealh of Sussex endowed Wilfrid with a vast estate at Selsey. Bede tells us what the great man did upon receiving this gift of 87 hides; he freed 250 *servi et ancillae*: male and female slaves (*Historia Ecclesiastica*, iv, 13). Query: what were these people supposed to be doing? Was it a matter of an agricultural workforce, or could we be looking at the domestic staff of something like a major Roman, or indeed Carolingian, *villa*? The reference to *ancillae* somewhat favours the latter supposition.

If for the sake of argument one assumes these things were connected, could the Pakenham great looms be part of a luxurious estate-centre weaving establishment, staffed by slaves and providing very high quality goods to the king which might be given to an archbishop of Mainz or even sold to an emperor? This is, of course, no more than a crude hypothesis to illustrate an argument, or rather a dilemma. It is this: how far were manufactured goods produced in association with lordship? Was it the possession of skilled slaves, toiling away in sunken-featured buildings, which gave great men control of manufacture, establishments such as that at West Stow being, so to speak, their factories? The interreaction between lordship, production and what we might think of as market-directed production was doubtless a complex one and involved attitudes and procedures contrary to our normal ways of thinking.

The economy which concerns us is that which paid for Bede. No interpretation of the economy (nor, I would venture to say, of the society) of seventh-century England can make sense if it does not take account of Monkwearmouth-Jarrow. Bede's monastery gives us an island of assured knowledge in a troubled sea, in which limited information is churned by cross-currents of speculation, not all of it happy. We have no doubt of the scale of the library of Monkwearmouth-Jarrow nor of the importance of the learning which was fostered there. We have no doubt about the Roman fineness of the buildings: not only are they described by Bede, their remains have been unearthed by Rosemary Cramp (for example Cramp 1976). Bede's account, his own writings, and the physical remains prove that Monkwearmouth-Jarrow was an immensely, an almost extravagantly, expensive enterprise. Biscop's repeated visits to Italy, his purchases of many manuscripts and other religious items there, the importation of craftsmen from Gaul to construct the fine buildings: all these things show him as a devout Maecenas, possibly at least as rich or richer than whoever was buried in Mound One at Sutton Hoo. By no means the least call on the funds for a founder was the maintenance of the community. Bede says that in 716 when Abbot Ceolfrith left on his fatal journey to Rome, there were nearly six hundred *fratres* in the twinned foundation of Monkwearmouth-Jarrow (Plummer 1896, i, 382). What did a *frater* cost? Writing on a rather later period and, of course, not in a position to give more than vague indication, Duby reckoned that it took thirty peasant families to maintain one monk of St Bertin (1978, 108). Maybe, one may say, English monks at an earlier date came cheaper. Bede, though possibly a distinguished exception in what he cost, can hardly have done so. Note that when, just before his death, he distributed his personal possessions, they included some pepper, which cannot have come from anywhere much nearer than southern India (Plummer 1896, i, clxiii). Monkwearmouth-Jarrow was outstanding but it was not unique as a monastery: far from it. All the evidence indicates that monasteries became very numerous in the age of Bede and by 800 there were some thirty in the diocese of Worcester alone (Stubbs 1862). Of course, there were monasteries and monasteries but we know just enough about some of the most obscure to recognise even them as centres of learning.

In short, England was a rich area. It almost looks like a booming area and its economy was such that the *emporia* must have played a big part. It was such that the study of 'productive' sites, the theme of this volume, can begin to be seen as representing part of an economic hierarchy (Ulmschneider 2000a, chapters 2 and 3). In such a hierarchy, one can begin almost to glimpse the economic mechanisms which linked the *emporia* to the free peasants whom early law codes assume, however reasonably or unreasonably, to have been capable of paying large fines, denominated in gold (Campbell 2000, 69–70). In this connection it is just about worthwhile to notice the number of gold or pseudo-gold coins found on 'productive' sites (Ulmschneider 2000a; 20, 22, 29 and 47–8).

Perhaps something like a commercial revolution was in progress linked, as Dr Ulmschneider emphasises, in more ways than one with the progress of the Church (*ibid.*, esp. 66–73). It may not have been for nothing that coining and Christianity seem to be introduced almost hand in hand. Bede tells how Bishop Wilfrid introduced new methods of sea-fishing to Sussex (*Historia Ecclesiastica*, iv, 13); this could be one instance among many of the introduction of new techniques by missionaries who, almost by definition, were men of wide experience. At the same time one should not lose sight of the possibility that economic progress depended largely on predation, and that behind the wealth which supported the minsters and the scholars lay the slave trade.

A familiar illustration of the role of the slave trade comes from Bede's account of the battle between Northumbria and Mercia in 679, the battle of the Trent (*ibid.*, iv, 22). After a Northumbrian nobleman, Imma, was taken prisoner his captor sold him to a Frisian at London. The incident illustrates the nexus, possibly the very important nexus, between (frequent) war and the slave trade (Pelteret 1995, 34). It is significant that the merchant was Frisian. The Anglo-Frisian connection, economic, monetary, linguistic and religious, is more than a mere background in our period.

The fruits of metal-detection and, in particular, the exploration of 'productive' sites are not only extending but transforming knowledge of the Anglo-Saxon economy in the Early and Middle periods. How can this knowledge be more fully extended and interpreted? I would suggest above all by surveying and studying similar material from later, better-documented, periods. Dr Ulmschneider rightly signals a problem when she indicates that the abundance of 'detectorist' finds in Lincolnshire may be connected with the outstandingly large number of deserted medieval villages in that county (Ulmschneider 2000a, 19). It is inevitable that such finds will, to a greater or lesser extent, be skewed towards sites at present uninhabited or thinly inhabited. The best way of estimating how far distribution patterns based on metal-detecting (and not from metal-detecting alone) truly reflect an overall economic position would be to make surveys of the later periods comparing what the 'archaeological record' and in particular its 'detectorist' element suggests with the comprehensive written evidence of such a source as Domesday Book.

CHAPTER 3

'Productive' Sites and the Pattern of Coin Loss in England, 600–1180

Mark Blackburn

The evidence for coin circulation in Early Medieval England has changed out of all recognition over the past twenty years. With the advent of the hobby of metal-detecting in the early 1970s, and its dramatic growth in the 1980s and 1990s, new data on coin single-finds was amassed on a scale never seen before. The timing was fortuitous, for Metcalf had already begun studying find distributions as a means of identifying the origin and circulation patterns of the early eighth-century pennies (the so-called 'sceattas') (Metcalf and Walker 1967; Metcalf 1974), and he took pleasure in publishing individual new finds at length as they were still something of a novelty (e.g. Metcalf 1976 and 1984b). As the numbers swelled and numismatists developed their contacts with the detecting community, the recording and publication of finds was put on a more systematic footing in the *British Numismatic Journal*, initially through a series of articles (Blackburn and Bonser 1984a; 1985; 1986) which in 1987 were subsumed into the annual 'Coin Register'. Several surveys of the find evidence from a particular period or region appeared (e.g. Rigold 1975; Rigold and Metcalf 1977 and 1984; Pirie 1986b and 2000; Blackburn 1993b; Bonser 1998; Metcalf 1998a), but they quickly became out-of-date and one could not readily be compared with another. Since 1999 an on-line Corpus of Early Medieval Coin Finds from the British Isles, 410–1180 (EMC: via www.medievalcoins.org) has provided greater access to this material.

It soon emerged that the finds, far from being evenly spread across the country, displayed a regional bias towards the eastern and south-eastern counties, and within those areas there were dramatic hot-spots – with certain fields yielding remarkable quantities of Anglo-Saxon coins and metalwork. The finds from two such sites were published in the 1980s – 'Sancton' (=Newbald, Yorks.) (Booth and Blowers 1983) and 'Near Royston', Herts. (Blackburn and Bonser 1986, 65–80) – and these could be compared with the equally prolific excavation finds from *Hamwic* (Southampton) (Metcalf 1988a). In 1989 a conference of numismatists and archaeologists organised in Oxford by Metcalf and myself considered the phenomenon of 'productive' sites, as these had by then become known, but regrettably the proceedings were not published. The term 'productive' site has always been problematic, for it was clear from the start that one could not make comparisons between sites simply on the basis of the number of coins found, as this depended so much on the area available for investigation and the opportunity and conditions of recovery. It is, however, helpful to distinguish fields that simply have little if any coinage or metalwork on them, from ones where there clearly was a considerable amount in the ground waiting to be recovered. It is true that the productive status of some sites only emerges very slowly as more finds are made, and that there is a graduation from sites that yield nothing to ones that are very prolific. Yet once recognised as 'productive' it highlights an aspect of the site that demands interpretation. That is not to say that a similar explanation will stand for all 'productive' sites, despite the temptation to regard them as the probable location of a market or occasional fair, for already we can see that they occur in a range of contexts: in urban and rural settlements, monastic sites, by rivers, roads and Roman forts.

The principal 'productive' sites are listed in the Appendix and their distribution mainly in the eastern counties of England is shown in Fig. 3.1.* Many of the finds have been published or are accessible from the web, but in only a few cases have they been discussed as site assemblages. Those reports should appear soon. The purpose of this paper is to consider the finds from a number of representative sites and set these in a context of the general pattern of finds across England. Before doing so, it is necessary to look at the theory of coin-find evidence and different approaches to its analysis.

* The histograms illustrated in this article are intended to reflect the likely date of loss of the coins, rather than their date of striking. To achieve this a simple adjustment has been made to the data, assuming that one third of the coins struck in any 25-year period remained in circulation until the following 25-year period, with the proviso that no coins were carried past the years *c.* 760, *c.* 792, *c.* 850, *c.* 862, *c.* 865, *c.* 875, *c.* 880, *c.* 973, etc., when fairly comprehensive recoinages appear to have taken place. Some of the histograms are based on a smaller sample of coins than the totals indicated in the Appendix, for reasons of consistency, reliability of data or convenience.

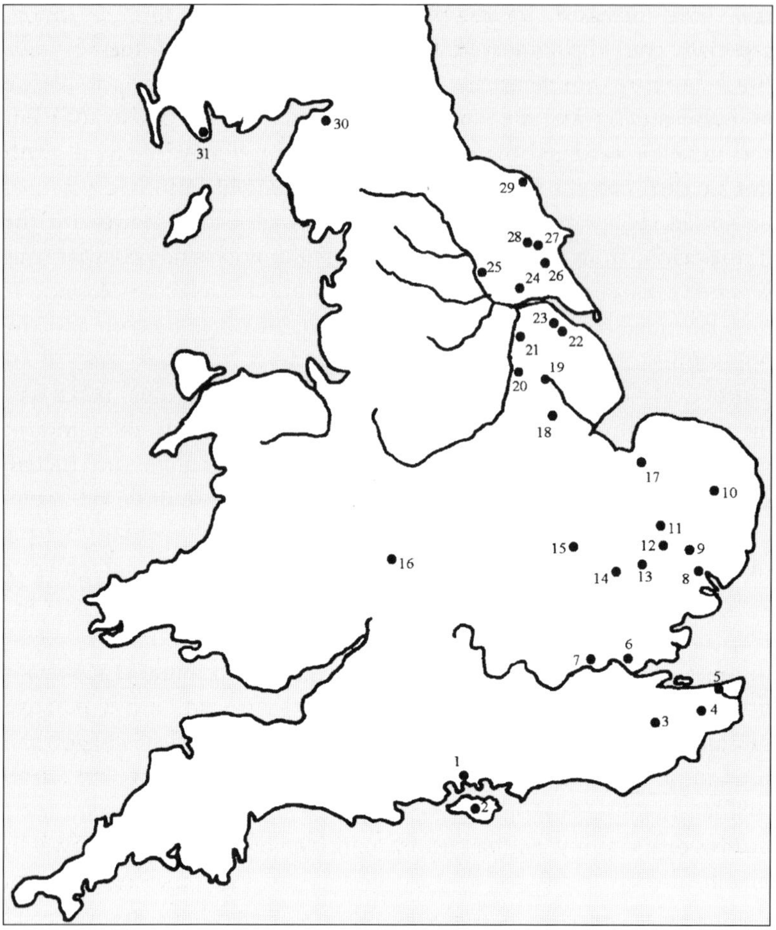

FIGURE 3.1.
Map of the principal 'productive' sites in Britain (see Appendix). 1. *Hamwic*; 2. 'Near Carisbrooke'; 3. Hollingbourne; 4. 'Near Canterbury'; 5. Reculver; 6. Tilbury; 7. London; 8. Ipswich; 9. Coddenham; 10. Caistor by Norwich; 11. Thetford; 12. Barham; 13. 'Near Cambridge'; 14. 'Near Royston'; 15. Bedford; 16. Bidford-on-Avon; 17. Bawsey; 18. 'South Lincolnshire'; 19. Lincoln; 20. Torksey; 21. Flixborough; 22. West Ravendale; 23. Riby; 24. South Newbold; 25. York; 26. Cottam; 27–8. 'Near Malton' 1 and 2; 29. Whitby; 30. Carlisle; 31. Whithorn.

The different nature of hoard and single-find evidence

There is a fundamental difference between the evidence provided by coin hoards and single-finds:

Hoards

Hoards are typically sums of money that have been put together and buried for safe keeping, and then for some reason not recovered by the owner. The coins may have been selected for the purpose and may not be representative of the money in circulation. Hoarding was a normal way of protecting money, but it may have been more intense in times of trouble or economic pressure, although these could also lead to the digging up of older hoards. What most affects the pattern of surviving coin hoards is the circumstances that led them not to be recovered by the owners or their families. The non-recovery of hoards may have increased, for example, when there was political turmoil, especially war, if people were killed or taken away from their homes. But that is by no means the only situation and it is wrong to seek a political context for every hoard discovered. There are also different categories of hoards – currency hoards, savings hoards, hoards with double peaks, grave deposits – each of which will influence the final composition of the hoard (Grierson 1975, 124–39). Hoards are the numismatist's primary tool for determining the chronology of a coin series and how long particular coin types remained in circulation.

Single-finds

Single-finds are assumed for the most part to be individual accidental losses from the money in circulation. They will have been lost in many different ways, some while changing hands in a transaction, others slipping from people's purses or pockets or having been dropped during a fight. Whatever the means, they should be a random sample of the coins in circulation, not specially selected because of their weight, fineness or coin type. Their chance of loss should not have been affected by political events as it was with hoards, so they ought to reflect genuine patterns of coin circulation. With some 6,500 single finds recorded from England 600–1180, they provide a much larger sample and a broader geographical and chronological coverage than the 250 or so English hoards of the same period (Blackburn and Pagan 1986).

The difference in the data presented by hoards and single-finds is vividly demonstrated in Fig. 3.2, which compares the incidence of hoards (above) with single-finds (below). Single-finds are plentiful during the first half of the eighth century, but become progressively fewer during the later eighth and ninth centuries. The hoards present a very different picture, there being very few in the eighth and early ninth centuries but swelling dramatically in the period 860–80, which coincides with the arrival of the great Viking army in 865 and its campaigns leading up to the conquest and settlement of the Danelaw in the later 870s. This is an unusually clear example of the impact a military campaign can have on the pattern of coin hoards.

In using the single-find data one should be aware of potential problems (Blackburn 1989a). Any coin that has been converted into jewellery by being pierced or mounted should be excluded from an analysis since it had probably ceased to have a monetary function. Some apparent single-finds may in fact come from disturbed graves, though this is really only a potential problem for the seventh century, as the practice of placing coins and other goods in graves died out in England at the beginning of the eighth century, while the few fifth-

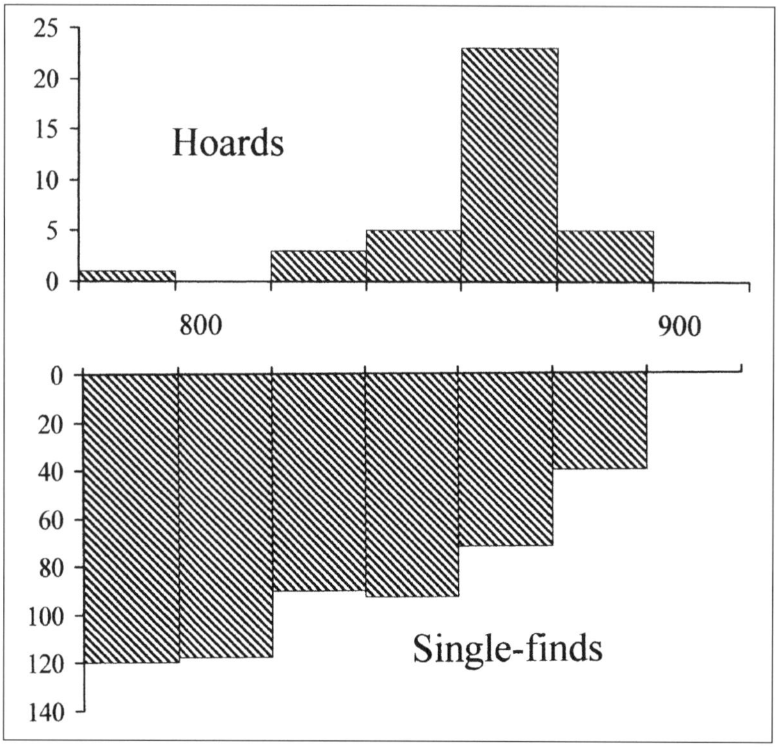

FIGURE 3.2.
Histogram comparing hoards and single-finds from England, 780–900.

and sixth-century coins in graves had usually been worn as ornaments. Some coins may be strays from disturbed hoards, although as the number of new hoards found in England is tiny compared to the number of single-finds any distortion of the evidence through the inclusion of the odd hoard coin should be small. That this does indeed appear to be so is indicated by the very different chronological patterns shown by the hoards and the single-finds. Suchodolski (1996) has also warned about the influence of votive deposits, such as coins placed in hearths or foundation trenches, but while this may be a factor in Poland, we have no evidence that such practices were followed in Anglo-Saxon England. Our confidence in the general reliability of the single-find evidence is bolstered by the similar patterns that recur at different sites and in different regions.

The interpretation of single-finds: geographical and quantitative approaches

The single-find evidence can be used for interpretation in two fundamentally different ways. One is studying their geographical distribution, taking them as evidence that the coins were in use at the places where they were found. The other is a more quantitative and chronological approach, looking at the number of finds from different periods in a particular place or locality.

We can use the geographical distribution of particular coin types to help identify where they were produced and how they subsequently moved in circulation. The simplest way is to plot the findspots on a map or series of maps, but Metcalf has developed a number of sophisticated statistical techniques to present and interpret the data. Thus he has used a form of regression analysis to compare the average distances and directions coins from different mints travelled before being lost (Metcalf 1998a and b; this volume). This showed that in the ninth century, coins from Canterbury and London generally travelled further that those from East Anglia and Wessex, a feature also seen in the eighth century. For the Late Anglo-Saxon period, after *c.* 973, he has investigated the velocity of circulation of coinage seeing how far coins had travelled during the short period in which each type was valid (Metcalf 1980, 27–31). These methods look at the distribution of coins of a particular type or mint, but one could equally concentrate on the origins of coins found at a particular site, seeing in which direction it had contacts. Thus, the 'productive' site in 'South Lincolnshire' is exceptional for its high proportion of Continental coins of the seventh and eighth centuries, implying it had a significant role in North Sea trade. However, before drawing conclusions about the significance of a group of finds, one must take into account the normal composition of the currency in that region and the indirect routes by which particular coins might have arrived.

The second approach to single-finds is a quantitative/chronological one. Here we are interested not in where the coins came from, but in how many have been found and what this tells us about monetary activity on a particular site or in a certain region (Blackburn 1989b). Any interpretation must take into account the fact that the rate of recovery of coins from different sites or localities will inevitably differ. The excavation finds from *Hamwic* have been prolific, yet only some one and a half hectares (three and a half acres) representing 3 percent of the estimated habitation area has been investigated. If the excavations had extended over 10 percent or 20 percent of the settlement, the number of coins found would be very different. Moreover, had the archaeologists excavated the same square metreage but in a different area of *Hamwic* they might have found very few coins. In the case of metal-detector finds, the sites that have yielded most coins have generally been worked on for hundreds of hours, often over many years, but the rate of discovery varies dramatically from year to year depending on soil conditions and the depth to which the land has been ploughed. The level of finds recording by numismatists or archaeologists also differs from region to region: a recent study of Celtic coins shows an unusually high density of finds in Oxfordshire, which is thought to be due to the fact that the Celtic Coin Index is based in Oxford (De Jersey 1997). Similar biases will undoubtedly have affected the Early Medieval find data.

Because of these factors biasing the sample, conclusions cannot be drawn based on the absolute number of coins recorded from a particular site or region. The data can, however, be used to draw comparisons between periods. A coin of the tenth century should have as much chance of being recovered in excavations or by metal-detector as one of the eighth or eleventh century, and most finders would be as likely to report one Anglo-Saxon coin as any other. There will be some distortions, with very rare coins having a greater chance of being recorded and the commonest ones or cut halves and quarters being passed over by some finders and professionals as being of lesser interest. This will particularly affect Henry II's cross-and-crosslet issue of 1158–80, which are uniform in type and badly struck. During the twenty years in which Michael Bonser and I have been recording finds we have always impressed on our contacts the need to report every single coin of the period 410–1180, irrespective of its rarity, legibility or condition. Let us start, then, as a control, by looking at three sites where we know that we have an unbiased sample: the excavated coins from *Hamwic*, and the metal-detector finds from 'near Royston' and Tilbury recorded by Bonser and myself.

Hamwic, Royston and Tilbury compared

The prolific coin finds from many seasons of excavations at *Hamwic* form a striking pattern when viewed as a histogram (Fig. 3.3a). This shows a dramatic start at the beginning of the eighth century to very high rates of coin loss which lasted for some forty to fifty years followed by an equally sharp decline in the middle of the century. After this coins continued to be lost at modest levels for another hundred years, before tailing off by the end of the ninth century. Three-quarters of the 129 excavation coins come from the period 700–50. This has been interpreted as indicating that *Hamwic* 'rose swiftly to commercial prosperity during the first quarter of the eighth century ... and declined again to a much more modest level of monetary exchanges in or before the last quarter of the same century. At that level it survived for at least another 80 or 100 years' (Metcalf 1988a, 25).

Archaeological evidence indicates that *Hamwic* was laid out as a town on a new site *c.* 700, and that it had been abandoned in favour of the defended *burh* to the west by 900. The coin finds are entirely

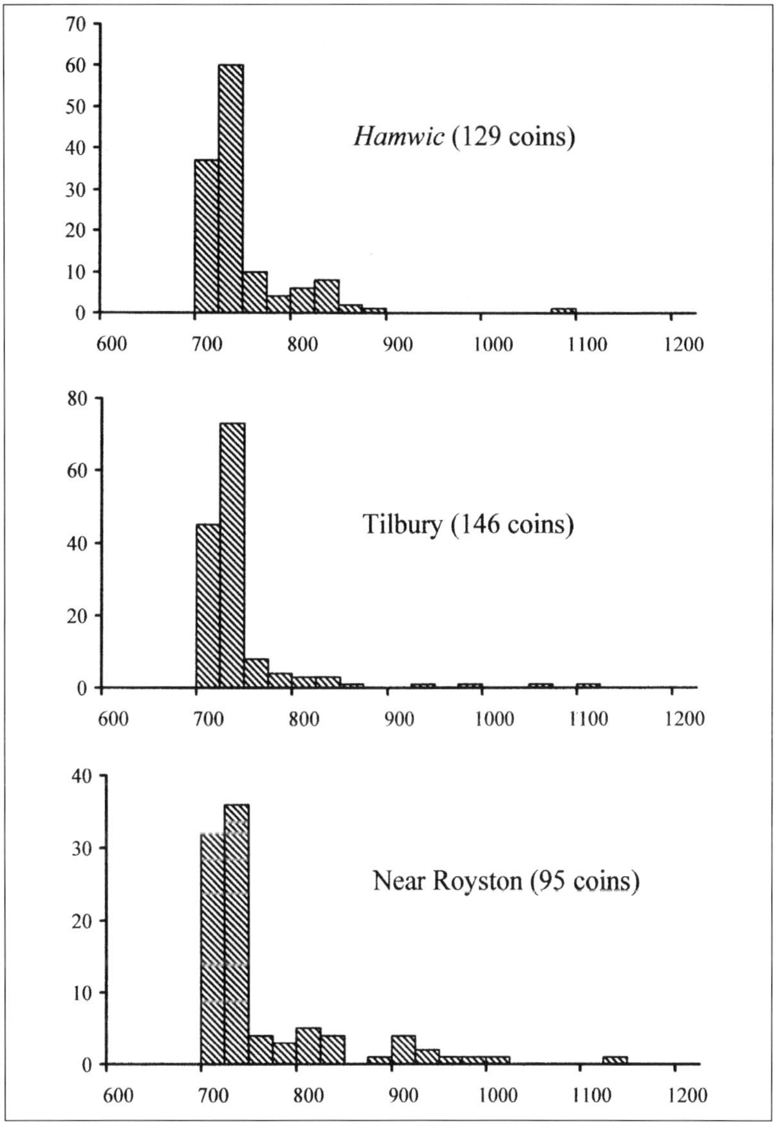

FIGURE 3.3. Finds from *Hamwic*, Tilbury and 'near Royston'.

consistent with this, but how far they can be used to chart the level of commercial activity at *Hamwic* during the intervening 200 years is something to be considered more closely.

Some 150 kilometres away at Tilbury, on the north bank of the Thames below London, two adjoining fields were a popular hunting ground for several metal-detector users during the later 1980s and '90s. Some of them reported their finds of coins and metalwork directly to us, so we have a significant and representative sample even if a much larger quantity of material has been found there. These 146 coins (Fig. 3.3b) present an almost identical pattern to those from *Hamwic*, with in this case 80 percent of the coins dating from 700–50. No seventh-century gold coins or primary sceattas have been found, but the intermediate sceattas (*c.* 700–15) are present in good numbers, and only four coins date from after 900. Some Middle Anglo-Saxon metalwork was seen by Leslie Webster but no archaeological survey of the site has been carried out.

Another eighty kilometres north, in a large field on the Cambridgeshire/Hertfordshire borders near Royston, two detector-users have found some 116 Early Medieval coins since 1979. Their histogram (Fig. 3.3c) again looks very similar for the period down to 900, but with a slightly lower concentration during 700–50 (65 percent) because the finds revive in the tenth century with a group of Viking and later issues. The metalwork from the site was not of high status and was predominantly from the eighth and ninth centuries, but continuing into the tenth century. Again, no archaeological survey has been carried out.

If the finds can be interpreted as a measure of general commercial activity, it does seem extraordinary that the fortunes of the sites at Tilbury and Royston should so closely have mirrored those of *Hamwic* a hundred miles away, despite their differing functions – *Hamwic* an international port and urban settlement, Royston perhaps a seasonal market serving the rural economy and Tilbury probably bridging local and inter-regional trade via the Thames. Nor do the different political circumstances at the three sites seem to have had a significant effect – *Hamwic* in Wessex, Royston in Mercia and Tilbury in Essex, the latter subject first to Mercian then to West Saxon domination. The coin types found at each site were rather different, especially during the first half of the eighth century, those at *Hamwic* being dominated by the locally-produced sceattas of Series H, while Tilbury and Royston had mainly Series K, L, S and Continental E but in differing proportions. In numerical terms the amount of coinage being lost may have been similar, but it was represented by the local currency.

The wider context

A comparable pattern can be traced at sites in East Anglia and Lincolnshire. At Bawsey in Norfolk (Fig. 3.4a) the finds begin somewhat earlier with gold shillings and primary sceattas, but there is still a build up *c.* 700 and a step down *c.* 750 into the broad penny period. Coinage is very sparse between the mid ninth and late tenth centuries, but then picks up in the eleventh century. Coddenham and Barham in Suffolk and Caistor-by-Norwich, Norfolk are three more sites that begin in the gold period, have some primary sceattas and many intermediate and

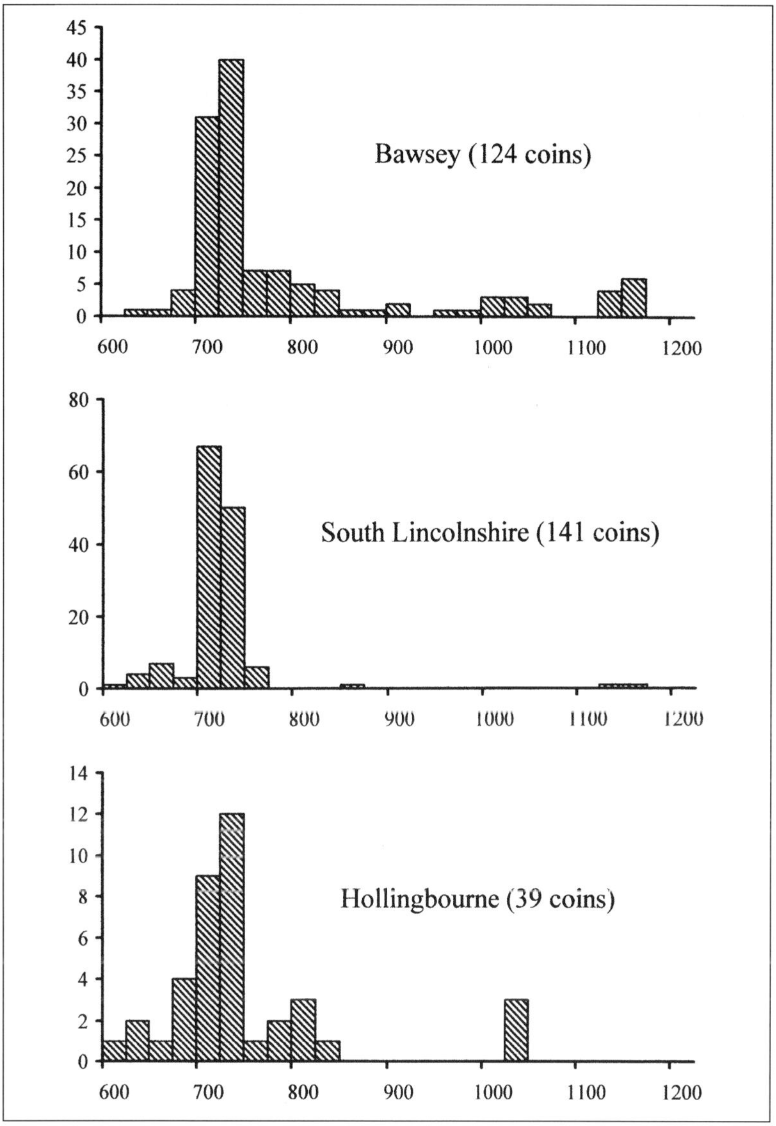

FIGURE 3.4.
Finds from Bawsey, 'South Lincolnshire' and Hollingbourne.

secondary ones, but very few broad pennies. 'South Lincolnshire' (Fig. 3.4b), Riby and Flixborough are three Lincolnshire sites dominated by Middle Anglo-Saxon finds, the first two having a distinctive seventh-century gold phase, but still with a sharp step up and down *c.* 700 and *c.* 750. Flixborough is unusual in having an additional mid ninth-century element, comprising 'Lunette' pennies of Burgred, Æthelred I and Alfred and Northumbrian stycas, arguably associated with the presence of the Viking army on the Trent in 872/3 (Blackburn 1993b), and this is certainly the cause of the distinctive pattern of coin and artefacts from Torksey (Blackburn 2002).

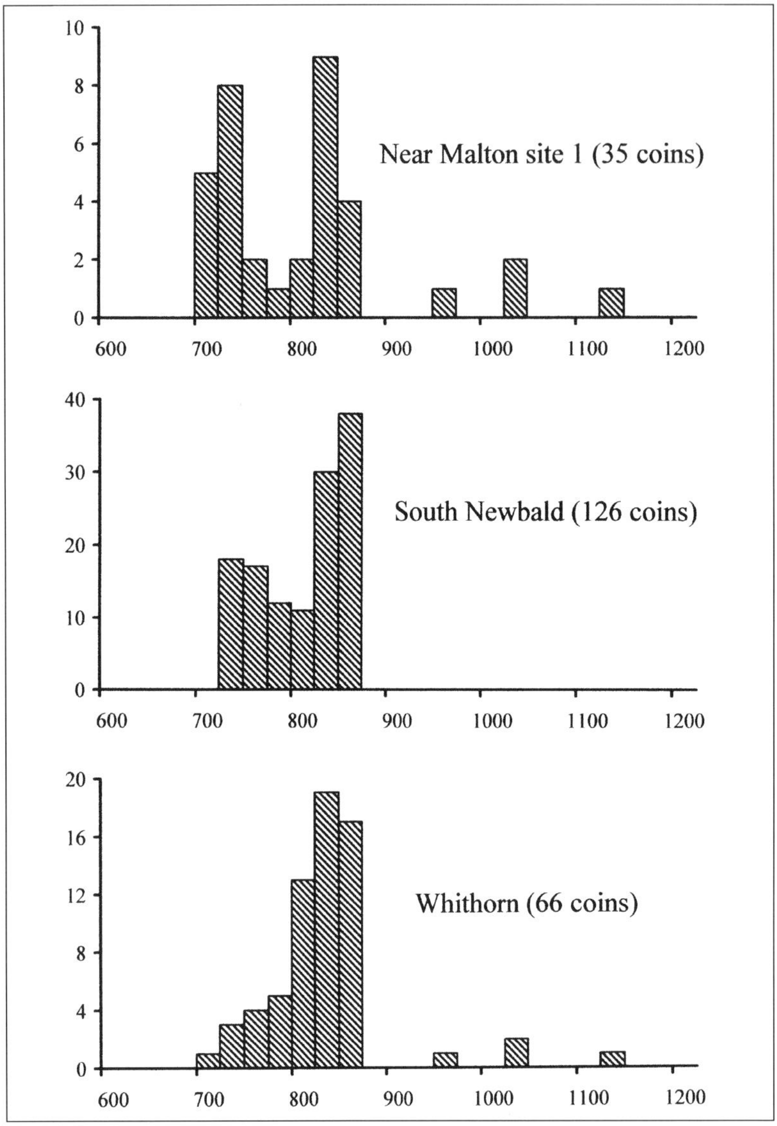

FIGURE 3.5.
Finds from 'near Malton' 1, South Newbald and Whithorn. The Northumbrian sites have a distinctive pattern due to the large quantity of base stycas circulating in the mid ninth century.

In Kent, the most prolific site, Reculver, produced at least sixty-five sceattas during the erosion of the coastline in the seventeenth and eighteenth centuries, but only a handful of broad pennies. At other Kentish sites broad pennies are better represented, but still sceattas predominate, as at Hollingbourne (Fig. 3.4c) which has four seventh-century gold coins, twenty-six sceattas and nine later pennies mostly of the late eighth or early ninth century. Another site near Canterbury with a similar distribution has yielded one gold shilling, nine sceattas, and nine broad pennies.

The Northumbrian sites, such as South Newbald (Fig. 3.5b), 'near

Malton 1' (Fig. 3.5a), 'near Malton 2', Cottam, Whitby, Carlisle, 'North of England' and of course York, have a distinctive pattern of their own, strongly influenced by the circulation of the base and low-value stycas in the ninth century. Into the same mould falls the only 'productive' site in Scotland, the Northumbrian monastic settlement at Whithorn (Fig. 3.5c).

The similarity in the pattern of coin loss at each of the sites we have looked at is too great to be the result simply of *ad hoc* changes in activity prompted by local circumstances. Could we be seeing evidence not of a change in the function of the sites but of a change in the use of money? Support for the view that these histograms mainly reflect a general monetary trend which is not site-specific is indicated by the pattern of 3,552 isolated finds from southern England excluding those from 'productive' sites (Fig. 3.6). The profile of this histogram between 600 and 900 has much in common with those for the sites in southern England discussed above. There is a small but increasing volume of finds during the gold phase, a step up with the primary sceattas in the last quarter of the seventh century, but a far more dramatic increase in the first half of the eighth. The sharp fall in the mid eighth century is just as clear as at the 'productive' sites, followed perhaps by something of a revival towards the end of the century, although the third quarter remains one of the most mysterious periods for the numismatist (Metcalf 1988b). For the ninth century, a steady decline in coin finds is seen more clearly among the isolated finds than those from 'productive' sites possibly because of the larger sample. After 900 the isolated finds provide a quite different picture, with a fairly progressive increase in the number of finds until the third quarter of the eleventh century, a falling back in the late eleventh and early twelfth centuries, and a rise again down to the end of the period in 1180. Even so, the highest point in the second half of the histogram is less than half the level attained during the first half of the eighth century. The proliferation of coinage in the early eighth century is one of the most remarkable features of the economy of Early Medieval England, and one we could barely have guessed at before the advent of metal-detector finds.

The histogram in Fig. 3.6 is an important tool, for it establishes a typical pattern of coin finds that might be expected in southern England from 'normal' monetary activity. When interpreting the finds from particular sites we should compare them with this control, and only if there are significant differences can we attempt to say something about the specific sites. Thus, the absence from *Hamwic*, Tilbury and Royston of any coins before 700 appears to be significant, and strongly suggests that those sites were newly established or, at least, changed

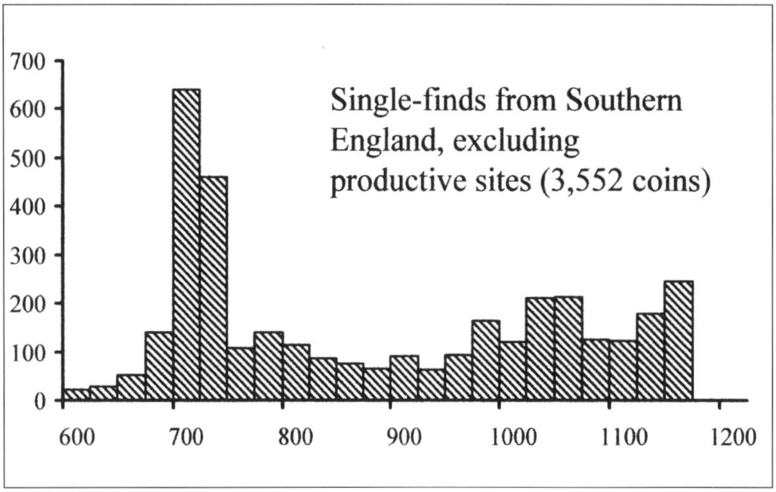

FIGURE 3.6.
Isolated finds from England south of the Humber.

their nature at the beginning of the eighth century. Their pattern of finds during the eighth and ninth centuries can now be seen to be unexceptional; towards the end of this period the finds are perhaps slightly lower than expected. The significant change for *Hamwic* and Tilbury comes at about the end of the ninth century and for Royston in the mid tenth century as the finds fail to pick up and match the profile of the isolated finds generally. Of the other sites reviewed, Bawsey, Coddenham, 'South Lincolnshire', Riby, Hollingbourne and 'near Canterbury' all have a sufficient quantity of early gold coinage to suggest that they had played a similar economic role throughout the seventh and eighth centuries, and possibly from an even earlier date. Some of them, such as 'South Lincolnshire', Hollingbourne and 'near Canterbury', may have suffered a real decline or been abandoned in the late eighth or first half of the ninth century, while Bawsey continued into the eleventh century. Coins may not have changed hands so frequently on these sites after the mid eighth century, but we should not assume that commercial activities suffered as a result, for other means could have been found to conduct business, such as barter or credit, as they would have been before 700. This view is supported by the finds of metal artefacts from the sites. Those from Royston, Bawsey and Barham were studied by Leslie Webster and Sue Margeson for the 1989 symposium and they reported that there was no parallel reduction in ninth-century metalwork, indeed at Royston and Bawsey this was the most plentiful group and the finds continued at a moderate level into the tenth century.

We are beginning to see the characterisation of quite a large number of Middle Anglo-Saxon places where coinage was regularly changing hands and metal artefacts were being dropped. Many of these declined or failed at some point during the ninth or tenth century, and did not develop into Late Anglo-Saxon towns. Today these are mostly located in open fields and have been readily accessible to metal-detector users. By contrast, those that continued to thrive and developed into towns in the Late Anglo-Saxon and later Middle Ages have not been investigated by metal-detector users to the same extent. The finds from towns and cities have often been recovered from small urban excavations and chance finds in gardens or on building sites. To obtain sufficient material to study from towns it is necessary to amalgamate such finds. Not surprisingly they present a very different pattern of finds from the more classic rural 'productive' site.

For London, Stott (1991) recorded 158 finds from within the City and from the settlement around Aldwych to the west, and their histogram (Fig. 3.7a) mirrors quite closely that of the isolated finds in Fig. 3.6. The eleventh-century finds are more plentiful than would be predicted from the 'normal' pattern, presumably reflecting London's growing importance as the capital of the newly unified kingdom of

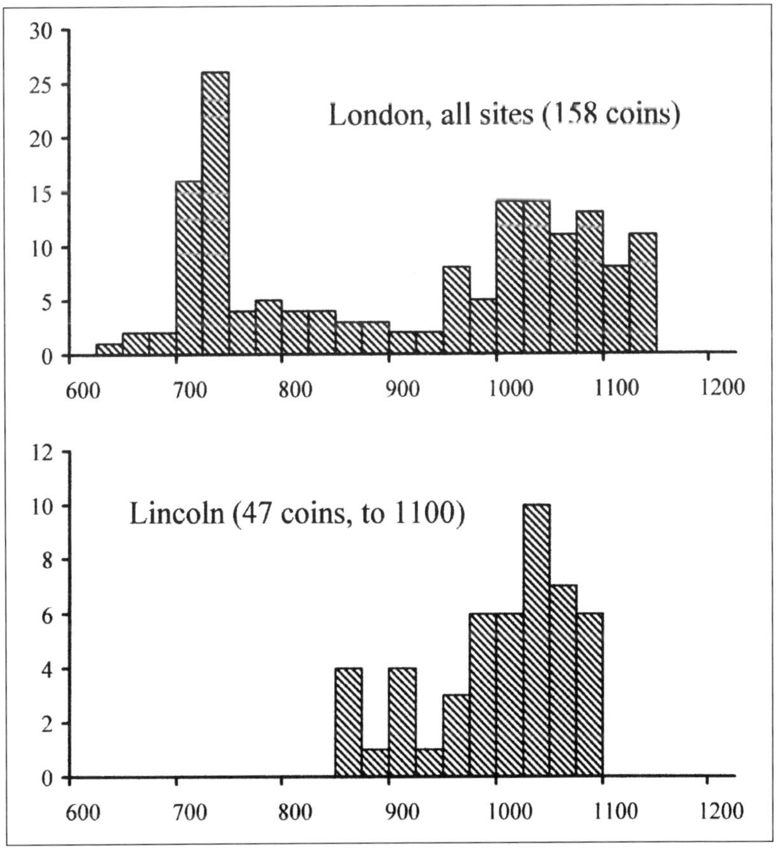

FIGURE 3.7.
Finds from London and Lincoln.

England. Yet even this is by a factor of less than two, confirming that in the Middle Anglo-Saxon period London was already a major commercial centre. Lincoln provides an interesting contrast. Archaeologists have yet to find evidence of a Middle Anglo-Saxon settlement in the town, and the accumulated coin finds (Fig. 3.7b) bear out the absence of this phase. They begin in the 870s and reflect the Scandinavian development of the town. If Lincoln had a Middle Anglo-Saxon precursor, comparable to *Hamwic* for Southampton or Fishergate for York, it must have been located elsewhere. Thetford has yielded many coins from the eighth century onwards, but their distribution is weighted to the eleventh and twelfth centuries as a prolific area of the Late Anglo-Saxon and later medieval town has been extensively investigated.

Economic factors

Having traced the changing pattern of coin finds in Early Medieval England, we have to ask what it is that we are really observing. Elsewhere I have argued that the finds reflect 'monetary activity' in a broad sense, not only changing hands in transactions but even being carried in people's purses, for the more money there was on the site, the greater the chance of coins being accidentally lost (Blackburn 1989a and b). The risk of loss could be increased by more rapid circulation of the same amount of money, but the most likely factor influencing it would be the volume of currency in circulation.

There is a well-documented parallel for the expansion and contraction of single-finds in the thirteenth to fifteenth centuries. Rigold (1977) observed a dramatic increase and decline in the number of coin finds from excavation sites which coincide with comparable changes in the volume of the English currency (Blackburn 1989a, 19–20; more accurate estimates for the size of the currency now available in Allen 2001 support the same conclusion). The contraction in the late fourteenth and fifteenth centuries was prompted by a general shortage of silver in Europe (Spufford 1988, 339–62). Arguably, we may be witnessing something similar in the Early Middle Ages, with large fluctuations in the amount of available silver as new sources were found to replenish the existing stock that was constantly being eroded. The dramatic rise in coin loss *c.* 700 took place at a time when the coinage of Frisia (sceattas of Series E and D) was expanding rapidly and flooding into England, where much of it was melted down and restruck as Anglo-Saxon sceattas (Grierson and Blackburn 1986, 152–4 and 167–9). New sources of silver had probably been discovered in central Europe, possibly in the Harz mountains in north Germany, fuelling the expansion of the coinage in north-west Europe in the first half of the eighth century. However, a debasement in the fineness of the silver sceattas during the second quarter of the eighth century apparently heralded a major contraction in the currency. In the mid ninth century a general shortage of silver is again suggested by debasements observed in the Carolingian and Anglo-Saxon coinages from *c.* 840 (Metcalf and Northover 1985 and 1989); in Northumbria it started earlier and was far more severe. Significantly, the ninth-century decline in single-finds found in England is also echoed in the finds from the Low Countries and Germany (Blackburn 1993a). There are other parallels; a number of sites, such as Domburg, Dorestad and Schouwen Island, thrived in the eighth and ninth centuries but then faded, just as many of the English 'productive' sites did. It seems, then, that we are really looking at common European economic trends.

Other aspects of this apparent contraction should be explored elsewhere. Die-studies of the coinage can shed light on the relative mint output, and these need to be brought into any consideration of how the economy operated. The price of silver will have varied with supply and demand, and so too the value of the penny. Historians should be aware, then, that a penny in the early eighth century is likely to have bought much less than one in the later ninth century. The new body of single-find evidence has provided us with a powerful tool for the study of the economy in the Early Middle Ages, but it is one to be used with considerable care.

Appendix: the principal 'productive' sites in Britain

Barham, Suffolk (50+ coins) (unpublished; 44 on EMC)

Bawsey, Norfolk (124 coins) (unpublished; 40 on EMC)

Bedford, near (19 coins) (unpublished; EMC)

Bidford-on-Avon, Warwicks. (14 coins) (Wise and Seaby 1995)

Brandon, Suffolk (20+ excavation coins) (unpublished)

Caistor-by-Norwich, Norfolk (23 unpublished, 19 sold Christie's 4.11.1986, lots 354–72)

Cambridge, near (15 coins) (Blackburn and Sorenson 1984)

Canterbury, near, Kent (19 coins) (Bonser 1997, 41)

Carisbrooke (area), Isle of Wight (15+ coins probably from a single site) (Ulmschneider 2000a, 171–2)

Carlisle, Cumbria (61 coins, various sites) (Pirie 2000, 49 and 76–7; EMC)

Coddenham, Suffolk (33+ coins) (unpublished; some Sotheby 4.10.1994)

Cottam, near Sledmere, N. Yorks. (40 coins) (Pirie 2000, 44 and 62)

Flixborough, Lincs. (53 coins, excavation and detector finds) (Blackburn 1993b, 87)

Hamwic (Southampton), Hants. (134 coins from several excavation sites) (Metcalf 1988a)

Hanford, Dorset (18+ coins) (unpublished)

Hollingbourne, Kent (39 coins) (Bonser 1997, 41)

Ipswich, Suffolk (*c.* 145 coins from several excavation sites) (unpublished, some on EMC)

Lincoln, Lincs. (47 coins from various sites) (Blackburn, Colyer and Dolley 1983; unpublished additions)

London (158 coins from various sites) (Stott 1991; EMC)

Malton, near, N. Yorks., site 1 (35+ coins) (Bonser 1997, 42)

Malton, near, N. Yorks., site 2 (57+ coins) (Bonser 1997, 42–3)

'North of England', E. Yorks. or N. Lincs. (112 coins, many unrecorded) (Bonser 1997, 43–4)

Ravendale, West, Lincs. (12 coins) (Blackburn and Bonser 1984b; Blackburn 1993b, 88 ('near Grimsby'))

Reculver, Kent (73+ coins) (Rigold 1975; Rigold and Metcalf 1984; Metcalf 1988c)

Riby, near, Lincs. (28+ coins, few described) (Ulmschneider 2000a, 146; EMC)

Royston, near, Herts./Cambs. border (116 coins) (Blackburn and Bonser 1986; Bonser 1997, 44; EMC)

'South Lincolnshire' (141 coins) (Bonser 1997, 41–2; EMC)

South Newbald ('Sancton'), S. Yorks. (126 coins) (Booth and Blowers 1983; Booth 1997)

Thetford, Suffolk (various sites) (109+ coins) (Blackburn and Bonser 1984a, 69–71; EMC and unpublished)

Tilbury, Essex (146 coins) (Bonser 1997, 44–5)

Torksey, Lincs. (50+ coins) (Blackburn 2002)

Whitby, Yorks. (169+ coins from 1920–8 excavations and other finds) (Rigold and Metcalf 1984, 265; Pirie 2000, 45 and 66–7)

Whithorn, Wigtownshire, Scotland (66 coins from excavations) (Pirie 1997)

York (150+ coins) (Pirie 1986a and 2000, 40 and 54–6; EMC)

CHAPTER 4

Variations in the Composition of the Currency at Different Places in England

Michael Metcalf

Bede tells us that when Earconberht became king of Kent in 640, his daughter Earcongota was a virtuous young lady then serving God in the monastery built by the Frankish princess Fara (i.e. Faremoutiers-en-Brie):

> At that time, because there were not yet many monasteries founded in England, numbers of people from Britain used to enter the monasteries of the Franks or Gauls to practice the monastic life; they also sent their daughters to be taught in them and to be wedded to the heavenly bridegroom; they mostly went to the monasteries at Brie, Chelles, and Andelys sur Seine. (*Historia Ecclesiastica*, iii, 8)

Earcongota died at Faremoutiers, and Bede actually speaks eulogistically of her as 'that gold coin' (*aureum illud nomisma*) which had come from Kent.

The list of Merovingian and other foreign gold coins found in England now runs to about 140 single finds from *c.* 530 to *c.* 670 (Rigold 1975, 653; Metcalf 1989, 267; Coin Register 1987-, *ad loc.*). It includes no fewer than five examples from the mint of Loco Sancto (Lieusaint-en-Brie), compared with only two from the far more prolific mint of Paris nearby. Three of the five are from Folkestone, one is from near Lincoln, and one (Coin Register 1989, No. 58) is from Heston, Middlesex. This is the only case which comes to mind, from seventh- to eighth-century England, where the distribution pattern of single finds of some particular variety of coin seems to reflect a non-commercial context. The emphasis on Folkestone is intriguing for the early history of the Kentish ports, but unfortunately it is not clear from the record whether they might not be from a single discovery, or even whether two of the finds may not be the same coin reported twice. Even so, four single finds or even two single finds and a hoard from this relatively obscure small Merovingian mint may be judged significant. There is only one French single find of Loco Sancto in Lafaurie's list, against eight from Paris (Lafaurie 1961, 275). I cannot resist quoting what Gough's edition of Camden's *Britannia* says about Folkestone, a delightful example of laconic brevity:

> In this towne there is a mayer; and this Lord Clynton's grant-father had there of a poore man a boote almost full of antiquities of pure gold and silver. A cony drawing his yerth betwyxt Folkestan and Hythe did cast up antique money' (Gough 1789, i, 246).

If I had got my hands on that rabbit, I would have put it out to stud.

In this paper I wish to address the specific question of whether it is possible to distinguish different categories of market sites by the nature of their coin finds, and the composition of the currency found at different sites. Were there any ascertainable differences between the currency circulating on the one hand in the English *wics*, and on the other hand in inland centres such as 'productive' sites or markets of the second rank, such as might imply a different character to monetary affairs in the smaller centres? The coins in use inland might, in principle, differ from those in the *wics* in a variety of ways. They might be slightly inferior coins, for example they might be more worn, or the heavier coins might have been culled. Neither of these differences, if they existed, would be easy to prove, although Frands Herschend has demonstrated the phenomenon in Scandinavia (Herschend 1989, 373). The most obvious and straightforward difference would be if the range of types represented inland (remember that there are more than a hundred different types of sceattas) was slightly different from the range encountered in the *wic*, either because certain coin types were not carried inland to the same extent, or because certain types were actually minted at inland centres.

This exercise, by its very nature, involves comparing one assemblage of finds with another. The comparison has to be statistical, whether one is comparing histograms of weights, or proportions of different types in a sample. So how do we define the samples we are to compare? Because there are so many different coin types, most of them scarce, we may sometimes need to group them, in order to create a sample of a statistically decent size. Those coins excavated from a *wic* offer a neat, ready-made sample from a clear and restricted topographical context, and those from an inland 'productive' site which has been conscientiously reported, without the selective withholding of common varieties by the finders, should provide a satisfactory, straight comparison. But the smaller inland centres are more difficult to handle statistically: the numbers, almost by definition, are not going to be large enough to be statistically adequate. We will leave that problem on one side for the moment. First, it is necessary to find some differences (if there are any), and only then can one dream up hypotheses to try to explain them, and look for ways of testing the hypotheses.

It is at least obvious that stark differences will not be found. At most there will be differences of degree, or tendencies, lying at the edge of what is statistically significant. The *wics* are certainly the best starting point: we have several well-excavated sites, from which at best a hundred or more sceattas have been recovered. Each *wic* is different in the range of types represented. *Hamwic* has a far higher proportion of the locally minted Series H than occurs anywhere else; York has a high proportion of the locally-minted Series Y. Ipswich, London, the east Kentish *wics* of the Wantsum Channel all tend to be more varied, with no predominant type. And indeed, even *Hamwic* has yielded a wide variety of English types from different mint-places, together accounting for about the same proportion of the total as Series H. Monetary circulation in England was compartmented into half-a-dozen big regions such as south Wessex, the Midlands, or East Anglia, but it was not tightly compartmented: coins from mints throughout England circulated throughout England, certainly in the primary phase (to *c.* 710), and to a lesser extent in the secondary phase (Metcalf 1998a, 276). In practice it is apparent that each of the *wics* was the gateway from the North Sea or the English Channel, into its hinterland: the mix of sceatta types in the inland parts of that region was broadly similar to what we find at the *wic*. That was because the minting of coinage was concentrated in the *wics* or in the coastlands. The currency needs of the inland parts were met by coinage being drawn in from the coastal mint-places, doubtless in a context of inter-regional trade. It follows from all this that we cannot legitimately or usefully compare one inland site with another in a different region.

Very generally, and in proportional terms, we can say that roughly 10 percent of the sceattas minted in England were minted in York, 30 percent in East Anglia, 50 percent in Kent and London, and 10 percent in *Hamwic*. Money originating in the south-east became widely diffused through the Midlands, whereas the other regions were rather more self-contained. At the 'productive' site near Royston, for example, Series R, from East Anglia, is noticeably lacking.

On top of this pattern, a good 20 percent of the English currency consisted of foreign sceattas, minted in the Rhine mouths area (and one percent or less consisted of the equivalent Merovingian silver coins). The Frisian coins entered England at all the major points of entry along the North Sea coasts and along the south coast. From the west, and from the Irish Sea coasts, there were virtually no inflows; and there were no English mints in the west. That, very briefly, is how English monetary circulation operated in the eighth century: recognizably much the same patterns as in the eleventh century. *A priori* it seems a forlorn hope to imagine that there might be significant differences between the inland centres and the *wics*. But let us not prejudge that question.

Inland we find a certain number of astonishingly 'productive' sites. Two or three adjoining fields will sometimes yield a hundred or more stray finds of sceattas. The eighth-century equivalent of a car-boot sale was perhaps a periodic fair held regularly at a traditional fairground. People would know where to come, in the same way that they knew the particular fields or pasture where the hundred court or the wapentake was held. We also find, throughout the countryside, stray finds in ones and twos, very widely distributed. In all, we have a data-base of over 2,360 single finds (plus a substantial number of coins from hoards, which cannot be used as evidence in the same way). The art of this research lies in deciding, or discovering, what constitutes a fair comparison. In southern Wessex, for example, we can say that at *Hamwic* Series H accounts for almost exactly 50 percent of the secondary sceattas, and ask how that figure compares with what we find in the hinterland. The scattered single finds are too few to give a statistically secure sample of the currency available in any particular locality. They need to be collected into larger groupings somehow before they can be compared, as to the proportions of different types, with the *wics*, or indeed with the 'productive' sites. How do we draw boundaries so that the stray finds so grouped neither obscure significant concentrations of sceatta types by lumping them together with material for which the context was different, nor create artificial significance by picking and choosing?

We can use a form of regression analysis in which we count up the total number of single finds within a circle of, say, twenty-five kilometre radius, and calculate the frequency of a particular type, for example Series H, as a percentage of that total. By repeating that procedure at numerous localities, we can create a map which is dotted with percentage figures. We can then interpret that information by drawing contour lines on the basis of the percentages, to reflect the districts where the type being studied was relatively more or less

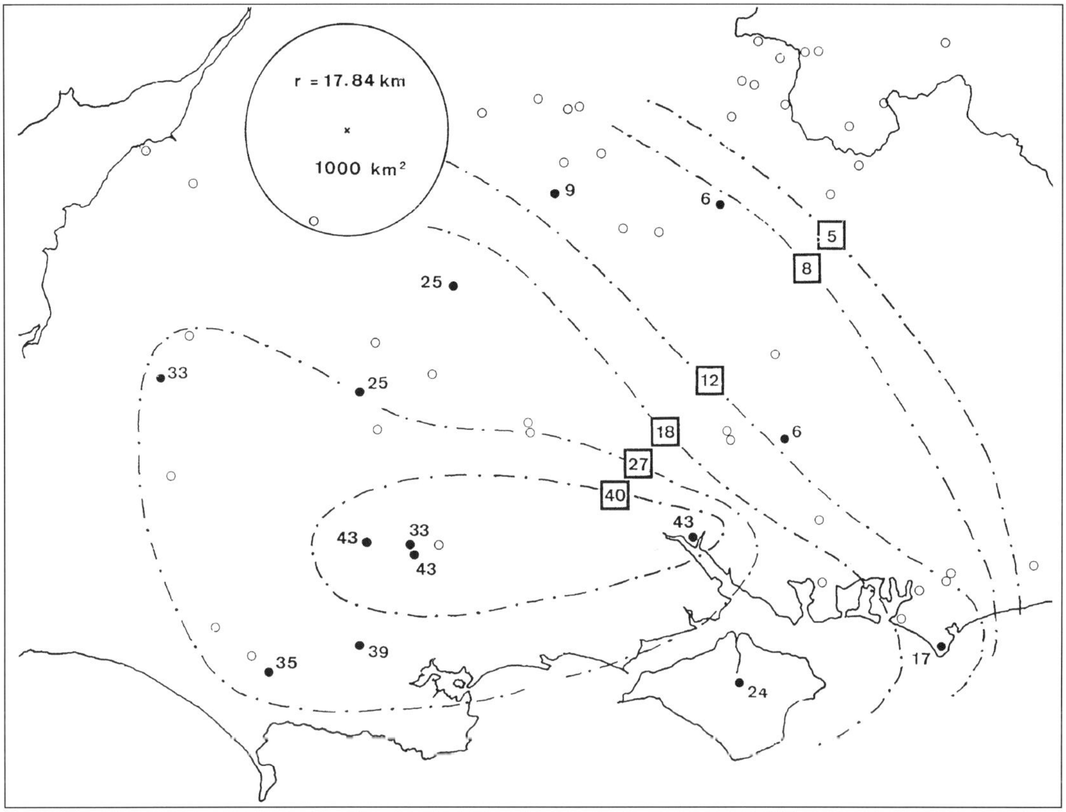

FIGURE 4.1.
Regression analysis showing the frequency of *Hamwic* coinage within Wessex, mapped in contours.

frequent. This procedure does not measure absolute quantities of coins: Series H could, in principle, be relatively frequent in a district where there was little coinage. A map of Wessex constructed in this way (Fig. 4.1) shows rather clearly that money from *Hamwic* was diffused into the hinterland westwards but not eastwards or northwards. The same technique has been applied to the finds from East Anglia (Metcalf 2001), in an attempt to discover the mint-places of Series R, and also to other sceatta types, the mint-places of which are debateable.

With this much encouragement from the study of English coin types, we turn back to the inland market centres where sceattas have been found, and to a regression analysis of the foreign sceattas. The *wic* was an interface; or, in the words of Bede, London was 'an *emporium* for many nations who came to it by land and sea' (*Historia Ecclesiastica*, ii, 3). But what of merchants from the Rhine mouths area, who brought so much money into England, especially in the primary phase, up to *c.* 710? Might not some of them have thought to cut out the middle-man, by travelling straight to the interior of England, rather than by buying at a *wic*? If that had happened, the proportion of continental sceattas might, contrary to rational expectation, be higher inland than at the *wic*. Practical experience suggests that it will be better to treat the primary and secondary phases separately. We will look in the first instance at the proportion of primary porcupines to all primary finds (Fig. 4.2). Regression analysis can be applied to a statistically very adequate sample of 153 porcupines from 96 localities, out of 744 primary sceattas from 292 localities. Porcupines were pervasive: there was no part of England which they failed to reach, or from which they were excluded. In more detail, however, the picture is complex and difficult to interpret. That should

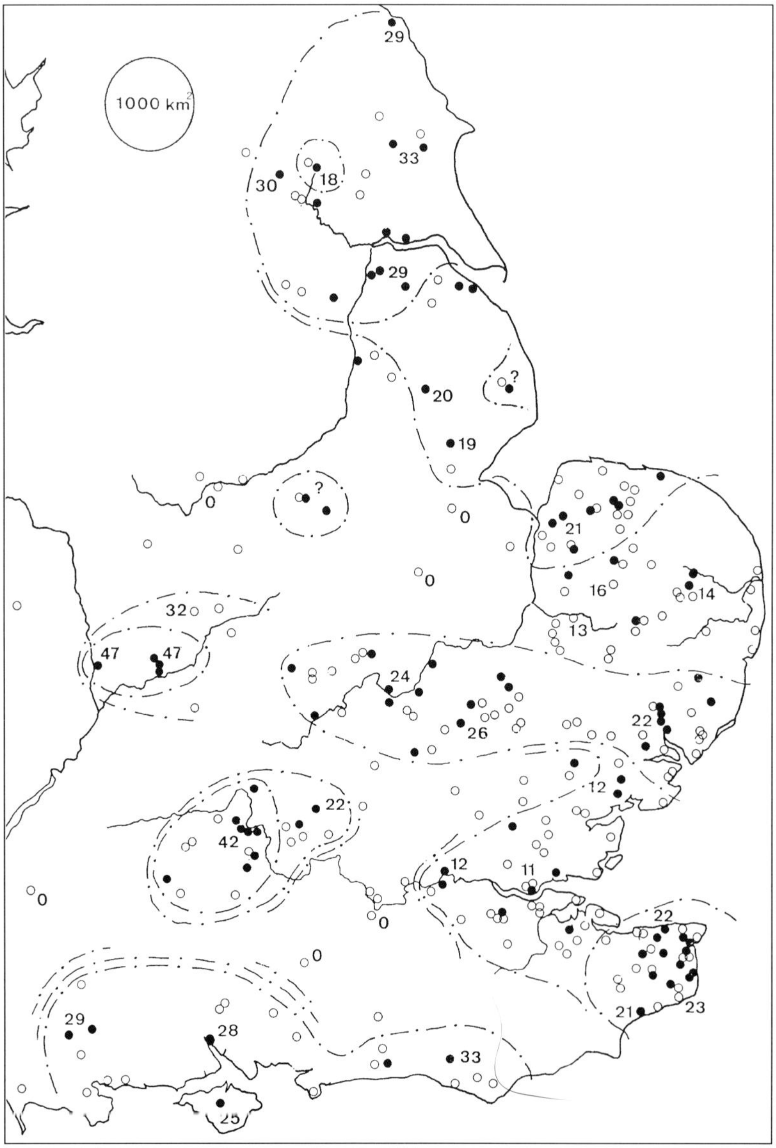

FIGURE 4.2.
Regression analysis showing the proportion of primary porcupine sceattas compared to all primary sceatta finds, mapped in contours.

not surprise us, because we are trying to isolate tendencies, in a human situation which was multifarious: some merchants may have decided to go inland, while others opted for coastwise trading, or for buying and selling at a *wic*. The only scientifically acceptable procedure is first to discover discrepancies, and then to try to explain them, through a hypothesis which seems to stand up to scrutiny.

The average proportion of primary porcupines, for England as a whole, is 20.6 percent. East Kent and much of East Anglia (where the evidence is numerically strongest) are close to the average. The south coast reaches 30 percent, as does Humberside. *Hamwic* is the focal point for diffusion westwards into Dorset but not eastwards – as we have already seen with Series H. London, the lower Thames valley, and Essex are distinctly below average, at 11–12 percent. The percentage figures marked in Fig. 4.2 are derived from all the primary sceattas lying within a circle of eighteen kilometres radius, that is, an area of 1,000 square kilometres. The size of the circle makes no difference to the argument. It is a matter of expediency: a larger sample permits a smaller circle which still includes enough single finds to be statistically indicative. Too large a circle is topographically vague. In the present case they may number anything from fifteen or twenty coins, up to eighty. If the total is smaller, the result will be less reliable, because even one porcupine more or fewer will alter the proportion appreciably. This applies to the fringes of the circulation-area of sceattas, but also to certain empty areas between the main concentrations that have been mentioned.

So far as one can judge from small numbers, there is a real contrast: the proportions of porcupines are genuinely low in the in-between areas. One can see how near to the edge of statistical significance the evidence is, even in the maximally favourable case of comparing 20 percent of the data, i.e. porcupines, against the whole. For many other types, the statistics are still very inadequate, even with an overall sample of 2,360 finds. But juxtaposed with the 'empty' areas there are also two or three 'hot-spots'. The Oxford region exceeds 40 percent, on the basis of a fairly adequate sample, while Bidford-on-Avon, from where we have a sample that is utterly reliable and complete, is close to 50 percent. If money had been carried to those two districts from London or the lower Thames, should not one have expected figures closer to 11–12 percent? Bearing Dorset in mind too, the glimmer of a hypothesis comes to mind, involving sheep on chalk uplands. One recalls that the abbess of St Peter's, Gloucester, at a date between 735 and 767, acquired land for use as a sheep-walk, and that the bishop of Worcester in 743/5 was freed from payment of toll on two ships at London (Sawyer 1968, No. 88). Finberg went so far as to suggest

20
22
29
21
21
25
10
7
50
2
2
1
1
2
4
25

that Mercian bishops and abbesses drew an important part of their revenues from the traffic in wool (Finberg 1957, 12). Whether the same was true at an earlier date, for example between 695–715, we can only speculate, as documentary evidence does not exist.

We should continue to view any 'hot-spots' with caution because the proportions could change as new finds come to light. Provisionally, one can say that they are intriguing, and that they chime in with other evidence. The numbers of single finds of primary porcupines which create the excess proportions are small in the general scale of things. They are important for Hwiccia, but they make up only a very modest proportion of all the primary porcupines which silted up in England. Series U, Types 23b and d, shows a polarized distribution, in the south-east and in the Oxford region, with finds of 23b from Abingdon, Dorchester-on-Thames, and Moulsford (Metcalf 1994, 552). Similarly, the London coins of the secondary phase include a large group of Type 15 etc., in the so-called 'Hwiccian' style, which again seem to reflect trade from London to the upper Thames region (*ibid.*, 406). Fig. 4.3 shows the coins in question consistently reaching proportions of over 20 percent in Hwiccia. The same style also occurs in the London (Thames) hoard, and it is noticeable at East Tilbury. The two specimens from Ford, near Old Sarum may or may not be a mini-hoard. They, and the finds from north of London, have been seen as tipping the balance against a Hwiccian mint-attribution. Whatever the location of the mint, the pattern of finds points strongly to the trade route along the Thames. The problem is best assessed by comparing the pattern for Series L in other styles, which is quite different (Fig. 4.4). The explanation could be partly chronological, but the contrast certainly gives pause for thought.

FIGURE 4.3.
Regression analysis of Type 15 secondary sceattas of 'Hwiccian' style, mapped in contours.

The 'hot-spots' are the nearest thing which I can find in the evidence to a different composition of the currency at inland sites, and the best-evidenced for statistical reasons. The context to which they point us is the opposite of what, perhaps, we might have assumed: not rural isolation, but rather the long arm of international trade. That perspective does not rule out the minting of a few sceattas at inland centres of the second rank. The obvious candidates, I suppose, for such attribution would be the various eclectic types which are mostly K- or L-related – the 'Animal Mask', 'Triquetras', and 'Celtic Cross' groups, for example (*ibid.*, 417, 423, and 447). They are so scarce that they would completely fail to pass any statistical test; but in any case they show no signs of clustering. They were carried about over long distances in southern England, as is demonstrated often enough by die-duplicate specimens found far apart.

A game that one can usefully play is to make an imaginary

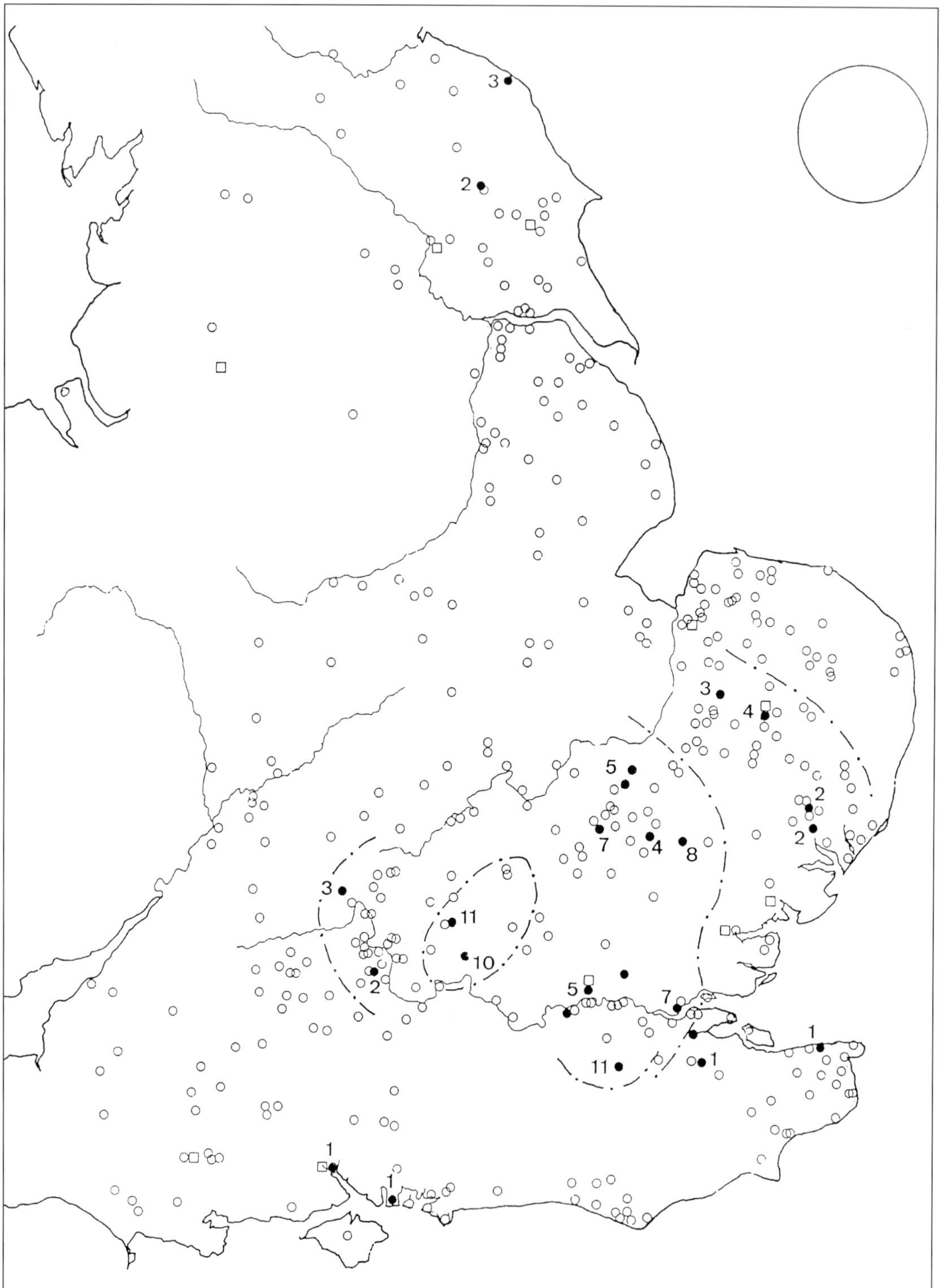
3
2
3
4
5
2
2
7
4
8
3
11
10
2
5
7
11
1
1
1
1

comparison with the eleventh century, when all the coins were mint-signed and when there were inland mints with relatively very tiny outputs. There tend to be very few single finds from those mints, naturally enough, and none from the towns where they were minted (Metcalf 1998a, 191–248). We can try to imagine the possibility of a similar framework of argument in the eighth century. In neither case, however, are there any grounds to suppose that the currency of those little inland mint towns was heavily coloured by the local issues: there are no grounds to postulate rural isolation.

The English monetary economy in the eighth century, it seems to me, was not only integrated regionally, with the *wic* as the focal point, but also it displayed the free movement of currency between regions (and between kingdoms). The distributional evidence suggests that by the first half of the eighth century it already functioned to create patterns that are remarkably similar to those from the eleventh century. The Aston Rowant hoard, from Oxfordshire, is a useful example of a large sum of money in transit, and which belonged (one imagines) to a wealthy merchant who was familiar with trading along the Thames valley. The hoard contained a lot of primary porcupines, but also sceattas of many other types. Behind the stray losses of single coins, which because they are random provide us with such splendid evidence, there lies big money. The great scale of the inflows of foreign currency is measurable *pro rata* through die-estimation of the contemporary English issues, and it offers a secure macro-economic perspective of which no historian of eighth-century England should be unaware.

I have tried to show how the evidence of single finds can be used through a version of regression analysis designed to be appropriate when it is unknown where a distribution is starting from. It has the merit that it sums up the totality of the evidence on a regional basis, and throws light on regional variation on a rolling basis all over England, thus permitting us to gain reliable perspectives on the ways in which coins circulated in the inland districts.

FIGURE 4.4. Regression analysis of Series L sceattas, mapped in contours.

Postscript

I am indebted to Mr David Holman, of Sandwich, who has pointed out that an abbey was founded at Folkestone in the later 630s by King Eadbald and his daughter Eanswythe, an aunt of Earcongota. Could it be, he asks, that the tremisses of Loco Sancto arrived there in the context of a family connection between the abbey and that of Faremoutiers, and the close ties between the Kentish royal family and their Frankish contemporaries? Given the probable date of the tremisses, it might be that the context of the use of coinage was the building of the abbey.

CHAPTER 5

The Hinterlands of Three Southern English *Emporia*: Some Common Themes

Ben Palmer

It has been traditional to study the *emporia* of England, and their place within the economy and society of the Middle Anglo-Saxon period by looking at, and extrapolating from, the physical evidence from these sites. The approach adopted in this paper is to place the *emporia* within their geographical and economic contexts by surveying the increasing evidence for contemporary rural sites in receipt of traded goods in their surrounding regions.

Figure 5.1 shows the major *emporia* or *wics* in southern England in the Middle Anglo-Saxon period at Ipswich, London (*Lundenwic*), and Southampton (*Hamwic*). It is the regions around these three southern *emporia* that form the basis of this paper. The *wics* are unusual for the period because they mark the first non-rural settlements of substantial size and with large populations in the post-Roman era. Consequently, they are sometimes regarded as the first towns of the Anglo-Saxon period. The semantics regarding this terminology have been heavily debated and this is not the place to go into it further; the key point to note is that these sites, in the archaeological and historical record of Anglo-Saxon England, represent a distinctly different and new type of settlement.

Since the 1970s, the study of the *emporia* has been central to the question of Middle Anglo-Saxon trade, and the impact of Richard Hodges' seminal *Dark Age Economics* (1989) has led to the development of something of an orthodoxy regarding the position of these sites within the Middle Anglo-Saxon society and economy. In brief, *emporia* have come to be regarded as an isolated and, ultimately, a failed experiment in the kingdom-building process. They were 'gateway communities' between the developed core (Francia) and the underdeveloped periphery (England and Scandinavia) in the Early Medieval world where native raw materials and craft products, the latter themselves produced in the *wics*, were exchanged for luxury goods from Europe. The *emporia* were royally created, supplied and controlled and were symbolic of a command economy, existing to provide the elite with a monopoly access to luxury traded goods, and hence to allow royal patronage, which was still very much the language of power (Hodges 1989a; Hodges and Whitehouse 1983; Astill 1985; Coutts 1991, 195). Small, occasional, rural markets may have existed, but they were unimportant to this system as a whole (Hodges and Whitehouse 1983, 101).

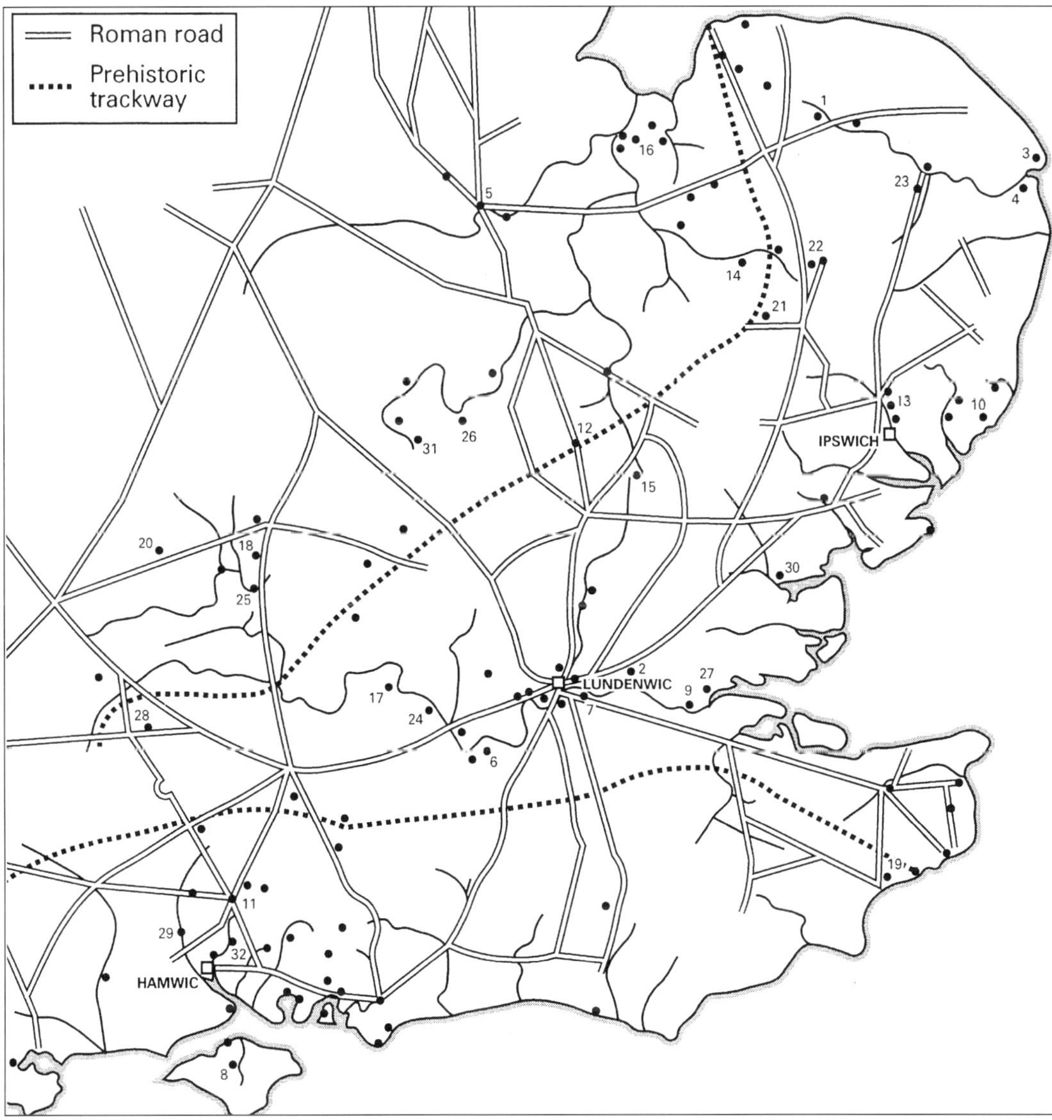

FIGURE 5.1. Distribution map of sites in receipt of traded goods, based on Palmer (1998). The numbers refer to sites identified in the text.

The decline and collapse of the *emporia* in the late eighth and early ninth centuries led to an hiatus of about a hundred years until a different set of royally-created settlement foci appeared. These were the *burhs* – walled population centres at key points in the West Saxon kingdom, originally developed as part of the defence of Wessex against the Vikings, and then extended as part of the policy of reconquest. Many became towns by Domesday as a result of their market functions. It was these royally-created, defended and legislated *burhs* that brought about the first inland production and trading centres – a development which led the way for the urbanisation and commercialisation of England (Scull 1997, 275).

This 'Hodgean' model of development has survived as long as it has partly because of the prevalence of the 'kings and bishops' school of Anglo-Saxon history, evident even in the recent *Cambridge Medieval History* (McKitterick 1995), and partly because it was believed that the archaeological evidence for rural sites of the Middle Anglo-Saxon period was insignificant. Discussion of Middle Anglo-Saxon exchange has therefore centered on the *emporia* themselves and inevitably *Hamwic*, as the best excavated and published example, has become something of a type site.

Early evidence for trade and settlement at *burh* sites that became towns by Domesday indicates that those which succeeded tended to have had several common elements, notably the siting of a seventh- or eighth-century minster on a navigable river or major road, with early evidence of trade, even if only on a small scale (Palmer 1997). This called into question just how much of an hiatus there was between the apparently outward looking command economy of the *emporia* and the later inland centres represented by the *burhs*. The latter were, after all, often sited on the very routes which led towards the *emporia* and along which Bede's 'many nations coming by land' probably arrived (*Historia Ecclesiastica*, ii, 3).

Several important regional surveys have emerged in recent years which, together with the conference papers in this volume, and from the 1989 'Productive' Sites conference, have pointed to the importance of new trends in research. Notable among these surveys has been the Ipswich Ware Project, currently in preparation by Paul Blinkhorn (see also Blinkhorn 1999), and Katharina Ulmschneider's work on 'productive' sites. The Ipswich Ware Project, a detailed survey and analysis of all known findspots of this first mass-produced domestic pottery of the Middle Anglo-Saxon period, has identified one hinterland of this *emporium* and has illustrated that not only was the distribution of the ware much wider than was previously suspected but that, as well as being almost ubiquitous within the East Anglian kingdom, it was not restricted merely to ecclesiastical and royal sites outside of that kingdom. Katharina Ulmschneider's work on 'productive' sites has for the first time tied together on a regional scale from Hampshire and Lincolnshire the increasing amount of information available from metal-detecting, pointing to an increasing number of hitherto unrecognised central places, many of which appear to have had some sort of market function (Ulmschneider 2000a).

It is in the spirit of these regional surveys that this paper offers a synthesis of the published evidence for sites in receipt of traded goods in the counties behind the three southern *emporia* (for a more detailed presentation, see Palmer 1998). Most importantly, the question of rural trade is addressed in order to set the *emporia* in the context of their surroundings. This has allowed a more regional, and therefore comparative, approach to the question of the *emporia*, and a multi-artefactual context in which to place the evidence from coin-rich sites discussed at this conference. A number of themes common to the development of the inland regions behind the *emporia* can now be addressed.

The distribution of rural sites in receipt of traded goods – some general observations

Figure 5.1 shows the distribution of the large number of Middle Anglo-Saxon sites which even a fairly cursory survey will identify as having had access to traded goods. In East Anglia, not all Ipswich ware findspots have been included because, as has already been observed, the ware is ubiquitous within this region; consequently only sites with exceptional concentrations of the pottery or with other imported goods have been included. A comparison with the map of navigable rivers *c.* 1750 (Fig. 5.2) prepared by Andrew Sherratt (1996), with reference to later prehistoric trade, shows quite markedly the influence of navigable waterways on the Middle Anglo-Saxon distribution.

Thus, the crucial role that navigable rivers, coastline and Roman roads had to play in the movement of traded goods is apparent even before the question is addressed of what sorts of sites received what sorts of goods. These transport routes, many of which follow those of antiquity, had a key part to play in shaping the hinterlands of the *emporia.*

The influence of ecclesiastical settlements

The next important factor that emerges is the key role apparently played by ecclesiastical centres within this distribution. Care must be

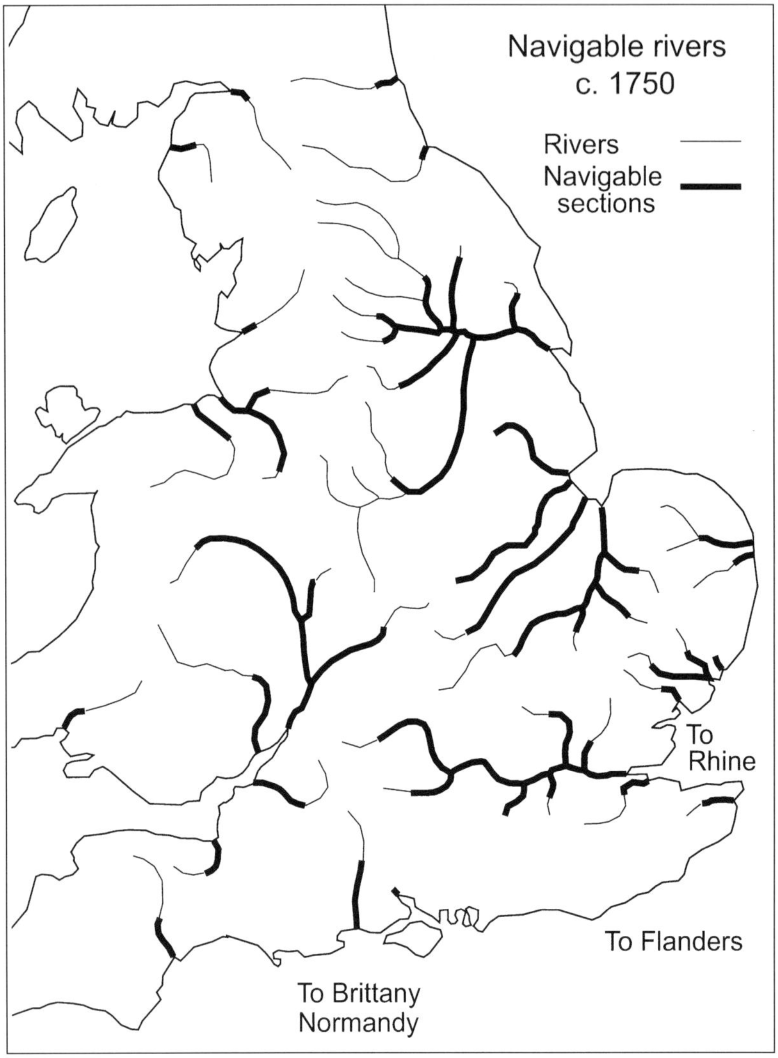

FIGURE 5.2.
Navigable rivers in England before the era of canals (after Sherratt 1996).

taken when handling this evidence as there has been something of a tendency in recent years to regard any particularly material-productive site as ecclesiastical. Nevertheless, in terms of their artefactual assemblages, positions within the landscape and interconnections, ecclesiastical sites and particularly the old minsters, do seem to have played a major part in the shaping of the hinterlands of the *emporia*.

For instance, these sites are usually the richest in terms of imports. North Elmham (Fig. 5.1:1), the seat of the posited northern see of the East Anglian kingdom, has produced about 30 percent of the imported sherds of pottery known from Norfolk (Wade-Martins 1980), while excavations at Barking Abbey (Fig. 5.1:2) have unearthed quantities of imported pottery and glass, styli, gold and silver artefacts and eight sceattas (Webster and Backhouse 1991; Redknap 1992). Furthermore, in purely geographical terms, minster communities (founded usually around the late seventh century) often occupy key positions within the distribution map. This is highlighted in the northern see of East Anglia. Burgh Castle (Fig. 5.1:3) and Caistor on Sea (Fig. 5.1:4) represent probable ecclesiastical foundations in receipt of traded goods (Johnson 1983; Rigold and Metcalf 1984; Darling 1993). They were situated on either side of the mouth of the major navigable inlet of the Yare, which was joined by a major east-west Roman road at North Elmham. At the other end of this route, where it joins Roman Ermine Street and the river route to the Wash, is Castor (Fig. 5.1:5), another site productive in imports, which is believed to have been attached to the Middle Anglo-Saxon nunnery of St Kyneburgha (Green *et al.* 1987). These routes encompass other sites in receipt of traded goods.

It appears that the founders and later heads of some of these minsters were well aware of the trade potential created by the location of their abbeys. For example, Bishop Eorcenwald (later a bishop of London) was instrumental in founding abbeys at Chertsey (Fig. 5.1:6) and Barking in the late seventh century at a time when *Lundenwic* was starting to expand. Eorcenwald had links with the Kentish royal family and held lands for Barking in Essex, Kent, Surrey, and Middlesex (Redknap 1991, 359; Dyson 1980). According to a charter of 672, he managed to gain land for Chertsey to the south of the Thames 'opposite where the boats tie up' at the confluence of the Thames and a public road (Whitelock 1955, No. 54; Dyson 1980). This land was probably at Southwark (Fig. 5.1:7) where Watling Street from Kent reaches the Thames, and where two sceattas have been unearthed (Youngs *et al.* 1986, 142; Youngs *et al.* 1988, 251). This suggests that both sides of the river were involved in trade and that there may have been a whole series of connections between the Thames riverbank and, especially, ecclesiastical sites in the hinterland. Such arrangements may even represent a precursor to references to bishop's *hagae* within the *burhs* at London and Worcester (Whitelock 1955, Nos 92 and 99).

The emergence of settlement hierarchies

In terms of the artefact assemblages, there seems to be something of a settlement hierarchy emerging, with those sites unusually rich in metalwork and coinage forming the upper tier of a variety of inland sites which, throughout the Middle Anglo-Saxon period, appear to have gained access to a wide range of traded goods. As this conference and its predecessor have illustrated, increased metal-detecting over the last two decades or so has led to the classification of a new kind of site, termed 'productive'. This may in some ways be slightly misleading as many of these sites have not been excavated and little is known about their context. However, the suggestion that the coin-rich sites in this category may have fulfilled an inland central place or market function does not appear to be misleading in terms of geographical relationships.

Predictably, some of the richest of these 'productive' sites were probably ecclesiastical. A sceatta-rich site on the Isle of Wight (Fig. 5.1:8) was possibly associated with an early minster of St Mary (see Ulmschneider 2000a and this volume). Certainly Tilbury (Fig. 5.1:9), which has now produced well over the originally published eighty-six sceattas (Newman 1999; Blackburn this volume), is associated with a monastic foundation by Cedd. Burrow Hill, Butley in Suffolk (Fig. 5.1:10), has produced several sceattas and Beonna proto-pennies. Given its enclosed, causewayed, construction and finds of styli, imported wares and glass, along with production evidence (Fenwick 1984 and 1985), it may also be an ecclesiastical settlement. Other coin-productive sites, however, do not have evidence suggesting ecclesiastical links and these may have been seasonal inland markets. Coin-find clusters at hillforts around Winchester (Fig. 5.1:11) have been interpreted in this way (Metcalf 1984a, 27 and 41), as have the coin finds from an unexcavated site near Royston (Fig. 5.1:12) (Blackburn and Bonser 1986). Barham near Ipswich (Fig. 5.1:13), however, has produced nearly fifty sceattas and some structural evidence, and the site has thus been claimed as a rural marketplace of more permanent character (Youngs *et al.* 1984; Newman 1999, 38 and 43; this volume).

At another level in the hierarchy are those rural sites with strong evidence for production, some of which may have had ecclesiastical connections. Brandon (Fig. 5.1:14), at which a church with attendant cemeteries has been unearthed, seems to have had a textile production role; a waterfront industrial area has been identified where dying and weaving materials have been found, associated with what seems to have been a wharf for vessels to tie up at (Carr 1985; Carr *et al.* 1988). However, there were non-ecclesiastical sites involved in specialised production. Wicken Bonhunt in Essex (Fig. 5.1:15) is one of the best examples of this. Although structurally it looks like a typical rural site, evidence for intensive meat production, in this case pig rearing and butchery, has been found. Its productivity seems to be reflected in the abundance of Ipswich ware, which made up 70 percent of the assemblage, and also imported Frankish wares which seem to have been shipped via London (Crabtree 1996; Wade 1980). The so-called Fen-edge sites near the Wash (Fig. 5.1:16), identified first by Ipswich ware scatters on the roddons (Silvester 1988), have subsequently produced evidence of specialist beef rearing. Some of this was doubtless for marketing on the hoof, but bone analysis and a salt pond found at Walpole St Andrew suggest that butchering and salting was taking place on at least some of these sites. Hay Green alone has produced over 1,000 sherds of Ipswich ware (Rogerson and Silvester 1986; Leah 1992, 55).

There is also an increasing number of rural sites which provide evidence for neither an ecclesiastical connection nor specialised production but which appear to have been involved in trade in some way, simply as a result of their location on major trade routes. A classic example of this is provided at Lake End Road near Maidenhead (Fig. 5.1:17), where a large concentration of refuse pits contained imported pottery, lava quernstones and Ipswich ware but which, despite extensive excavation, has revealed no evidence of metalwork or permanent settlement (Blinkhorn 1998, S. Foreman, pers. comm.). Yarnton in Oxfordshire (Fig. 5.1:18) represents another apparently ordinary rural site which had access to the trade routes along which Ipswich ware and lava quernstones were shipped in the Upper Thames (Blinkhorn 1998). Sandtun at West Hythe, Kent (Fig. 5.1:19), is an inhospitable site on Middle Anglo-Saxon coastal routes. It has produced imported pottery and stone but very little metalwork. There is some supposition that the site was attached to Lyminge minster but it seems to have owed its imported assemblage primarily to its position as a natural harbour. Analysis of fish bones from the site suggests seasonal occupation (M. Gardiner, pers. comm.). Such small and sometimes seasonal sites were probably trading in occasional surpluses in textiles, or consumables.

While the *emporia* have been touted as production centres, none of the household units at the *wics* would have looked out of place in the countryside, and production at the *emporia*, although diverse, does not seem to have been on a scale even close to the amount needed to support the trade which appears to have passed through them. Given the ubiquity of weaving evidence at rural sites, it would be hard to argue that many of the textiles reaching the *emporia* were not already in a finished state. Early sceattas associated with weaving debris at Shakenoak on the Upper Thames (Fig. 5.1:20), and lava querns and Ipswich ware found in weaving sheds at West Stow (Fig. 5.1:21), may support this (Blair 1994, 82; West 1985).

The development of inland central places or areas with their own hinterlands

As the archaeological and historical landscape behind the *emporia* of eighth-century England appears more clearly, the development of inland central places or areas, with their own hinterlands, are starting to emerge. This has been touched upon with regard to ecclesiastical sites and their interconnections. With artefactual evidence from individual sites, the Brandon finds assemblage illustrates how local, regional and long distance trade could come together at an ecclesiastical settlement. It has been suggested that the plant remains at the site suggest a consumer-type economy and certainly the raw materials for the textile production would have been acquired locally. The large number of oyster shells at the site must have come from the coast however, and the large range of imported finds attest to the association of the site with longer-distance trade networks (Carr 1985; Carr *et al.* 1988). This type of assemblage is not unique to religious sites: a similar assemblage of goods of varied provenance is visible at Lake End Road, which seems to have been supplied with Emmer wheat (a bulk import not known since Roman times), tidal and coastal fish and Continental pottery (S. Foreman, pers. comm.).

It is also possible that multi-settlement focal areas were emerging in the Middle Anglo-Saxon period which developed more fully later. This is particularly visible in what became the Danelaw where, in the Middle Anglo-Saxon period, coin-rich sites are found near Thetford (at Middle Harling: Fig. 5.1:23) and Norwich (at Caistor St Edmund: Fig. 5.1:22), both of which later became urban centres (Wade-Martins 1997, 38; Rogerson 1995). The same may be true in the Middle Thames region in the Old Windsor/Staines area (Fig. 5.1:24); in the Upper Thames around Oxford (Fig. 5.1:25); and in the Bedford area (Fig. 5.1:26) (Palmer 1998).

The distribution of lava quernstones from the Eifel region of the Rhineland to a large number of insular rural sites of all kinds is becoming increasingly apparent. This artefact distribution in itself points to the development of a multi-tiered system of distribution and exchange which mirrors indicators already highlighted at the level of individual settlements. Unfinished stones are known from the *emporia*, from Thetford and from Linford in Essex (Fig. 5.1:27) (Parkhouse 1997; 97, 102 and 104; Freshwater 1996, 42–5; Dunning 1956, 232; Barton 1968), which suggests that they were imported in block form and finished nearer to or on the sites at which they were found. These lava querns, despite being better than their native competitors, were still utilitarian items whose distribution indicates how widely they were traded. This would make sense, as such bulky and friable items would have to have been traded in large quantities to make profit viable. Here then, we may see artefactual evidence of bulk trade in agricultural goods which tallies with the evidence for the increasing mobilisation of resources in the English countryside at all levels.

Evidence for growing specialisation and organisation

Economic specialisation at sites such as Wicken Bonhunt and Brandon has been mentioned, and what appear to be iron production centres at Ramsbury (Fig. 5.1:28) (Haslam 1980), Romsey (Fig. 5.1:29) (Scott 1993 and 1996), and Little Totham (Fig. 5.1:30) (Adkins 1989) are also known.

There is also evidence that at some sites the arrival of traded goods accompanied a change towards a more commercial economy. Pennyland (Figs. 5.1:31) has been regarded in this way by Paul Blinkhorn (1999, 15–16). In the Early Anglo-Saxon period the settlement existed as a fairly typical, unenclosed, scattered hamlet. The late seventh to early eighth century saw the first use of domestic enclosures, though the artefactual evidence suggests that at this stage the settlement was still engaged in a broad-based subsistence economy. However, when Ipswich ware started arriving at the site, apparently in association with lava quernstones, the enclosure system appears to have been abandoned for domestic use in favour of stock rearing and the domestic buildings retreated to a smaller cluster to the west. Blinkhorn suggests this indicates a major shift in the economy towards a less labour-intensive and more profitable stock rearing function (*ibid.;* Williams 1993).

The Fen-edge also appears to show an expansion of rural activity. This area had been exploited in the Roman period but then fell out of use, partly due to climatic conditions. The Middle Anglo-Saxon period saw fresh advantage being taken of the good pastureland, communication routes and saltings at least for seasonal commercial purposes (Silvester 1988; Leah 1992). Another example of the re-organisation of resources can perhaps be discerned at Old Windsor. From the middle of the eighth century, imported goods, notably pottery, started to reach the site. By the end of the third phase of the settlement in which these contacts first appeared, there was a large three-wheeled mill in existence, contemporaneous with the introduction of a man-made leat and large-scale deforestation of the area, which would seem to indicate increased exploitation of the agricultural resources of the region from the late eighth century (Wilson 1958).

We can see that, particularly in the counties around London and Ipswich, evidence for what appears to be a quite complex and multi-tiered system of trade is emerging. This is represented by a range of sites, among which those termed 'productive', played a prominent but far from exclusive role. It further seems that geographical considerations, previous trade routes and the role of minsters and ecclesiastical settlements as central places had a major role to play in the shaping of these hinterlands. The growth of trade in goods, both agricultural and industrial, was a feature of the countryside as well as the *wics*. However, one of the most interesting conclusions to emerge from this survey is that, when we look at *Hamwic* and Hampshire, we are dealing with a different situation.

Anomalies in Hampshire

The hinterland of *Hamwic* does appear to have exhibited an unusual degree of royal control in its development. In retrospect, the clues were there from the start. The *wic* was laid out *c.* 700, after the other two *emporia* in question had started trading from more modest origins. The context of this foundation is also significant, coming as it did immediately after Cædwalla had captured the Jutish provinces on the south coast, providing the Gewisse with direct access to the sea. After this point, the tribe of the Gewisse starts to be recorded in documents as the West Saxon kingdom (Yorke 1989). Furthermore, the West Saxon kingdom was the first to organise its lands around a manorial system of royal estates with associated minsters. *Hamwic* itself, according to Hase, may have represented one of these estates and the recent discovery of a high-status cemetery close to the *emporium* may support this proposal (Hase 1988, 45). Such observations accord to an extent with the suppositions made by Hodges and those deductions which have been made from the excavations within the *emporium* itself.

Certainly, the survey outlined in this paper highlights trends in the development of the Hampshire hinterland which are substantially different to those seen in the remainder of the study area. There are many fewer 'productive' sites in Hampshire than in other regions (Ulmschneider 2000a; Palmer 1998) and those sites which were associated with production and the movement of goods to the *emporium*, such as cattle from Bishopstoke (Fig. 5.1:32) and iron from Romsey, appear to have been tied in to the estate system (Nenk *et al.* 1992, 233; Scott 1993 and 1996). Furthermore, very few imported goods are known from rural sites in Hampshire.

Communication routes were still of undoubted importance in the shaping of the hinterland, for instance Roman roads are clearly important in the distribution of coinage (Fig. 5.3). However, *Hamwic* had a very narrow hinterland. A re-examination of that area shown in Figure 5.2 illustrates that the Hampshire hinterland stands out rather pitifully in contrast to the extensive navigable networks spreading out from London and Ipswich. The rather restricted geographical extent of this late-formed kingdom may have been another reason for the royal impetus required in the control of the economy of the area.

FIGURE 5.3. Coin-productive sites (excluding hoards) and Roman roads in Hampshire (after Ulmschneider 2000a, Map 21).

There are indications of some limited rural trade in Hampshire, as

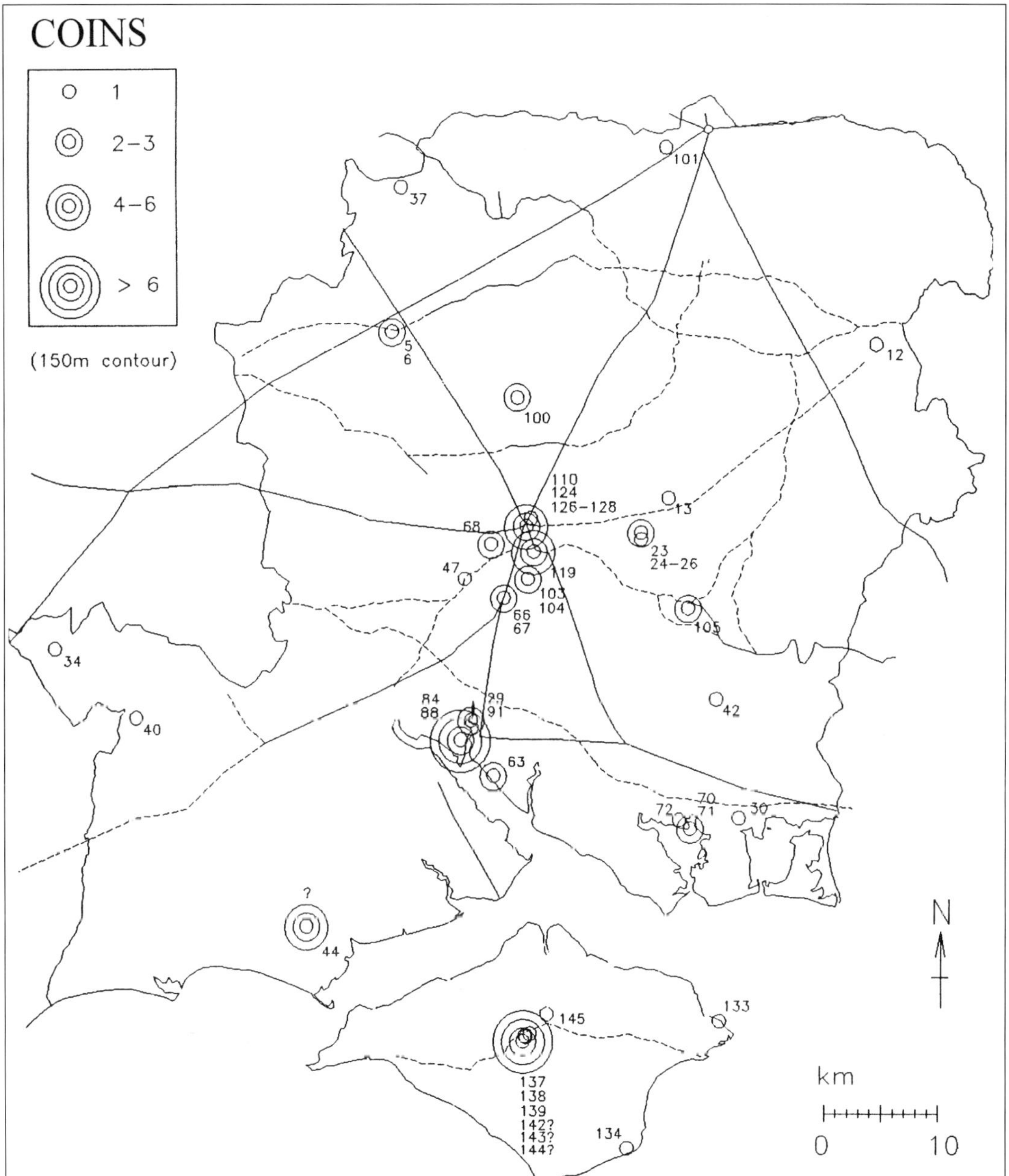

would be expected, for instance in iron bars for smithing, oysters and local hand-made pottery; but these sorts of trade do not seem tied to the *emporium* and there are no rural sites which seem to have boomed in response to increased trading opportunities provided by the development of the *wic* (Palmer 1998).

Even the distribution of the *Hamwic*-minted sceatta coinage, Series

H, is anomalous, the vast majority of examples having been found inside the *wic* (Metcalf 1993–4, iii, 321–33). It has been suggested that this represents a positive balance of trade, but in the light of the other evidence, all it may represent is that this currency was primarily used as an internal token of exchange within the *emporium* and that monetary transactions had not spread into the hinterland.

Hamwic is the best-studied *wic* site, at least partly due to its archaeology having been less disturbed than that of London or Ipswich because it did not survive beyond the ninth century. This early demise may be due to the artificial nature of the original foundation: the *emporium* was unable to survive the disruption of its Continental trade because it had no strong tradition of inland trade to fall back on. In this light, it is ironic that it has become the type-site for the English *emporia.*

Conclusions

In a survey of limited scope one can only hope to raise possibilities and questions rather than solid conclusions. This may be a healthy thing, as for too long we seem to have been concerned with debates over semantics and, as several contributors to this volume point out, a rehashing of a fairly limited dataset that has been known for decades. With increasing data becoming available, in terms of extensively excavated sites, the publication of rescue excavations, and increased numbers of single finds, now seems to be an opportune time to try out new multi-disciplinary approaches to Middle Anglo-Saxon trade.

II

Trading and 'Productive' Sites in the British Isles

CHAPTER 6

Markets and 'Productive' Sites: A View From Western Britain

David Griffiths

Discussions of 'productive' sites in Early Medieval Britain tend to focus exclusively on the eastern and southern counties of England. Yorkshire, Lincolnshire, East Anglia and the South-East account for almost all of the known 'productive' site locations. Rarely mentioned, by contrast, are the areas towards the western side of Britain, commonly referred to as the 'Celtic West' but which were affected in varying degree by Anglo-Saxon settlement (south-west and north-west England, Wales and its borders, and south-west Scotland), which have far fewer sites. This pattern begs the question as to whether this distribution pattern is real, or simply a reflection of greater metal-detecting and/or archaeological recording in the East and South-East. If, as argued here, it is to a large extent 'real' in that it broadly indicates the spread of sites rich in Anglo-Saxon non-ferrous metalwork in the seventh to tenth centuries, is this a reflection of economic 'backwardness' in the West? Or, is the relative lack of such sites more to do with a lower (but still detectable) circulation in the West of the characteristic Anglo-Saxon metalwork of the eastern sites, rather than a genuine absence of market activity? Following these basic questions, it seems a useful point to ask whether we should hold to a rigid definition of the 'productive' site as a wholly Anglo-Saxon material-culture phenomenon, and thereby make it a distant factor in understanding contemporary market sites in the West. Alternatively, should we adopt a definition which puts the widest possible range of indicators of market activity at the heart of our interpretation, and make the presence in sufficient numbers of deterministic 'productive-site' Anglo-Saxon metalwork types a secondary consideration?

This brief survey of western Britain illustrates the marked difference between East and West in the quantity of 'productive' sites, if strictly defined as the presence of medium to large assemblages, perhaps over fifteen objects, of Middle to Late Anglo-Saxon period metalwork and coins (assuming one accepts the validity of the term at all – *cf.* Richards 1999b and this volume). West of a line drawn between (approximately) the Dorset/Hampshire border on the south coast and the English/ Scottish border on the east coast at Berwick upon Tweed, there are very markedly fewer sites than to the east. Interviews by the present author of finds liaison officers within the Portable Antiquities Scheme financed by the Heritage Lottery Fund, have confirmed the general pattern. Although in mid-2001 the scheme has not yet covered the whole United Kingdom, Dorset and Somerset, the English West Midlands, Wales and the North-West (defined as Cheshire to Cumbria) are under the remit of this programme. However, the picture in the West is not completely negative.

Metalwork of the eighth to tenth centuries AD is known from a number of locations in western Britain (see below). There is considerable metal-detecting activity, and this has led to some interesting discoveries. One such is the collection of material, including bronze Anglo-Saxon strap-ends and a pin, together with ironwork and a fine ninth-century openwork bronze plaque, from Asby Winderwath Common, near Appleby-in-Westmorland, Cumbria (Youngs 1999). Possibly indicative of a market site on a trans-Pennine routeway, the Asby Winderwath material shows that there is some potential for the eastern distribution of sites to extend northwards and westwards. In the Midlands, a site producing a range of Anglo-Saxon metalwork at Bidford-on-Avon in western Warwickshire (Wise and Seaby 1995; A. Bolton, pers. comm.), also pushes the distribution pattern westwards. A recent study of Germanic-Celtic interaction in the post-Roman period by John Hines includes a useful survey of some recent Anglo-Saxon finds in the South-West (Hines 2000), but unlike the Asby Winderwath material, for instance, these are largely individual discoveries, and cannot be said to resemble the traditional Anglo-Saxon 'productive' site artefact pattern. It is remarkable, if also ironic, that the great ninth-century hoard from Trewhiddle, Cornwall, should have become so emblematic in studies of contemporary Anglo-Saxon metalwork styles, yet was discovered in a region where comparable site finds have been so meagre.

Regarding the distribution of sites producing metalwork of the eighth to tenth centuries, however, one significant difference seems to be that such sites in the West are predominantly coastal or near-coastal, whereas most 'productive' sites in the East are situated away from the sea. Two sites in particular which the author has been closely involved in researching, namely Llanbedrgoch (Anglesey, Wales) and Meols (Merseyside, north-west England) form relevant case-studies. The situation in western Britain challenges us to be flexible in our definitions for markets and 'productive' sites, and suggests that a longer-term perspective is necessary.

The idea of the 'productive' site has not yet made a great impact on the terminology of sites in the west of Britain, but there is no doubt that in its loosest sense it could be applied to sites with a large quantity of imported material. Tintagel, for example, is extremely 'productive' in terms of post-Roman pottery of Mediterranean origins. Imported material from less dominant sites in the South-West such as Gwithian and Bantham echoes Tintagel's external contacts. The work of Charles Thomas and Ewan Campbell in mapping the spread of African and Phocaean Red Slip tablewares ('ARSW/PRSW', also known as A ware), East Mediterranean amphorae (B wares), and western Gaulish D and E wares, together with Continental glass beakers, shows that the mid-first millennium AD in the West was characterised by patterns of exchange which still reached well beyond north-west Europe (Thomas 1990; E Campbell 1996). Major secular defended settlements such as Dinas Powys in south-east Wales and Dunadd in Dál Riata, western Scotland, show evidence of indigenous production of high-status portable objects such as penannular brooches (e.g. Lane and Campbell 2000). As the present author argued in an article published in 1994 by the Gudme Project in Denmark (Griffiths 1994), it seems that the imports – the fine tablewares, wine, honey and colourful dyes represented by the ceramic evidence and glass – and the locally-produced metalwork, were part of a system of re-distribution within tribal or kinship territories based on tribute and reciprocal obligations. Feasting and inauguration ceremonies would have provided a focus for consumption. The Mediterranean contacts and increasing wealth of the early Christian Church certainly played a role in the pattern of exchange, and we can point to good evidence for imports and production in the vicinity of monasteries, Whithorn being an obvious example (Hill 1997).

One group of sites which forms part of the exchange network in the West, but for which there is almost no historical information, are those loosely termed 'beach markets'. At a number of marginal coastal locations around the Irish Sea, mostly characterised by sand dune landscapes, there have been finds of metalwork comparable in type if not in quantity to the 'productive' site assemblages known further to the east and south. At Luce Sands, Galloway, south-west Scotland (Cormack 1965), stycas and bronze Anglo-Saxon strap-ends (among a range of other earlier and later material) have been found in eroding sand formations on Torrs Warren behind the beach. Stevenston Sands, Ayrshire (Callander 1933) is a comparable site, if smaller in the range of objects. A similar situation where Early Medieval metalwork has been found unstratified together with a range of prehistoric items is documented at Murlough Dunes, Dundrum Bay, Co. Down in Northern Ireland (Jope 1966).

These are not recent finds, but careful re-examination of the assemblages and their context can be surprisingly informative. The eighth- and ninth-century metalwork finds, if abstracted from the wider assemblages of material from these sites, begin to look like a sparser version of the classic 'productive' site phenomenon. (The presence in the West of contemporary Anglo-Saxon metalwork is also attested by hoards, including the Trewhiddle Hoard from Cornwall (see above) and the Talnotrie Hoard from Kirkcudbrightshire, south-west Scotland.) However, where the sand-dune sites are concerned, the presence of earlier metalwork, including sub-Roman and post-Roman penannular brooches, together with Iron Age and also later Medieval metalwork, confirms that the material dating to AD 700–1000 must be seen as part of a long-term pattern of importation of traded objects at these sites. Elsewhere in the 'Celtic West', the presence of coastal redistribution centres is indicated by varied ceramic assemblages at highly marginal sites, of which Dalkey Island off the Dublin coast (Liversage 1967) is a good example, although Longbury Bank in south-west Wales (Campbell and Lane 1993) should also be mentioned in this regard. This author's interpretation for the coastal market sites as a group is that they represent small non-elite and largely undefended settlements which occasionally functioned within a very long-lived tradition of seasonal markets at these specific locations. Indeed, a seasonal function has even been suggested for Tintagel by Charles Thomas (Thomas 1988). These seasonal events, possibly taking place on set days in the calendar, would have drawn trade largely from within the region, but the presence even in small numbers of merchants from much further afield would have been an undoubted attraction for the elites and their representatives. If one is permitted to infer back from more recently documented traditions, the annual 'wakes' of north-west England would be a good example.

From the late eighth century onwards, the Vikings clearly played a role in circulating material culture, mostly but not exclusively of insular origin. In all but the earliest phase of the Viking presence, it would be simplistic to view raiding activity as the predominant theme in this context; many apparent market sites in the West which show evidence of sixth- to eighth-century material also show Viking influence. There was a tradition in contemporary Scandinavia of non-urban markets in boundary zones, where a number of metalwork-producing sites have been recorded (e.g. Larsen 1985).

One significant coastal 'beach market' site is Meols (pronounced

'Mells', from Old Norse *Melr*, meaning 'sand dune'). Situated on the north coast of the Wirral peninsula facing Liverpool Bay and mid-way between the river estuary mouths of the Dee and Mersey, this site is currently the subject of a full site history and catalogue being written by the author and Dr Robert Philpott of Liverpool Museum (Griffiths and Philpott in prep.). Over 3,000 objects from the site exist in five museum collections, dating from the Mesolithic to the post-Medieval periods, but it is from the Middle Iron Age to the fifteenth century AD that Meols seems to have acted as a regional market. Most of the finds were collected by antiquarians in the period 1846–1900 as coastal erosion gradually exposed ancient settlement. The coastal retreat was stopped in the late 1890s by the construction of sea defences. Led by the Rev. Abraham Hume (Hume 1863), a handful of antiquarians searched for artefacts and made some interesting, if poorly-located, observations of burials, wattle round houses succeeded in upper layers by rectangular long houses, trackways, walls and fences. The surviving objects represent, of course, an unknown fraction of the original number, but leave no doubt as to the regional importance of the site. The antiquarian story is fascinating in itself and we have to remain constantly aware of the need to be source-critical, but for the most part the collections are coherent, with regional parallels, and their provenance at Meols seems secure. There has been a trickle of finds since 1900, mostly chance discoveries, but in recent years metal-detector users have begun to contribute some important pieces. All of these subsequent finds confirm themes already inherent in the antiquarian collections, and in some cases have provided identical objects.

The similarities and correspondences at Meols to our familiar idea of the 'productive' site concern the eighth to tenth century material (for discussions of some of this material see Bu'Lock 1960 and Dolley 1961). The coins, although not large in number, are a case in point. Two Frisian Primary sceattas, still unusual on the west coast (an area once described by Michael Metcalf as 'the back of beyond' in monetary terms: 1987, 365) were found here, together with a handful of ninth-century Northumbrian stycas. Stycas are slightly more common in the North-West than sceattas, with hoards and single finds known from Otterspool (Liverpool), Lancaster, Grange, Kirkoswald and Carlisle (Pirie 1986b). Other characteristic Middle and Late Anglo-Saxon objects at Meols include a bossed silver disc pin, a group of bronze hooked tags, a probable 'Winchester style' openwork strap-end, and an iron disc pin which has been referred to elsewhere as a stylus, but which is now not regarded as such (T. Pestell, pers. comm.). There are also a number of biconical-headed and faceted bronze pins

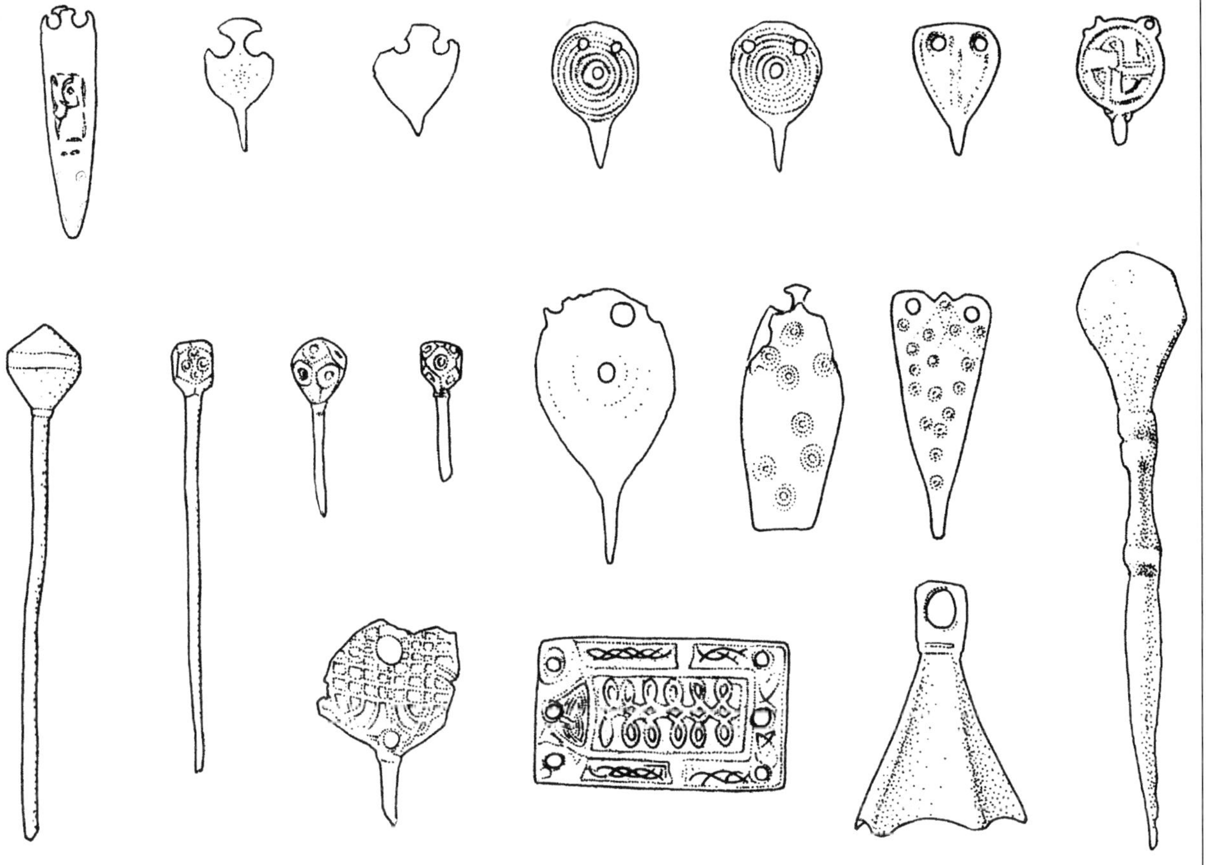

FIGURE 6.1.
Some eighth- to eleventh-century finds from Meols, scale 1:1 (drawn by Mark Faulkner).

(Fig. 6.1). These are accompanied by Irish Sea regionally-derived material including an interlaced carved mount, a bronze hexagonal pyramidal bell and the largest single group of Hiberno-Viking ringed pins outside Ireland.

There are close to thirty tenth- and eleventh-century Anglo-Saxon silver coins from Meols (Dolley 1961), although the whole pre-Norman coin series looks small compared to the Roman and Medieval coins which number several hundred. This reinforces the point that the Early Medieval objects are an important but still fairly small part of a very long-lived assemblage which includes, apart from imported material, much of the standard equipment of everyday life in the form of iron tools, leather, Roman and Medieval pottery and even some manufacturing evidence in the form of crucibles and metal wasters. Meols may have acted as a regional *entrepôt* for trade in Cheshire salt or lead mined in the Flintshire Hills across the Dee estuary (Griffiths 1996).

Further evidence for possible sites linked to Meols within the surrounding river systems comes from a small group of ninth-century Anglo-Saxon metalwork objects, including a bronze strap-end with an enamelled zoomorphic design and a Trewhiddle-style circular silver disc pin head, found by metal-detectorists at Hale, on the north bank of the Mersey (Philpott 1999), although their context has not been investigated archaeologically. At Altmouth, on the Lancashire coast across the mouth of the Mersey opposite Meols, some Roman and eleventh-century Norman coins have been discovered, but as yet no Anglo-Saxon material.

One of the aims of the current Meols publication project is to integrate more recent and reinterpreted finds. Several Iron Age dress pins have been rescued from century-old labelling as Medieval, and a curious glass 'necklace', presumably assembled by a Victorian museum assistant, has been disaggregated to reveal a collection of Roman, Anglo-Saxon and Medieval beads. One of the more fascinating twentieth-century discoveries at Meols, by a local man digging for lugworms on the foreshore in the 1950s, was a small pilgrim's pottery flask or *ampulla* from the shrine of St Menas, Lower Egypt, dated to the sixth or early seventh century.

Recent metal-detecting activity around Meols has added some significant pieces to the existing assemblage. An 'Aucissa'-type Roman brooch from the first century AD, found on the foreshore, is identical to one in the antiquarian collections. Further recent finds have cast some exciting new light on long distance contacts. Indications of Mediterranean links in the Iron Age come in the form of three Carthaginian *drachmae* recorded among the nineteenth-century finds (three other Iron Age coins, two of Armorican and one of British origin were also found). These contribute to a small but important stock of evidence for Iron Age trade in the region (Matthews 1999). The St Menas flask is an indication that Mediterranean links via the Atlantic seaboard of western Europe (*cf.* Cunliffe 2001, 421) may have survived throughout the Roman period, obscured perhaps by the difficulty of detecting these distant links within the more general Roman influence on Britain between AD 43 and 400, or alternatively were resurrected in post-Roman times. From the hinterland of the site have come three sixth to early seventh-century Byzantine coins, including a *follis* of Justin I (518–27) a *decanummium* of Justinian I (527–65) and a *follis* of Maurice Tiberius (582–602). The coin of Justinian was a chance find, the other two were metal-detected (Philpott 1998). These add to the small but increasing stock of evidence for Byzantine contact in the Irish Sea region, including the probable inscription (*c.* 540) *in tempore iustini consiliis* at Penmachno in North Wales (Nash-Williams 1950, 93) and the recent discovery of an intaglio together with an insular penannular brooch at Cefn Cwmwd, Anglesey, during a road-widening scheme (White *et al.*, in prep.). Traded objects imported directly via early Byzantine contacts in western Britain (for a discussion, see Fulford 1989) have often been dismissed as an over-interpretation of a small, if exotic, group of material. Other explanations, such as modern loss, have been sought for the presence of this material (e.g. Boon 1991). However, as further pieces come to light, we are surely right to begin cautiously to appreciate its significance within the patterns of exchange in western Britain (*cf.* Dark 2000, 162–3) and to see its role in fostering and continuing markets, and thereby the market tradition, which in some cases attracted traders bringing the type of material more commonly associated with 'productive' sites. To stretch this argument still further, it may even be that some of the Byzantine high-status metalwork found in Anglo-Saxon contexts may have found its way there via these western routes.

It is perhaps no accident that the Isle of Anglesey (Ynys Môn), forming the north-western part of Wales and at the centre of the Irish Sea region, has been the scene of the discovery of relevant material. A historic centre of power within the Welsh kingdom of Gwynedd, its relatively fertile and low-lying pastures have contributed to the island having an impressive range of archaeological sites of most periods, which form a significant concentration in western Britain. Until the 1990s the period 600–1000 was not well represented (Redknap 2000). However, there has been considerable metal-detecting activity in Anglesey over the past decade, to which the National Museums and Galleries of Wales has been quick to react. In an example of beneficial co-operation between metal-detectorists and museum archaeologists, one result has been the discovery of a major new site of the Early Medieval period, unknown before 1989. In the early 1990s, from Glyn, Llanbedrgoch, just inland from the east coast of the island near Benllech, metal-detector users reported eighth- and ninth-century coins and metalwork to Dr Mark Redknap of the National Museum. Dr Redknap initiated a major archaeological investigation which continued annually until 2001 (supervised in part by the present author in 1997–9).

One of the first indications that the metal-detectorists had stumbled across an extraordinary site was the discovery of an Anglo-Saxon penny of Cynethryth, wife of Offa (757–96) and a number of lead merchants' weights. There was also the discovery by this method of several ninth-century coins, namely a penny of Wulfred of Canterbury, two *deniers* of Louis the Pious, one of Charles the Bald and one of Pepin II of Aquitaine. The subsequent discovery of a small collection of pins and brooches pointed to a Viking or immediately pre-Viking context. Also found were some classically Irish Sea Viking material such hacksilver and a bronze hexagonal bell, which emphasise the trading links of the site and which are close parallels for finds from Peel Castle on the Isle of Man and Meols.

At one of a small number of locations investigated archaeologically (with the active on-site assistance of the original metal-detectorists who discovered the material), geophysical survey followed by excavation began to reveal a defensive ditch forming an enclosure around a small spring. Subsequent seasons have revealed that this enclosure,

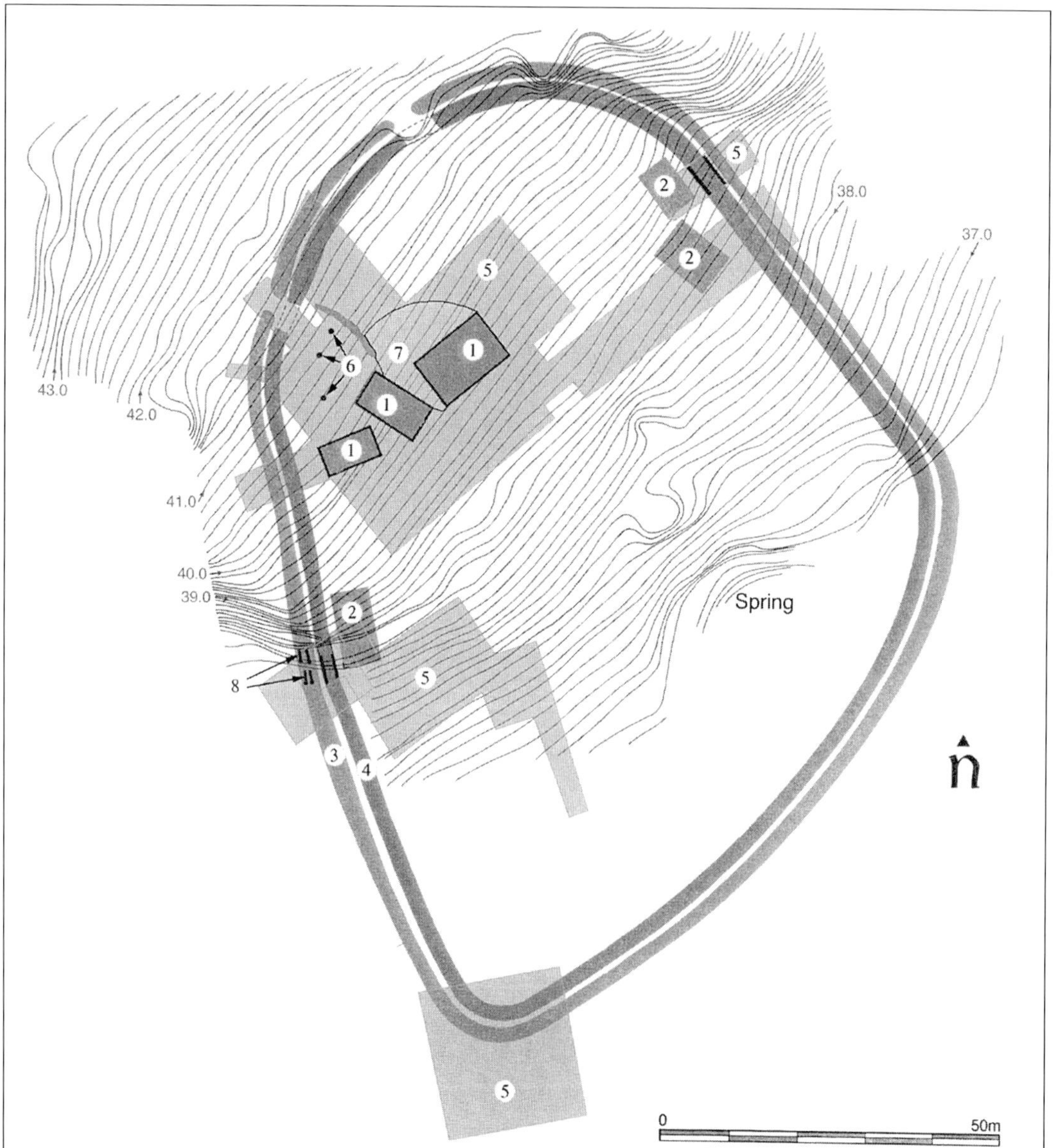

fortified in places by a massive wall, was intensively occupied during the ninth and tenth centuries, with at least three (and possibly up to six) timber buildings of long-house type, extra-mural inhumations, extensive middens and metalworking hearths (Fig. 6.2). These latter two contexts have produced two Northumbrian stycas, and elsewhere the excavation has produced tenth-century Anglo-Saxon silver pennies and an Arabic *dirhem.* When begun, this excavation was designed principally to investigate the context of the Viking-period metalwork, but gradually more and more indications of pre-Viking activity have been discovered. It is now clear that the spring at the centre of the site has been the location of activity since the Neolithic period, and there is a sequence of artefacts (including a polychrome bead and a seventh-century bird-headed brooch) supplemented by radiocarbon dates, and a possible round house stratigraphically below one of the long houses, indicating settlement in the pre-Viking period. A nearby scatter of Roman pottery, some Late Roman coins in the form of a clipped *siliqua* and a barbarous radiate, together with the proximity on the same farm of the known sixth- to eighth-century settlement site of Pant y Saer (Edwards and Lane 1988, 99–101), go far towards completing a long-term context for the eighth- to tenth-century imported metalwork. The site was almost certainly a native Welsh site which experienced significant influence, and probably settlement, by Irish Sea Vikings from the later ninth century.

FIGURE 6.2. Llanbedrgoch site plan (drawn by Tony Daly © National Museums and Galleries of Wales). Key: (1) Definite buildings; (2) possible buildings; (3) ditch; (4) wall; (5) areas of excavation up to 1999; (6) bowl hearths (ninth century); (7) metalled/paved surface; (8) burials.

Despite the Anglesey site not being in an immediately coastal situation (although it is only one kilometre from a sheltered coastal inlet), the artefactual parallels between Llanbedrgoch and Meols are striking. Both seem to have been the setting for more-or-less permanent settlement in the Early Medieval period, but the trading contacts evident in the metalwork assemblages in particular point to an elevated role as market sites, or a very close connection to a market location. Given the chronological range emerging from studies of these sites, it may well be that we are detecting here long-term traditions of seasonal markets at territorial and topographical boundary zones. These may relate, possibly in the case of Meols at least, to a basic or 'prime' commodity which was available here along with metalwork for personal ornament, salt and lead being the most likely materials.

There is no evidence that there is any difference in the strength and quality of archaeological response to the discovery of 'productive' site type material in the west as opposed to the east of Britain. Indeed the Portable Antiquities Scheme, for example, presently covers at least as much of the west as the east of England and Wales, with only Devon, Cornwall and the English southern border counties in the Welsh marches exempted in the West. Therefore, we have to accept that there are simply far fewer obvious candidates for designation as 'productive' sites, and the general circulation of seventh- to tenth-century Anglo-Saxon metalwork is markedly lower. However, as illustrated above, there are a number of market-influenced sites in western Britain which conform to some of the general characteristics of 'productive' sites, whether in their method of discovery or artefact assemblage. A sufficiently broad and flexible attitude to the concept (perhaps seeing such sites simply as reflecting non-urban market activity in liminal zones) may well bring the western sites within the remit of the debate. There is a clear difference in scale of the characteristic metalwork assemblages between West and East, which must in part be due to a lesser or more diffuse Anglo-Saxon cultural influence in the West (*cf.* Hines 2000). Braudel's *longue durée* is a useful interpretative backdrop to patterns of trade and external contact in those parts of western Britain bordering the Irish Sea region, which Mackinder once referred to as the 'British Mediterranean' (Mackinder 1902, 20). Consideration of artefact patterning across several millennia from the Iron Age through to the Late Medieval period is a key interpretative tool here, and might very well stand as a conclusion relevant to other areas.

Acknowledgements

The author would like to thank Katharina Ulmschneider and Tim Pestell for inviting him to contribute on this subject. Mark Redknap of the National Museum of Wales provided an invaluable commentary and permitted the use of Figure 6.2.

CHAPTER 7

Markets Around the Solent: Unravelling a 'Productive' Site on the Isle of Wight

Katharina Ulmschneider

For many years research on Middle Anglo-Saxon trade in the Solent area has focused mainly on the great *emporium* at *Hamwic*. This is not surprising given the quantity and variety of finds from this important trading place, its recording as a *mercimonium* in the eighth-century *Vita Willibaldi*, and its wide European contacts (Morton 1992; Andrews 1997; Bauch 1984, 40–1). However, it is clear from the same written source that *Hamwic* was not the only market in operation at that time. When, in about 721, Willibald set out on his travels to a place near Rouen, it was not from *Hamwic*, but from a place nearby, which in Hugeburc's *Vita Wynnebaldi* was described as another *mercimonium* at Hamblemouth (Bauch 1984, 136–7). Unfortunately this market and shipping place at present remains undiscovered, but it serves as an important reminder that other trading places would have existed alongside the major coastal *emporia*.

Indeed, archaeological support for such likely trading sites is now increasingly being provided by metal-detector finds, which have led to the identification of 'productive' sites in many parts of eastern England (Ulmschneider 2000b, 62–3; authors in this volume). This paper, based on a study currently being undertaken on the Isle of Wight, charts the development of such a metal-detected 'productive' site in the south of England. It will begin by reviewing the current archaeological evidence from the site, before attempting to answer questions about how, when, and why this site may have evolved, and about its role and importance within the wider area.

The 'productive' site and its surrounding landscape

The first thing to notice about the site, and a characteristic of nearly all 'productive' sites, is its striking location, situated in the centre of the island close to major lines of communication (Fig. 7.1). The site lies in the Bowcombe valley, near Carisbrooke, in an area of great geographical importance. In this area the central chalk ridge, running approximally west to east across the island, is intersected by river valleys accommodating important north-south routes. The major land route from the west to the east of the island, believed to have been in use since prehistory, ran along the crest of the ridge and descended near Bowcombe to cross the valley of the Lukely Brook, formerly the Carisbrooke (Ulmschneider 1999, 23). It is not known exactly where this crossing point might have been in the Anglo-Saxon period, but an important ford, one of three in the valley, survives at Clatterford near to our site, where there are also the remains of a substantial but largely unexplored Roman villa (Basford 1980, 31, 33 and 123). Having crossed the brook, the route would have continued eastwards, crossing the River Medina at another major ford near to the better-known Roman villa at Shide (*ibid.*, 31–3 and 129; Tomalin 1977), before climbing to continue along the chalk ridge. The site can thus be seen to lie in the immediate vicinity of the crossing of a minor tributary of the Medina by the most important west-east land route across the island, and to have good communications to an agriculturally rich hinterland via the river valleys. The twelfth-century town of Newport,

FIGURE 7.1.
The location and geography of the Isle of Wight.

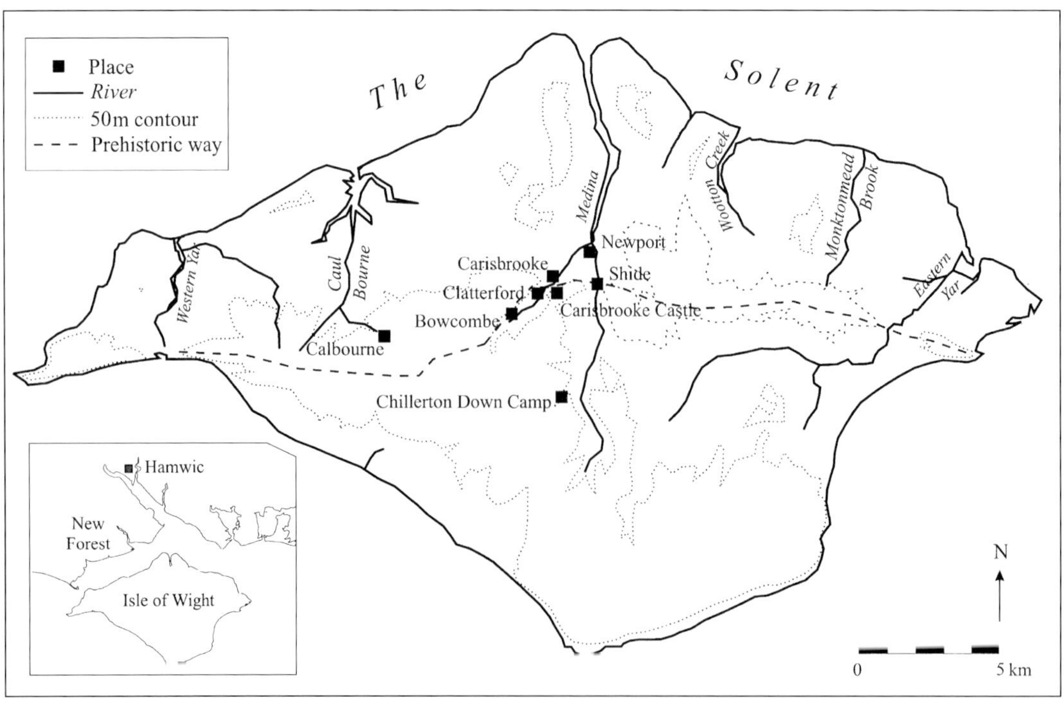

about three kilometres from the site, lies at the head of navigation of the River Medina, from which point the river provides a major shipping route into the Solent and beyond.

The second important characteristic of this, and other 'productive' sites, is the large amount of Middle Anglo-Saxon coinage they produce. When finds from the site were first discussed in 1999, there were certainly nine, and probably as many as eighteen coins attributed to it, making it more coin productive then any other site in Hampshire, apart from *Hamwic* (Ulmschneider 1999, 30–3, with detailed literature on the published finds). Since then, co-operation between two of the finders, archaeologists on the island, and Michael Metcalf has doubled this number to thirty-seven or thirty-eight finds (M. Metcalf, pers. comm.), making this 'productive' site completely unique for the whole area. These finds immediately raise some very important questions: when, how, and why did this site start, what were its connections, and when and why did it cease to function?

A detailed assessment of the coinage is currently being carried out by Metcalf (M. Metcalf, pers. comm.), but a few observations may be made. Of the thirty-seven finds, eleven are silver sceattas of Series E and two of Series D. All originated from the area of the Rhine mouth, while one further find, a sceatta Series X, originated from Jutland. The coins of Series D and one of the seven specimens of Series E which were available for examination, are of primary date i.e. before *c.* 710–15, although their date of loss may have been later. Other Continental finds comprise one Merovingian *denier*, and perhaps a very rare Series E Type 12/5 'mule'. The second largest group in the assemblage is formed by sceattas of Series H, minted at *Hamwic*. These comprise seven coins, one of them of the early Secondary Type 39, five of the later Type 49, and one which still needs identification. Of the remaining thirteen finds, twelve are English sceattas of Series C2, F, H Type 48, J, O, R derivative, V, W and a Series W related mule, four of them primary, the rest secondary. Finally there is a penny of Offa, and possibly yet another sceatta, Series O Type 38.

Coin use on the site therefore appears to have started late in the primary sceatta phase, perhaps from around 700–10 onwards, when both Continental and English issues reached the site. This coin use intensified greatly during the course of the eighth century but seems to have declined towards the end, following a general pattern of decline found at other sites of the period (Blackburn, this volume; Grierson and Blackburn 1986, 155–89; Metcalf 1988b, 230–53). However, there appears to have been no re-generation of coin use on the island site, which appears to have ceased, or moved to another place, by the early ninth century.

The origins of the coins also indicate a wide range of connections. Among them, the most important one appears to have been with the Rhine mouths area, and probably Dorestad (Metcalf 1993–4, 170–81). However, we cannot assume that all of these coins would have necessarily arrived directly from the place they were minted, although this seems likely for those from *Hamwic.* Perhaps more significant is the number of unusual or extremely rare finds. These include, amongst others, the Merovingian *denier* (unpublished) and the two sceattas of Series R derivative (Coin Register 1993, 147 No. 177), currently the only ones of their type known in Hampshire. The really outstanding finds are the Series E Type 12/5 mule, probably of Continental origin (Ulmschneider 1999, 39–40 and fig. 6e), and the Series W related mule (unpublished). Both coins are extremely rare. Only two other specimens of the Series E mule are known at all, one of them on the Continent, and all three from the same dies (Metcalf 1993–4, 531 and 536), while there is only one other, unpublished, find of the Series W related mule (M. Metcalf, pers. comm.). From this preliminary analysis it is already becoming clear that we are dealing with a very important 'productive' site, a picture which is now beginning to be mirrored in other find categories.

The third characteristic of this and other 'productive' sites is that they invariably produce other non-ferrous metalwork, and sometimes unusual high-status finds. In 1999 one strap-end was known to have come from this site (Ulmschneider 1999, 39–40 and fig. 6d), but since then it has become clear that other finds have been made during the last decade, and there is now a pressing need to establish a full corpus of these objects. One such new find, very kindly brought to my attention by Leslie Webster, is a very unusual copper-alloy fitting with a runic inscription, now in the possession of the British Museum (L. Webster, pers. comm.; BM Acc. No. 1999.4–1.1). The object, still unpublished, is of eighth- to ninth-century date, but its function currently remains unknown. It seems highly likely that we have not yet seen the full range of finds available from this site. This may also be underlined by a surprising lack of pins so far, which are almost always found on other 'productive' sites (Ulmschneider 2000a, 32, 51 and 60, and maps 6 and 22).

Interestingly, it is now also becoming clear that the site is producing a scatter of finds from many other periods, for example Roman coins, brooches, and even some pottery (Isle of Wight SMR 2161 and 2156). There was clearly a focus of Roman activity in the valley (Fig. 7.1), and three Roman villas are currently known: at Carisbrooke, Clatterford, and Bowcombe (Basford 1980, 123). This focus appears to have continued in the Early Anglo-Saxon period, for which important high-status burials with outstanding Merovingian objects are found at Carisbrooke Castle (Morris and Dickinson 2000, 86–97), and on Bowcombe Down (Stedman 1998, 115–18). Early Anglo-Saxon finds, including brooches, have also been reported from the same two or three fields as the 'productive' site, together with Medieval, and many other, undated finds (Isle of Wight SMR 2161, 2156, 2388). Unfortunately, the information provided at present does not allow the identification of different foci of activity within the fields, which await fieldwalking.

A local place of importance

Current evidence therefore points to a major market or 'productive' site in an area of very dense activity in the centre of the island, which clearly had close connections with both *Hamwic* and probably the Continent. Perhaps one of the most intriguing questions surrounding this site is: why is it located in this particular place? Here answers may be provided by the surrounding landscape (Fig. 7.2).

One possible explanation for its location, which has already been touched upon, is that the valley was clearly a centre of communications and activity from a very early date (Fig. 7.1). A few kilometres to the south is the only definite Iron Age hillfort on the island, at Chillerton

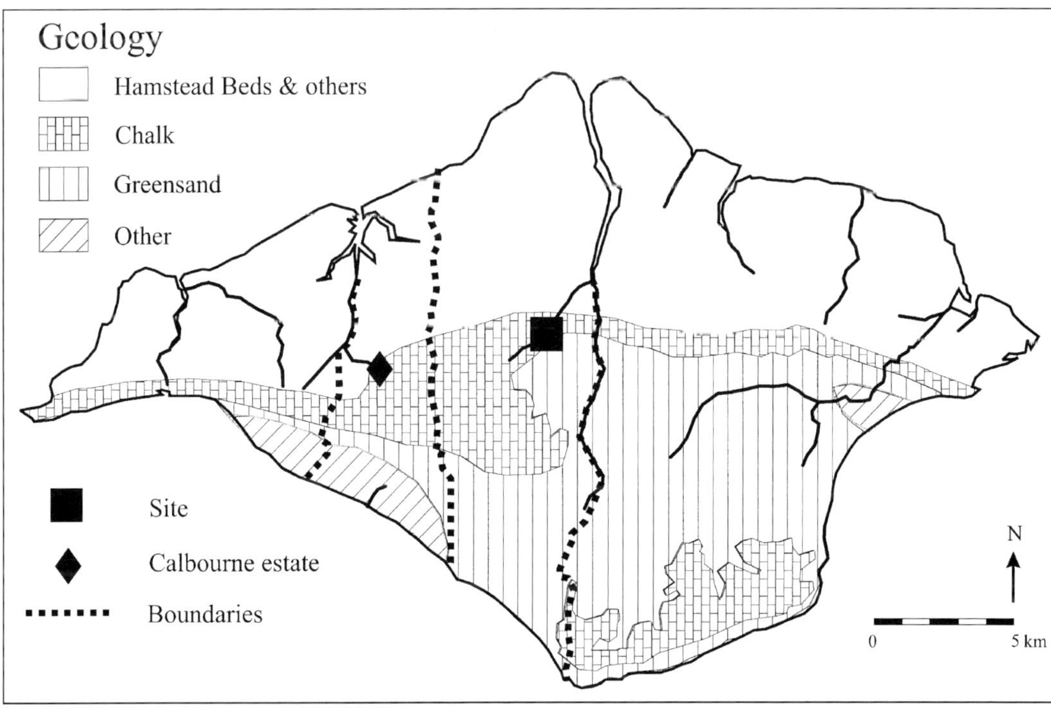

FIGURE 7.2.
A simplified map of the geology of the Isle of Wight. Estate boundaries indicate the early use of different geological zones.

Down (Basford 1980, 27 and 121; Dunning 1947). Then, during the Roman period, three – or including the Shide villa, four – of the eight known villas on the island were concentrated here (Tomalin 1987, fig. 1). From the Early Anglo-Saxon period, two very important cemeteries with Merovingian imports are found, one of them possibly within a highly tentative Late Roman enclosure (Young 1983, 283–4 *versus* Rigold 1969; Young 2000, 12, 18 and 190–1). There was also an important ford and crossing point of major routes in the valley.

However, there may have been other reasons influencing the choice of site. Why, for example, was it not located at the second important fording point at Shide in a possibly even better geographical position, or indeed lower down the Medina, where it becomes navigable? Here the local geology and soils (Fig. 7.2) may provide some important clues. Unlike the largely infertile sands and clays following much of the lower valley of the Medina (Hamstead Beds and others), the 'productive' site was situated in a rich agricultural and pastoral landscape where the downlands meet the fertile greensands (Welldon-Finn 1962, fig. 90; Bird 1997, fig. 1). This location in an area where large blocks of very different soil types meet is of great importance, as the site would have been able to exploit two or probably three major ecological zones. This practice may have originated much earlier (see Fig. 7.2), and is perhaps preserved in the boundaries of the ninth-century Calbourne estate (Sawyer 1968, No. 274), and the territories from sea to sea of the early churches at Domesday (Hockey 1982, 1–8, map inside cover for parish boundaries). Not only was the site situated at the junction of three major ecological zones, it also lies in an area where porous chalk meets with less permeable greensand formations (Geological Survey, Drift Sheet 330). In these areas fresh-water springs often break out, and at least two springs are known within the close vicinity of this 'productive' site.

This preliminary assessment of the surrounding landscape therefore seems to argue for a 'productive' site heavily involved in the exploitation of natural resources. But what were they? While the wooded north of the island is likely to have been used, among other things, for pig-rearing, hunting, and as a source of timber, the chalk downs would have been very well suited to sheep farming. But perhaps the most important resource was the loamy greensands in the south. These provided excellent soils for grain and were intensively exploited throughout the Roman period and in the later Middle Ages (Isle of Wight County Council 1992, 24; Hockey 1982, 105–8).

Of potential importance here may be the only pre-Conquest record of a mill on the island, at Bowcombe in a charter of 964×975 (Sawyer 1968, No. 821; Kemble 1839–48, No. 599). Unfortunately, the charter is complicated, and the mill may not actually have stood in Bowcombe itself but within its hundred (Finberg 1964, No. 109 at 51–2, 97–8 and No. 352 at 107–8). Nevertheless, the general idea deserves serious attention. In Domesday Book two mills are recorded at Bowcombe (*DB Hampshire*, fo. 52b), which has been identified with Carisbrooke (Margham 1992), and at a later date at least two are known to have belonged to Carisbrooke castle and the priory (Hockey 1982, 239). Also intriguing, although maybe completely co-incidental, is the record of an eighteenth-century paper mill in the immediate vicinity of the 'productive' site, marked on the 1864 first edition Ordnance Survey 25″ map (sheet 95.5). Could it therefore have been grain, milled or un-milled, that was purchased by the *Hamwic* sceattas? The island greensands provide the only soils of their type in the Hampshire Basin (Welldon-Finn 1962, fig. 90), and such perishable foodstuffs could have quickly and easily been shipped down the Medina.

Regional and international importance

If we are to understand the full significance of this site in the future, it will also be necessary to look more closely at its wider context (Fig. 7.3).

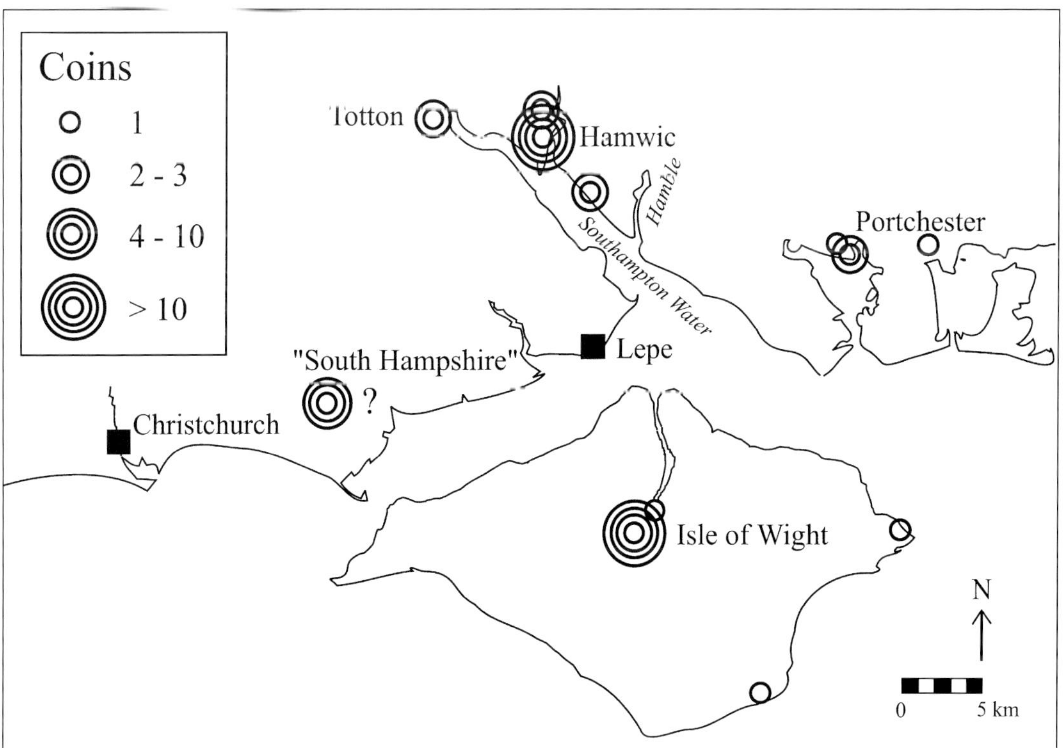

FIGURE 7.3. Coin-productive sites and markets around the Solent.

One line of enquiry that immediately springs to mind is the relationship between the 'productive' site and the *emporium* at *Hamwic*. How did these trading sites compare and differ? What were their respective origins, functions, and were they in competition?

Again a few trends may be suggested. As noted above, the large number of *Hamwic* sceattas found on the island site clearly indicates a strong trading connection with the *emporium*, particularly from the second quarter of the eighth century onwards. Both sites also show large numbers of coins from the Rhine mouths area (Metcalf 1988a, 19–20 and 37–9), some of them probably arriving directly from their place of origin, although it could be argued that the Isle of Wight finds may have arrived via *Hamwic*. Indeed, as far as can be said at present the 'productive' site does not seem to have pre-dated the *emporium* (M. Metcalf, pers. comm.). Neither is there any evidence to suggest that it would have had an active mint-place of its own (Metcalf 1988a, 18–19), being, it seems, largely under the monetary influence of *Hamwic*. However, this is not to say that all its contacts would have necessarily led via the *emporium*. Not only is there a small, but probably significant, number of sceatta types from the island that have not yet been paralleled in over 130 sceatta finds from *Hamwic*, or indeed the rest of Hampshire (such as Series R derivative, O Type 38, and F variety b: Ulmschneider 2000a, Appendix 2; Metcalf 1988a) – there are also the two extremely rare 'mules', of which only one or two other specimens are known at all.

While *Hamwic* out-lived the 'productive' site (Metcalf 1988a, 22–5 and 52–7), both markets must have operated side by side for about a century, and despite their possibly different outlooks, the Isle of Wight site would always have remained closely connected with the mainland of Hampshire. Indeed, important trading and shipping routes existed across the Solent, and from the Roman period onwards there is evidence for the transport of goods such as stone, salt, grain, and probably wool from the island (Ulmschneider 1999, 33–6).

Not all traffic of goods would necessarily have been connected with trade. Some of the high-status objects on the island may have arrived as a result of gift-exchange, while other commodities are likely to have been redistributed to supply different parts of large estates. Here another important line of enquiry, which has not received much attention, is provided by the early manorial relationships across the Solent. The evidence provided by eleven Anglo-Saxon charters referring to the island (Sawyer 1968, Nos 274, 281, 543, 766, 821, 842, 1391, 1507, 1581 and 1662–3) and Domesday Book is complex, and points to many changes taking place during the later Anglo-Saxon period. Nevertheless, there is a likelihood that some of the Domesday entries may indicate more ancient ties. For example, there appears to have been a strong connection between the island and the New Forest area on the mainland (Fig. 7.1 inset; Fig. 7.3), with five New Forest manors recorded holding land in the Isle of Wight, and another manor apparently being held from the island (Eling, Holdenhurst, Ringwood, Braemore, Twynham, and Stanswood: Welldon-Finn 1962, 291; Golding 1989, 18–21). Of these, the entry for the church at Tywnham, later Christchurch, claims that the Isle of Wight lands had 'always been' in the lands of the church (*DB Hampshire*, fo. 44b).

Could these entries reflect even earlier connections? (Fig. 7.3) When the West Saxon king Cædwalla conquered the Jutish Isle of Wight in 686, two young princes are reported by Bede to have fled to a place called *Ad Lapidem* (*Historia Ecclesiastica*, iv. 16), which has been identified as Lepe in the New Forest, in what would have been the adjoining mainland territory of the Jutes (Yorke 1989, 90). Estate ties between the island and mainland are also attested in a charter of 826, which records the grant of a large estate at Calbourne (see above) to the bishop of Winchester. One therefore must assume a fairly regular network of contacts and flow of goods between parts of royal and ecclesiastical estates in the two areas, and it seems likely that other landing and probably market places would have existed.

Perhaps one of the most interesting questions is how and why this 'productive' site came into being. At present it appears from the coinage that the market would most probably have been established, or started to function, fairly shortly after Cædwalla's conquest of the island in 686, in the immediate aftermath of which a quarter of the Isle was given 'for God's use' to Bishop Wilfrid (*Anglo-Saxon Chronicle*, *s.a.* 686; *Historia Ecclesiastica*, iv. 16). Patrick Hase has long argued for the existence of an early mother church for the island at Carisbrooke, the ancient rights of which are preserved in the Cartulary of Carisbrooke, and the *parochia* of which by the twelfth century still appears to have comprised the vast area from sea to sea between Northwood and Shorwell/Chale (Fig. 7.2; Hase 1975, 323–33; Hockey 1982, 1–13, map in cover). Could the 'productive' site have been associated in some way with the foundation of an early mother church in the area? The suggested date of its foundation would certainly be consonant with that of five other mother churches around the Solent in the late seventh to early eighth centuries (Hase 1988, 45–8 and fig. 9). Unfortunately, in the absence of any corroborative written or archaeological sources, the evidence must remain highly speculative and entirely circumstantial.

There is no further information about the area until Domesday, when Bowcombe was the site of the most important royal manor and hundred on the island, encompassing a church, mill, salt-house, and a toll worth thirty shillings. All the tithes of Bowcombe belonged to this church, to which were also attached a second mill and twenty smallholdings, inhabited by bordars (*DB Hampshire*, fos. 52b and c). Both the presence of the bordars as well as the toll all point very strongly to the existence of a market at Carisbrooke in the Late Anglo-Saxon period (Dyer 1985, 100–1).

Where would this market have been located? There is certainly no evidence at present to suggest a continuation of the 'productive' site. So did it shift to another site? The only Late Anglo-Saxon coin so far known in the area is a penny of Æthelred II (985–91), found at Carisbrooke Castle car park. However, the find is said not to have been *in situ*, and may have arrived in soil carted from Newport (Jones 1959, 157–9). As the excavated remains of substantial timber buildings attest, the later castle site was clearly important during the Late Anglo-Saxon period (Young 2000, 53–5 and 191–2), but other places also need to be considered, not least areas in the vicinity of the priory church, on the opposite site of Lukely Brook.

Finally, a third line of enquiry must focus on the relationship between the island and the Continent. It is now becoming increasingly clear from its burials that perhaps already by the late fifth, but certainly during the sixth century, the 'Jutish' Isle of Wight exhibited considerable wealth and wide trading connections (Arnold 1982a; Morris and Dickinson 2000). Equally significant are the historically and archaeologically well-attested links between the Jutish island, the Jutes of Kent, and the Continent, at a time when both Kent and the Isle of Wight appear to have held a monopoly of southern cross-Channel trade (*Historia Ecclesiastica*, i,15; Huggett 1988; Welch 1991). But what were the routes in operation, and how did they change over time? Their continuing use is now reflected both in archaeology and in early written records which, at least from the late seventh or early eighth centuries onwards, point to the growing importance of travel routes to Northern France and the Seine area (Le Maho, this volume; Johanek 1985, 222–5 and 234–44), Willibald's ship perhaps being bound for the important early fair at Saint-Denis (Bauch 1984, 40–1 and 136–7).

In conclusion, there is now evidence for a major 'productive' site evolving in an area that commanded important coastal routes and cross-Channel links from the earliest times. Access to these, as has been argued elsewhere, was probably one of the foremost reasons for the final West Saxon conquest of the formerly Jutish areas by the late seventh century (Ulmschneider 1999, 36–8). By the early eighth century, a number of trading posts existed in the area (Fig. 7.3), including the major *emporium* at *Hamwic*, the landing place at Hamblemouth, the 'productive' site on the Isle of Wight, and possibly other places, such as one recorded as 'South Hampshire', perhaps south of the New Forest (Rigold and Metcalf 1977, 47). In addition, Metcalf has suggested that the minting place for the West Saxon coinage of Series W may have to be sought in this area or a little further west (Metcalf 1993–4, 152–7 and 684), while ninth century coins are now emerging from a site at Eling Creek, Totton (Dunger 1997; EMC 1999.0098). Are we therefore beginning to observe a network of markets in operation, each seemingly bound to a major inlet?

More research is needed, particularly on the chronology and interaction of these sites, before any such pattern can be proposed more confidently. Future research will also have to try to explain two other important observations: First, why, despite much metal-detecting activity, have 'productive' sites on the scale of those in the eastern counties not been discovered in the south of England (Ulmschneider 2000a, 107 and maps 5 and 21)? Second, how can the outstanding wealth of the Isle of Wight 'productive' site be explained? Apart from *Hamwic*, no other sites anywhere near its scale are known along the south coast, or within a fifty-mile radius inland (EMC, December 2000). Probably the most important explanation, cross-Channel trade, has already been suggested, but other factors also need to be considered such as the strategic position of the island, which provided important access to Winchester and the Thames Valley – a fact not lost on the Vikings (*Anglo-Saxon Chronicle, s.a.* 897 [896], 998 and 1001). Ultimately, part of the answer may also lie in the nature of Southampton Water and the Solent itself. Could some of these multiple markets have supplied ships or fleets anchored in and around the greatest natural harbour on the south coast?

CHAPTER 8

The Early Anglo-Saxon Framework for Middle Anglo-Saxon Economics: The Case of East Kent

Stuart Brookes

Introduction

Recent contextual approaches to Early Medieval socio-economic development have stressed the important relationship between trade or exchange and political power in the formation of increasingly hierarchical structures of social dominance. Given the dearth of archaeological evidence for the nature of these early changes, such approaches are marked by the application of social theory to numerous multi-disciplinary lines of argument, to model wider developments on the basis of recognised social features. As such, the identification of seemingly specialised commercial or trading settlements (*wics* or *emporia*) during the seventh century, has been linked to wider theories regarding the increasingly centralised economic and political power of emergent polities during this period (for example Hodges 1978; 1988; 1989a and b; Arnold 1988; Carver 1989; Scull 1992 and 1993).

In part fuelled by the importance of such trading sites and imported artefacts in archaeological literature, many interpretations of the social processes during the period have privileged the competitive exchange and consumption of foreign exotica as a causal dynamic to institutional change. The distribution pattern of these objects has been argued to represent a 'prestige-good exchange' apparatus operating between the kinship-dominated societies of the Early Anglo-Saxon period. As gift-giving and loyalty in military service formed the basis of social relations, a monopoly of the trade in luxury goods ensured political dominance within the competitive peer-polities. The coastal zone (including Kent, the Thames Valley and the East Anglian headland) in which these objects are primarily clustered, and the evolutionist models proposed by analogy with the later *emporia* sites within this geographical area, have combined to emphasise early Kentish material within macro-economic interpretations. In part explainable by the inevitable shipping patterns around the East Kent headland, Kent has historically been presented as the focal node of impact for diffusionist patterns of settlement, trading connections, state formation, and Christianisation. Certain documentary sources attest to an East Kent/Frankish connection, in the form of Frankish claims of authority over Kent, royal alliances and tribute extraction (Wood 1983), and these have often been utilised to explain the particularly dense patterns of imported goods in the county in the Early Anglo-Saxon period (Huggett 1988; Welch 1991). Additionally, some evidence for inter-regional trade is supported by eighth-century toll remissions at the ports of Sarre and Fordwich (Kelly 1992). Despite little concrete archaeological evidence for comparable trading settlements therefore, Kent has often been presented as the first kingdom to adopt monopolising control over long-distance trade, a move that placed the sixth- and early seventh-century kingdom in a pre-eminent position over its neighbours.

Such models of Early to Middle Anglo-Saxon socio-economic development suggest a number of further areas of investigation. The reconstruction of the spatial framework of increasing inter- (and by implication, intra-) regional trade and exchange suggested by the works of Hodges for example, can be explored both through the distribution of commodities in space (Renfrew 1975 and 1977) or the arrangement of hierarchies of settlement with respect to the tenets of central-place theory (Davies and Vierck 1974; Arnold 1988, fig. 5.5; Aston 1986). Carol Smith's (1976) thesis on regional economic systems, from which Hodges drew much inspiration, also showed through a number of empirical studies, that the regional organisation of hierarchical central-places was crucially tied to modal networks, particularly in disarticulated, periodic market systems (*ibid.*, 26). Following Stine (1962), Smith argued that, within a predominantly agrarian economy, traders need to be mobile in order to maximise the consumer demand range beyond the minimum range of goods traders need to offer to survive. Periodic markets, fairs and other specialised centres by their very nature therefore, are tied to trader mobility. Sedentary commercialised settlements, Hodges' 'type B' *emporia*, could only occur when the consumer range increased enough to support permanent traders. These sites, be they *emporia*, inland settlements or markets, are expected to occupy key nodal positions within a region; straddling environmental zones, major routeways and frontiers, to maximise the demand catchment-area (Hodges 1989a, 52–3).

Straight models of such economic central-place hinterlands show a decrease in demand density with increasing distance from the commercial centre. Close to markets, high demand density and transport efficiency enable continuous commercial activity (Plattner 1976). As the distance to the market increases, the zone of viable commerce is determined by a ratio between the periodic trader's minimum daily income threshold and transport costs. Finally, a zone is defined, where demand falls below the trading threshold, and the transportation costs are so expensive, that even itinerant trade cannot be sustained. A model of key regions comprising the trading hinterland implies that the comparative pattern of consumption of individual communities is expected to vary regionally. Gateway communities or elite residences should demonstrate markedly different patterns of consumption and access to wealth markers than contemporary productive settlements. As part of this phenomenon, there should also be some evidence for cultural features associated with increasing specialisation, such as production, provisioning and distribution. Finally, institutional changes of the type suggested by Hodges, should also manifest themselves in increasing forms of centralised control.

Corridors of movement, settlement and exchange

Although this economically deterministic model runs the risk of oversimplification, there is some evidence for such restricted commercialisation in Early to Middle Anglo-Saxon Kent. Reconstruction of the region's Anglo-Saxon transport geography presents a useful framework to examine the siting of many of the important settlements of the period. Drastic geomorphological change to the landscape of East Kent, as a result of Holocene sea-level changes and local coastal responses, means that many of the settlements of interest are now up to several kilometres inland (Fig. 8.1). Of particular importance amongst these, are those around the former Wantsum Channel in north-east Kent which have been continually argued to represent comparable, though possibly earlier, specialised trading sites to those excavated in other parts of England. In addition to such evidence of past riverine and coastal movement, the network of Roman roads radiating out from the *civitas* capital of Canterbury, and some Iron Age and Prehistoric trackways, continue to be preserved in part as contemporary routeways (*cf.* Margary 1946 and 1948; Knox 1941). Finally, the evidence for Anglo-Saxon and Medieval detached pasture, in the form of *-den* place-names, High Medieval lists of extra-manorial demesne and other charter evidence, has prompted some authors to posit a number of possible ancient droves existing as trackways and sunken lanes linking the northern coast with the Weald in the south-west (for example Everitt 1986, 36 Map 1).

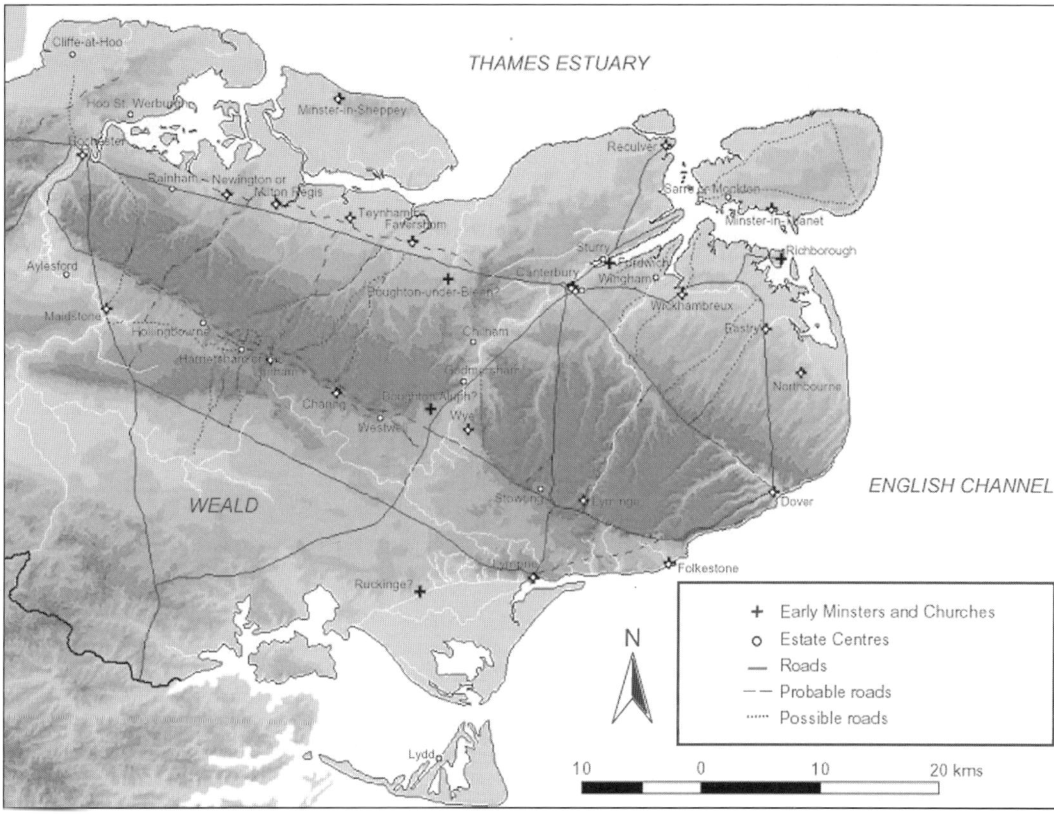

FIGURE 8.1.
Map of East Kent, showing the reconstructed coastline *c.* 800 and its relation to some of the sites and roads mentioned in the text. The digital elevation model of East Kent was produced in ARCVIEW at 50m pixel resolution from 10m Ordnance Survey digital contours provided by the Digimap Project (http://edina.ac.uk/digimap/).

Spatial analysis in the form of Kolgomov-Smirnov testing of Early Anglo-Saxon cemetery distribution in East Kent suggests that these were significantly structured in relation to existing routes of communication, i.e. Roman roads, navigable rivers or the coast. Approximately 85 percent of cemeteries are seen to lie in highly visible locations within 1.2km of these routes, while the location of the remaining sites can be argued to correlate closely to predicted droves, linking thirteenth-century estate centres with their appurtenant Wealden pig-pasture. Although the antiquity of these latter routes is uncertain, the case argued by historians (e.g. Everitt 1986; Witney 1976), the number of *denns* mentioned in Anglo-Saxon charters from the mid-eighth century onwards (such as Sawyer 1968, Nos. 24–25, 30, 33, 37, 123 and 125), the correlation of these routes with computerised GIS 'least-cost path models', and places-names containing the element *-ora* (Brookes forthcoming), all suggest a clear tendency for sites to be located close to roads or routeways. Given the conspicuous use of above-ground markers in Kentish cemeteries (in the form of secondary interment in prehistoric barrows or Roman monuments, as well as primary burial in Anglo-Saxon barrow cemeteries or cemeteries with other visible grave structures – Shephard 1979; Hogarth 1973) and the close association of burial throughout the period with the prevalent routes of communication, a deliberate rite can be suggested, determined in the first instance by selection of places in the landscape visible from the patterns of movement of the living.

The evidence from the distribution of Early Anglo-Saxon cemeteries offers a picture of fossilised social movement from which to compare the pattern of hierarchical locales. In this regard, Tatton-Brown's Kentish gazetteers of early towns (1984) and ten 'old minsters' (1988) finds close topographical correlation with both this pattern of Early Anglo-Saxon mortuary structures and Late Roman settlement. Utilising further documentary sources and the distribution of archaeological complexes, Everitt (1986) has also argued for a number of 'seminal place' estate-centres, forming the nucleus of colonising tenurial holdings in the North Downs and Weald. His hypothesis has stressed the importance of diverse economic conditions in the make-up of early estates by looking at the ancient patterns of land usage in terms of their detached lands and ancient common rights (*cf.* Witney 1976 and 1982; Everitt 1979 and 1986). Significant links between the more intensively cultivated lowland estates in the northern coastal fringe and Holmesdale valley and dependent appurtenances in the Weald and North Downs have been argued to reflect not merely the pattern of economic settlement, but also the underlying basis of later administrative structures. Thiessen Polygons constructed around these settlements confirm the contrasting economic zones of agrarian resources underlying their topographical shape, and the importance of their location, almost equidistant, along the routes of communication (Fig. 8.2).

If Everitt's interpretation can be accepted (1986, 339–41), that a relatively established system of estates with its origins in the pattern of Romano-British settlement, formed the basis of seventh-century ecclesiastical foundations, the importance of network utility becomes clear both as a component of Middle Anglo-Saxon economic organisation and as a link to earlier patterns of ostentatious consumption. In the purely functional terms of an integrated regional system, nodal settlements could be predicted at the junction of major modal networks, where the costs of transference are minimised. As central-places for tenure spanning a variety of agrarian resources, and the further administrative implications such a pattern of estates suggests, manorial centres therefore needed to be sited at the nexus of inland routeways. Similarly, the link between trader mobility and periodic markets stresses spatial organisation circumscribed by geographical and social restrictions. The importance of Sarre, for example, has been

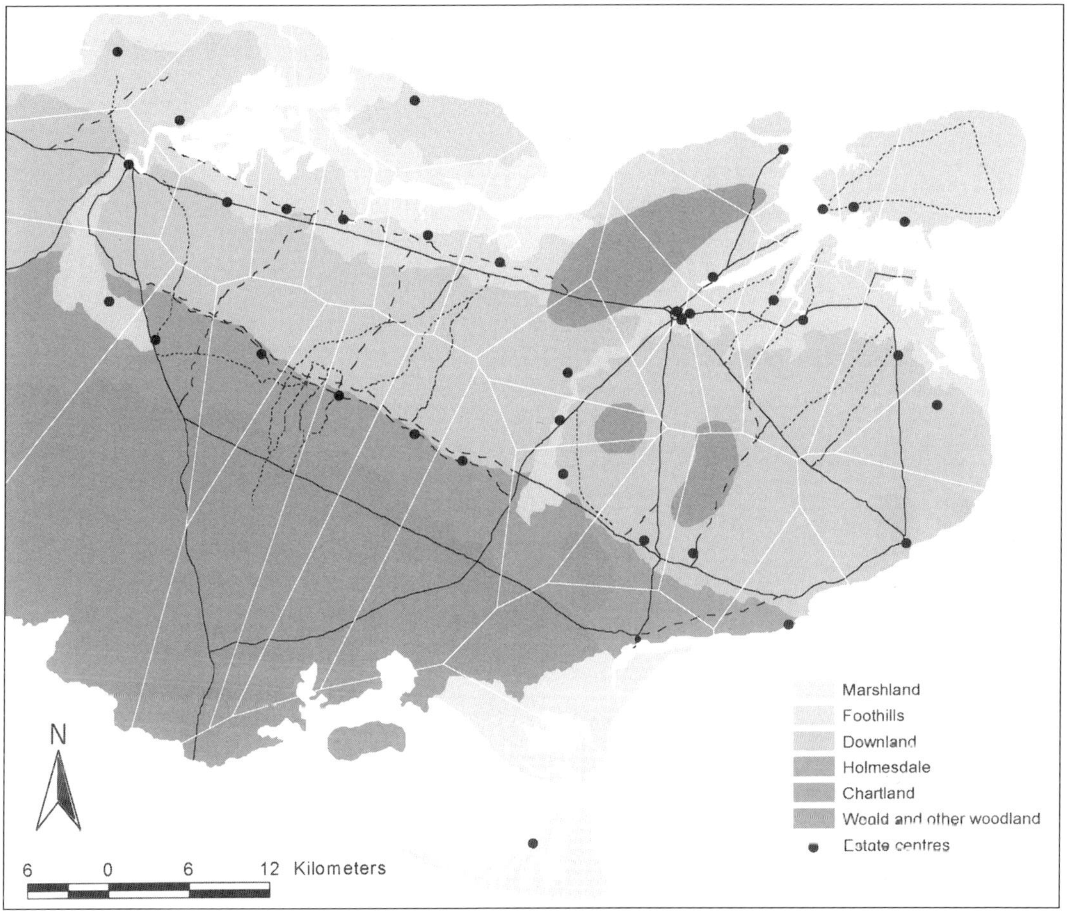

FIGURE 8.2.
Thiessen polygon interpolation, showing the environmental *pays* of Kent and their relation to early estate-centres, as defined by Everitt (1986).

seen with respect to its location at both the major Roman crossing point and at the conflux of the double tidal waters of the Wantsum Channel (Brookes 1998, 29–32). Fordwich's significance has been stressed due to the settlement's position at the tidal head of the Great Stour, and its probable role as the *emporium* for the nearby *villa regalis* at Sturry and Canterbury itself, while also offering the most likely point of trans-shipment between the sea-going Channel and coastal vessels, and the inland riverine modal network. Equally, Sandwich's strategic position at the southern entrance of the Wantsum, adjacent both to the Roman roads to Dover and Canterbury and the large sheltered haven of the *Meacesfleote,* offered it topographical attributes which would secure its importance until well into the medieval period.

These general functional characteristics of settlement appear to be supported by inland settlement also, and the tentative case for a continuity of central-place functions from Romano-British territorial organisation seems unavoidable. Central to this interpretation of the settlement pattern of early Kent is a bridging argument, linking reoccurring observed phenomena rather than verified empirical data. An example of this line of argument is offered by the settlement of Eastry, though it could just as easily be Faversham, Milton Regis or Maidstone. Eastry appears as a Roman road-side settlement occupying the cross-roads of the Richborough-Dover road (Margary 100 or Stane Street) and a prehistoric trackway from Sandwich to Wootton (O'Grady 1979, 114). Roman finds are also known from the immediate environs (*ibid.*, 113) and a Roman cemetery at Walton (Gibben 1902) indicates a level of pre-Saxon settlement. A number of Early Anglo-Saxon cemeteries and burials surrounding the village at Updown ('Cemetery III': Hawkes 1974; 1976; 1979), Buttsole ('Cemetery I': Meaney 1964, 113; Hawkes 1979), Eastry Mill ('Cemetery IV': Hawkes 1979) and at Eastry House* ('Cemetery II': Hawkes 1979), are testimony to a substantial local population, often linked to an inferred Anglo-Saxon *villa regalis.* The latter suggestion relies on the validity of some Late Anglo-Saxon documentary evidence detailing seventh-century events having occurred at Eastry (Hasted 1799, iv, 216) and the association of the place-name with the modern settlement (*cf.* Arnold 1982b, 121). 'Eastry', documented as *Eastorege* in a ninth-century charter, has been interpreted as 'the eastern district capital' (Hawkes 1982, 75) and is taken to indicate both the existence of administrative sub-districts in Late Anglo-Saxon Kent and the importance of the settlement within the royal estate system. The latter argument has prompted the identification of Eastry Court Farm as a potential Anglo-Saxon administrative centre or royal residence (Hawkes 1979, 95) despite little archaeological justification (Arnold 1982b, 135; Parfitt 1999, 50) and suggested the association of Eastry with the unnamed twelfth-century great church listed in the *Domesday Monachorum* (Tatton-Brown 1988, 107). The correlation of Iron Age, Romano-British and Anglo-Saxon archaeological complexes, topographic suitability, place-name evidence, historical allusions and early ecclesiastical associations all indicate a form of ideological, if not necessarily physical, continuity.

The above example could be restated for a number of different settlements and it seems clear, certainly from the point of view of early ecclesiastical centres and *villae regales,* that an association with the Roman past was deliberately fostered. Roman precedents are known by Sturry (Rigold 1972; Brookes 1998); Faversham (Philp 1965, lii; Jessup 1970, 189; Detsicas 1983, 131–3; Everitt 1986, 109–12); Milton

* Recent excavations in the immediate vicinity of this burial suggests that this may actually be an isolated burial (Parfitt 1999, 52).

Regis (Kelly 1978, 267; Detsicas 1983, 81), Lyminge (Kelly 1962, 205; Detsicas 1983, 143–4), Wye (Detsicas 1983, 84, 97 etc.) and Wester Linton, near Maidstone (Detsicas 1983) among others. The influence residual Romano-British finds had on the siting of early churches is equally apparent as is demonstrated by the association of Roman buildings with churches at Lyminge (Detsicas 1983, 143–4), and the minster foundations at Reculver and Richborough for example (Gem 1995, 42; Bushe-Fox 1928, 34–40).

If the Romano-British settlement pattern prejudged the distribution of later economic centres, the routes of communication themselves constrained the flow of wealth through the kingdom. Certainly, restrictions on movement and exchange and the importance placed on negotiated places of social interaction are implicit in documentary sources. Evidence, particularly from palynology, stresses the importance routes of movement took in the construction of social space. Roads are seen as delimiting boundaries (e.g. Hooke 1985, 58), operating as hundredal meeting places (*ibid.*, 102) and provide functional benefits to military and economic endeavours. Movement along the defined routes, on the other hand, must be seen with respect to contemporary social conditions. The Kentish law-codes of the seventh century offer some evidence of concerns for the movement of people and goods. The wording of the Laws of Æthelberht, and particularly those of Wihtred and of Ine of Wessex, stress the importance of roads for movement throughout the kingdoms, with heavy penalties being exacted for unannounced travel off the established routes of communication. Specific laws protecting travellers on roads from robbery, such as is evidenced by Æthelberht 19 and 89 on the other hand, suggest both the importance safe transit through the kingdom held for the king, and that highway crime was sufficiently common-place it required explicit measures for it to be suppressed.

Given the high number of laws dealing with foreigners, strangers and traders (e.g. Æthelberht 19; Hlothere and Eadric 15; Wihtred 4 and 28) it is conceivable that these measures indicate increasing levels of royal control placed on the movement of people and goods through the kingdom; an observation many commentators have associated with taxation (e.g. Carver 1993; Reynolds 1998a, 237). Certainly, other evidence suggests that systems of taxation were becoming more widespread during the mid seventh and eighth centuries (such as the Tribal Hidage: Davies and Vierck 1974, 136–41), but just how much the archaeological pattern of coin loss, for example, can be taken to represent top-down legislation or bottom-up decentralised trading, is debatable. Given the hypothesised economic constraints of the period, wherein goods of inelastic demand were traded in order to bear the costs of transport through sufficient profit, and the environment with little state provisioning of public goods and uncertain and dangerous transport patterns, it is suggested that it was in the interest of traders themselves to restrict alienable exchange to areas protected by law-codes and higher authorities, i.e. roads, fairs and markets.

Distributional patterns of consumption

The characterisation of the period in terms of increasingly exploitative relationships between dependent social classes, offers a further hypothesis by which to compare the differential distribution of commodities among communities accessing common distribution networks. Attempts at investigating mortuary evidence to explain economic concepts of accessibility and consumption of goods, and their use to express wealth (accumulation), social standing (differentiation) and cultural position (where possessions 'flag' certain cultural discourses) are well attested in archaeological practice. Recent distributional methods differ in their attempt to quantify the interment of commodities, with respect to units of economic consumption, such as

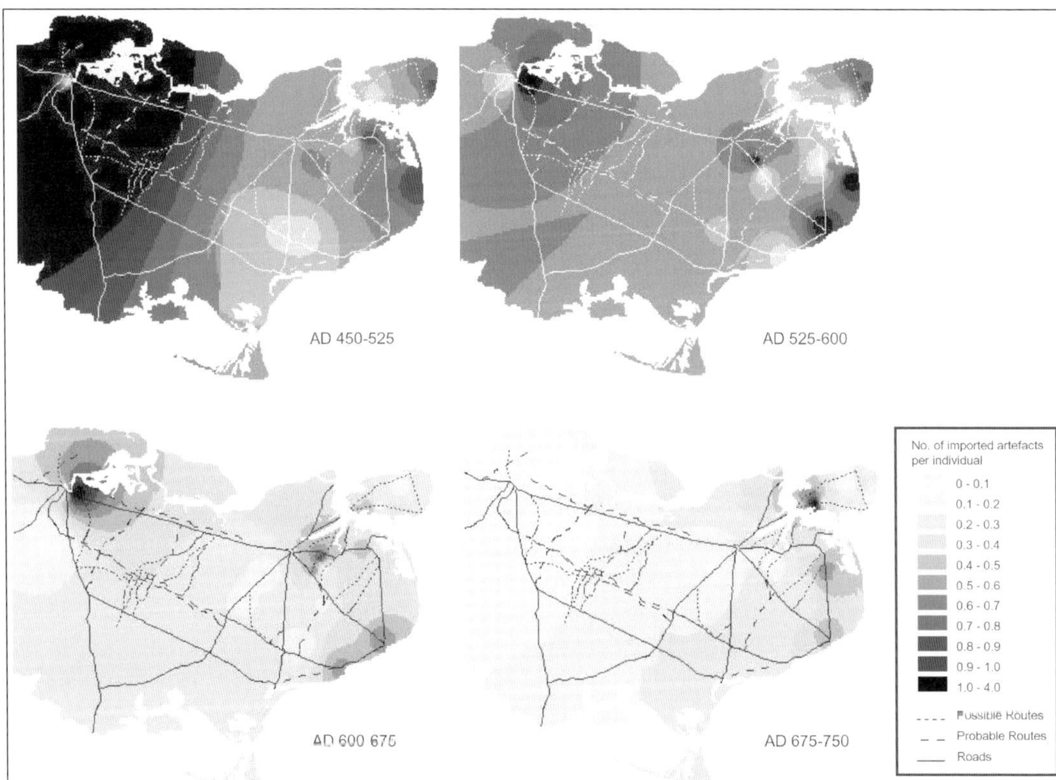

FIGURE 8.3. Trend surfaces produced from the average number of imported artefacts interred with each individual in Early Anglo-Saxon cemeteries of East Kent. The interpolated surfaces were produced in ARCVIEW on the basis of an inverse distance weighting (IDW) regression function from the twelve closest sampled points.

individuals, households, or communities (Loveluck 1994 and 1996; Hirth 1998).

Trend surfaces derived from counts of foreign or local objects within cemeteries, and the percentage of the interred population with such goods, reinforce an impression of wealthy coastal communities, particularly along the Wantsum and Dover coasts (Fig. 8.3). Inland redistribution, by contrast, focuses mainly along the Dover–Canterbury road, also identified as a major routeway by the distribution of Early Anglo-Saxon cemeteries. To the south and west of the kingdom, a noticeable fall-off in the amount of both imported and locally provenanced material further demonstrates the polarisation of wealth along the Thames estuary/Continental axis. An immediate impression gained from these regression models, is the stark contrast between imported artefact consumption prior to and after AD 600. Although the distribution pattern for both periods is roughly similar, with particular conspicuous consumption visible among the communities of the eastern and northern coasts (including a particular dense cluster in the Canterbury environs), the sharp decline after 600 in the deposition of imported goods suggests a changing role in the mobilisation of these objects. Sonia Hawkes (1970, 191; 1982, 72 and 76) has suggested that the later sixth century witnessed increasing royal control over foreign exchange contacts from the basis of inferred military components in the communities of Sarre and Dover. That these overtly military phases are followed by a period of decreased material consumption, despite evidence from documentary sources and coin finds to the contrary, suggests imposed change in the social role of objects.

The pattern of supply and demand underlying the differential consumption of wealth during the sixth and seventh centuries, can be compared with the patterns of seventh- to ninth-century coin finds in East Kent (Fig. 8.4). The generally coastal distribution of areas of high coin loss fit well with the model of important coastal trading suggested by the distribution of imported goods and media of exchange such as weights and measures (*cf.* Scull 1990) during the Early Anglo-Saxon period. Given issues of specialised alienable exchange, implicit in monetary transactions, this distribution pattern sits favourably with the idea of foreign trade and it is perhaps telling that the zone of monetary exchange extends further south along the coast than in previous periods, to include Lympne and the Romney Levels.

The lack of coin finds near the estate centres of the Swale and Holmesdale, by contrast, suggest an interpretation of differential regional access to the means of exchange. Despite the lack of clear Early Anglo-Saxon cemetery evidence from the Swale region from which to extrapolate a model of local consumption, the density of

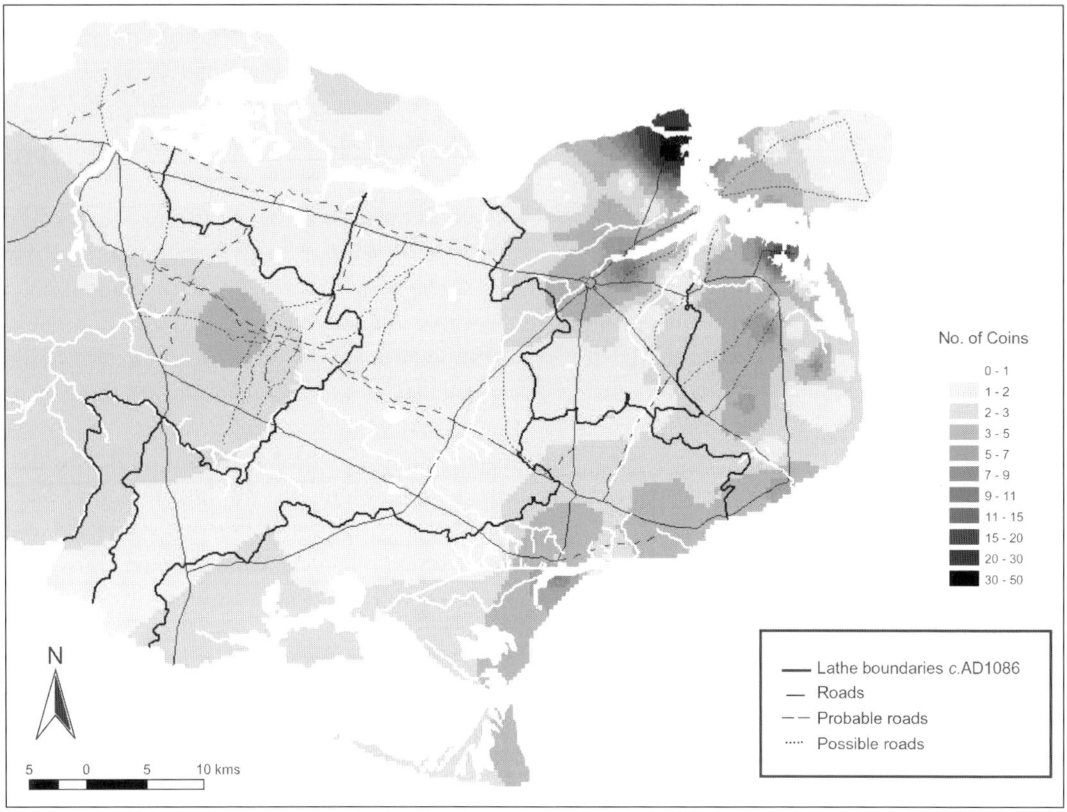

FIGURE 8.4.
Trend surface of Early Medieval coin finds in East Kent. Surface produced from coins *c.* 500–899 listed in the EMC up to 6 July 2001 in ARCVIEW at IDW12 regression.

Anglo-Saxon estate centres in this region, and the clear pan-environmental structure of these settlements, suggests an economic basis operating primarily through non-monetary means. By contrast, the communities of the Dover and Wantsum coast and their immediate hinterland, such as Eastry and Northbourne/Great Mongeham and indeed Canterbury itself, can be recognised both to access foreign commodities from the sixth century, and as peaks of coin loss in the seventh. The coincidence of coin finds in this area with the pattern of earlier imported good deposition suggests that these regions probably engaged in limited price-making markets. The model of the highly fragmented nature of Middle Anglo-Saxon markets, meant that only communities with direct access to alienable trade could engage in monetary exchange.

That areas of particularly low coin loss can in some cases be equated with known important Late Anglo-Saxon estates, such as the *regio* and minster of Milton or the lathe of Wye discussed by Everitt and Jolliffe respectively (Everitt 1986, 302–32; Jolliffe 1933), raises the possibility that these areas can be identified as regions where exchange through the estate mechanism restricted active participation in price-making markets. In contrast to the monetary zone of alienable exchange identified along the eastern margin, the inland 'productive' site of Hollingbourne offers the only comparable example of such negotiated exchange in the west. The location of this settlement at the important cross-roads of routeways linking the historically discrete territories of East and West Kent, the *denns* between the settlements of the Swale and their Wealden appurtenances, and the environmental junction of the *pays* of Chart, Holmesdale, Downland and Weald, all single out its suitability for localised trading. Beyond favourable topographical criterion, Hollingbourne's importance, as is probably the case with the 'productive' sites of Reculver and Richborough, may well be related to the ecclesiastical foundations of the seventh century. Church involvement in the resettlement of Richborough and Reculver have already been mentioned, and it is possible that Hollingbourne represents an ecclesiastical foundation, without substantial Early Anglo-Saxon precedent, as part of the original minsterland of Maidstone of which it is a named dependency in the *Domesday Monachorum* (Everitt 1986, 332).

A comparison between the regression models of Early Anglo-Saxon consumption and Middle Anglo-Saxon coinage demonstrates the importance of 'new' sites within the pattern of controlled exchange. Unlike communities close to the estate centres and coastal sites of the Early Anglo-Saxon period which demonstrate both high numbers of imported goods and Middle Anglo-Saxon coin losses, those of Richborough, Reculver and Hollingbourne are unremarkable in their consumption of wealth during the earlier period. By contrast, the almost unparalleled number of sceatta and tremissis finds at the two coastal sites (Rigold and Metcalf 1984, 258–60) and the clear peak of coin loss at Hollingbourne, may well be indicative of large-scale monetary exchange on a scale only achievable by, and under the protection of, institutions such as the Church.

Conclusions

The Middle Anglo-Saxon economic development of the kingdom of East Kent, of which 'productive' sites are only one phenomenon, can be related both to the topographical attributes of the region and local issues of consumption and exchange. A comparison between Early Anglo-Saxon centres of wealth consumption and the distribution of Middle Anglo-Saxon coin finds in East Kent presents clear implications for the interpretation of developing settlement hierarchies. Important similarities in the geographical structure of Early Anglo-Saxon consumption and later manorial organisation stress, not least, the importance corridors of communication took in structuring the social and economic landscape. Significantly, these same roads and routeways are seen as central to the structure of Early Anglo-Saxon mortuary structures.

That the pattern of Middle Anglo-Saxon estate centres finds close correlation with these same places, suggests at the least a continuity of integrated regional production from the earliest phases of settlement. As one of the criteria governing wealth circulation, access to focal points within the spatial network of routes, can also be argued to underlie differential patterns of consumption within these interred communities. The fall-off curves in imported good deposition within Early Anglo-Saxon cemeteries indicate the importance of specific coastal settlements for the redistribution of these objects, as has been suggested by other lines of historical and archaeological enquiry, and may well provide evidence of so-called 'gateway communities' discussed in geographical anthropology. Of importance, nevertheless, is the recognition of substantial change in the mobilisation of these resources after 600, with particular *foci* of consumption being suggested at known Middle Anglo-Saxon estate centres during the later seventh century. In support of these patterns of exchange, trend surfaces of seventh to ninth-century coin finds indicate the importance of coastal location for active engagement in alienable exchange. In addition, areas of few coin finds and certain sites of unusually high coin-loss possibly reflect local responses to the framework of large-scale institutional exchange and associated restrictions.

CHAPTER 9

Exceptional Finds, Exceptional Sites? Barham and Coddenham, Suffolk

John Newman

The large number of non-ferrous metal finds of all periods recovered by metal-detector users and reported, in East Anglia at least, over the last twenty-five years has prompted a far reaching reassessment by archaeologists, historians and numismatists of how past social and economic systems functioned. In particular for the seventh- to ninth-century period, a number of apparently exceptional site assemblages have been recorded from eastern and southern England that are now collectively called 'productive' sites. But are these site assemblages exceptional or is their study and interpretation thrown off-balance by the wealth of material recovered, in what is often an intensive but largely unsystematic method? Finders will, after all, inevitably concentrate on 'productive' areas with a consequent lack of detector searches across 'non-productive' parts of the countryside. Much as the spectacular discoveries at Sutton Hoo caused a major revision of previously held ideas about the later pagan period following their excavation in 1939, the 'productive' site phenomenon of the seventh to ninth centuries needs to be set against existing data for that respective period, in order to be fully assimilated in what must be an environment of continual research and revision.

Historians would probably say that there should be little surprise caused by the wealth of post-Roman archaeological material that has been recovered over the last two decades. These are the traces of an Anglo-Saxon society which by the seventh century had developed to a level of sophistication capable of supporting various major developments that must, to some extent, be reflected in the archaeological record. These developments included the emergence of kingdoms, with their ability to collect, concentrate and distribute resources; and the foundation and growth of the early Church with similar abilities to control resources as society in general supported both secular and clerical elite groups. Inter-linked with the growing power of these groups, the ever-increasing importance of both internal and international trade can also be seen through the foundation of the trading ports or *wics* and more common use of gold and, subsequently, silver coinage with general standards of weight and purity accepted across north-western Europe. How these developments might be reflected in the archaeological record is crucial to the interpretation of the so-called 'productive' sites.

At this point, it is as well to remember that such sites were known before the widespread use of metal-detectors began in the mid 1970s. Known 'productive' sites include those which can be linked to historical explanations for the seventh- to ninth-century period, such as the early monastic sites at Whitby and on the Kentish coast, in addition to the early trading port of *Hamwic*, Anglo-Saxon Southampton. If these 'productive' sites cause few worries in interpretation, might the same also be true of the recently discovered ones when they are set against systematic survey results giving the full range of the seventh- to ninth-century settlement hierarchy? Similarly, useful information can be gained from what are, admittedly, later historical sources that may give clues relating to the status and function of particular sites in the seventh- to ninth-century period. This information can help in the interpretation of known 'productive' sites and may be able to suggest where other ones await discovery and why they appear to be at the upper end of the settlement hierarchy. Finally, such comparative studies may help to justify the apparently arbitrary terminology that

FIGURE 9.1. South-east Suffolk, showing the position of Barham and Coddenham in relation to Ipswich, other Middle Anglo-Saxon sites and the local system of Roman roads (sources: Margary 1973; Moore 1988).

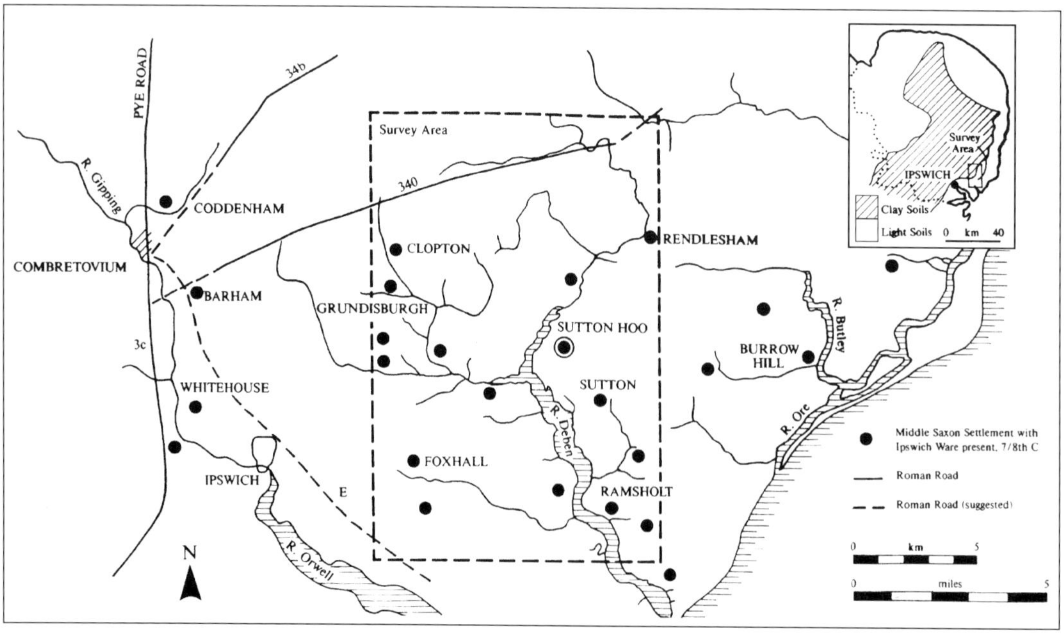

sees some sites as 'productive' and, by definition, others as 'non-productive'.

As noted above, numerous metal-detector finds have been reported and recorded in Suffolk since the late 1970s. The Ipswich area in south-east Suffolk has been particularly well covered by various detector users. By happy coincidence, this concentration of casual detecting coincides, in part, with the area in the Deben valley covered by the South-East Suffolk Survey as part of the Sutton Hoo Research Project which ran between 1983 and 1991 (Fig. 9.1). The survey was initiated as a clear and explicit project to systematically fieldwalk all the available arable land in a 200 square kilometre block centred on Sutton Hoo and Woodbridge (Wade and West 1983). The primary aim of the survey was to locate and then to characterise Anglo-Saxon sites through extensive and intensive field survey (Newman 1989 and 1992). The creation of a settlement hierarchy based on the size and density of pottery scatters then became possible, and it is fortunate that some of these sites have seen subsequent metal-detector searches. It is therefore now possible to present comparative data, against which any 'productive' site can be checked, to see if it is exceptional in terms of the size or character of the finds assemblage recovered.

In south-east Suffolk for the seventh- to ninth-century period the exceptional or 'productive' sites are at Barham and Coddenham. While they are not in the survey area shown in Fig. 9.1, they do form part of a settlement pattern which includes the Deben and Gipping valleys. Of the two, Barham is perhaps the better known and more directly comparable with similar sites in eastern England. The site is located on a ridge forty-six metres above sea level, overlooking the River Gipping eight kilometres north-west of Ipswich. It has commanding views over the wide valley to the south and south-west, while to the north the land rises gently onto the nearby boulder clay plateau. The soils at Barham are relatively light and the underlying drift geology is a mix of sand and gravel. Adjacent to the site is the parish church of St Mary's (Fig. 9.2), which at Domesday owned sixteen acres (*DB Suffolk*, fo. 383b).

The Gipping valley is rich in archaeological finds of all periods as it contains large areas of light and easily worked soils which have attracted settlement from the earliest times. However, the valley also forms a natural routeway from the coast around the natural harbour of the Orwell estuary over a relatively low watershed to the Lark valley, providing access to west Suffolk and the Fen-edge as shown in Fig. 9.4. The Gipping/Lark corridor presents a convenient cross-country route to the densely settled Fen margins and a viable means of avoiding the longer and probably more perilous sea route around the north Norfolk

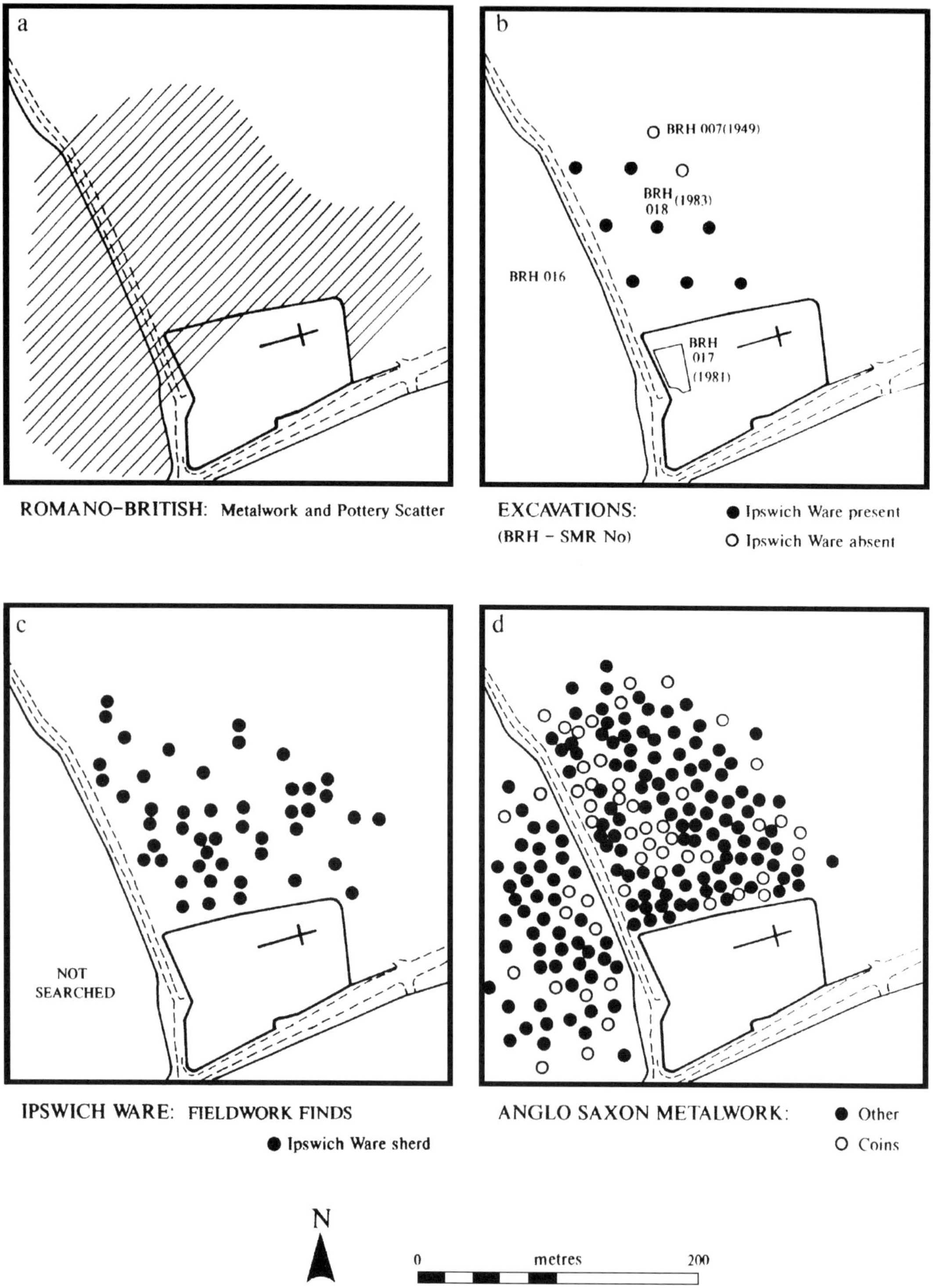
a
ROMANO-BRITISH: Metalwork and Pottery Scatter
b
BRH 007(1949)
BRH 018 (1983)
BRH 016
BRH 017 (1981)
EXCAVATIONS:
(BRH - SMR No)
Ipswich Ware present
Ipswich Ware absent
c
NOT SEARCHED
IPSWICH WARE: FIELDWORK FINDS
Ipswich Ware sherd
d
ANGLO SAXON METALWORK:
Other
Coins
N
0
metres
200

coast. For the Roman period, the importance of the lower Gipping part of the corridor across Suffolk can be seen by the presence of the small town of *Combretovium* in Coddenham parish, three kilometres north-west of Barham. Here, a major Roman route, the Pye Road (Margary 1973), enters East Anglia from the south and crosses the River Gipping before heading north for Caistor-by-Norwich (Fig. 9.1). Continued use of the Pye Road into the post-Roman period is confirmed by the presence of the modern A140 on this same alignment, a continuity which could not have been achieved without its use by the Anglo-Saxons. Both Barham and Coddenham sit at a natural crossroads, where various Roman roads converge to ford the River Gipping and link into the valley route which crosses Suffolk (Fig. 9.1).

Barham is a multi-period site initially noted when Roman material was reported in 1949. Subsequent minor excavation by Ipswich Museum confirmed the Roman settlement evidence but it was not until the advent of metal-detectors in the late 1970s that an Anglo-Saxon presence came to light. As the initial post-Roman finds included a Merovingian tremissis and a gold stud set with garnets it rapidly became apparent that an important Anglo-Saxon site had been discovered. To date, some 1,000 finds of all periods have been recorded from the site by the Archaeological Service at Suffolk County Council and many of the Anglo-Saxon artefacts have subsequently been published (West 1998, 6–8). Most of the Anglo-Saxon coins and artefacts have subsequently been acquired by the British Museum. Finally, it has been possible to fieldwalk most of the site systematically and to carry out small-scale trial excavation (Fig. 9.2).

FIGURE 9.2.
Barham, Suffolk, showing the distributions of artefact-types.

By combining the evidence from the metal-detector finds, small-scale excavation and fieldwalking it is possible to get some idea of the nature of the site at Barham. There is some prehistoric material and Iron Age sites are known nearby. The Roman material covers an area of some five hectares with a coin series running up until *c.* 380. Other finds include brooches and pins as well as an extensive pottery scatter and a moderate amount of tile. Taken together, this probably represents a relatively prosperous rural settlement situated close to a known small town: the small-scale excavation indicates the division of the site into numerous small plots of a probable agricultural origin and there is no indication of high status in the Roman period.

The site at Barham has not produced any evidence of fifth-century activity although there are a few copper-alloy artefacts of probable sixth-century date. In addition, the excavation of nine six-by-six metre trial trenches in 1983 did reveal a scatter of handmade pottery sherds in association with some post-holes that could indicate sixth-century settlement activity. A slightly larger excavation area, of some 500 square metres, was examined in 1981 prior to the construction of a car park for the parish church and this revealed evidence for two timber-built structures of Roman or post-Roman date and two ditches containing Late Anglo-Saxon pottery sherds.

The scatter of seventh- to ninth-century material at Barham covers a similar area to the Roman finds, of around five hectares (Fig. 9.2). The Middle Anglo-Saxon assemblage includes some 50 coins and nearly 150 non-ferrous artefacts. This is clearly an impressive group with the bulk of the coinage dating from between the mid seventh and the mid eighth century and the artefacts indicating an intense level of activity extending into the early ninth century. Later eighth-century coinage is generally rare in East Anglia and Barham has produced relatively few later ninth- or tenth-century coins or artefacts although the presence of Thetford-type ware pottery sherds does indicate a Late Anglo-Saxon domestic presence at least.

In brief, the mid seventh- to mid eighth-century coins from Barham includes the tremissis noted above, which is from the Quentovic mint, two 'Pada'-type thrymsas, a range of sceattas that covers many of the series including a number of Frisian types, and a high proportion of local Series R coins plus two Beonna pennies. The non-ferrous artefacts have been published in detail (West 1998) and include numerous dress items of probable local origin. In addition, a few Continental items such as a 'Saint' brooch (*Heiligenfibel*), a Merovingian buckle-plate, and some hanging-bowl escutcheons of Celtic origin have been recovered.

Barham, therefore, has a wealth of seventh- to ninth-century metalwork indicating contacts outside East Anglia to the other kingdoms in the south-east of England as well as across the North Sea and to the west into the Celtic, or British, areas. The pottery collection from the site, on the other hand, is typical for the area in most respects. Gridded fieldwalking recovered some forty sherds of Middle Anglo-Saxon Ipswich ware, produced *c.* 700–850, which is directly comparable with other, less 'productive' sites nearby and it is likely that a continuous, domestic, rural settlement presence underlies the apparent wealth of Middle Anglo-Saxon Barham. This presence continued once the site had lost its apparently pre-eminent role by the later ninth century. The fieldwalking did recover one imported, Continental, pottery sherd of Middle Anglo-Saxon date which is unusual for a rural site, but which reflects the foreign contacts indicated by the metalwork finds.

For the Middle Anglo-Saxon period at least, therefore, Barham appears to have fulfilled a more complex and central role within the local settlement hierarchy which involved extensive and far-reaching contacts outside of East Anglia at the time Ipswich was growing as a *wic*, or trading port (Wade 1993), a little lower down the Gipping valley. It appears likely that their functions were at least non-competitive if not complimentary. However, before going into Barham's possible role in more depth another 'productive' site at Coddenham should also be considered.

The first finds from the 'productive' site at Coddenham were reported in 1987 as previous metal-detector searches in the parish had concentrated on the area around the small Roman town of *Combretovium* some two kilometres to the south. The Anglo-Saxon site, where the artefact scatter covers an area of nearly six hectares, lies in a small tributary valley just to the north of the main Gipping valley (Fig. 9.1). The line of the Pye Road runs across the valley mouth as it climbs northwards away from the river towards the nearby boulder clay plateau of central Suffolk. Coddenham village with its parish church lies one kilometre to the east of the site. The drift geology in this area is made up of sands and gravels over chalk, giving rise to light, easily worked, soils and a cluster of Early Anglo-Saxon sites around the main Middle Anglo-Saxon finds scatter indicates that this was a preferred area for settlement. While the site is tucked away into a relatively secluded valley it had easy access to the Gipping valley 'corridor' and to the Pye Road.

From its initial discovery, the 'productive' site at Coddenham has produced a great wealth of coin and non-ferrous artefacts with the bulk of the high quality material being of seventh- or very early eighth-century date. The great majority of the finds from Coddenham were recovered between 1988 and 1996 as the site was intensively searched and re-cultivated several times each winter in order to deter illicit detecting. Most of the artefacts remain with the finders and landowner and have recently been published (West 1998, 20), while the bulk of the coin finds went to auction and are now in various private collections following recording by the British Museum and Suffolk County Council.

For the purposes of this study it is only possible to give a brief summary of the material recovered in order to try and characterise the site. Coddenham has produced some evidence for prehistoric activity including four Iron Age coins which are, curiously enough, slightly unusual examples for Suffolk. Roman finds have been found scattered across the field with enough material to indicate the presence of a small to medium farm site with coinage going through to the mid-fourth century. As with Barham, material from the fifth century is absent although a sixth-century presence is indicated by standard East Anglian brooch and wrist-clasp finds, in addition to a few imported items. This site is one of a small group within a one square kilometre block with potential domestic or cemetery use in the sixth century.

By the early to mid seventh century, activity within the valley became more concentrated on the one, main, site with a wealth of material indicating undoubted high status and far-reaching contacts. The coin group for Coddenham runs from the early seventh century, with a worn late sixth-century tremissis, through to the very early eighth century before coming to an abrupt end. Later Anglo-Saxon coinage on the site is rare, comprising a penny of Eadwald and a tenth-century penny. With over sixty early coins, Coddenham must be seen as 'productive' and the composition of the group is exceptional with three tremisses, twelve English thrymsas and some fifty early sceattas. Of particular note is a cut quarter of a tremissis, which indicates real coin use rather than the simple transfer of bullion, as do two contemporary forgeries of Merovingian coins. In addition, an adjacent findspot some 150 metres from the main group has produced a Visigothic tremissis, three early sceattas and a folding balance.

Just as the coin finds are exceptional, so too are the seventh- and early eighth-century artefacts from the site (Fig. 9.3). To date, over 200 items of early Middle Anglo-Saxon date have been recovered, comprising a wide range of copper-alloy dress accessories, fittings, mounts, pins and two fragments of styli. In addition, a number of gold items of the highest quality have been recovered, including a cosmetic scoop (Fig. 9.3a and b), two finger rings and various items of scrap jewellery. The latter items are of particular interest as microscopic examination of one piece (Fig. 9.3c) has shown that the inlaid cloisonné garnets it originally had were prised from their cells, suggesting a possible workshop presence. Similarly some of the copper-alloy material is scrap or off-cut while other artefacts are unfinished, again indicating a workshop on the site.

FIGURE 9.3.
Finds from Coddenham.
(a) and (b) Side and front views of a unique seventh-century gold cosmetic spatula.
(c) Early seventh-century gold ?cross fragment, robbed of its cloisonné-inlaid stones.
(d) Sixth- or seventh-century cast copper-alloy mount, possibly from a box or casket.
(e) Sixth-century copper-alloy bird brooch with traces of an iron spring on the tail reverse.

The case for 'productive' sites having extensive external contacts is made elsewhere in this volume, and Barham and Coddenham exhibit an even more varied pattern with Merovingian and Visigothic coinage in addition to North Sea links shown by the sceatta finds (within this latter group Frisian examples are in a high proportion as are ones from south-east England). Finally, contacts with the West should not be overlooked as Coddenham also has a few items of 'Celtic' origin.

Coddenham is undoubtedly the most impressive early Middle Anglo-Saxon assemblage from Suffolk but, at first glance, its interpretation appears problematic. Systematic fieldwalking has produced no Ipswich ware making a domestic origin look unlikely. However, it now appears that Ipswich ware was not produced in large quantities until the early

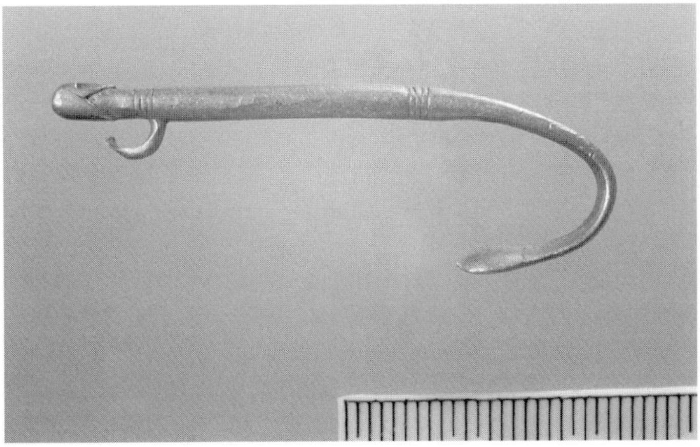

a

b

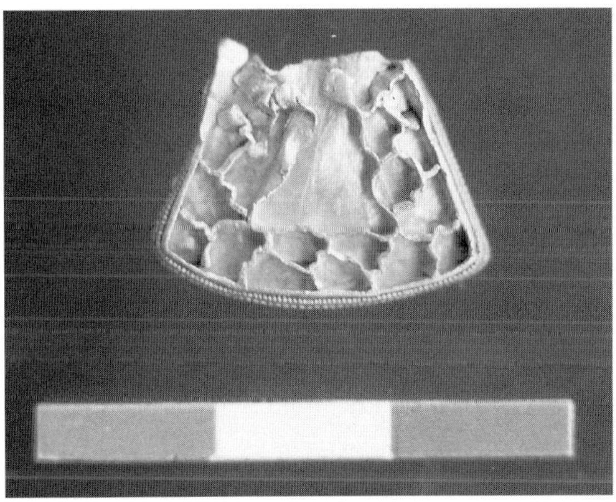

c

d

e

eighth century and the coin evidence indicates that activity at Coddenham decreased dramatically soon after *c.* 700. Therefore, any domestic pottery on the site is likely to have been of a more fragile, handmade, type prone to agricultural erosion. A funerary interpretation for the Coddenham assemblage also appears unlikely as it includes workshop waste and too high a number of coins. In addition, archaeological excavation work on a quarry site some 600 metres south, and overlooking the main Coddenham site, has revealed a wealthy cemetery of seventh- to early eighth-century date, with furnished barrows and a bed burial. Grave-goods from the cemetery include copper-alloy bowls of Merovingian type, a Merovingian pot, a tremissis of Dagobert reused as a pendant and an imported fauchard or iron axe. Early eighth-century coins from here mirror the status and contacts of the main site in the valley below.

With a cemetery of at least fifty graves, and evidence for high status among the burials, a contemporary settlement of similar status should be located nearby. The settlement in question is probably represented by the large artefact scatter, or 'productive' site, at Coddenham with its evidence for metalworking, extensive external contacts and literacy. With this high-status seventh- and early eighth-century settlement evidence in mind, it is interesting to note that Coddenham parish has been suggested as a possible early minster site from its complex Domesday Book entry which mentions the ownership of parts of four churches (Scarfe 1999, 52; see also Pestell, this volume). Any link between a possible minster status and the 'productive' seventh-century site is difficult to prove or substantiate but the historical sources do indicate that Coddenham parish had a central role in the Anglo-Saxon period.

A good case can therefore be made for Coddenham being a high status settlement with a range of social and economic contacts, and functions as reflected in the finds assemblage. What then of Barham? Here, direct comparison with nearby Ipswich ware pottery scatters in the Deben valley is instructive. At Sutton for example (Fig. 9.1) a similar, gridded, fieldwalking search recovered a comparable quantity of Ipswich ware from a four-hectare area close to the parish church. However, intensive metal-detector searches over some years have yielded only four sceattas, an Offa penny and ten Middle Anglo-Saxon artefacts. Similarly at Ramsholt in the Deben valley (Fig. 9.1), a gridded search recovered fifteen sherds of Ipswich ware from some two hectares while intensive detector searches located three sceattas, an Eadwald penny and six Middle Anglo-Saxon artefacts. Excavation work on Middle Anglo-Saxon sites in the Deben valley also indicates that the metalwork assemblage from Barham is exceptional and indicative of more than simple, domestic, activities on the site. At Grundisburgh, an area of some 800 square metres was examined close to the parish church revealing a post-built structure associated with Ipswich ware. However, no Middle Anglo-Saxon coins or metal artefacts were found during detector searches on the site. Similarly at Foxhall, open area excavation revealed evidence for two structures, Ipswich ware, but only two copper-alloy artefacts. Here, the metal-detector searches covered the excavation area and a large part of the adjacent field just to the east of the site of the now-demolished parish church. Finally, on the Whitehouse Industrial Estate overlooking the River Gipping to the west of Ipswich, excavation revealed an enclosed Middle Anglo-Saxon settlement. Evidence for three hall-type structures, and a small burial ground without a church was recorded, but the site yielded just one sceatta, a Beonna penny, and no copper-alloy artefacts of any note.

From this comparative evidence, Barham is clearly exceptional for its metalwork assemblage. The key to this outstanding quality may, at first, appear elusive but an examination of historical sources indicates that Barham was a major estate of four carucates belonging to Ely Abbey in the Late Anglo-Saxon period (Hart 1966, 67). While this acquisition by Ely Abbey was late in the Anglo-Saxon period it does, perhaps, indicate the presence of a large estate at Barham which may well have

FIGURE 9.4. Sceatta finds from Suffolk showing the number of coins known from each site (source: Suffolk SMR).

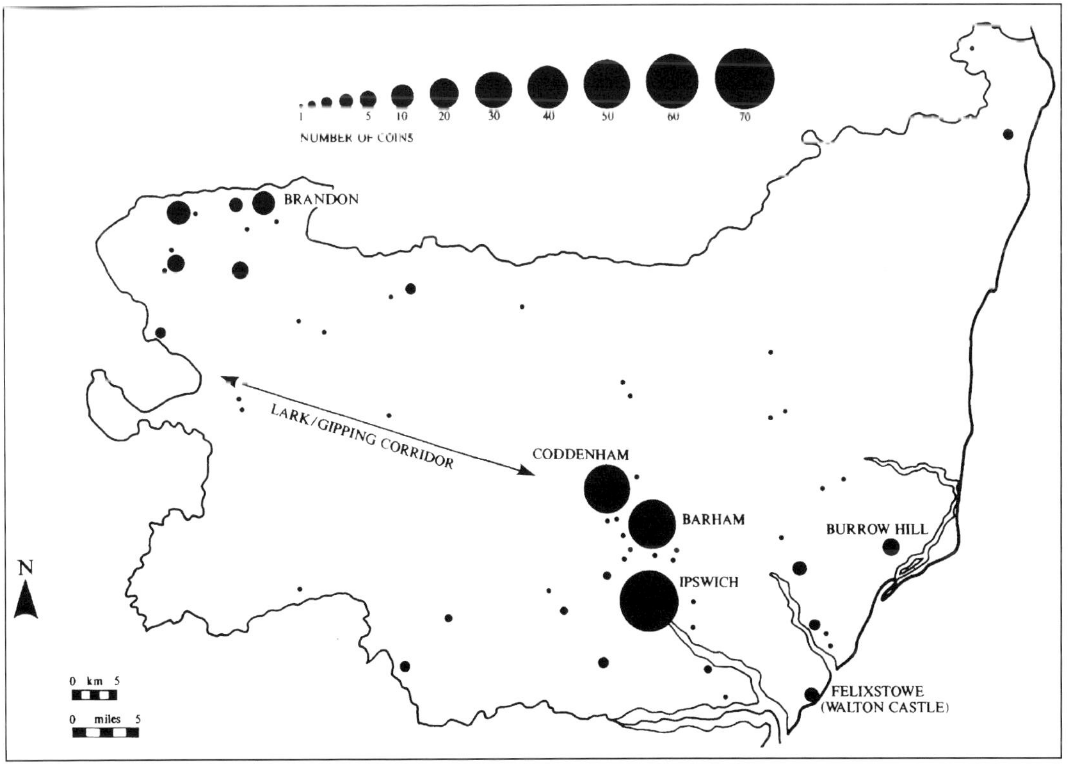

had some pedigree by the tenth century. It was, moreover, an estate that had escaped fragmentation and which may have belonged to the Church or a powerful local family in the Middle Anglo-Saxon period.

Within south-east Suffolk, where survey and excavation work has located and characterised a number of Middle Anglo-Saxon sites, Barham and Coddenham can therefore be seen to be extraordinary for their range and size of respective metalwork assemblages. Not only does it seem justifiable to call them 'productive' sites; they also appear to be in a productive Middle Anglo-Saxon landscape. As Fig. 9.4 shows, sceatta finds are concentrated in the Orwell estuary/lower Gipping valley end of the Gipping/Lark corridor, which so conveniently links sea-borne access to the Continent and south-east England with the agriculturally rich Fen-edge in west Suffolk. The metalwork finds from the 'productive' sites in eastern England emphasise external contact as much as status and wealth with Frisian sceattas and Merovingian- and Celtic-derived artefacts. Therefore, it should perhaps be of little surprise that exceptional sites developed where commerce, contact and control could so easily be exercised as at Barham and Coddenham, natural nodes on major communication routes. By way of further comparison it is also interesting to note that the Gipping valley has yielded a high number of Iron Age coins, again emphasising a corridor of economic activity and contact. This corridor is still of economic importance, having been highlighted for modern-day growth along the A14 between Cambridge and Ipswich.

In conclusion, Barham and Coddenham have produced exceptional assemblages which rise above an almost obscured, but nonetheless present, domestic level of activity on each site. It is easiest to interpret and accept the wealth and range of material recovered from Barham and Coddenham if they are put into a local context as part of a complex social and economic hierarchy, where central places regulating the collection and redistribution of resources were to become ever better established from the mid seventh century. At the top of this hierarchy, in economic terms at least, must come the growing *wics* or trading ports and it is worthy of note that Barham, Coddenham and Ipswich must have co-existed in the late seventh century before Coddenham and then Barham slipped back to a more simple, rural, existence. A link to estates controlled by the Church can also be discerned at Coddenham, with its possible minster status, and, possibly, at Barham. The early Church is now seen as a major influence on Middle Anglo-Saxon economic development and here it is worth noting that Walton Castle at Felixstowe on the Suffolk coast, now destroyed by the sea, may also have been a 'productive' site. It has been argued that Walton Castle was the site of *Dommoc*, the first seat of the bishops of East Anglia (Rigold 1961, 55) and recent research indicates that the 'Woodbridge Hoard' of sceattas comes from Felixstowe (Newman 1996, 217). There is, in addition, an antiquarian collection of Anglo-Saxon finds from around Walton Castle (West 1998, 38). Walton may, therefore, constitute another 'productive' site at Felixstowe. Like Barham and Coddenham, this 'productive' site will only be better understood once the complex nature of Middle Anglo-Saxon society is acknowledged, and when these exceptional sites are seen against systematic survey results which help to illuminate the complete settlement hierarchy for the period.

Acknowledgements

Many thanks to Emma Parker for producing a presentable text and to Sue Holden for preparing the figures.

CHAPTER 10

Six Middle Anglo-Saxon Sites in West Norfolk

Andrew Rogerson

Introduction

Twenty-five years of archaeological effort in Norfolk, expended in recording finds of all periods made by fieldwalkers and metal-detector users, have been used to recover 'invaluable information about economic, political and social developments' (Ulmschneider 2000a, 101). In Norfolk, for the most part, little of this information would have been forthcoming from formal archaeological excavation on its own. The time is now ripe for attempting to interpret the meaning of what is an immense body of new, and almost entirely unpublished, data held in the county Sites and Monuments Record. Most periods from the Bronze Age onwards might benefit from such work, but a transformation in the size of the Middle Anglo-Saxon dataset makes it especially suitable for analysis. More than 1,200 'sites', separate geographical entities, have so far yielded finds of Middle Anglo-Saxon date. One masterful but not widely circulated paper (Andrews 1992) clearly showed the potential of the material then available for the study of the whole range of settlement types, but was of necessity very brief. As brevity governs this paper too, and although only markets, fairs and 'productive' sites are under consideration, the area of just one of the seven district councils in Norfolk, the Borough of King's Lynn and West Norfolk, has been chosen for examination (Fig. 10.1).

The selected area, a local government entity created in 1974, comprises 143,000ha (approximately 27 percent of Norfolk), 102 civil parishes, and covers three complete Domesday hundreds and most of a fourth, half of a fifth and part of a sixth. It has the greatest variety of soil types within the seven council districts; in the west are peats and silts of the Fen basin, with Breckland sands in the south, mixed sands, clays and carstone in the centre (the West Norfolk Lowland), and in the north the Chalk Scarp which forms the northern and

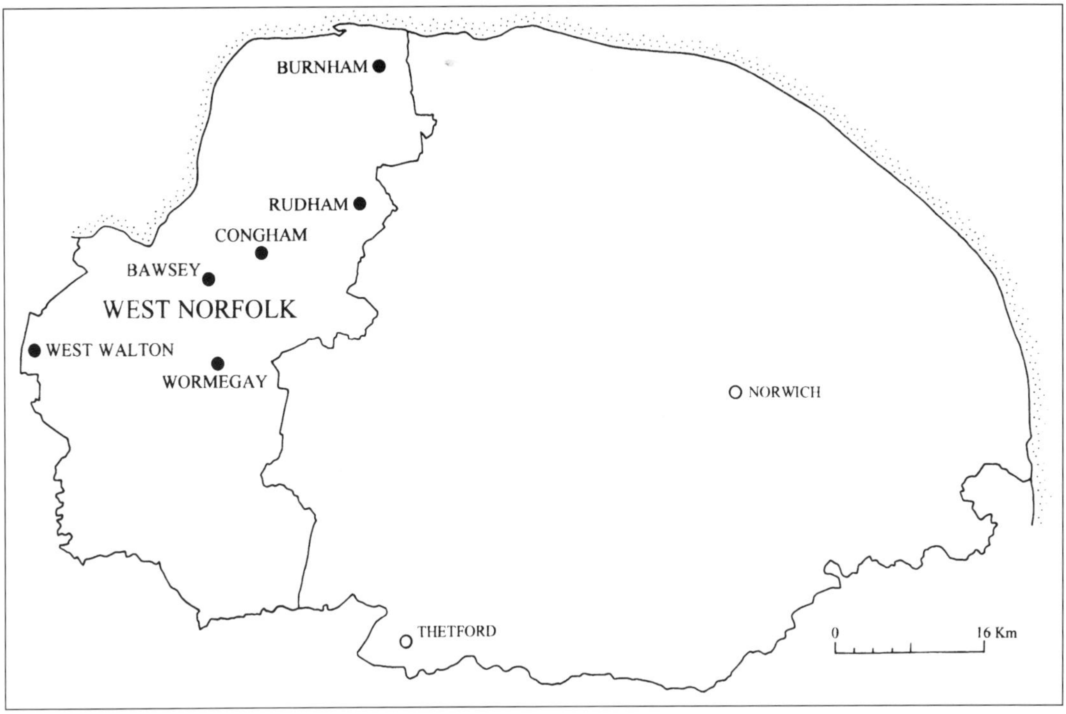

FIGURE 10.1. Location map of sites discussed in the text.

western boundaries of an upland zone of mixed but predominantly light soils known as the Good Sands (Corbett and Dent 1993).

The study area has been slightly more abundant than elsewhere in most major categories of Middle Anglo-Saxon finds, as the following rather blunt statistics indicate. Totals of sites on which some of the main categories of finds have been recorded, with the county total in brackets, are as follows: pottery 236 (658), coins 49 (158), brooches 41 (176), pins 56 (200), and strap fittings, i.e. predominantly strap-ends, 59 (179). Thus, it is only in the case of brooches that West Norfolk's proportion of the county total of sites falls below 27 percent. This relative abundance is enhanced when the substantial zone of low-lying peat-covered Black Fen in the southern part of the district, which was uninhabited throughout the Early Middle Ages, is taken into account. A clear indication of the level of wealth in the upland part of the west of the county is given by an early ninth-century hoard of six silver disc brooches found by accident in the churchyard at Pentney, about nine kilometres south-east of Bawsey (Wilson 1984, 96 and fig. 120; Webster and Backhouse 1991, 229–31).

Although there are wide variations in the numbers of recorded episodes of field survey and metal-detecting across the county (Gurney 1997), it is evident that the relative frequency of finds in each area is real and will not be altered to any great degree by further work. The same holds true for sites that might be regarded as in some way 'productive'. At present in other parts of the county there are few such places, only Burgh Castle, Caistor St Edmund, Thetford (Andrews 1995, 26–7), Middle Harling (Rogerson 1995), Hindringham and Quidenham being contenders.

Within West Norfolk six places stand out as exceptional or 'productive'; Bawsey, Burnham, Congham, Rudham, West Walton and Wormegay. Brief archaeological summaries of these six will follow, while the historical backgrounds of each, and of other important Middle Anglo-Saxon sites in the county, are discussed by Tim Pestell elsewhere in this volume. That these six places are outstanding vis-à-vis others in the area can be seen from the following simple figures: Middle Anglo-Saxon coins have been recorded in twenty-nine out of a total of 102 West Norfolk parishes, of which thirteen records are of a single coin. It should be noted that all of the single coin and many of the non-coin parishes have been subjected to recorded metal-detecting, often on a considerable scale and over long periods. (This is not to suggest, however, that further outstanding sites may not be identified in the future, both in previously unexplored places and in those where metal-detecting has hitherto gone unreported and unrecorded.)

Bawsey

This site is the most 'productive' in Norfolk. Settlement within the modern parish is severely reduced, although decline set in during the later Middle Ages. Bawsey featured in the first list of Norfolk deserted villages and at Domesday was a mere berewick or dependency of nearby Glosthorpe, which features in the same list (Allison 1955; 120, 127, 143 and 147). The Anglo-Saxon site lies four kilometres east of King's Lynn and sits on a very pronounced and striking hill capped with glacial sand and gravel, a peninsula thrusting out into the valley of the River Gaywood. Now a minor watercourse, this drained west into the Wash on the north side of what is now King's Lynn. Open water lay very close to the site in the Middle Anglo-Saxon period. The hill is entirely given over to arable farming except for a small area of grass at the highest point, at 15m OD, surrounding the ruined Norman parish church of St James (Fig. 10.2).

Since 1984 metal-detecting by Mr Steven Brown has enabled the recording of over fifty Anglo-Saxon coins, almost all dating from the late seventh to mid ninth century, as well as of very numerous metalwork finds of the same date-range, including six styli. Numerous coins, including two late seventh-century *tremisses*, found by another

FIGURE 10.2.
Bawsey: an aerial view of the site from the north-west, 17/7/89. (*Photograph: D. A. Edwards, Norfolk Museums and Archaeology Service*)

person in the 1980s are unfortunately unconfirmed, and remain unexamined by numismatists. Three Iron Age gold torcs (including two found in the 1940s) show some pre-Roman specialised use of the site, but a small Romano-British settlement on the northern slope, represented by finds of pottery, tiles and coins is unexceptional. Early Anglo-Saxon material is quite sparse, but the site has yielded many tenth- to thirteenth-century finds. A systematic fieldwalking survey has yet to be attempted, but sufficient quantities of Ipswich Ware sherds have been recovered to indicate that much of the hill-top and slopes was occupied with some intensity in the eighth and ninth centuries. Middle Anglo-Saxon finds are, in the main, restricted to a ditched enclosure recorded by aerial photography and subjected to trial trenching in 1998. However, they do occur outside the enclosure down to the base of the northern slope, i.e. close to the River Gaywood.

In late 1989 a summary of finds was prepared for publication (Blackburn, Rogerson and Margeson unpublished) and in 1998 the Channel Four television programme *Time Team* carried out geophysical survey and excavations in the form of trial trenches. In view of the hope that a report on the results of all work so far conducted will soon be published, no further details will be given here. Seven objects from the site were exhibited at the British Museum in 1991 (Webster and Backhouse 1991, 231–2).

Burnham

The substantial medieval and modern village of Burnham Market lies on the Chalk Scarp some three kilometres south of the north Norfolk coast. The Middle Anglo-Saxon site is situated above the five metre contour immediately north and east of the village on both sides of the Goose Beck, a stream draining through the village and east into the River Burn which flows north off the Good Sands plateau into the North Sea. The stream and its junction with the river, at a point where its valley begins to widen out towards the estuary, seem to be the focus of the settlement. It is probable that a safe haven for coastal traffic was available here in the Anglo-Saxon period, although scientific work on valley sediments is yet to be conducted.

Three modern civil parishes join within the Middle Anglo-Saxon site, Burnhams Market, Norton and Overy; a small portion of another, Burnham Thorpe, enters the south-eastern corner. Burnham Market is made up of four former ecclesiastical parishes, Burnhams St Andrew, Sutton, Ulph and Westgate. An eighth former parish, Burnham Deepdale lies on the coast to the north-west. This present day complexity is reflected in Domesday Book, which gives the name Burnham in seven entries. Thorpe is alone in not being so named.

The site was discovered by Mr John Smallwood and his A-level pupils from King Edward VI School, King's Lynn, who carried out fieldwalking from 1983. In addition to Romano-British building debris and a few Early Anglo-Saxon sherds, considerable quantities of Middle Anglo-Saxon pottery, including several Continental imports, were recorded. In 1990 when, with this author's encouragement, metal-detecting was begun by Mr David Fox and Mr Philip West, it soon became apparent that this was an exceptional site. Very large amounts of fifth- to seventh-century metalwork, including material of Continental origin, betoken intense activity with a strong funerary element. Prolific eighth- and ninth-century metal finds include pins, hooked tags and strap-ends. The Middle Anglo-Saxon coin assemblage of fifteen coins begins with a Series Va sceatta (670–80) and ends with a *denier* of Louis the Pious (822–40). The latest sceatta is a Series R derivative (730–50), while a Beonna protopenny of the moneyer Wilred (*c.* 760), though the subject of a coroner's inquest, is of questionable provenance.

A systematic fieldwalking programme of sufficient extent to identify the boundaries of the pottery spread associated with this 'productive' site has not yet been carried out. At present the main area of metalwork and pottery at the confluence of the Burn and Goose Beck appears to extend to six hectares. On the other hand, recent excavations carried out by the Norfolk Archaeological Unit to the east and south-east of this site in advance of development have considerably extended the known areas of Middle Anglo-Saxon occupation. However, no coins and few metal finds were recorded, and it is clear that these interventions were located outside the main settlement. The largest excavation, to the north of St Æthelbert's, the ruined former parish church of Burnham Sutton, showed that Middle Anglo-Saxon activity was present only at the southern end, i.e. close to the church and not continuous with the 'productive' site lying *c.* 400m to the north-west.

Congham

Middle Anglo Saxon Congham sits next to the very small modern village, just above the twenty-metre contour line at the foot of the Chalk Scarp, on the sandy soil of the West Norfolk Lowland. Heavier clay soils occur to the west. The River Babingley, which flows westwards into the Wash, is two kilometres to the north, but a minor watercourse rising at a spring immediately north of the site feeds into the river. The western, lowland, branch of the Icknield Way, a prehistoric trackway which was used as a route in the Roman period (Gurney 1993), passes through the site. A Romano-British masonry building, probably a villa, lies next to the above-mentioned spring just east of the northern end of the site. The Domesday entry is unremarkable, and three churches in the Middle Ages (All Saints', St Andrew's and St Mary's) need not, by Norfolk standards, indicate any special status.

Finds of Ipswich ware were recorded in the late 1960s, while Early and Middle Anglo-Saxon metalwork was first recovered in the mid 1970s. A small-scale excavation by Keith Wade in 1970 revealed the clay floor and post-holes of a Middle Anglo-Saxon building (Webster and Cherry 1972, 157). Since 1993 a very detailed metal-detector survey has been carried out by Mr John Wells and Mrs Pat Wells. This has recorded Middle Anglo-Saxon metal finds in a one kilometre long band aligned north-north-west to south-south-east, which appears to follow the general line of the Icknield Way. The three churches lie strung out along the western edge of the finds area. In common with most of the other sites discussed here a detailed fieldwalking survey has not yet been attempted, but yet again small-scale and casual collections of Middle Anglo-Saxon potsherds have shown that occupation debris is present in all areas yielding metalwork and coins, suggesting that the site may have covered as much as ten hectares. A wider and more abundant spread of Early Anglo-Saxon metal finds is evidence for the presence of cemeteries involving both cremation and inhumation.

The quality and range of Middle Anglo-Saxon metalwork are not particularly exceptional although the total of finds is large. The post-Roman coins, on the other hand, form an interesting group. Eight sceattas begin with Series BII (700–10) and end with a Series R derivative (730–50). There are three *tremisses*, of Goademar II of Burgundy (524–32), Dorestad (sixth century) and Quentovic (mid-seventh century), as well as a Merovingian *denier* of the first half of the eighth century. The Continental numismatic theme ends with a gold Carolingian coin. In contrast only one sheard of Continental imported pottery has been reported.

FIGURE 10.3. Selected finds from Rudham, scale 1:1. (a) Gilded copper-alloy fragment of the head of a pin or possibly stylus, eighth century. (b)–(d) Three silver strap-ends, each with Trewhiddle-style animals on a niello-inlaid ground, two rivets and empty eyes, probably once filled with glass pellets. Mid ninth century. (e) Carolingian copper-alloy strap-distributor with four empty perforations which would have once held dome-headed rivets. The arms are decorated with plant ornament, the tendrils probably picked out in silver wire against a niello ground (now silver coloured). The object has not been scientifically analysed. Later ninth century. Drawn by Sue White

Rudham

This is in reality two geographically discrete sites. The substantial paired villages of East and West Rudham lie at 50–60m OD in a valley of one of the River Wensum's upper tributaries, in the open Good Sands country. Thus, although this land drains east towards Great Yarmouth and sits on the wrong side of the county's central watershed (Williamson 1993, 14–19), it is emphatically a part of the north-west Norfolk uplands. On the boundary between the two parishes south of the modern villages an unexcavated Roman masonry building is situated on arable land, and a possible Roman road approaches from the north-east. A Roman main road, the Peddars Way, runs on a north-west to south-east alignment about six kilometres to the west (Gurney 1993).

The Middle Anglo-Saxon significance of Rudham became evident in 1991 when Mr David Fox and Mr Philip West undertook metal-detecting and fieldwalking in the western parish. Profuse finds of metalwork were accompanied by many sherds of Ipswich ware. Since 1994 the work has continued under Messrs Barry and Ashley Mears. To the south and west of St Peter's, the parish church of West

Rudham, an area of about five hectares has produced Middle Anglo-Saxon material including two sceattas, of Series D and E (710–15 and 710–30) and three ninth-century silver strap-ends (Fig. 10.3 b–d). A small number of objects have been recovered outside this well-defined area, but only to the north around the present village (Fig. 10.3 a and e).

The situation in East Rudham is far less clear. Some 1.4km north-east of the western site, metal-detecting carried out by Mr Barry Mears over a very limited period in a field no longer under arable produced three sceattas, of Series BII and C (700–10) and R (730–50), and a cross-shaped brooch. A few Middle Anglo-Saxon sherds were also recovered. The site lies 300m from St Mary's parish church. The nearest part of a contiguous arable field has yielded a further Series E sceatta. Despite providing restricted opportunities for survey East Rudham is without doubt more numismatically productive than its western neighbour.

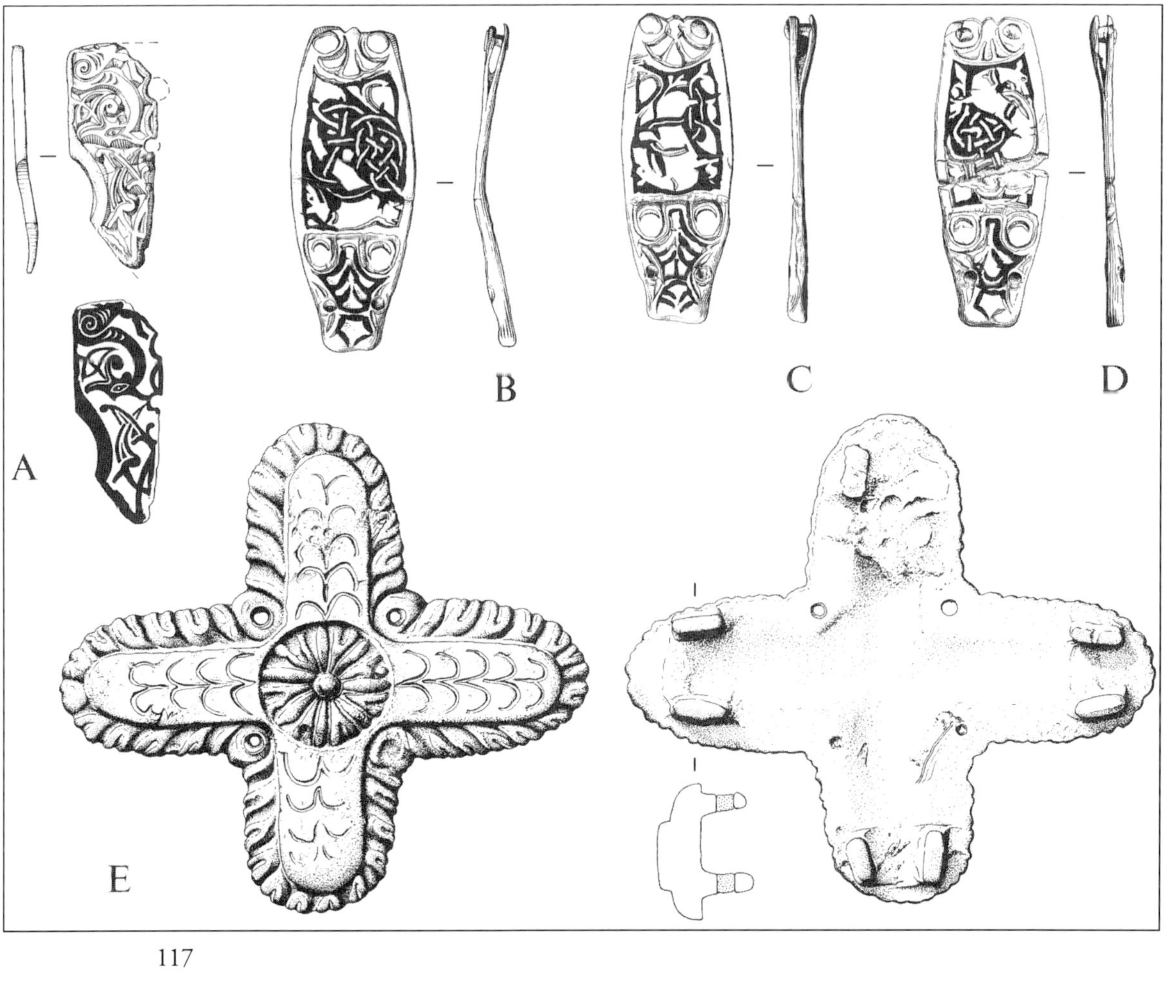

In common with Burnham and Congham, Middle Anglo-Saxon Rudham is set against a background of prolific amounts of Early Anglo-Saxon metalwork which have been recorded over a much larger area and which must, at least in part, be derived from inhumation burials. However, unlike the other two places the seventh-century component is not strong, although undoubtedly present. In the Rudhams metal and pottery finds of the tenth and eleventh centuries are more numerous and widespread than those of the Middle Anglo-Saxon period, but could not be described as remarkable.

West Walton

At the extreme western edge of Marshland, an area of silt soils south of the Wash, and only one and a half kilometres from the River Nene which forms the boundary between Norfolk and Lincolnshire, lies the only known 'productive' site in the Norfolk fenland. The modern village, with its splendid medieval church, has seen considerable growth in modern times.

The site was discovered by Bob Silvester during fieldwalking for the Fenland Survey in the early 1980s (Silvester 1988, 92), with Ipswich ware spread over fields to the north and south of the parish church of St Mary. The Sea Bank, a sea defence earthwork now considered to have been constructed in the Late Anglo-Saxon period (Crowson *et al.* 2000, 229) runs *c.* 800m to the west. Middle Anglo-Saxon finds are confined to areas of very slightly elevated ground which Silvester demonstrated were the confluence of the raised silt banks or 'roddons' of relict Iron Age watercourses. A detailed field survey by Silvester and the present author was left unfinished, and as a result an incomplete and unsatisfactory plan has been published (Andrews 1992, fig. 4d). A second Middle Anglo-Saxon site in West Walton, a smaller concentration of finds 1.6km to the north, has more recently been subjected to trial excavation (Crowson *et al.* 2000, 216–7).

Regular searching with a metal-detector was begun by Mr Michael Carlile in 1987. The Fenland Survey recovered no evidence for Early Anglo-Saxon activity at West Walton which, because of unfavourable environmental conditions prevalent over most of Marshland at that period, was not suitable for settlement. This absence has been confirmed by metal-detector survey. Likewise, changes in Late Anglo-Saxon times with the onset of a more dispersed settlement pattern (Silvester 1988, 92), are mirrored in the distribution of tenth- and eleventh-century metalwork

Small quantities of Middle Anglo-Saxon metal finds have been recovered south of the parish church and include one Series G sceatta

(710–25). To the north, a rather well-defined area of profuse finds is similar in size and location to what is known of the pottery distribution and covers *c.* 2.8ha. Recording of findspots has been of sufficient detail to demonstrate that metalwork does not occur very close to the churchyard, indicating that the 'productive' zone is not continuous with the area of Middle Anglo-Saxon occupation to the south. The northern field has produced a substantial group of unremarkable metal finds, along with six sceattas, four of Series E (710–30), one of Series Q (715–30) and one unidentified. In contrast, only four sceattas have been recorded from other Norfolk Marshland sites (two each from Walpole St Peter and Walsoken), while Hay Green in Terrington St Clement, by far the largest of the group of nine Middle Anglo-Saxon settlements (Rogerson and Silvester 1986), has proved almost devoid of Middle Anglo-Saxon metalwork.

Wormegay

In common with West Walton, the archaeology of Wormegay island, an outcrop of mineral soil within the peat-filled lower valley of the Nar, has benefited from the attentions of the Fenland Survey (Silvester 1988, 143–50). Ipswich ware was first recovered from the Middle Anglo-Saxon site, the sole one on the island, in 1970. A detailed 'sherd-by-sherd' survey, completed in 1991 recorded a crisply defined area of Ipswich ware extending to 1.8ha next to the edge of the island on a southern-facing slope (Andrews 1992, 21). St Michael's parish church is close by to the west, while the medieval and medium sized modern village, with its motte-and-bailey castle, sits one and a half kilometres away on the western edge of the island.

Metal-detecting, which commenced in 1993, has been carried out chiefly by Mr Steven Brown, on far fewer occasions than on the other sites under consideration. The distribution of metal objects matches very closely that of the pottery. The assemblage includes nineteen pins and two styli, as well as six sceattas, of Series B and BII (700–10), Series D (710–15), Series E (710–30), Series J (710–50) and Series R (730–50). The latest coin is a *denier* of Louis the Pious (814–40). The likelihood that concentrations of possible iron-smelting slag to the south-west of St Michael's church are Middle Anglo-Saxon (Andrews 1992, 21) remains unproven. The material is more likely to be Romano-British given the distribution of other finds of that date.

Evidence for Early Anglo-Saxon activity on the site is sparse, consisting of fragments of two sixth-century brooches and one sherd. The 'handful' of Thetford-type ware sherds (Silvester 1988, 146) is insufficient to indicate occupation continuing into the tenth century, a point borne out by a corresponding lack of Late Anglo-Saxon metal finds. Exceptions to this are two fragments of a Viking gilt-bronze oval brooch (or possibly a pair) found within an almost sherd-free gap in the Middle Anglo-Saxon pottery distribution on its south-west side (Andrews 1992, fig. 7). It may be significant that a spread of human bones coincides with this gap, and a Scandinavian burial may be indicated.

Discussion

Pre-Domesday Norfolk suffers from a paucity of documentary sources which contrasts strikingly with the wealth of archaeological evidence. The latter, though, is heavily skewed towards non-excavated surface collected data. No large excavation of a Middle Anglo-Saxon site has been conducted since work at North Elmham ceased in 1971 (Wade-Martins 1980). None of the sites under discussion has seen more than trial trenching, and all six owe a recognition of their significance to non-invasive surveys, largely carried out by amateurs.

Bawsey is undoubtedly the pre-eminent place in terms of 'productivity' and in common with the other five it was certainly a settlement, rather than a periodically visited and sporadically occupied fair or market. It is tempting to see it as a more obvious candidate than Wormegay for 'one of the estate centres from which the Middle Saxon settlement of Marshland was organised and controlled' (Crowson *et al.* 2000, 225). Its total of six styli (the highest in Norfolk) certainly suggests literacy, but it would be dangerous to insist on a monastic role solely from these objects. An administrative function at an aristocratic or royal centre, which required the presence of clerical men, seems as plausible. Nor should Bawsey's role as a minor *wic* be ruled out, given its near-coastal location. Like West Walton and Wormegay it was of little importance in the fifth and sixth centuries, but unlike them it had its origins in the seventh.

West Norfolk forms part of a large sector of the county which remained unurbanised until the twelfth century despite a largely above-average population in the Late Anglo-Saxon period (Atkin 1985, fig. 2). Bawsey and another coastal site and potential *wic*, Burnham, could be proposed as candidates to fill this lacuna, at least in the eighth and ninth centuries, although thereafter this part of the county remained strictly rural until the emergence of the major port of (King's) Lynn in the 1090s. Burnham was to survive as a minor market town in the Middle Ages but Bawsey dwindled, almost to the point of desertion, under the twin threats of inadequate access to the sea and the proximity of Lynn.

The permanent settlements at Congham and the two Rudhams were at inland locations, and both were places of significance in the Early Anglo-Saxon period. Communication, in the form of the Icknield Way rather than the tenuous links with the River Babingley, probably contributed to Congham's role as a centre of trade, but it is difficult both to pinpoint the forces behind the amount of activity that is evident in East and West Rudham and to characterise its function. A more complete knowledge of the Roman road network in that area might provide an explanation for its location.

The role of West Walton must surely be closely linked to its eight companions along the arc of Middle Anglo-Saxon settlements in Marshland. The surfaces of all nine sites are characterised by profuse quantities of animal bone, and trial work at three has recovered evidence for salt making (Crowson *et al.* 2000). A large-scale meat production and export regime, presumably under the control of one or more great monasteries, or even the East Anglian king, has yet to be demonstrated (Silvester 1988, 158). Yet, if this were the case, then as well as an administrative and trading centre at Bawsey, a subsidiary port on the banks of the Nene at West Walton might well have been necessary.

The best interpretation of the restricted and short-lived, almost exclusively Middle Anglo-Saxon, insular site at Wormegay, might be that it was monastic. Its topographic setting is reminiscent of the three probably monastic sites in Suffolk, at Brandon, Butley and Iken (Carr *et al.* 1988; Fenwick 1984; West *et al.* 1984). An additional indicator may be the presence of an inhumation cemetery, admittedly unexcavated and undated.

In all the above there has been only a superficial treatment of the material and much surmise, despite the small and anachronistic area chosen for study. Without a major study of the evidence now available for the whole of Middle Anglo-Saxon East Anglia, we can go little further in understanding the economic, political and social dynamics which were at play during the seventh to ninth centuries. Markets, fairs and 'productive' sites must be set alongside their more numerous low status neighbours, some of whose inhabitants were surely the consumers of a proportion of what passed through the former. It is hoped that Stanley West's presentation of the artefactual evidence for Anglo-Saxon Suffolk (West 1998) will soon be followed by a Norfolk volume, to be assembled by the same author. As well as corpera and syntheses of what has been recorded, on a par with what has been achieved for Lincolnshire and Hampshire (Ulmschneider 2000a and 2000b), there remains a pressing need for more detailed surface surveys of known sites of every status and size, including the six above examples, followed by carefully targeted and high quality excavations.

CHAPTER 11

The Afterlife of 'Productive' Sites in East Anglia

Tim Pestell

In this paper I shall consider 'productive' sites from a rather different perspective, namely their Late Anglo-Saxon and Norman landscape histories. Although this approach might at first seem strange, sites notable simply for having unusually large metalwork assemblages clearly need to be placed within the context of wider settlement hierarchies. Moreover, when a whole region such as East Anglia has little in the way of early documentary sources, we have little choice but to pursue these later clues for any hints they may give us about the earlier landscape in which 'productive' sites operated. The region is almost devoid of historical sources until 1086 when, in contrast, the richness of Little Domesday Book provides a detailed snapshot of the Early Norman landscape, albeit one with limitations in focus and scope. Finally, a later perspective is required when casual observation seems to indicate East Anglia has a high coincidence of Middle Anglo-Saxon 'productive' sites and important later land units, in particular the locations of post-Conquest monasteries.

FIGURE 11.1. Locations mentioned in the text.

Clearly, back-projecting provides no secure interpretation for the origins and nature of Middle Anglo-Saxon 'productive' sites. Is it therefore possible to discuss the presence and distribution of different archaeological site types, separated by two or three hundred years, in any meaningful way? I aim to show that we can, and that in so doing, 'productive' sites can indeed be seen as distinct and of above-average importance in Middle Anglo-Saxon settlement hierarchies, rather than 'normal' types of site from which greater numbers of artefacts have been recovered by metal-detection (Richards 1999b and this volume).

In addition to studying the documentary evidence for those 'productive' sites discussed by Andrew Rogerson and John Newman elsewhere in this volume, I shall consider five other sites which appear 'productive', namely Hindringham, Caistor St Edmund and Burgh Castle in Norfolk and Burrow Hill and Brandon in Suffolk (Fig. 11.1).

Congham and West Walton

Of those six west Norfolk locations identified by Andrew Rogerson, four came to have monasteries founded on or close to the known 'productive' sites. At Congham and West Walton, however, there was no such direct religious involvement. Indeed, the later history of Congham has very little to recommend it as of especial interest. Domesday Book records only small landholdings here, held by William de Warenne, one of the greater Domesday tenants-in-chief. There was

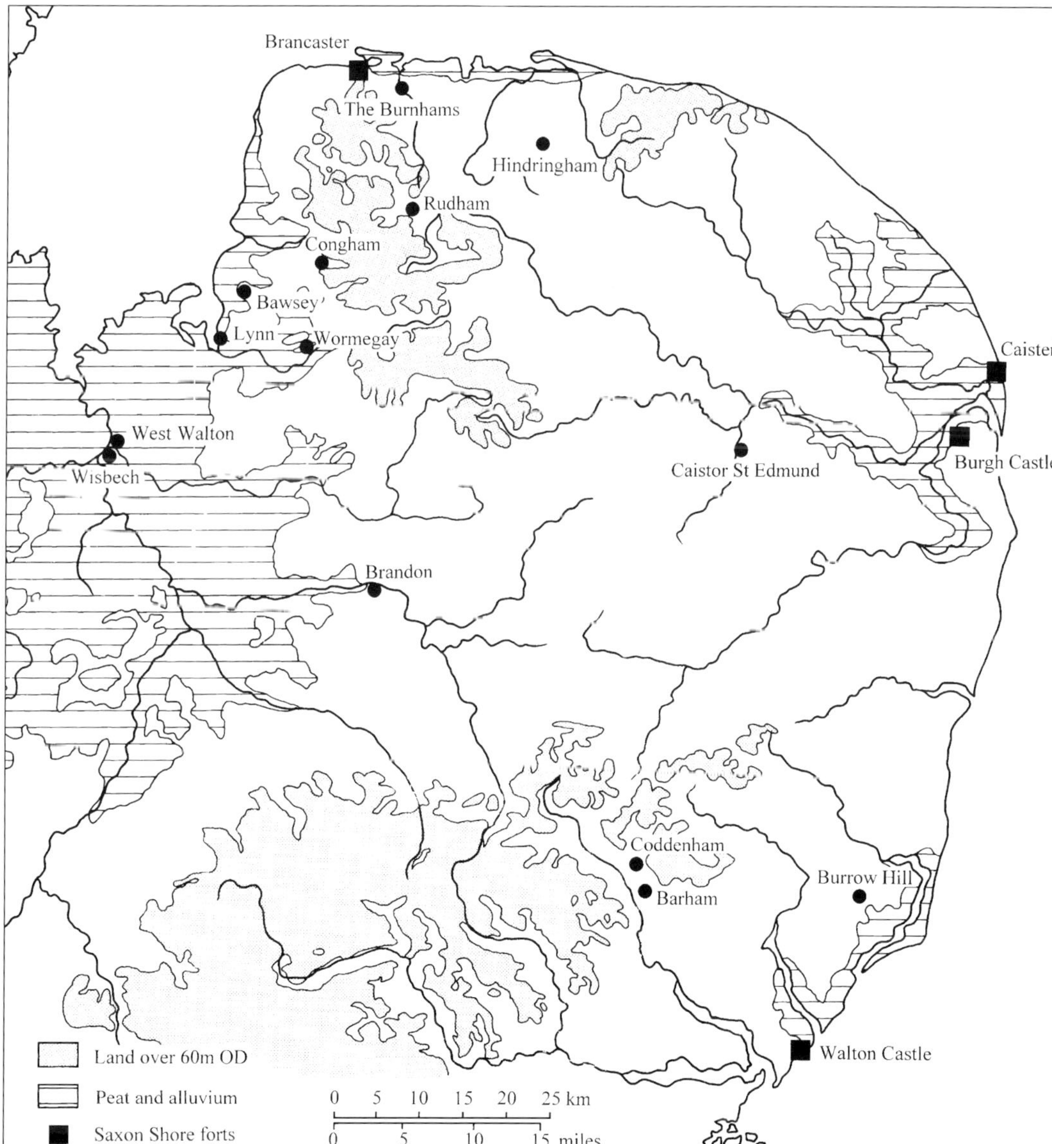

a church, but the entry is interlined in the Domesday text and no value is given (*DB Norfolk*, fo. 161a). Congham therefore appears to be a location best understood tenurially as simply being a minor holding of the Warenne lands.

West Walton has a far more interesting history. Located on the very western edge of Norfolk, traditionally it appears to have looked west rather than east. It was adjacent to Wisbech, one of the richest manors belonging to Ely Abbey, and enjoyed an association which appears to have continued into at least the thirteenth century. Wisbech came to Ely about 1016, as the gift of the East Anglia bishop Ælfwine, and formed a *ferding* or quarter hundred with a ten-hide valuation. Edward Miller pointed out that this arrangement possibly had an earlier origin (Miller 1951, 31–3), and a hundred court met at an unlocated place called *Modich*, probably in or near Wisbech, certainly by the twelfth century when mentioned in the *Liber Eliensis* (written 1169×1174) (Blake 1962, 125).

Wisbech became a nodal point through which riverine traffic passed from the Midlands to the sea at the Wash, leading to its wealth by Domesday at £6 in 1066, 100*s* in 1086 (*DB Cambridgeshire* fo. 192a). The town itself has an uncertain origin, but a recent small-scale excavation revealed very deeply stratified deposits caused by the frequent and sometimes deep accumulation of fine silt from episodic flooding. At 3.80m OD, three metres down, only mid thirteenth-century levels had been encountered while auguring indicated archaeological deposits extending to at least 2.60m OD (Hinman 1999, 15). The trading potential of this site in the Middle Anglo-Saxon period is extremely difficult to assess, but it is conceivable that the twelfth-century situation represents a repositioning of an earlier trading focus. If West Walton had been part of an hundredal centre, later developed at Wisbech, it might explain why above-average quantities of eighth-century metalwork have been found here. Indeed, a fluidity in market location may well have been enforced by the very fluidity of the ground upon which the merchants traded.

FIGURE 11.2.
(a) Bawsey and its surrounding parishes;
(b) East and West Rudham and surrounding parishes;
(c) Hindringham and its surrounding parishes.

Bawsey

Bawsey arguably represents another Middle Anglo-Saxon redistributive centre which moved in response to changing topographical considerations. Bawsey is today a parish surrounded by seven others (Fig. 11.2a) and its strange zig-zag shape strongly suggests that it was carved out of an earlier surrounding land unit. That this probably included Gaywood and Mintlyn is of interest because these manors belonged to the East Anglian bishops. When Herbert de Losinga became the

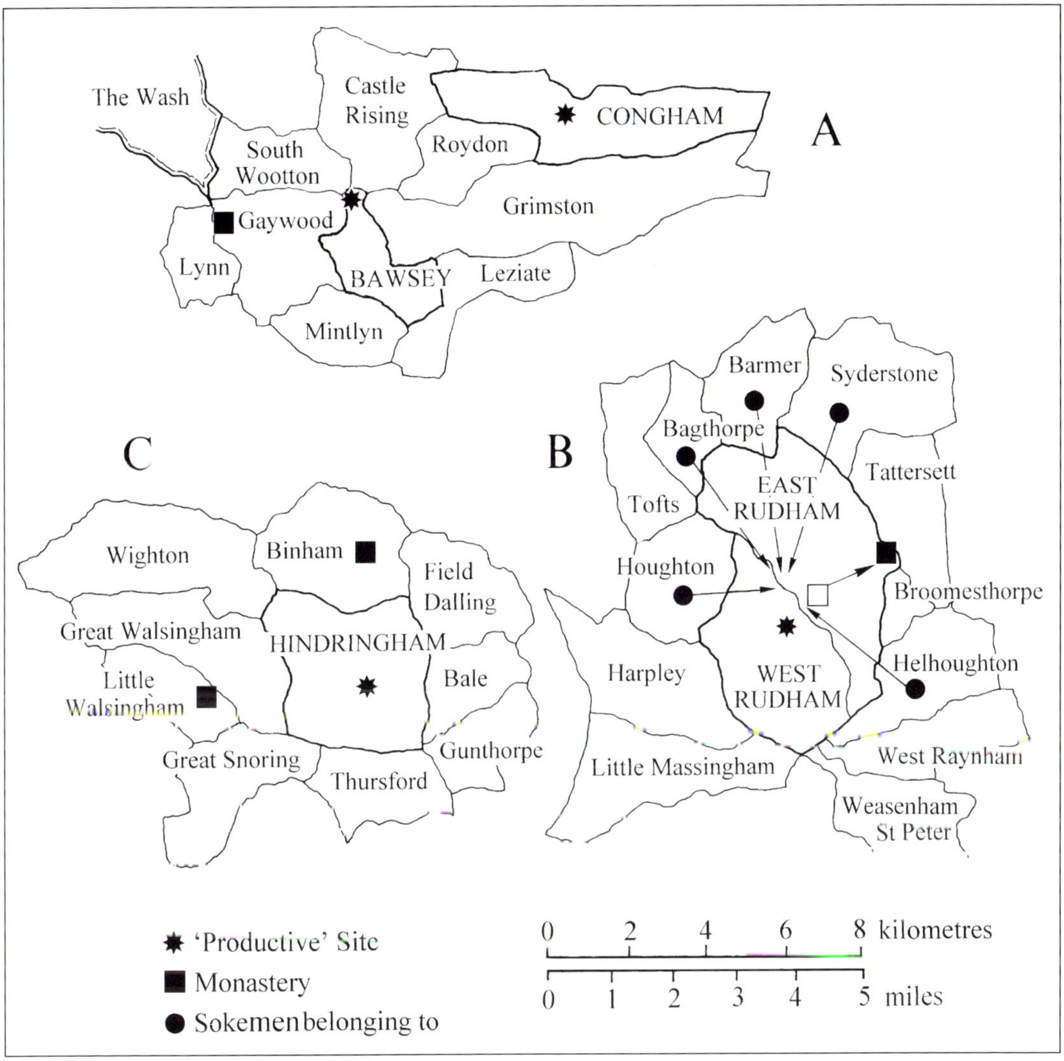

diocesan in 1091 he embarked upon an impressive programme of monastic patronage whereby he established a Benedictine community in his new cathedral in Norwich to which were attached a series of monastic cells, including St Leonard's in Norwich, St Nicholas' in Yarmouth and St Margaret's in Lynn (Pestell 2001a). The first two cells involved the suppression of wealthy Anglo-Saxon churches but no similar institution was present in Lynn to be redeveloped. Instead, as archaeological excavation has shown (Clarke and Carter 1977), this settlement was a 'new' town developed by the bishop to the west of his manor of Gaywood, to exploit the evolving configuration of river and water systems in the Fenland basin. Its principal trade rival was Wisbech, then also being developed by Ely Abbey. The control of trade was clearly the principal motive behind Losinga's foundation at Lynn and this probably represents the reconfiguration of an earlier trading centre originally located at Bawsey. In the Middle Anglo-Saxon period, Bawsey was more directly approachable by the sea, but by the twelfth century it seems to have become increasingly marginalised either by falling sea levels or by other more commercially advantageous river systems then evolving in the Wash area.

Losinga's monastic cell at Lynn may, therefore, also have had an Anglo-Saxon precursor and it should be noted that one carucate of the bishop's demesne was granted from Gaywood for the maintenance of Lynn priory. The difficulty is proving a clear link between Bawsey and the bishop's manor at Gaywood by 1086. Domesday Book mentions Bawsey only twice; once as the holding of a freeman, Wulfgeat, holding half a carucate of land in Bawsey and nearby Ashwicken of Count Alan, valued at only five shillings; and second, in the holdings of Robert Malet, as a carucate of land in Bawsey forming a berewick of Glosthorpe (*DB Norfolk*, fos 149a–b and 153b).

The tenurial history of this area is difficult to reconstruct from Domesday alone, for instance Glosthorpe subsequently disappeared into Bawsey parish. The parish of Leziate to the south-east of Bawsey and slightly larger in area, makes only one appearance in Domesday, within the annexations of Baynard at the end of the Norfolk entries. Robert Malet was recorded as having two free men here with sixty acres and four of meadow worth five shillings (*ibid.*, fo. 276b). The present parish is much larger than this, implying an acreage recorded under another landholding. More work needs to be done to resolve the early tenurial structures and parish boundaries, but two observations can be made. First, the 'productive' site at Bawsey lay only a mile to the north of Mintlyn church and close to the Mintlyn parish boundary. Bishop William de Raleigh created a park in Gaywood about 1240, apparently incorporating land in Mintlyn. Second, the entire distance from the new church at Lynn to that at Bawsey is just over four kilometres, with Lynn itself representing a western movement in settlement, on an ancient demesne holding of the bishop. Although not certain, it seems likely that a landholding once including the 'productive' site at Bawsey, was originally owned by the East Anglian bishops. Not only might this provide an explicable context for why the bishops held what was an isolated holding in this western area of Norfolk, but why the village became deserted in the Middle Ages – if its former trading role had become shifted to Lynn.

More certain associations between Middle Anglo-Saxon 'productive' sites and subsequent medieval religious houses come from our remaining three West Norfolk sites, at Burnham, Wormegay and Rudham.

FIGURE 11.3.
The parish church of Burnham Overy St Clement's from the south.

Burnham

Some time in the late twelfth century, an Augustinian priory of Peterstone was founded by an ancestor of the Cheney family, dedicated to St Peter, in Burnham Overy (Knowles and Hadcock 1971, 170). Overy is one of seven parishes, once nine, which comprise the Burnhams. Covering nearly forty square kilometres with the large recorded population of 133 people at Domesday, this whole group of parishes almost certainly once formed a substantial multiple-estate; its name incorporates the early *-ham* place-name ending which would apparently support this early importance. A variety of entries in Domesday Book shows Burnham to have been broken down into a number of manors, of which the most important were held by the king at Burnham Overy, with three carucates of land and another two carucates as outliers, and by William de Warenne at Burnham Thorpe, with two carucates of land and a church with eighty acres of land (*DB Norfolk*, fos 128a and 169a). Trying to reconstruct the form and origins of Burnham is dangerous because the area has received little archaeological investigation, although some dependent settlements are suggested in the north and south *tuns* of Burnham Norton and Burnham Sutton.

Most problematical is the interpretation of Burnham Thorpe and Overy. Not only would Thorpe suggest a later and subsidiary settlement, so too might 'Overy', meaning 'over the river', being on the east bank of the River Burn (Mills 1991, 63). These, however, were the two largest manors by Domesday. Thorpe's church with eighty acres suggests the presence of a community of priests here by the Conquest, yet, its dedication to All Saints, and the surviving church which shows modest work no earlier than thirteenth-century in date, do little to reinforce this. By contrast, such evidence does appear in the royal manor of Burnham Overy where St Clement's church was built in the eleventh century as an aisleless cruciform building, its central tower now partially demolished (Fig. 11.3). Further investigation here is deserved and it is of potential interest that Burnham, in Domesday *Bruneham*, may conceivably have been the royal vill of *Bruna*. According to the early twelfth-century Bury St Edmunds chronicle, the *Annals of St Neot's*, the East Anglian bishop Hunberht is said to have consecrated the martyr Edmund as king of East Anglia here on Christmas Day 856 (Dumville and Lapidge 1984, 51). Although the identification is uncertain, the former status of Burnham as a royal estate would be perfectly acceptable and provides a readily understandable context for the appearance here of above-average quantities of coinage and prestige metalwork in the Middle Anglo-Saxon period.

Rudham

Rudham provides another challenge in reconstruction but, like Burnham, would appear to have been the centre of a multiple-estate, the division into East and West forming the first hint at a formerly larger land unit (Fig. 11.2b). Domesday Book makes this more explicit, including in its valuation two churches with sixty acres, and within the extensive holdings of William de Warenne, a number of outliers, including Bagthorpe, Houghton, Barmer, Syderstone and Helhoughton (*DB Norfolk*, fo. 169a-b). The fact that a church at Houghton had no land attached suggests it was a chapelry dependent upon Rudham. Finally, the fact that sixty-nine sokemen were attached to Rudham again infers an earlier estate centre. The discovery here of an increasingly large quantity of Middle Anglo-Saxon material would appear to root this place's importance back to at least the eighth and ninth centuries. Rudham came to be the site of a medieval priory founded in about 1140 by William Cheney, for which the two churches in Rudham, of St Mary and St Peter were given as an initial endowment. From aerial photographs of an otherwise unknown large cruciform church, it would appear that construction of the monastic buildings was never completed before it was moved to a new site within East Rudham by which the priory was subsequently known, as Coxford (Knowles and Hadcock 1971, 155).

Wormegay

The 'productive' site at Wormegay, located on a sandy island in the Nar valley, was found close to the unspectacular medieval church of St Michael. Recent research into Wormegay's Domesday entries has indicated an antecessorial pattern suggesting a pre-Conquest estate centre, probably the manorial *caput* of Thorketel, antecessor to the Domesday tenant Hermer de Ferrers (Liddiard 2000, 31–3). This possibility is made more likely by the island subsequently being chosen as the location for a castle by Reginald de Warenne, who married Alice de Wormegay, heiress of the honour of Wormegay and a descendant of Hermer. Not only was a castle established, but an Augustinian priory, of the Blessed Virgin Mary, Holy Cross and St John the Evangelist, in 1174–5 (Vincent 1999). There therefore appears to have been a received importance to Wormegay in the eleventh and twelfth century which echoes a similar situation in the Middle Anglo-Saxon period.

Other Norfolk sites

Let us now turn to consider three other 'productive' sites in Norfolk. On the basis of coinage recovered, Hindringham in north Norfolk has some claim to be 'productive', having yielded four sceattas, a penny of Offa and a Louis the Pious gold *solidus* forgery, in addition to an array of Middle Anglo-Saxon pins and strap-ends. This cluster of finds (SMR 24909 and 25071) is to the east of St Andrew's church, in a parish which is large but otherwise has little particularly to recommend it. Despite no mention of a church in any of the Domesday entries it was a substantial estate of four carucates, held by the bishops of East Anglia (*DB Norfolk*, fo. 192a). Hindringham is also of interest in sitting adjacent to three important parishes (Fig. 11.2c). Great Walsingham has also yielded quantities of Middle Anglo-Saxon metalwork while in Little Walsingham, presumably once a part of a larger land unit, the Augustinian priory of the Blessed Virgin Mary was founded *c.* 1153 by Geoffrey de Fervaques (Knowles and Hadcock 1971, 177). Little Walsingham was certainly a minster church in the Late Anglo-Saxon period, before its Norman refoundation: Domesday Book reveals that within the lands of Ranulf Peverel, the manor of Walsingham included one church with sixty acres of land, three times the average valuation for a church in Norfolk and Suffolk (*DB Norfolk*, fo. 254a).

To Hindringham's north-west is Wighton, a royal manor and the hundredal manor for North Greenhoe (Williamson 1993, 102). The proximity of a major royal estate with one held by the local diocesan may again point to some earlier relationship. Finally, to the north, in Binham a Benedictine priory of the Blessed Virgin Mary was founded by 1093 by Peter and Albreda de Valognes (Knowles and Hadcock 1971, 52). The evidence for any post-Conquest importance to Hindringham itself is weak and should not be overstressed. It is of note, though, that the 'productive' site forms a focus of activity in an area with other parishes of interest, to one of which Hindringham may potentially once have been attached, to form a larger single land unit.

I will end this consideration of Norfolk 'productive' sites with Caistor St Edmund and Burgh Castle. Both are Roman sites, Caistor a walled town which was formerly the administrative centre *Venta Icenorum*, the latter a Saxon Shore fort, possibly the *Gariannonum* of the *Notitia Dignitatum* (Davies 1996; Gurney 1996). By 1086 Caistor was held by the abbey of Bury St Edmunds as a manor of three carucates, having a church with eleven acres valued at sixteen pence (*DB Norfolk*, fo. 210a). The only other tenant-in-chief with an interest in Caistor was Ralph de Beaufour, possibly a relative of the then Bishop of Thetford, William de Bellofago (or Beaufour: Harper-Bill 1990, xxviii). Ralph's holding was modest and assessed with his landholdings at Markshall, the adjacent parish. The appellation 'St Edmund' is only likely to have been attached to Caistor after Bury came to hold the lordship here, some time after *c.* 1020 (when the abbey was regularised as a Benedictine foundation). This landholding stands isolated from Bury's few other Norfolk estates which in itself makes it curious as to why or how Bury should have come by Caistor. The location of St Edmund's church in the corner of the walled town is reminiscent of a number of Middle Anglo-Saxon minster foundations (Blair 1992, 235–46) suggesting a similar origin here too. The lack of direct evidence for this may reflect not only East Anglia's limited documentary sources, but Bury Abbey's own administrative regime. Any wealth the church at Caistor may once have had would be unlikely to have survived long because dues would soon have been re-directed towards the abbey itself, leaving only the modest valuation of the parish church, eleven acres at sixteen pence, to support a priest. This is certainly the case at Horningsea, where *Liber Eliensis* (ii, 32; Blake 1962, 105) describes a royal minster being given to Ely Abbey on its refoundation *c.* 970; by Domesday the estate was still of seven carucates but the church there was not even mentioned (*DB Cambridgeshire*, fo. 191a). Bury's ownership of Caistor would also have ensured that no post-Conquest monastery would have ever been founded in this particular vill.

At Burgh Castle, another Roman site has yielded much Anglo-Saxon metalwork and a number of sceattas. An association has also been made, on little evidence, for Burgh being the site of *Cnobheresburg*, a monastery mentioned by Bede as founded by the Irish monk Fursa (*Historia Ecclesiastica*, iii, 18–20). Excavations by Charles Green in three short seasons between 1958 and 1961 revealed evidence for Middle Anglo-Saxon occupation including a cemetery with 167 individuals excavated, three of which had radiocarbon dates varying between AD 600±70 and AD 720±70 (Johnson 1983, 112). Sadly, Green's excavations were too small-scale and unclear in their dating and phasing to provide any useful indication of the site's character. Although a Christian cemetery is indicated, no trace of any accompanying church was found. By Domesday, Ralph the Crossbowman held Burgh as a manor of four carucates and although a church was included in the holding, its attached acreage was the entirely unexceptional ten acres.

The present church at Burgh Castle is outside the walls of the Roman fort and three possibilities appear to exist. First, there may have never been a church within the walls of the fort; alternatively, an Anglo-Saxon church may have fallen out of use – perhaps a minster, becoming abandoned. Finally, and most probably, the construction within the Roman walls of a Norman castle may have led to the church being re-sited, not least as the motte was located in the south-western corner of the fort, the same area in which the Middle Anglo-Saxon cemetery was found. Little is known of this motte's construction, but a common feature of many Norman castles was the removal of a church or chapel from the area of the bailey to a site outside, for instance at Walton Castle under the Bigod family, and at Castle Acre under the Warennes. While the castle's builder is unknown, it does not seem to have been a later construction from the 'anarchy' of Stephen's reign. In conclusion, Burgh Castle's Domesday entry reveals a reasonably-sized estate which, with subsequent motte, suggests a significance was attached to this landholding attracting its redevelopment, again echoing a Middle Anglo-Saxon importance.

'Productive' sites in Suffolk

Restrictions of space permit only a limited discussion of the Suffolk sites, beginning with Brandon, on the Norfolk-Suffolk border. This 'productive' site is well known despite its limited publication (Carr *et al.* 1988). By Domesday, Brandon was held by only two landowners – Ely Abbey, which had a substantial manor of five carucates including a church with thirty acres, and Eudo the Steward's minor holding of six sokemen in Brandon and adjacent Lakenheath, which were subsequently acknowledged also to belong to Ely (*DB Suffolk*, fo. 403a). The *Libellus Æthelwoldi episcopi*, a vernacular Ely source translated into Latin 1109×1131, describes Bishop Æthelwold buying five hides of land at Brandon and Livermere from a Wihtgar for fifteen pounds, in the late tenth century (chapter 46; Keynes and Kennedy, forthcoming). The purchase of Brandon occurs in the *Libellus* following a description of Ely's acquisition of Horningsea in Cambridgeshire, and it precedes an account of how Sudbourne, Woodbridge and Stoke, all in Suffolk, came to the abbey. The significance of these places rests not simply in their being large estates but in all probability having minsters, most clearly Horningsea, which was described as 'minster of royal rank' (*ibid.*, chapter 42). The other places should not be regarded any less lightly. For instance, Sudbourne appears to have been a large royal estate in the Sandlings, the royal heartland of the East Anglian kings, and to have included Iken, almost certainly the site of *Icanho*, a monastery founded in 654 by Saint Botolph (Whitelock 1972, 10). In buying Brandon, Ely Abbey may again have been taking possession of both a large estate and one with a minster. Naturally, whether we can equate the excavated Middle Anglo-Saxon site at Staunch Meadow in Brandon with such a former minster remains open, but it should suffice to state that another 'productive' site can be seen to lie within a later landholding of importance to a monastery.

If we turn next to consider the 'afterlife' of those sites described by John Newman, Barham and Coddenham, a mixed picture is apparent. At Barham, the majority of the landholdings mentioned in Domesday Book belonged to Ely Abbey, most notably an estate of four carucates, including the church with a modest sixteen acres (*DB Suffolk*, fo. 383b). The land was, however, more fragmented at Domesday than many of the estates we have considered so far. In *Liber Eliensis* (ii, 97), the estate at Barham is described as being bought from Earl Ælfgar during the abbacy of Wulfric (*c.* 1052–65) (Blake 1962, 152n and 166).

At Coddenham, Domesday Book preserves evidence for a minster church. In the holdings of Roger Bigod, sometime sheriff of Norfolk and Suffolk, half a church with 2½ acres of land valued 'always' at the paradoxically high 36*s.*; a church with 12½ acres of land at 25*d.*, and another church with 8 acres valued at 16*d.* are mentioned (*DB Suffolk*, fo. 338a). More churches were within the holding of Odo, the Bishop of Bayeux at Coddenham, one with 3 acres valued at 6*d.*, another with 1 acre at 2*d.* and 'two acres belonging to the [unidentified] church valued at four pence' (*ibid.*, fo. 375a). In Ranulf Peverel's holdings at Coddenham was 'a part of three churches' as well as a church with 3 acres at 6*d.* (*ibid.*, fo. 417a); Roger of Rames had 'the fourth part of a church and of what belonged to it' (*ibid.*, fo. 422a) while various undertenants (described as *vavassors*) held a priest, Frideb (possibly Old English *Friðubeorht*) with half an acre *in elemosina*, valued at a penny (*ibid.*, fo. 447a and endnote). Such a number of churches or parts of churches associated with one named place suggests they may represent possessions of a minster church and, as Norman Scarfe has suggested, a former large *parochia* (Scarfe 1999, 52). With these possessions it should come as no surprise to learn that Coddenham was the intended location for a house of Cistercian nuns by Eustace de Merch in the time of Henry II (1154–89). In the event, the foundation was never made and by 1184 the church was instead given as an endowment to Royston Priory (Knowles and Hadcock 1971, 154).

I shall end by considering Burrow Hill, a settlement explored in limited excavations between 1978 and 1985. Lying in the parish of Butley, on numismatic grounds alone it might be described as 'productive', five proto-pennies of East Anglian king Beonna, five sceattas and a Kentish penny of Cuthred having been excavated (Sherlock 1984, 44–52). In fact, a variety of objects demonstrates the high status occupation here, including a silver repoussé vandyke, Continental imported pottery and a substantial decorative iron cauldron chain (Fenwick 1984). Butley appears in Domesday Book in the holdings of three landowners, Count Alan, Robert Malet and Roger of Poitou (*DB Suffolk*, fos 294a; 327b; 348a). None of these holdings were of any size or particularly exceptional, and certainly do nothing to suggest a place of any importance. However, *c.* 1171 the Augustinian priory of St Mary was founded in Butley by Rannulf de Glanville and his wife Bertha de Valognes (Mortimer 1979, 1). Butley provides a useful final location to consider purely because its 'afterlife' appears entirely unexceptional from the documentary evidence. Despite this, it came to have a monastery founded in the twelfth century. If for no other reason than this, we need to consider whether yet another instance of an important Middle Anglo-Saxon site subsequently coming to have a religious house founded nearby in the twelfth century is pure coincidence.

Discussion

The presence of many medieval monasteries on or near Middle Anglo-Saxon 'productive' sites is curious and interesting. Of the thirteen sites considered here, five subsequently had a monastic house founded on them or nearby while a sixth, Coddenham, nearly did. Instead, Coddenham and a further three 'productive' site locations came to act as endowments for monastic houses. To what extent was this a result of chance or the deliberate policy of such earlier sites being especially selected? Two issues seem particularly important here, topography and continuity.

Topographical considerations

The siting of monasteries has most usually been seen in terms of their location on isolated sites or in quiet valleys. In fact, this isolation is increasingly understood to be as much a mental projection on the part of monastic inmates as reflecting a true existence within harsh or liminal settings (Menuge 2000). A brief examination of the wider geography of monastic settlement in medieval East Anglia is required. In the years between 1066 and 1199, seventy-one monasteries, of a wide variety of orders, were founded in the diocese of Norwich. However, from this we may exclude those thirteen 'alien' priories which acted essentially as small land endowments for Continental houses. The remaining fifty-eight monasteries show a distribution favouring certain areas, in particular to either side of the clayland central watershed which runs up East Anglia, dividing Norfolk and Suffolk into east and west. Within these areas there were other concentrations and absences, for instance monastic foundation appears to have been retarded in west Suffolk by the presence of Bury St Edmunds Abbey.

Essentially those areas of more dense monastic foundation relate to prevailing soil conditions. The reason would seem to be not a preference as such for certain soil types but the influence topography had on population density and tenurial control. An ideal foundation endowment was a unified block of land over which the monastic founder had control. Domesday Book shows that land held by free men predominated in certain areas, for instance, in Norfolk their distribution was most strong to the south and east. Sokemen, who owed slightly more services to estates, predominated in areas of greater lordly power. While far more free individuals held land in the east of Norfolk, the west was more bound to a smaller number of single lordship vills – precisely those areas where land of suitable area and tenurial control might make an acceptable or unified foundation endowment.

This picture is reiterated in Bruce Campbell's analysis of medieval manorial structure, using the 1316 *Nomina Villarum*. This record of the names of vills and their lords, arranged by hundred, shows that the complex lordship attested in Domesday was maintained into the early fourteenth century. Only 23 percent of vills were held by a single lord, but of these, many were in the west of the county, and usually of high value (Campbell 1986, 227–30). Not only was this the area in which we find many of Norfolk's medieval monasteries, it is the location of many 'productive' sites. While it would be unwise to suggest similar ties of lordship pertained in the 300 years between 800–1100, as did in the 230 years from 1086–1316, it is of note that the overlapping pattern of monasteries and 'productive' sites extends also to the east of Suffolk.

Religious continuity

The second issue arising from our discussion of 'productive' sites' afterlives concerns the number which subsequently came into monastic ownership. With evidence for several sites having had Anglo-Saxon minsters, this ownership may be seen as a process of monastic refoundation, a process which allowed incoming Norman families to reorganise indigenous priestly communities in their own Continental image. Indeed, one of the striking features in East Anglia is just how many monasteries appear to have had some form of an Anglo-Saxon 'past', especially in the earlier period of post-Conquest foundation when the larger, better-endowed, houses were established.

Of the fifty-eight monasteries, seventeen or 29.3 percent had some definite locational importance in the Anglo-Saxon period, a further nine or 15.5 percent a possible earlier importance. Thus, 44.8 percent of these monasteries probably had some former importance suggesting monastic foundations had a locational rationale associated with topography, existing settlement and the tenurial implications of lordship (Pestell forthcoming). Does this mean that we should see in the 'productive' site an ecclesiastical origin, attenuated at times but frequently recast as a monastery in the years following the Conquest? The documentary evidence from Burnham and Coddenham, and to a lesser extent Rudham, could be argued to point this way. The problem is that some form of 'importance' to a site, for instance in having large quantities of coinage, is not the same as providing evidence for Anglo-Saxon minster communities.

Other ways to identify 'productive' sites as minsters have been proposed, notably through the presence of styli. These writing implements have been found at a number of East Anglian 'productive' sites including Bawsey, Brandon, Coddenham, Wormegay and perhaps Burrow Hill, and have frequently been seen as an accoutrement of religious life. No-one can deny the pre-eminent position of the Church in the practice of literacy and that we might expect to find styli most often on religious sites. Unfortunately, this is not the same as saying writing implements always indicate a minster. There is increasing evidence for lay literacy from archaeological sources, in addition to recent reassessments of the documentary evidence. Additionally, many styli are appearing on perfectly normal Anglo-Saxon sites. A stylus metal-detected at Otley in Suffolk came from an area with Ipswich ware but little to suggest a high-status or 'productive' site, and still less can be said about the stylus finds from Grimston and Tibenham in Norfolk. The two styli recovered in excavations at Sedgeford, also in Norfolk, derive from a site with no evidence for being anything other than a nascent manor. It may be that these finds indicate various literate and butter-fingered clerics stalking the countryside but if they do, we may well question what they were doing. An obvious answer is carrying out bureaucratic and administrative duties, as likely for the secular elite as the Church. This also does not preclude the laity from being literate themselves and using styli on occasions.

With some 1,300 vills in Norfolk and Suffolk, the high coincidence between the fifty-eight post-Conquest monasteries and handful of 'productive' sites is striking and insistently suggests a link between them. One explanation is that many 'productive' sites were minsters in which a strand or tradition of religious life continued to be maintained. The role of the Church in trade in the eighth and ninth centuries similarly provides an easy explanation for the artefactual wealth found on 'productive' sites. That so many sites do not appear 'religious' by the time of Domesday Book need occasion no surprise, as much land appears to have been secularised by the West Saxon kings in the wake of the First Viking Age (Fleming 1985; Dumville 1992). Indeed, as Hadley has pointed out, a burgeoning land market operated by the tenth century, in which even the humble bought and sold, contributing to the dismantling and creation of multi-vill territories (Hadley 2000, 158). Some sites, like Coddenham, have good evidence for an ecclesiastical component while others, such as Bawsey, can arguably be inferred. The difficulty is that extrapolating such links on the basis of one or two examples is unhelpful and at worst obscures what is likely to be a far more complex picture. Wormegay and Butley, for instance, have no hard evidence for any ecclesiastical origin in the Middle Anglo-Saxon period, despite religious foundations occurring at each after the Conquest. More seriously, other sites like West Walton and Hindringham at best have an association with other, adjacent, centres. At Congham and Barham, the wealth that was generated by trade in the eighth and ninth centuries appears to have had no successors.

We have, perhaps, become too obsessed with the idea of identifying and categorising site types. The example of styli illustrates how difficult it is to use finds to make specific identifications of a site's secular or ecclesiastical character. In the same way, Flixborough has recently been argued to represent a settlement which featured both lay and clerical occupation, possibly in different periods of the site's use (Loveluck 2001). We may see a very similar picture in any number of our other sites. While the Church may frequently have represented a stable locational presence in the landscape and produced documents with vastly greater chances of survival than those of the laity, this should not encourage us simply to accept an ecclesiastical origin to all sites. It was royalty and the secular aristocracy, after all, who patronised the Church, granting it lands, rights and goods. If the Church was of fundamental importance in bringing mechanisms to exploit and run estates more efficiently, we can hardly be surprised if the laity did not also rapidly adopt these tools.

Finally, the difficulty in tracing the afterlife of several 'productive' sites may reflect the fluid nature of trade and redistributive networks themselves. Just as the Fen basin proved to be constantly evolving as sea levels changed and old watercourses silted up or were redirected, so sites like West Walton and Bawsey arguably became re-sited; others like Barham and Congham simply went out of business. To explain the nature and presence of 'productive' sites, the influence of topography and soils must, arguably, not be ignored. The fluidity in trading settlements and their survival (or not) owed much to the development of tenurial control. The principal feature of the East Anglian sites' afterlives is their usual association with larger land units in places which came to have high concentrations of single lordship vills. Their very survival as land units, in a majority of cases, reflects this tenurial importance. This was to result in the continuation, renewal or creation of religious life through monasteries or monastic endowment, but also in two cases, Wormegay and Burgh Castle, in castle building. The challenge in interpreting 'productive' sites may not, therefore, be to question whether they are really 'normal' or 'above-average' sites revealed by metal-detection, but what they can tell us of local settlement hierarchy and why, in a few cases, they failed. The evidence from East Anglia suggests 'productive' sites are indeed exceptional and must relate to the origins of land organization and social control. Certainly, their development had a lasting effect on landscape organization beyond the Norman Conquest.

CHAPTER 12

Middle Anglo-Saxon Lincolnshire: An Emerging Picture

Kevin Leahy

Recent years have seen a revolution in our knowledge of the Early Medieval period in Lincolnshire. An increase in archaeological excavations and the work of metal-detector users has produced large numbers of finds and previously unknown sites.* This paper will look at the overall picture presented by these finds and will then go on to look in detail at one 'productive' site and attempt to place it in context.

The distribution maps (Figs 12.1–12.3) show all Anglo-Saxon and Viking metalwork from Lincolnshire known to the writer as of December 2000. This includes 1,186 metal-detector finds, with additional information from the Lincolnshire County Sites and Monuments Record. A problem inherent in all distribution maps is whether the pattern revealed represents an historical reality or merely concentrations of fieldwork. The figure shows a fairly good coverage, but with some areas where finds are lacking or sparse. These lie along the coastal margins, around the Wash and inland to the south of Lincoln; all are marshland areas where the Domesday Survey recorded a low population (Darby 1977, 87–94, figs 34–6). A further gap in the pattern of finds, in the central section of the Wolds, may correspond to an area of woodland at Domesday (*ibid.*, 193, fig. 64). It appears then, that the recorded pattern of metal-detector finds

FIGURE 12.1.
Finds of Early Anglo-Saxon metalwork from Lincolnshire. Much material will have come from previously unknown cemeteries but, set against a background of single finds, a hierarchy of cemeteries may be inferred.

* This paper is based on finds recorded over the last twenty years, first as a personal initiative by the writer but for the last three years with the assistance of Mrs Marina Elwes, as Finds Liaison Officer. The material recorded has not been removed from its stratigraphical context by the metal-detector users. Lincolnshire is one of the most heavily cultivated areas of England: on average 46 percent of the land in an English county is under crop or fallow but in North Lincolnshire 78 percent of the land is ploughed. The damage done to the historical environment is appalling. The metal-detector finds often represent all that survives of a destroyed historic landscape and it is vital that this material is recorded.

5th- to 7th-century finds
Number of finds
40
20
4
Known Cemetery

is providing us with a credible distribution of Anglo-Saxon metalwork in Lincolnshire from which we can begin to discuss settlement patterns.

To place the Middle Anglo-Saxon material into its historical context it is necessary to consider the earlier and later Anglo-Saxon finds. The 1,186 recorded items of Anglo-Saxon and Viking type recorded break down as follows:

Table 12.1. *The breakdown of Early Medieval metalwork recorded in Lincolnshire to December 2000.*

Total finds	*5th–7th century*	*8th–9th century*	*10th century*	*Viking*
1186	522	417	135	112

The distribution of fifth- to seventh-century finds presents a startling picture (Fig. 12.1). This material is surprisingly common and, in some areas, it appears that every parish (to use a later term) had a cemetery. In addition to the cemeteries, there are many single finds of Early Anglo-Saxon metalwork. Some pieces must represent casual losses, but other finds probably represent small family burial sites. A phenomenon recently observed in Lincolnshire is polyfocal cemeteries where one parish contains a number of small, separate burial places, perhaps again relating to individual family plots.

Until recently our knowledge of Middle Anglo-Saxon Lincolnshire was restricted to a few isolated finds of fine metalwork,* and it came as something of a revelation to find that metalwork of this date is both common and widespread (Fig. 12.2). This suggests a high level of prosperity in the Middle Anglo-Saxon period with small metal objects becoming common.† It might also reflect the homogenisation of the population with 'Anglo-Saxon' culture no longer being the preserve of one social group.

The finds suggest that Middle Anglo-Saxon Lincolnshire was divided into three zones: a northern zone where finds are common and with some 'productive' sites; a south-western zone where Middle Anglo-Saxon metalwork is also common, but without 'productive' sites; and a south-eastern zone where finds are rare. This pattern of finds may be explained in political and geographical terms. The three zones equate to the historic 'Parts' of Lincolnshire: the kingdom of Lindsey

FIGURE 12.2. Middle Anglo-Saxon finds from Lincolnshire and imported material of similar date. Roman roads and early trackways are shown as broken lines.

* Such as the eighth-century silver pins and bowl from the River Witham (Wilson 1964, 132–4, pls. IIc and XVIII). With the work of the East Midlands Early Anglo-Saxon Pottery Project on Maxey-type ware (Vince and Young 1990–1, 38–9) we are beginning to understand the regional ceramic sequence.

† Fig. 12.2 does not include coins, the distribution of which has been discussed elsewhere (Blackburn 1993b, 80–90; Ulmschneider 2000b, fig. 6).

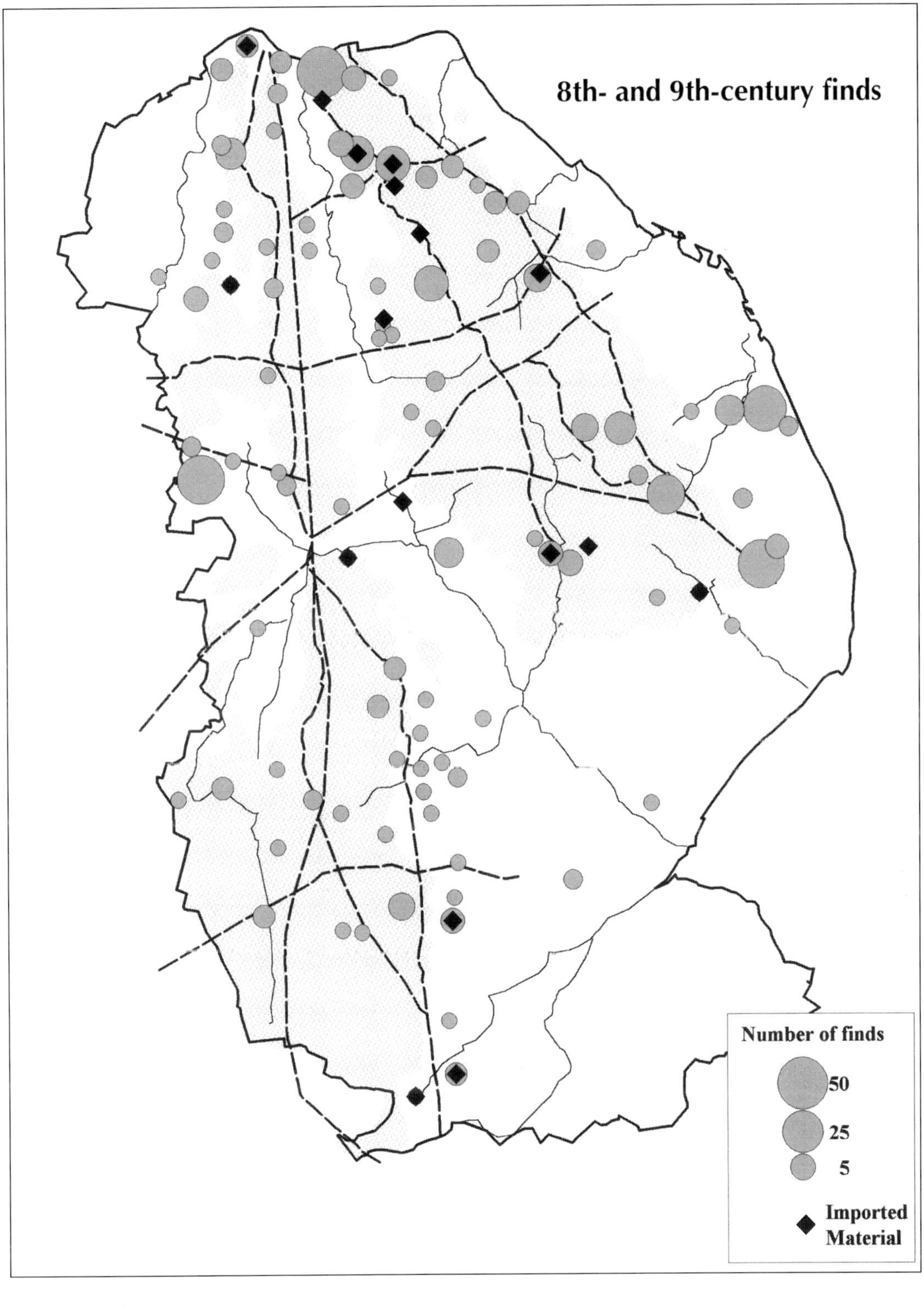
8th- and 9th-century finds
Number of finds
50
25
5
Imported Material

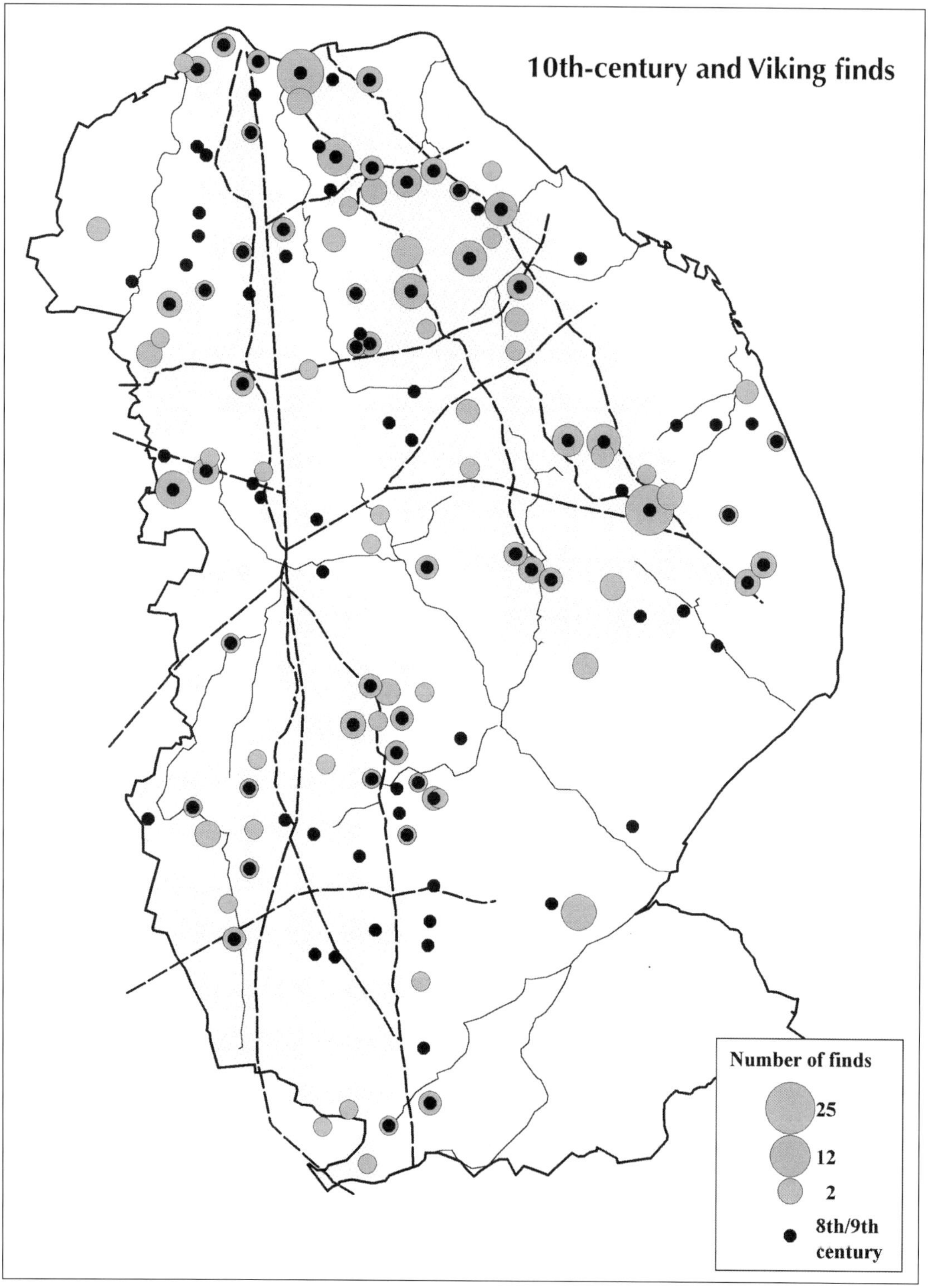
10th-century and Viking finds
Number of finds
25
12
2
8th/9th century

in the north, Kesteven to the south-west and Holland to the south-east. Lindsey was an ancient Anglo-Saxon kingdom (Foot 1993) and likely to have had a well-developed economy and identity. Indeed, the quantity of Middle Anglo-Saxon metalwork and coins from Lindsey led Mark Blackburn to suggest that it was one of the wealthiest regions of England during the eighth and ninth centuries (Blackburn 1993b, 83). Holland, to the south-east, was largely marshland and carried a low population density at Domesday (Darby 1977, 87–94, figs 34–6). It is interesting that the two recorded finds of Middle Anglo-Saxon metalwork from Holland come from the area where the Fenland Survey found a concentration of Middle Anglo-Saxon sherds (Lane 1993). The absence of 'productive' sites in Kesteven may have been due to its heavy soils and higher level of woodland. A lack of political cohesion, on the edge of Mercia, may also have played a part. Comparisons between the zones suggest, therefore, that there were factors which allowed the development of 'productive' sites in some areas but not in others.

Ulmschneider (2000b, 63–5) drew attention to the strong correlation between 'productive' sites and lines of communication. Fig. 12.2 draws on the same data as her work, and shows that increasing numbers of finds have reinforced her observation that these rich sites are linked into trade routes. Imported metalwork is most common in Lindsey and is, again, found along lines of communication, one group of findspots running down Caistor High Street, Barton Street and Middlegate, the main north-south routes through Lindsey. A second group runs across the Fen-edge from Welton le Marsh towards Lincoln and, in the south of Lincolnshire, finds of imported metalwork probably mark routes inland through the rivers entering the Wash.

FIGURE 12.3. Tenth-century and Viking metalwork shown against the pattern of Middle Anglo-Saxon finds. Only earlier Scandinavian objects (Borre and Jelling styles) have been included on the map. The findspots of eighth- and ninth-century metalwork are included to illustrate the changing pattern of settlement.

The 'productive' sites appear to have come to an end with Viking settlement after 877 (Leahy and Paterson 2001, 189). Viking and tenth-century Anglo-Saxon metalwork is common in Lincolnshire (Fig. 12.3) and, while it occurs on some of the 'productive' sites, finds are too few to suggest that they survived in anything other than an attenuated form. This may have been a result of the division of estates among an incoming Danish population, or of more complex social and economic changes.

While the regional distribution of finds is of great interest, it is important to look at individual sites and place them into their historical and geographical context. A particularly interesting 'productive' site lies on the edge of the Lincolnshire Wolds between the parishes of Melton Ross and Barnetby le Wold. Here, systematic metal-detecting has resulted in the recovery of large quantities of Anglo-Saxon metalwork and coins.* The site lies on major lines of communication, the east-west route through the Lincolnshire Wolds passing close by, to cross the marshes of the Vale of Ancholme at Brigg, their narrowest point. Melton Ross is also on Middlegate Lane, the ancient north-south track leading along the edge of the Wolds to the River Humber at South Ferriby.

At Melton Ross the finds came, in the main, from four areas. Most of the Middle Anglo-Saxon coins and metalwork was concentrated in area marked 'A' on Fig. 12.5, with a further patch of finds to the south, 'B', an area which also produced some Early Anglo-Saxon metalwork. Both Early and Middle Anglo-Saxon pottery has been found on the field together with large quantities of lead melt, a common feature of Lincolnshire 'productive' sites. Although few of the coins have been seen by the writer,† they included Frisian sceattas of Series E, sceattas of Series J and R, Northumbrian stycas, and broad pennies of Coenwulf (796–821) and Æthelred II (986–1016), together with some Medieval sterling pennies. Perforated Roman coins, commonly found on Early Anglo-Saxon sites, were found in area 'B'. Around 300m to the west of the main findspot is a group of finds near to a spring feeding the Welbeck stream, 'C'. Material from this area suggests the presence of a Romano-British settlement followed by one of Anglo-Saxon date. Finds of Early Anglo-Saxon metalwork from an area 350m to the south show the presence of a cemetery, 'D', and burnt objects indicate that the cemetery contained cremations as well as inhumations.‡

One hundred and two pieces of metalwork have been found at Melton Ross, which can be broken down as shown in Table 12.2, opposite. Analysed by type, the finds may be broken down further, as shown in Table 12.3.

Seen in the context of the other Middle Anglo-Saxon sites in Lincolnshire, Melton Ross is only relatively 'productive'. However, the detectorist, Mr Parkin, was only able to search part of the site

---

* The writer is indebted to the generosity of Gary Parkin on whose finds, records and advocacy with other detectorists this paper is based. Without his work we would know nothing of this important site. While the finds come from the parish of Barnetby, rather than Melton Ross, the site is referred to by the latter name, this being the closest settlement. The area of the site in the northern field is in different ownership and Mr Parkin was unable to obtain permission to detect.

† I am indebted to Marion Archibald for her comments on some coins from the site shown on a photograph.

‡ While one burial rite tends to predominate in Lincolnshire Anglo-Saxon cemeteries there is usually some mixing with the cremation cemeteries containing inhumations and vice-versa.

Table 12.2. *The breakdown of metalwork from Melton Ross, by date.*

Roman	9
Fifth century	1
Sixth–seventh century	36
Eighth–ninth century	49
Tenth–eleventh century	4
Medieval	3
Total	102

Table 12.3. *The breakdown of Anglo-Saxon and Viking metalwork from Melton Ross, by type. N.B. Objects represented by only single finds are not included in this table.*

Brooches (Roman)	4
Brooches (Early Anglo-Saxon)	27
Wrist clasps (Early Anglo-Saxon)	4
Mounts (eighth century)	5
Pins (eighth/ninth century)	26
Strap-ends (ninth century)	15
Hooked tags (ninth/tenth century)	5
Knives	5

and large areas remain unknown. Some items of high quality eighth-century metalwork have been found at Melton Ross suggesting a settlement of some importance (Fig. 12.4). In common with other sites in Lindsey, the ninth century saw a general fall in the quality of the metalwork but an increase in quantity. Tenth-century and Medieval finds from Melton Ross indicate that activity continued at a reduced level or moved to a site nearby while Stamford and Torksey ware (of the tenth to eleventh century) has been found in a garden between sites 'A' and 'C'. The continued importance of the location is demonstrated by Domesday Book and the presence of Ross Castle, a large moated site in the adjacent field.*

The Domesday survey of 1086 provides useful information on Melton Ross and Barnetby le Wold. Barnetby was a soke centre and included a holding in the port of Barton on Humber (Hart 1992, 235, map 8.2a). In 1066, it was in the possession of Earl Harold and been valued at £15 (*DB Lincolnshire*, fos 349b, 353d and 362b). Unusually,

* National Monument 21250, listed as a 'moated site with adjacent fish ponds'.

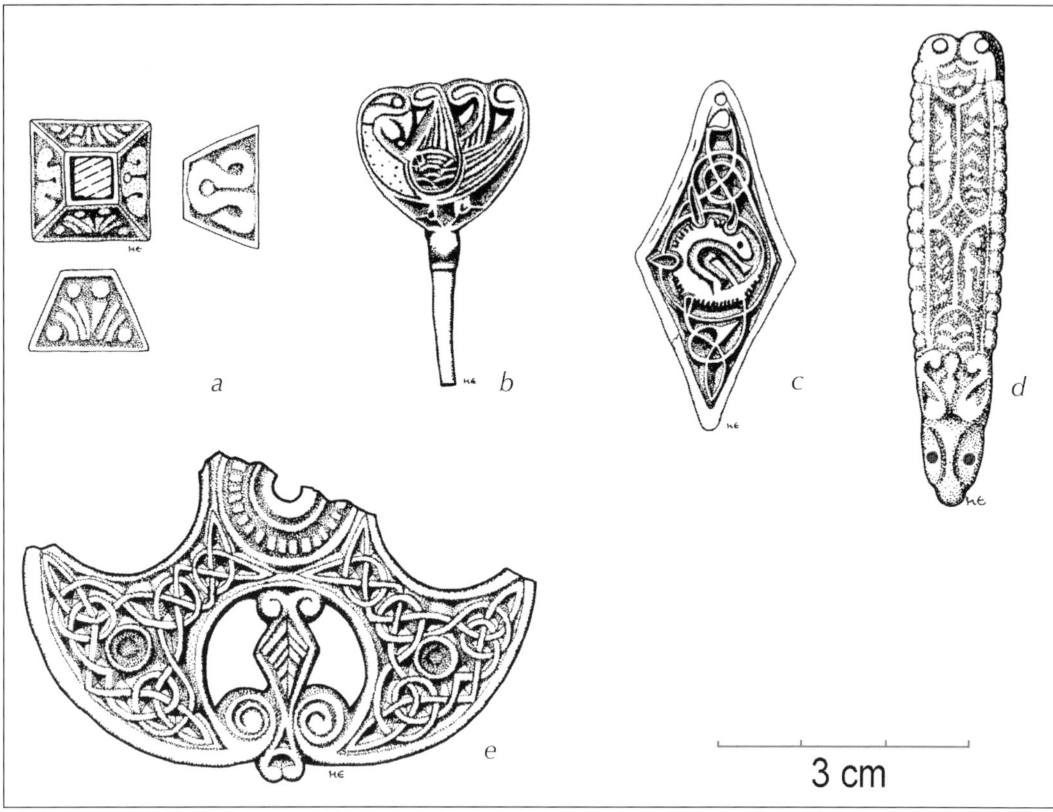

FIGURE 12.4.
Selected finds from Melton Ross. (a) Early seventh-century gilt copper-alloy sword pyramid, the apex inlaid with a square garnet and each of the four faces bears a simple curvilinear motif. (b) Eighth-century silver-gilt pinhead decorated with the stylised figure of a standing bird, left, looking back over its body. The wings and tail are raised and have club-like terminals, the shoulder bears what appears to be a panel of blundered interlace; the feet are also crudely executed. Drawn from a photograph, scale uncertain. (c) Eighth-century lozenge-shaped silver-gilt mount decorated with the figure of an animal, the limbs, ears and tail of which extend into interlace. (d) Ninth-century copper-alloy strap-end inlaid with niello. Two silver rivets at upper end, traces of silvering on back. The main field is divided into five panels containing Trewhiddle-style motifs. The terminal's animal head has inset blue glass eyes, a feature of a number of items of Middle Anglo-Saxon metalwork in Lincolnshire including the eighth-century Witham pins. (e) Fragment of a gilt copper-alloy mount in the form of a disc containing an interlace-decorated cross pattée. There is a central perforation and each of the surviving arms contains the traces of a rivet or nail. Such mounts are generally considered to be mounts from book covers or shrines, which may have implications for the interpretation of the Melton Ross site.

by 1086, its value had risen to £20 16*s*. Melton Ross was valued at £6 in 1066 and, as with Barnetby, its value had increased and in 1086 it was worth £8 (*ibid.*, fo. 362b). The assessments make reference to a church and a priest in Melton Ross and half a church in Barnetby.

Aerial photographs of the Melton Ross site show a series of enclosures marked by double-ditched droveways (Fig. 12.5) characteristic of

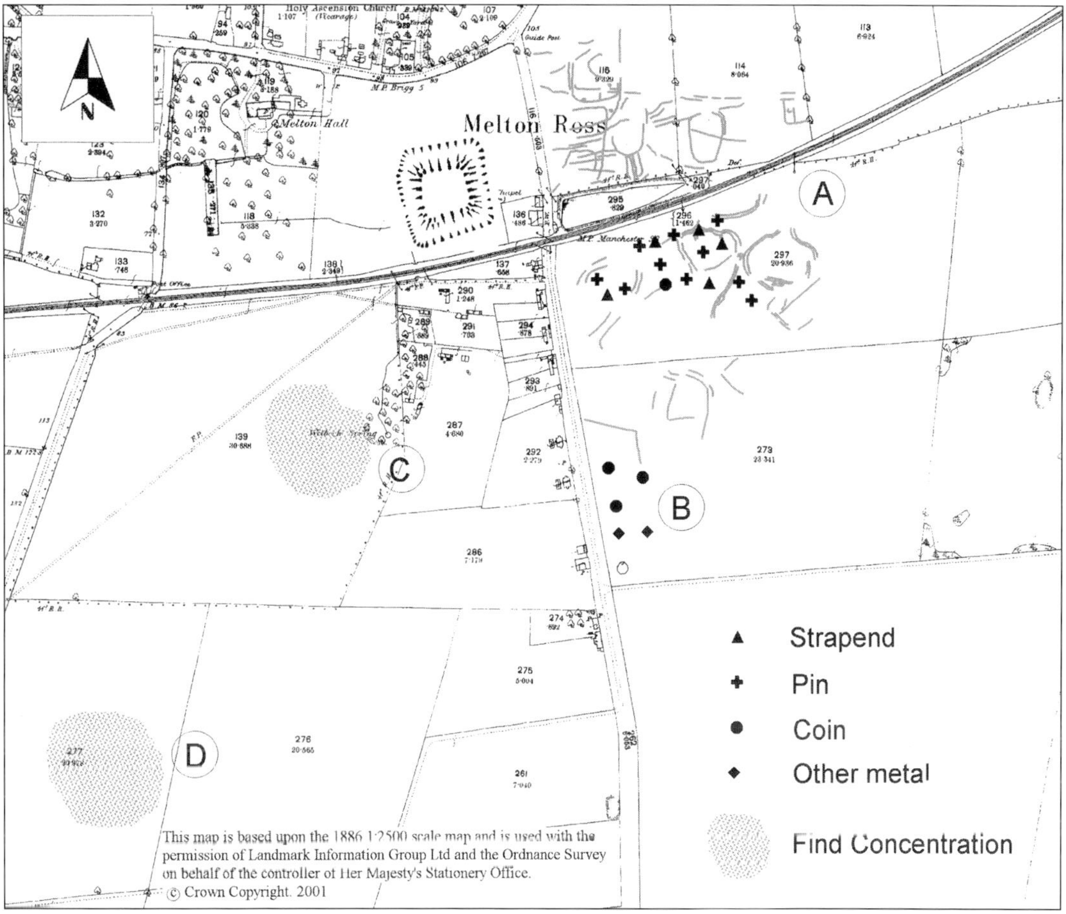

FIGURE 12.5.
The site at Melton Ross, showing the findspots, cropmark plots and the location of Ross Castle.

the so-called 'Butterwick' type sites known from the eponymous site at Butterwick in East Yorkshire (Stoertz 1997, 58–9, fig. 30.1). Butterwick lies in a bend of the Gypsy Race, the main stream in the Yorkshire Wolds. It was identified from the air and assigned to the Anglo-Saxon period on the basis of rectangular marks within the enclosures which, it was suggested, were *Grubenhäuser*. The double-ditched enclosures that typify Butterwick sites can also be seen at Cottam B, a site which has produced large quantities of Middle Anglo-Saxon metalwork (Richards 1999a). A Butterwick-type settlement has been recorded at Riby Cross Roads, eleven kilometres to the east of Melton Ross (Steedman 1994). In 1991, excavations conducted in advance of pipe laying provided a transect through this site, revealing ditches but no structures. Metalwork similar to that recorded from Melton Ross was found, together with large quantities of Early and Middle Anglo-Saxon pottery. It is rumoured that this site has produced large numbers of coins but few other objects.

Parallels can be drawn between the siting of Melton Ross and the 'productive' site at South Newbald in East Yorkshire, which lay near the junction of the Roman road leading north from the Humber Estuary and the roads to York and Malton (Leahy 2000). Like Melton Ross, South Newbald was discovered and investigated by metal detector users who found 126 coins and 114 items of Middle Anglo-Saxon metalwork (*ibid.*). Early Anglo-Saxon material was absent and the finds suggest that activity on the site ended in the later ninth century, perhaps in 867 when York fell to the Vikings. Unlike Melton Ross, the Newbald site has produced no settlement debris suggesting that

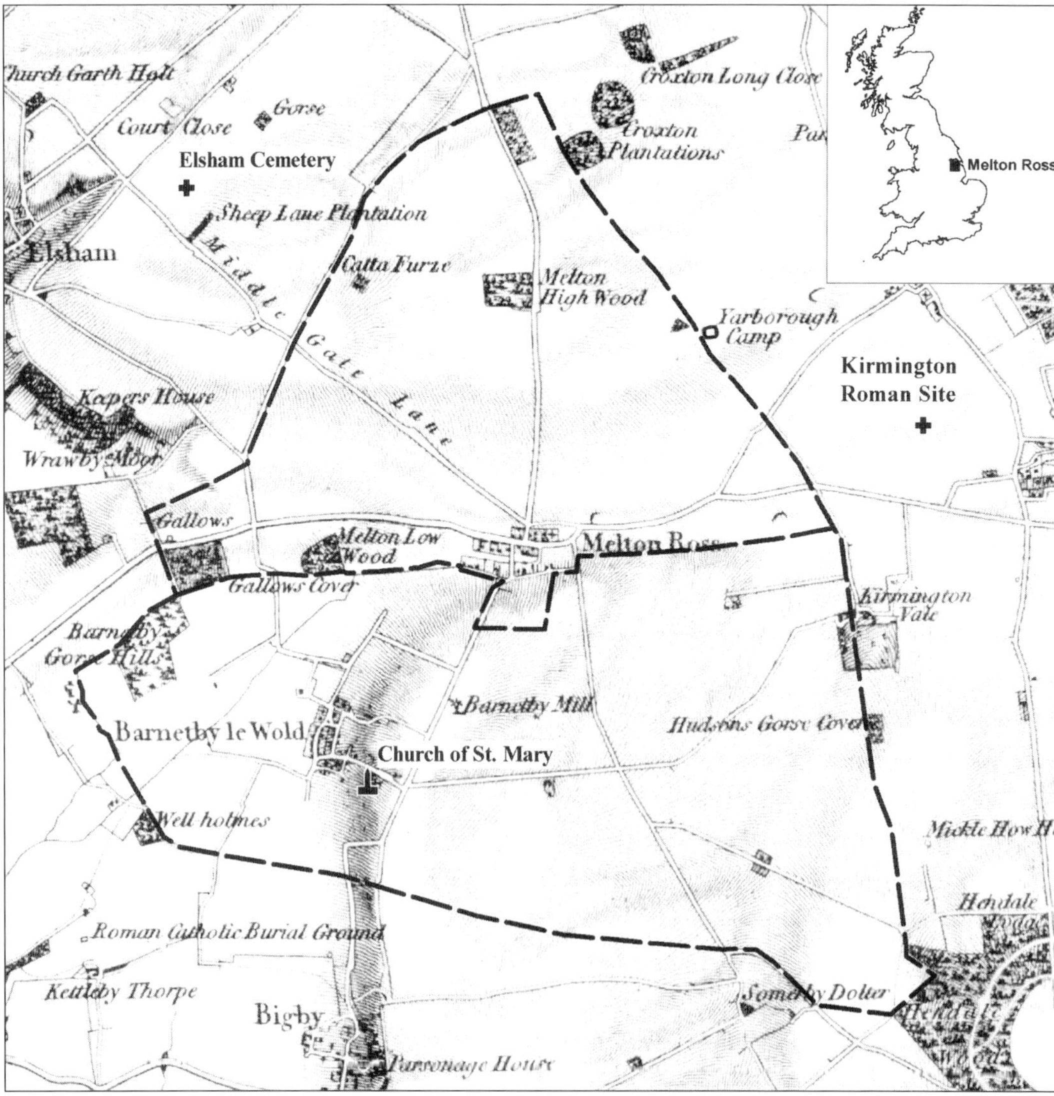

it had a different function, perhaps as a market site focused on a putative minster which would fit into a gap in the pattern of East Yorkshire minsters. Later the manor became a prebend of York, the fate of a number of former Yorkshire minsters (Morris 1989, 138). North Newbald church is a magnificent late Romanesque cruciform structure, looking 'more akin to a miniature cathedral than a parochial building' (*ibid.*, 283), again suggesting the importance of the parish.

The boundary between the parishes of Melton Ross and Barnetby is diverted in the area from which the finds come so that a tongue of Melton Ross parish extends down into Barnetby le Wold (Fig. 12.6). The parish of Barnetby was enclosed in 1766–8 but there is no map with the Award, our first detailed map of the parishes being the Tithe Award of 1849. This shows the tongue of Melton Ross extending south of the parish boundary but includes a smaller area than that seen on the modern map, stopping just east of the Welbeck spring. The present boundary between Melton Ross and Barnetby appears to be a secondary feature, dividing an original, roughly triangular, area of land in two. At South Newbald the parish boundary also deviates from its line to bisect the site (Leahy 2000, 54–5). Originally this section of the parish boundary was very complex with alternate fields belonging to the two parishes, giving a chequer-board like pattern, an arrangement apparently described in a charter of 963 (*ibid.*). The significance of the deviations near these sites is difficult to explain. Most English parishes appear to have been defined between 950 and 1150 as landowners built churches on their estates and allocated tithes to support them. The boundary thus often followed the limits of the earlier estate. At Melton Ross the deviation may have been to retain the Welbeck spring, or an associated site, within Melton parish: it is suggested that the adjustment at South Newbald allowed two parishes or estates to share in an important market/minster site. Like Melton Ross, Newbald lay at the centre of an estate that included all of the hundred of Cave (*ibid.*). Parishes within the hundred were inter-related, with Newbald having ancient rights of common and pasture in other parishes, and with another parish having a detached outlier.

FIGURE 12.6. The combined parishes of Melton Ross, Barnetby le Wold and the surrounding sites, taken from the 1887 2″ Ordnance Survey map (Sheet XX.7). Parish boundaries are shown by a broken line.

Both Melton Ross and Newbald are close to large Early Anglo-Saxon cremation cemeteries. On Middlegate Lane, three and a half kilometres to the north-west of the Melton Ross was the Elsham cemetery (Leahy 1993, 40) and, just over six kilometres to the north of Newbald, again in an adjacent parish, is the Sancton cemetery (Myres and Southern 1973). Paul Everson has suggested a relationship between these large cemeteries and later Domesday soke centres, the Cleatham cemetery being linked with the great soke of Kirton in Lindsey, and South Elkington linked with Louth (Everson 1993, 98). Everson considered

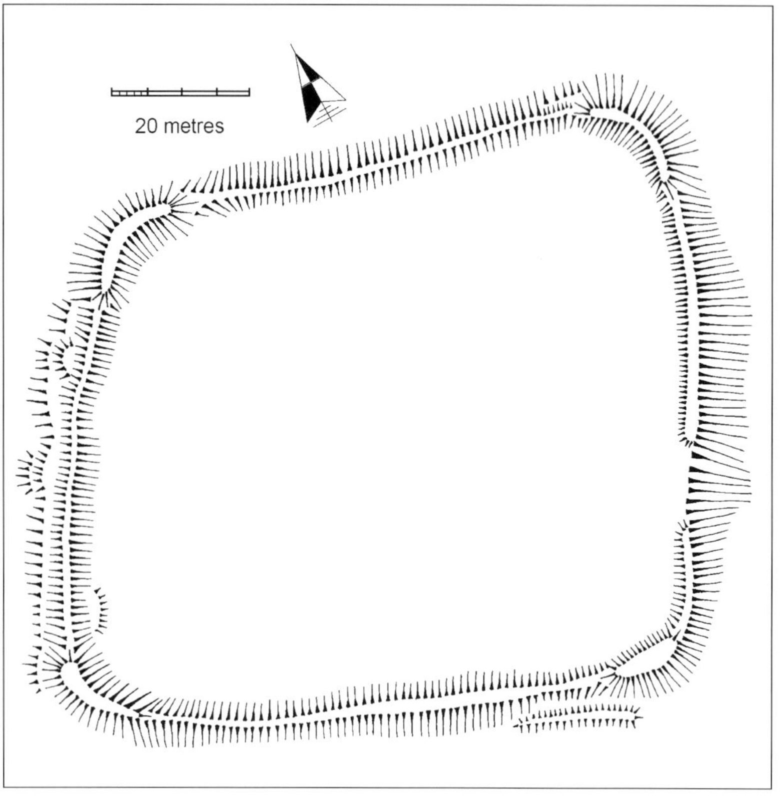

FIGURE 12.7. The Yarborough Camp earthworks. Plan based on a survey carried out by K. A. Leahy and J. C. Dyson in May 1984. The ditch was filled with leaf litter and was located by probing.

that Elsham was too far away from Caistor to be linked with it, but it now seems possible that Elsham was linked not to Caistor, but to the soke centre in the adjacent parish of Barnetby. Both Melton Ross and South Newbald are also close to Early Anglo-Saxon inhumation cemeteries, the cemetery at Newbald being just over a kilometre away from the site (Leahy 2000, 54).

Two kilometres to the north-east of Melton Ross, on the boundary with the neighbouring parish of Croxton, is Yarborough Camp, a 0.62ha trapezoid enclosure (Fig. 12.7).* The monument is now obscured by woodland, but a survey showed it to consist of a bank and surrounding ditch. At each of its four corners is a mound, probably representing the remains of a bastion and a ten-metre wide gap in the east side of the enclosure may mark the position of an entrance. This monument is difficult to date on morphological grounds. It was visited by the antiquarian William Stukeley in 1724 who recorded:

> Two miles west of Thornton (Curtis) is a great Roman camp, called Yarborough which surveys the whole hundred dominated

---

* National Monument 32623, scheduled as 'a large univallate hill fort'.

from it, and all the sea coast. Vast quantities of Roman coins have been found here: Mr Howson of Kenington (Kirmington) hard by, has pecks of them, many of Licinius (Stukeley 1776, 101).

As no coins have been found at Yarborough Camp in recent times it has been suggested that Mr Howson's coins came not from the Camp, but from the Roman site at Kirmington two kilometres from Melton Ross (Scheduled County Monument 217). Occupation at Kirmington started in the Iron Age and following a brief military phase, the site went on to become a large, unenclosed civil settlement. When metal-detecting was allowed on the site it yielded large quantities of Romano-British metalwork but very little Anglo-Saxon material, activity having perhaps moved from Kirmington to Melton Ross.

In the collection at North Lincolnshire Museum are four sherds of pottery found by archaeologists at Yarborough Camp in 1967. One sherd is Bronze Age, two are of Romano-British greyware but the fourth is of Early Anglo-Saxon gritty ware. There is also a record of the bases of two Romano-British pots being found in the south-east corner of the enclosure. Perhaps the most significant feature of the site is its name. 'Yarborough' comes from the Old English *eorburg*, 'earth fortification' and this name was also applied to the Yarborough wapentake in which it lies.* This suggests that the camp was the centre of the wapentake and acted as the moot or meeting place. *Eorburg* is the word the Anglo-Saxons used for pre-existing earthworks, their own fortifications being referred to as *burh* (Cox 1996, 50). This would support the evidence provided by archaeology for the earthwork's prehistoric, or possibly Romano-British origin. Barry Cox has suggested that Yarborough Camp and the other Yarboroughs in Lindsey represent the remains of a late Roman defensive system (*ibid.*, 59) or formed part of a defensive system dating from the seventh century wars between Mercia and Northumbria (Cox 1994, 53–4). Late Roman fortifications employed bastions but those at Yarborough Camp differ in that they fail to extend beyond the defensive line and would not have allowed flanking fire. We may instead be looking at a seventh century *burh*. Yarborough wapentake is not unique in being centred on a prehistoric earthwork. Dickering ('dike-ring') wapentake in East Yorkshire was centred on the massive 120m diameter Bronze Age

---

* Wapentakes were district assemblies of free men. While the word is Scandinavian, the institution is far older and Sawyer (1998 134–6) has pointed out that most of the wapentakes in Lincolnshire have English, not Scandinavian, names. Yarborough Camp retained some importance into later times, acting as one of the mustering points during the 1536 Lincolnshire Rising.

earthwork at Thwing; Thwing may be derived from *thing*, the Old English word for a meeting place.*

Excavations carried out at Thwing between 1973 and 1987 revealed, in addition to the prehistoric remains, evidence that the enclosure had been re-occupied from the eighth to the tenth centuries AD (Manby 1988). Buildings, including a large *Grubenhaus*, were erected within the earthwork which was surrounded by a series of palisades and enclosures forming ditched drove-ways resembling those seen on the Butterwick-type settlements. In spite of the clear importance of Thwing, the amount of Middle Anglo-Saxon metalwork found was relatively small, with only thirty-seven copper-alloy objects and sixteen coins. Many of the coins appear to be 'as struck' suggesting that they were being issued from the site. In the centre of the earthwork was a cemetery of 132 close-packed graves containing the remains of men, women and children aligned roughly west-east, and some graves had been used for successive burials (Manby 1986, 1–8). Thirty of the graves contained iron coffin fittings, marking them as burials of some quality. Just outside of the cemetery were two graves containing the remains of individuals who had been executed, suggesting that the site had a judicial role.

Some of the 'productive' sites may also have had a judicial role. The 1852 Ordnance Survey map records that eighteen human skeletons were found on the Newbald site but gives no further details. It is possible that they were linked to a minster, but eighteen is a low number for a churchyard and no further bones have been seen by the detectorists. They could instead have been placed around a gallows linked to the market/administrative functions of the site. By the side of the former main road just over two kilometres from the Melton Ross site stands a simple gallows. While the present structure is a modern replacement, this is an old place of execution. Gallows were recorded here on the 1824 Ordnance Survey map and the Hundred Roll of 1276 refers to a *furc* at Melton belonging to Robert de Ross (Illingworth 1812, 377b).† In describing the Melton furc the Roll uses

---

* The place name 'Melton' is derived from 'middle ton' (Cameron 1998, 87) showing that it, at least, was a central place, the *-ton* element unlikely to date to before eighth century. 'Ross' comes from the family who held the manor in the thirteenth century and whose name is linked to 'Ross Castle'. 'Barnetby' is less interesting, Cameron suggesting that it comes from an otherwise unrecorded Anglo-Saxon personal name, *Beornede*, to which has been added the Danish suffix *–by* (*ibid.*, 10).

† The word *furc* appears in a number of contexts amongst which are *furcae suspensivae* in 1317 (Fisher 1968) and *furcae judiciales* in 1296 and 1305 (Latham 1965, 204). Elsewhere in the *Rolls* the word *furc* is used in conjuction with *tumbrell* and *pillor*, again suggesting an unpleasant function.

the term *antiqui conquest* showing that they were not a newly-installed amenity, but pre-dated the Norman Conquest. Again the parish boundary is diverted, here to include the gallows within the parish of Melton Ross. At this point the boundaries of the parishes Melton Ross, Barnetby, Elsham and Wrawby meet. Locations in elevated positions, on parish boundaries, are characteristic of gallows sites (Reynolds 1998b).* The Newbald boundary may also have been diverted to include a gallows.†

To summarise, there is in the area around Melton Ross/Barnetby le Wold a remarkable concentration of Anglo-Saxon material and evidence. We have, in a relatively small area, the 'productive' site itself with its concentration of finds and settlement debris; cropmarks; an Early Anglo-Saxon cemetery and settlement; deviations in the parish boundary in the area of the finds and the gallows; the crossing of two major routes with implicit commercial activity; the wapentake centre at Yarborough Camp; gallows; and an important Medieval manorial centre.

Here are most of the main elements of Middle Anglo-Saxon administration, the main omission being the absence of any direct evidence for an ecclesiastical function, although gilt copper-alloy mounts like the example shown on Fig. 12.4e occur on monastic sites such as Whitby and Hartlepool. The parish church at Melton Ross was built in 1867, replacing an earlier structure. At Barnetby however, the redundant church of St Mary contains Anglo-Saxon work.‡

In conclusion, the large number of finds recorded as part of the Portable Antiquities Scheme has presented us with new opportunities to study the Anglo-Saxon period. The metal-detector finds cannot be seen in isolation and must be evaluated on both a site-specific and an inter site basis. Every available source of evidence, archaeological, historical, topographical must be integrated, allowing us to move from the mere amassing of data to something more interesting and exciting.

---

* The best known Anglo-Saxon gallows site is that excavated at Sutton Hoo (Carver 1998, 138–42). These burials date from between the seventh and the eleventh centuries but in view of the exceptional nature of Sutton Hoo any parallels must be treated with caution. References to gallows, or at least to the feudal right to exact the death penalty, are not uncommon in medieval Lincolnshire and, on average, gallows appear to have been set about eight kilometres apart (Platts 1985, 53–5, fig. 19). The very survival of the Melton gallows suggests their importance.

† Trial excavations carried out around the gallows by the University of Sheffield have shown the subsoil to be severely truncated with no remains surviving.

‡ This building is Norman with medieval additions but contains a curious key-hole shaped window bearing the figure of a cat-like animal and some crude interlace. It is difficult to date but the Taylors favoured a Saxo-Norman date on the basis of the way in which the window opening was formed (Taylor and Taylor 1980, 47–8, fig. 24).

Acknowledgements

I should like to thank Marion Archibald, Mark Bennett, Marina Elwes, Sarah Golland, Dave Haldenby, Mike Hemblade, Nick Lyons, Terry Manby, Gary Parkin, Rex Russell and Alison Williams. The drawings of the finds on Fig. 12.4 are the work of Marina Elwes. The digital mapping is the work of Mike Hemblade and the plan of Yarborough Camp, Fig. 12.7, is the work of the writer.

CHAPTER 13

The Anglian and Anglo-Scandinavian Sites at Cottam, East Yorkshire

Julian D. Richards

Introduction

This chapter is based upon fieldwork carried out at the so-called 'productive' site at Cottam (East Yorkshire) from 1993 to 1996, the first two seasons of which have been published (Richards 1999a). On the basis of the results from Cottam, I have argued elsewhere (Richards 1999b) that the term 'productive' site is unhelpful as it generally reflects a method of finds recovery, based upon the use of metal-detectors, rather than a distinct activity in the past. Somewhat controversially for a volume including the term 'productive' site in its title, in this paper I will attempt to outline and develop this argument. I will suggest that not all sites which have been labelled 'productive' are especially rich in finds; that they do not have to have been involved in artefact production; nor need they have been primarily markets. In fact, excavation of such sites is beginning to reveal that the term 'productive' masks a range of activities which themselves evolve through time. We should seek to refine our typology of Middle Anglo-Saxon sites by more detailed study of metalwork assemblages alongside other material. Most critically, we urgently require further excavation of sites which have attracted the 'productive' label.

Cottam: the archaeological evidence

Excavation reveals that the site at Cottam is in fact not just one 'productive' site but three, developing and shifting through time (Fig. 13.1). Each of the sites is related to an ancient droveway which follows the side of a typical Wolds dry valley. Although the droveway apparently ceased to function during the medieval period it is still visible on recent aerial photographs as a linear crop mark which continues northwards up the side of the valley and then joins a major east-west route, the 'High Street', running along the Wolds top. If the alignment of the droveway is projected to the south then it would intersect a second major east-west route, the Roman road running

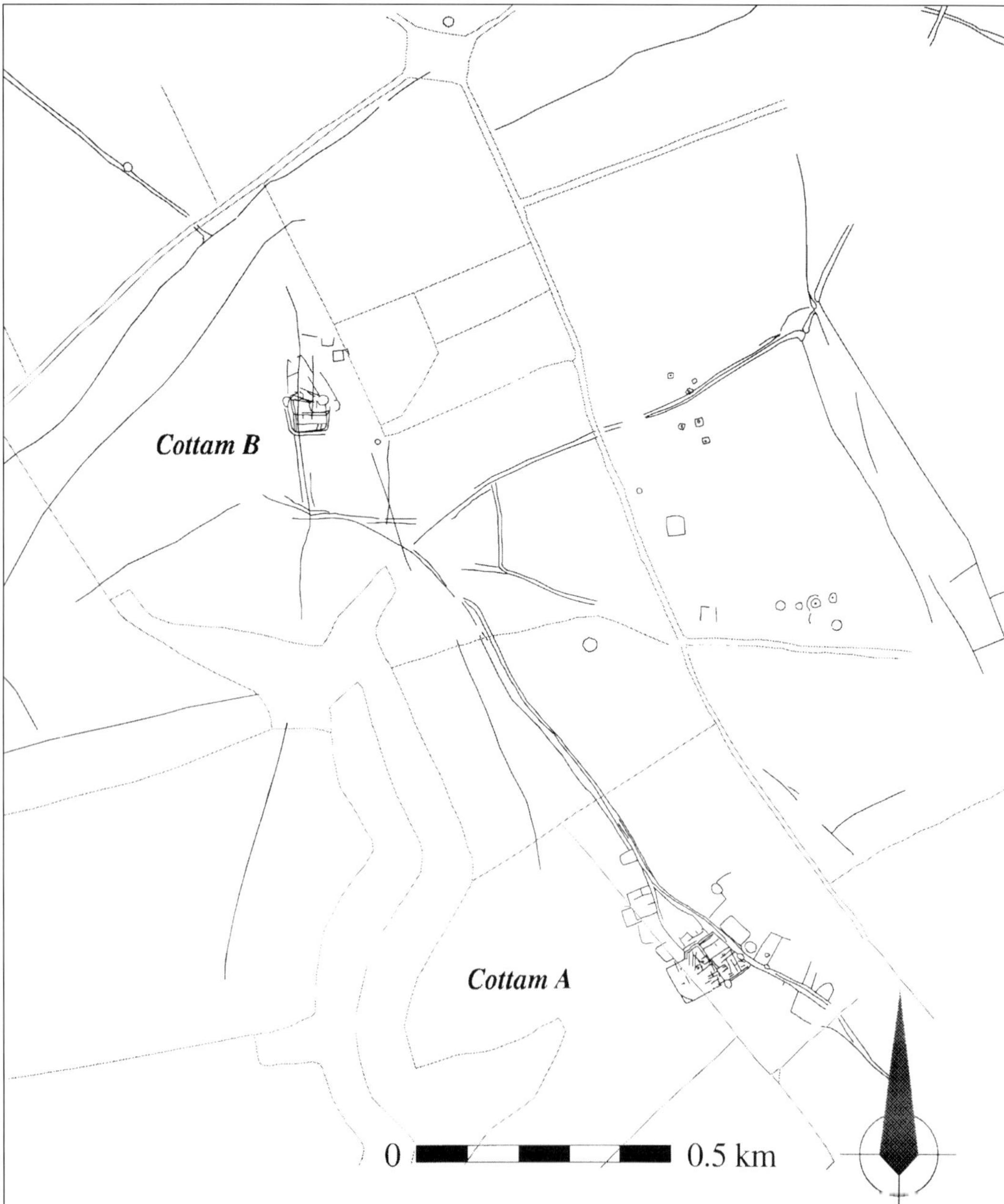

FIGURE 13.1.
The location of the sites at Cottam. Evidence from fieldwork demonstrates that settlements shifted through time.

from Bridlington to York. It appears from the positioning of Iron Age square barrows adjacent to the Cottam droveway that it goes back at least as far as the Iron Age, and is of a type found throughout the Yorkshire Wolds (Stoertz 1997). It certainly continued in use during the Roman occupation and survived to influence the Anglo-Saxon settlement pattern.

The southernmost settlement, adjacent to Cottam Grange Farm, is known as Cottam A; the two settlements to the north, adjacent to Burrow House Farm, have been described collectively as Cottam B. Cottam A begins as a standard Romano-British 'ladder' settlement with a series of rectilinear enclosures developing on either side of the droveway, from which metal-detectorists recovered a standard range of brooches and coins as might be associated with a reasonable high-status Romano-British Wolds farm. However, they also recovered a relatively small number of Northumbrian stycas, strap-ends and dress-pins, numbering some twenty Anglo-Saxon and Anglo-Scandinavian objects in total (D. Haldenby, pers. comm.). They also found a chalk thatch or net weight, possibly depicting an incised ship (Richards 1995).

Excavation found few clear Anglo-Saxon settlement traces other than a few post-holes reflecting ephemeral structures. It seems as if the main focus of the site in the ninth and tenth centuries was a large quarry hole, which may have been used as a watering hollow by herdsmen following the line of the droveway from the sites at Cottam B, to the north (Richards, in prep.).

Cottam B was first discovered by a group of metal-detector enthusiasts in 1987. Over sixty pieces of eighth- and ninth-century date were found over the following two autumn seasons, during approximately 200 man-hours of searching by five metal-detector enthusiasts (Haldenby 1990, 51), at a recovery rate of one object per three hours of detecting. The importance of the site was appreciated at an early stage and the non-ferrous metal finds were systematically plotted (Haldenby 1990, 1992 and 1994). No attempt was ever made to recover non-metallic artefacts, other than unusual finds, although the presence of pottery and bone has been acknowledged by the metal-detector enthusiasts and substantiated by the results of fieldwalking (Didsbury 1990; Richards 1999a, 15–16). Metal-detecting continued during 1990, although the rate of recovery had by now decreased to approximately one artefact per six hours of detecting (Haldenby 1992, 25).

The detected finds from Cottam B include some sixty-eight dress pins, thirty-four strap-ends, seven rings, four brooches (including one with Jellinge-style decoration), eight lead weights, over thirty-five iron knife blades, and two so-called Norse bells. There are also some nineteen Roman coins, three eighth-century sceattas, and twenty-two ninth-century stycas.

All the finds recovered have been found in ploughsoil, close to the surface. The site has been regularly ploughed for cereal cultivation but, on at least one occasion, it has also been 'subsoil ploughed' for the planting of potatoes, resulting in disturbance of material to a depth of *c.* 0.4m (15 inches), which led to the recovery of additional metalwork (D. Haldenby, pers. comm.). Several of the metal items were quite corroded, having suffered from agricultural disturbance, whereas much appears to have only been ploughed up in recent years and was still in a good state of preservation. During the subsequent excavation most of the objects recovered were found resting in the archaeological layers immediately at the base of the ploughsoil. In certain places the 'tram-lines' left by the sub-soiling equipment could be seen cut into this layer, providing a graphic demonstration of the site formation processes which create a 'productive' site (Richards 1999a, illus. 19).

By plotting the distribution of the metal finds it became apparent that there were two main concentrations at Cottam B (Fig. 13.2). These clusters are believed to be real, as the surrounding fields were also intensively detected and did not yield these densities of artefacts. Activity was clearly focused on these two areas. The southern concentration coincided with an enclosure visible as a crop mark, but there was also a general spread of metal artefacts to the north of this. The Cottam B southern crop-mark enclosure fits within a type identified by Stoertz as a curvilinear enclosure complex:

> Each site comprises a nucleated cluster of distinctive elongated and irregular curvilinear enclosures, tightly grouped and occasionally overlapping. They contain faint and superimposed traces of small internal features; rectangular pits are also found in association with these enclosures. The perimeter ditches appear to have been recut many times. Although linear features may be present in the vicinity of curvilinear enclosure complexes, the two are not directly related (Stoertz 1997, 55).

Although Cottam is not as complex as many of these examples it can be seen to comprise a single module which is often included within a larger complex. Stoertz identified eleven curvilinear enclosure complexes within the RCHME Wolds survey area, including Butterwick, Rudston, Huggate, Low Caythorpe, Willerby, Garton, West Lutton and East Lutton. Of these most clearly defined examples, two are located on slopes in similar situations to Cottam, while the rest occupy low-lying positions, on the floor of the Great Wold valley. At each of these sites rectangular pits are visible as crop marks and Stoertz

FIGURE 13.2. The distribution of metal-detector finds (marked by crosses) superimposed on crop-mark features of the Cottam B enclosures. The modern field boundaries of Burrow House Farm are to the east.

suggests that these represent Anglo-Saxon *Grubenhäuser*. On this basis she has suggested that the whole class of sites may be post-Roman. To date, rectangular pits have never been identified on aerial photographs of Cottam, but one was excavated in the southern enclosure (cut *3026*: Richards 1999a, 31–3). Although the fill was clean and no dating evidence was recovered, it has been suggested that it was a *Grubenhaus* (D. Powlesland, pers. comm.). Certainly *Grubenhäuser* have been recovered in Middle Anglo-Saxon contexts at West Heslerton and at Wharram Percy (Milne and Richards 1992) and appear to be used quite late in the Anglo-Saxon period, at least in East Yorkshire. It is quite plausible therefore that the curvilinear enclosure complexes of Butterwick type identified by Stoertz are in fact Middle Anglo-Saxon sites (see Leahy, this volume), and may represent a stage in the evolution of rural Anglo-Saxon settlement towards enclosed sites with droveways and individual farmstead enclosures, such as that excavated at Catholme (Losco-Bradley and Wheeler 1984). It would be interesting to know if 'productive' sites from elsewhere in Eastern England were associated with similar enclosures, although the Wolds may be exceptional for the quality of its crop-mark evidence.

A similar site is known from Riby, Lincolnshire (Steedman 1994) where excavation has revealed a number of curvilinear enclosures defined by ditches, here seen as foundation trenches for fences or hedges. At Riby, the enclosures are also linked by droveways but despite domestic refuse being recovered from the enclosures, no post-hole buildings were found, although four possible *Grubenhäuser* were recorded. Occupation appears to have commenced in the sixth or seventh centuries, and to have ceased by the second half of the ninth century.

Excavation at Cottam B has revealed that, as well as various pits and a corn-drier, the southern enclosure includes a number of post-built structures, in use over at least two phases. The settlement debris includes thatch weights and ceramic lamps, which provide further support for the existence of residential accommodation, but would not have been recovered by metal-detector survey alone. In addition, there were several whetstones which had clearly been used in the sharpening of metal tools, possibly including scythes and sickles as well as knives. These may have related to metalworking; there was limited evidence for copper-alloy metalworking, in the form of some tiny fragments of molten lead, but greater quantities of fuel ash slag, as might be associated with a smithy. There was also a weathered female skull in a pit, sealed by a layer including a coin of Æthelberht of Wessex, 858–62. The pit also acted as a trap for frogs and voles and probably dates to the abandonment of the enclosure, which is therefore placed in the late ninth century. It seems unlikely that the skull would have been left lying in a pit while adjacent buildings were occupied. I have suggested that it may represent the victim of an execution killing of a type investigated by Andrew Reynolds (1998a). Kevin Leahy (this volume) has noted the possible judicial function attached to some 'productive' sites, specifically Melton.

At that stage settlement at Cottam shifts to the north where, although it was invisible as crop marks, magnetometer survey revealed a series of sub-rectangular farm enclosures, with a massive entrance way with bank and ditch, and possible gatehouse. By the tenth century the settlement form appears to have evolved to match the Catholme model more closely (Fig. 13.3). The gatehouse reminds one of the

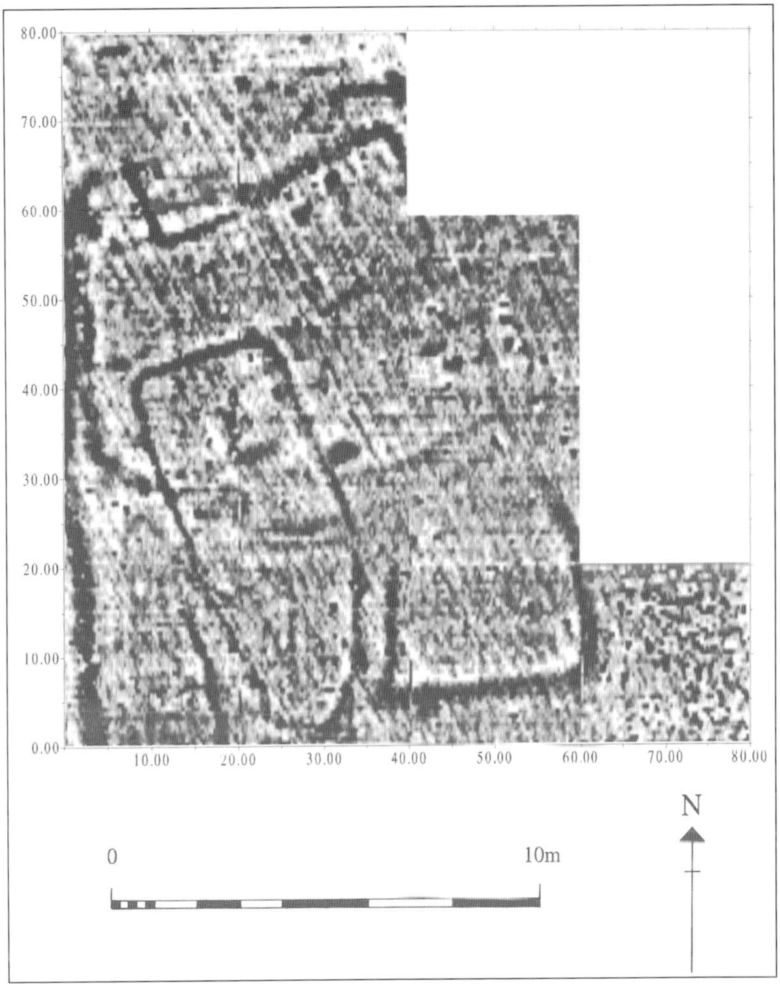

FIGURE 13.3. The Anglo-Scandinavian farmstead at Cottam B, seen as a magnetometer plot. The entrance is at the south with enclosures on either side of the trackway.

need, recorded by Archbishop Wulfstan of York in an eleventh-century text, for a thegn to possess a *burh-geat* (Williams 1992, 225–7).

This settlement shift and the replacement of the Anglian enclosure by an Anglo-Scandinavian enclosure is reflected in the distribution of pottery recovered by fieldwalking. All the Torksey ware, which is introduced in the late ninth and early tenth centuries, is found in the northern area.

The metal-detector evidence shows the same pattern. Objects datable to the eighth and ninth century are predominantly, but not exclusively, found in the southern group, while those of the later ninth and tenth century are predominantly but not exclusively in the northern group (Fig. 13.4). Most of the stycas were also found in the southern group; this would also be consistent with a settlement shift to the north as coin usage on rural sites in Northumbria is believed to decrease in

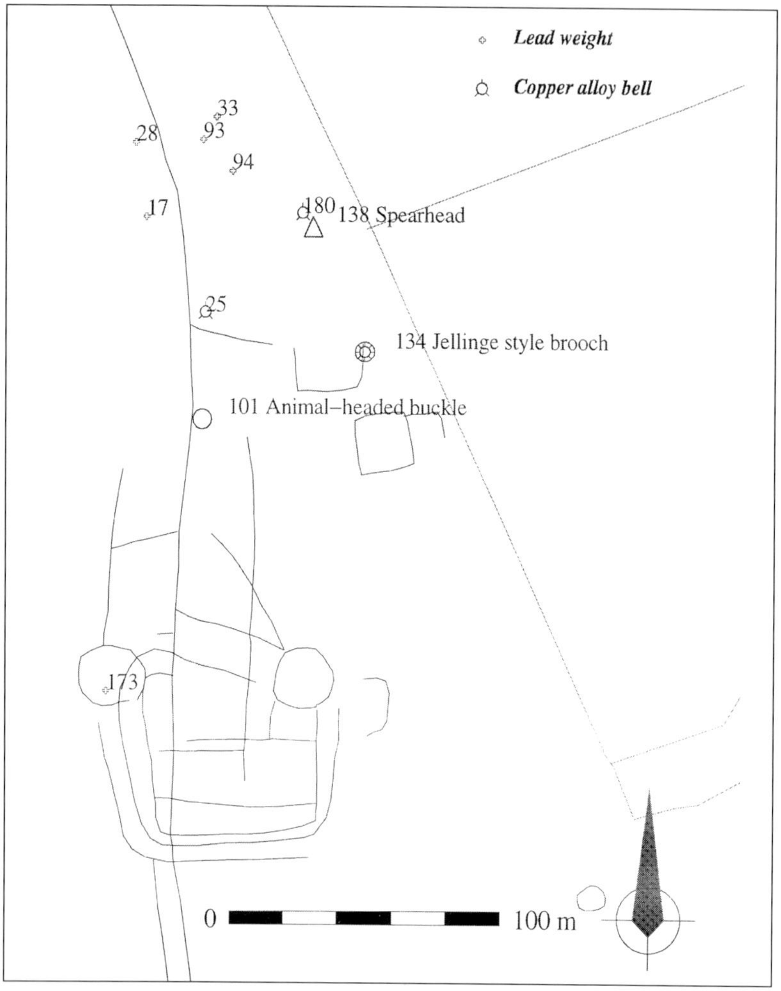

FIGURE 13.4.
The distribution of lead weights, Norse bells, and other objects attributed to the tenth century, superimposed on the crop-mark enclosure and the suggested northward settlement shift.

the tenth century (Blackburn 1993b). The lead weights were originally published as spindle whorls (Haldenby 1990, 59; 1992, 36) but should now be seen as weights, of a type recovered from Dublin (P. Wallace, pers. comm.). Their distribution is focused entirely upon the northern enclosures, also reflecting the reversion to a barter economy. Some artefact types, such as the dress pins, appear to be chronologically undifferentiated, each type occurring in both the south and north enclosure areas. When other categories of find are grouped by type, interesting differences in distribution begin to emerge, reinforcing the value of using locational information for plough zone finds in order to develop artefact typologies.

The strap-ends fall into two broad categories. These groups can be described as zoomorphic (those employing animal motifs, including Trewhiddle-style strap-ends), and geometric (those not employing

FIGURE 13.5.
The distribution of strap-ends. While zoomorphic types are found in both groups, the geometric forms are predominately associated with the southern enclosure of Cottam B.

animal motifs). These broad types have been further sub-divided into twenty-one groups by Haldenby (1997; 1998a; 1998b) on the basis of a study of some 400 strap-ends recovered by detectorists. It is apparent from the distribution that, with the exception of a single outlier, the strap-ends with geometric ornament are confined to the area of the south enclosure, while those decorated with zoomorphic ornament are found in both concentrations (Fig. 13.5). The zoomorphic strap-ends with Trewhiddle-style ornament are also found across both areas. This would suggest that geometric types went out of fashion at the end of the ninth century, and were not used in the tenth century. This is at odds with Haldenby's view that the geometric Arc and Step type (his Group 19) is late in the sequence, but it is proposed that the evidence from horizontal stratigraphy from the excavations at Cottam B should lead to a revision of that typology, based as it is on the assumption that the generally lower level of technical accomplishment seen on the Arc and Step type is indicative of a debased and later production date. On the other hand, the presence of both examples of the Animal Mask type (Haldenby Group 13) in the northern group might lend some support to his other proposal that these are an Anglo-Scandinavian type produced in York (Haldenby 1998a, 40). Finally, four of the Cottam strap-ends – each in the southern group – have been recognised as members of a distinctive type which have traces of inlaid silver wire ornament, generally set in rectangular panels. These four are seen as outliers of a distribution which is focussed on East Anglia (Thomas 1996). Their coincidence with the south enclosure at Cottam B supports the ninth-century dating of the type.

The Anglo-Scandinavian site was itself short-lived and abandoned later in the tenth century, in favour of the Medieval villages, represented by deserted Medieval village earthworks at Cottam and Cowlam. The latter is about one kilometre from the Cottam B enclosures, on the other side of the valley. Excavation of the Post-Medieval farmstead at Cowlam by Brewster, prior to its destruction, also yielded some earlier structures associated with Torksey ware (Brewster and Hayfield 1988). Although the site has now been ploughed out, metal-detecting there has yielded exclusively tenth-century and post-Conquest artefacts, in much smaller numbers (D. Haldenby, pers. comm.).

The project as a whole illustrates the value of combining evidence collected by metal-detector users with various forms of remote sensing, including aerial photography and magnetometry and resistivity, alongside targeted excavation. It also demonstrates the potential of combining aerial photographic data from the English Heritage National Mapping Programme with finds spots collected via the Portable Antiquities Scheme.

I have argued that when compared with other Middle Anglo-Saxon sites Cottam is not exceptional (Richards 1999c, 51–2). Although it is difficult to derive accurate figures for the total area of the settlement, it seems reasonable to calculate this based on the total area from which artefacts have been recovered. For excavated sites the artefact density can be based on the density of finds within the excavation trenches. Although some thirty-four strap-ends have been recovered from Cottam B it has to be borne in mind that this is from an area of *c.* 30,000 square metres. The density of strap-ends per square metre is identical to that from the South Manor at Wharram Percy, and actually lower than that at Fishergate (York), Flixborough, and Whitby. Similarly, although there were sixty-three copper-alloy dress pins recovered at Cottam B, the density of these finds is lower than that at Wharram Percy, Fishergate, Flixborough and Whitby. Even the density of ninth-century coins at Cottam is lower than that of the other sites. When one also takes account of the fact that the use of metal-detectors both before and during the excavations at Cottam has led to a higher rate of recovery of small copper-alloy objects than is probably typical, one is forced to conclude that the rate of loss of these objects fits well within the continuum of sites.

These sites therefore represent a range of functions; the use of metal-detectors at some sites artificially inflates the rate of recovery of metal finds. These sites need to be assigned to a hierarchy of settlement types: rural, urban, secular, monastic, trading and farming. A large quantity of metalwork does not by itself denote a special distinctive class of inland trading site, though I am not suggesting that such sites do not exist (*cf.* Naylor 2001; Ulmschneider 2000b).

The role of Cottam

What was the function, therefore, of the 'productive' site at Cottam? The animal bone assemblage reflects both production and consumption. Sheep/goat are the most common species, followed by cattle. The wide range of size of sheep was particularly noted, indicating a breeding population (Richards 1999a, 85). The presence of wool combs indicates that the sheep were being kept for cloth production, as well as for their contribution to diet. Pig, domestic fowl and geese appeared to be very poorly represented, although there is limited evidence for some variety in the diet, including salmon bones, eggshell, and deer bones. The contribution of arable crops to the economy is more difficult to assess, given the poor preservation of botanical remains. Nevertheless, imported quernstones and a corn-drier at least indicate the cultivation and processing of cereal crops.

Some local metalworking may have taken place, and although there is little evidence for iron smelting, pieces of fuel ash slag probably indicate the presence of the smith who would have been required to manufacture and maintain farm implements. A small piece of gold sheeting and a silver ring indicate that Cottam was part of a wider network, and the coins include a non-local Secondary phase sceatta (Naylor 2001, 87). Nonetheless, the balance of evidence suggests that Cottam was not free to import goods from the *wic* sites. All the honestones recovered from this phase of activity are from sandstone available locally in the Wharram area. Similarly there is no evidence for imported pottery, either for foreign imports as seen in York and Flixborough, or for Ipswich ware from the South. This is despite the fact that Cottam's location only fifteen kilometres from the coast and on the surviving Roman road network (see above) might have put it in a good position for traders coming ashore on the east coast and moving around the countryside.

Generally, the artefactual evidence suggests a low level of trade, just as the dietary evidence suggests quite a low level of subsistence. In contrast to the contemporary settlement at Flixborough (Loveluck 1998) Cottam appears distinctly impoverished. This is the same situation as that observed at Wharram Percy, where there was little trickle-down from the thriving *wic* site in York (Richards 2000). At this stage Cottam and Wharram Percy may both have been excluded from direct contact with this developing market.

I have suggested that one possible explanation for this is that Cottam was itself under royal control during the Anglian period (Richards 1999a, 91–2). Chris Loveluck (1996, 25) has suggested that there was a significant Northumbrian royal centre at Driffield and that there may have been a substantial royal landholding in this part of the Yorkshire Wolds. Naylor (2001, 88) suggests that the coin finds at Cottam and Kilham may be related to trade and exchange taking place through that estate, in which case one would assume that such trade was controlled from the centre.

Conclusion

In summary, therefore, we can say a bit more in answer to the questions posed at the start of this volume. In the case of Cottam, excavation of this particular 'productive' site has demonstrated that it actually represents a sequence of settlements, whose role and social context changes through time. At Cottam B there certainly is settlement activity, including farming, but possibly as part of a royal estate. Trading may have taken place, and this must explain the context of the metal finds, but it was generally of a local nature. That activity is associated with monetary exchange, at least in the eighth and ninth centuries, but not in the tenth century when there is reversion to a barter economy. Activity was initially under elite control, possibly from a royal vill at Driffield, but the occupants broke free from this in the Anglo-Scandinavian phase.

By using the evidence of 'productive' sites provided by the controlled use of metal-detectors we can certainly advance our knowledge of the Anglo-Saxon period, and of the range of sites, but only if we break away from simplistic classifications, and assess the metalwork alongside other forms of archaeological evidence.

III

Markets and Settlements on the Early Medieval Continent

CHAPTER 14

Markets and Fairs in Norway and Sweden Between the Eighth and Sixteenth Centuries

Peter Sawyer

There is very little written evidence for fairs or markets in Norway and Sweden before the thirteenth century, and there are few references to them being held in particular places before about 1400. Information about tenth-century trade in Icelandic sagas is sometimes treated as reliable evidence although there is no reason to believe that the authors, writing in the thirteenth century, relied on well-remembered traditions. They were, rather, elaborating their accounts of the distant past with details drawn from what they knew about trade in their own time. There are, however, two texts written in the late ninth century that give valuable information about trade in Scandinavia; the *Vita Anskarii*, and the accounts of voyages by Ohthere and Wulfstan that were included in the Old English translation of Orosius' *Historiarum adversum Paganos* that was made for King Alfred (Lund 1984).

The sparsity of historical evidence means that our knowledge of trade and trading places in Scandinavia depends largely on archaeological investigations which have not only given substance to the references to trading places named in the texts but also identified many others, large and small, that are not. Archaeological evidence also shows that some goods were transported great distances within Scandinavia before and during the Viking Age. In Norway, for example, different types of whetstones have been found far from their sources (Resi 1987), while iron from Norway and soap stone from Norway or Sweden has been found in Denmark. Similarly quernstones from the Eifel region that were imported through Ribe and Hedeby in the eighth and ninth centuries, were widely distributed; fragments have been found in almost all the contemporary Danish settlements that have been excavated (Roesdahl 1982, 88–91). Then, as later, such things, as well as ornaments, tools, weapons, combs and other craft products were distributed in various ways; by peddlers, itinerant craftsmen, by farmers, landowners and traders, but the fairs and trading places discussed here had an important role in the process (Fig. 14.1).

Place-names are a less rewarding guide to early trading places. Many were called in Old Norse *kaupang(r)*, which has become *köping* in modern Swedish and *købing* in Danish. There is general agreement that it was a loan from the Old English noun *ciping*, which can mean 'market', and many scholars think that it was borrowed fairly early in the Viking Age (Schmidt 2000, 86–8). That is, however, most unlikely. It was rare as a place-name in England and only occurs twice in Domesday Book, at Chipping and Chippindale in Lancashire, names

FIGURE 14.1.
Markets and fairs in Norway and Sweden mentioned in the text.

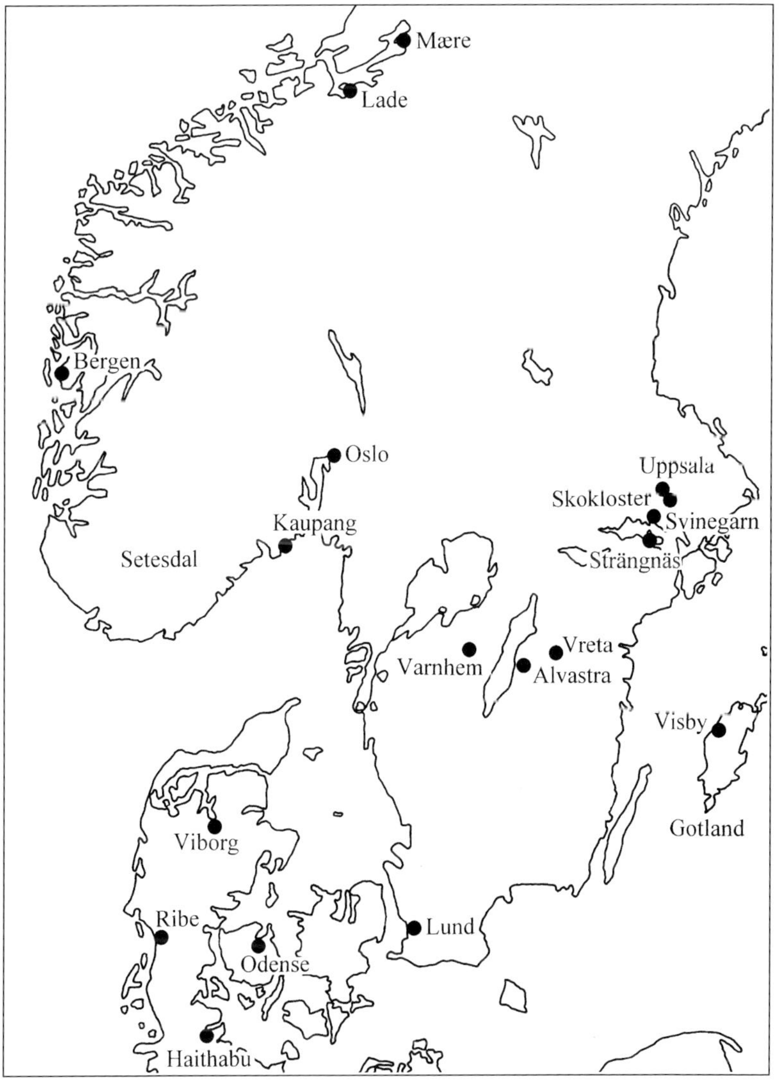

such as Chipping Camden or Chipping Norton being later (Harmer 1950, 335 n. 2). Old English *ciping* could also mean 'market dues' owed from places that were variously called *tun, port* or *burh* (*ibid.*, 342–4). Kaupang names in Scandinavia are therefore probably no older than the eleventh century and cannot be used to identify earlier trading places. It is worth noting that the trading place in south Norway that Ohthere visited is now called Kaupang, but that name was first recorded in 1401 (Schmidt 2000, 91 n. 16): in the Old English text it is called *Sciringes heal.*

Numerous Scandinavian place-names mean that they were suitable places for loading boats. A well-known example is Lade, meaning 'landing-' or 'loading-place', across the River Nid from the site of the Medieval city of Trondheim. In Norway there are several places called Laberg or Lahelle, names that are closely related to Lade, and in Denmark there are two places called Ladby (Sandnes and Stemshaug 1980, 198; Dalberg and Sørensen 1979, 177–9). Some of these may have been trading places but most probably served one or more neighbouring farms. Such names are, therefore, little help in locating early markets.

By combining the various strands of evidence, it is possible to show that there were many places throughout Scandinavia where annual fairs were held at which native inhabitants could exchange their produce. Some of them, especially in Norway and Sweden, were held in winter when travel was easier than at other times of the year. The main other season for annual fairs was the autumn, when the summer produce could be exchanged (*Kulturhistorisk Leksikon*, xi, cols 445–53; Staf 1933). Most of these fairs continued to be held in or near later towns that owed their existence, in part, to the fairs. Many towns probably developed on, or very close to, the site of an earlier assembly and its fair, but some apparently took over fairs that had been held some distance away.

For example, Lund began to develop *c.* 990, the date of its earliest church and churchyard. However, there are reasons to think that it was in some respects the successor of an Iron-Age centre at Uppåkra, five kilometres to the south, where abundant evidence has been found of trading and workshops until the mid tenth century (Hårdh 2000). Traces of three burial mounds that were surrounded by relatively undisturbed areas suggest that these had some religious significance. As one of the fairs later held in Lund was called the 'Three Mounds Fair' it appears that it had been transferred from Uppåkra (Andrén 1998). There is no doubt that many fairs had ancient roots. Some were held in places with names showing that they had been pagan cult centres, for example, the name of the Danish episcopal city of

Viborg meant 'hill(s) by a *vi*', that is, a temple or place of worship. Viborg not only had an important fair in January but was also the place in which Jutlanders chose, or recognized kings (Jørgensen 1982, 142). Similarly, the cathedral city of Odense on the Danish island of Fyn first appeared in 988 in the Latinized form *Othenesuuigensem* meaning 'Odin's *vi*' (Hald 1963).

These fairs were originally held in connection with assemblies in which local communities regulated their own affairs. These assemblies had religious, political and legal functions, as well as providing opportunities for people to buy and sell. Some fairs were held in connection with festivals celebrated at cult sites that were not linked with such assemblies. A well-documented Swedish example was held at a spring at Svinegarn, near Enköping in Uppland. Before the Reformation, votive offerings were made at the spring and to the nearby church by people of both high and low status (Ahnlund 1922). In Denmark over thirty similar fairs were held at springs, and some of them survived until quite recently (Christensen 1933, 186–7).

After the acceptance of Christianity most of these assemblies and fairs were 'converted' and linked with Christian festivals. One exception was the winter fair held at Uppsala, called Distingen 'the *ting* of the Díser [goddesses]'. Throughout the Middle Ages it was held when the first new moon after midwinter was full (*Kulturhistorisk Leksikon*, iii, cols 112–5). Its date could therefore be worked out by all who attended it, including non-Christian trappers and traders from the far north who would know from experience when to set out. At least two others were based on the lunar calendar. Winter fairs held in Strängnäs in eastern Sweden and in Oslo were not linked with Christian festivals, but were held in the first week of Lent when, as with Distingen, the moon was growing (*Kulturhistorisk Leksikon*, xv, cols 25–7; Koht 1921, 25–8). It was also in the winter that the Saami brought their furs, skins, feathers and other produce to landing places on the Norwegian coast in or near their winter camps to render as tribute, of the kind received by Ohthere, or to exchange for metalwork and other produce supplied by the Scandinavians.

There were many other places in which the produce of different regions was exchanged. Some were inland. A good example is a site in the valley of Setesdal in south Norway which received imports from all directions in the Viking period. It seems likely that there were seasonal fairs then much like those reported in the nineteenth century, when men travelled to Setesdal from the coast to exchange salt, cloth, leather and fish for hides and skins (Larsen 1980). Many more were on coasts. In Gotland, for example, where many farms had their own landing places, there were at least six harbours that seem to have served several farms, and where trade was done and at which craftsmen worked throughout the Viking Age (Carlsson 1991). Such a concentration was exceptional, but there is no doubt that there were many along all Scandinavian coasts. Some are shown to have been operating even before the ninth century by the fact that, thanks to the land uplift since the Ice Age, the traces left by traders and craftsmen have been found several metres above the present sea level. The town of Bergen was established in the eleventh century close to a site of this kind, which was soon covered by the expanding settlement (Helle 1985, 8–9).

Towns had to have markets in which the inhabitants could buy provisions, clothing and tools. From the thirteenth century, and probably earlier, efforts were made to protect these urban markets from the competition of traditional rural markets nearby. By the twelfth century, the network of towns with markets covered most of the Danish kingdom, but in other parts of Scandinavia there were few towns, and large areas had no easy access to urban markets. It is therefore unsurprising that in many parts of Scandinavia unlicensed rural markets continued to flourish despite repeated prohibitions. They clearly served a useful purpose and efforts to abolish or transfer them elsewhere met with resistance: as late as 1775 there were at least 150 such rural fairs throughout Sweden (Staf 1933).

Some of these rural markets were associated with churches. In 1488, illegal markets held at the Cistercian nunnery of Skokloster and at a church called *Ness* were ordered to close (Sawyer 1986, 69). Christian churches that had replaced pagan cult centres continued to provide opportunities for buying and selling, although there is little direct evidence of Sunday trading in Scandinavia as there is in England. Swedish market charters beginning in the late thirteenth century are concerned only with weekday markets (*Kulturhistorisk Leksikon*, xviii, col. 480), but the thirteenth century law of Gotland provided for the sale on Sundays of cheese, butter, fish, fowls and meat, but not flour, seeds or other goods (Sawyer, 1986, 71). In 1531 Gustav Vasa complained that illegal fairs were becoming so frequent that there would soon be one held at every church festival (*ibid.*). We may suspect that fairs were often held on church patronal festivals and that unlicensed markets were commonly held on Sundays long before the sixteenth century.

Certainly, Medieval coins found in Scandinavian churches support the idea that they were places in which trading took place. Excluding hoards that were deliberately concealed, larger concentrations of Medieval coins have been found in the excavation of churches than in farms, castles or even town sites. In some churches very large numbers of coins have been found. The Cistercian monastery of Alvastra in

Östergötland is the extreme case, with 1,380 coins of the sixteenth century or earlier scattered in the church itself, in the chapter house and in other abbey buildings and grounds (Malmer 1981). Large numbers of Medieval coins have also been found in other monasteries, for example Vreta and Varnhem (both Cistercian), and in Birgitta's foundation, Vadstena, as well as in the cathedral church of Linköping. Smaller concentrations have been found in many less important churches. The Swedish evidence has been systematically studied by Henrik Klackenberg (1992), who has analysed some 7,000 Medieval coins that have been found in 200 rural churches in Sweden. In 1986 I suggested that although some may have come from disturbed graves the most natural explanation for these coin finds is that churches were used for buying and selling as well as for worship. Churches not only offered the best opportunities for regular meetings, they also provided sheltered space that was badly needed for much of the year (Sawyer 1986, 71). Klackenberg objected that as most coins have been found at the east end of churches, around the altars, they are more likely to have been lost when offerings were made. In many churches, however, coins have been found away from the altar. Svanhild Sortlind, of the Archaeological Institute in Trondheim, has drawn my attention to the excavation of Mære church, at the head of Trondheim Fjord, where 575 coins from the eleventh to the nineteenth centuries have been found; 313 of them were in the nave. The interpretation of such evidence is complicated by the fact that there were many burials in the nave from the earliest phase of the church (Lidén 1970). She has also pointed out that the churches in Trondheim have yielded remarkably few coins. That may be, in part, because they had better paving than most rural churches, but it may also be because in towns there were other opportunities to buy and sell than in the countryside.

Most of the fairs and markets discussed here were places in which natives could exchange their surpluses. Scandinavia was, however, not a closed economy. Long before the Viking period it was a source of exotic luxuries, especially furs, that were exported to the Mediterranean and western Europe. In return, Scandinavians obtained fine metalwork, jewellery, glassware and other high quality goods that have been found in burials. It was in the eighth century that the dramatic development of commerce across the English Channel and North Sea led to the creation of *emporia* in Scandinavia and beyond, across the Baltic to Staraja Ladoga in North Russia (Clarke and Ambrosiani 1991). These were visited by merchants in the summer and, with the exception of Visby on Gotland, were not associated with traditional cult centres. They were alien institutions and were not self-sufficient. They depended for supplies of raw material, food, and goods for export on the complex network of fairs that had been long established. Later, in the eleventh century, the Scandinavians began to export bulkier produce, timber, skins and, most important of all, dried fish as food in the winter and spring for the rapidly expanding towns of England and neighbouring parts of the Continent (Sawyer and Sawyer 1993, 156–9). Some of these exports may have come directly from the estates of rulers and magnates, but some were certainly gathered through the network of exchanges that had existed for centuries.

CHAPTER 15

Manor and Market at Lake Tissø in the Sixth to Eleventh Centuries: The Danish 'Productive' Sites

Lars Jørgensen

Just a few decades ago the picture of Scandinavian settlement from the Iron Age and Viking Age appeared relatively unsubtle, the known settlements mainly comprising agrarian villages with only a few standing out from this pattern. However, the excavation of Danish settlement sites over the past twenty-five years, especially since the introduction of the metal-detector, is revealing a more complex society with a clear stratification in settlements. It now seems that we can divide Danish settlements from the sixth to eleventh century into seven main groups:

1. *Aristocratic sites* with an unusually high density of buildings and evidence for extensive resource consumption in the form of many metal finds. These include Lejre (Christensen 1991 and 1997), Gudme (Jørgensen 1994; Sørensen 1994a and 1994b), Tissø and Toftegård (Tornbjerg 1998).
2. *Early towns/emporia* from the eighth century and onwards (Hedeby and Ribe: Jensen 1991 and 1993).
3. *Landing/trading places* with trading and craft activities. A large site of this type is Sebbersund in North Jutland (Christensen and Johansen 1992; Birkedahl and Johansen 1993). Small sites are numerous along Roskilde Fjord on Zealand and along the south coast of Sweden (Ulriksen 1994 and 1998).
4. *Specialized production sites* (especially for textiles) like Næs (Møller-Hansen and Høier 2000) and Selsø on Zealand (Sørensen and Ulriksen 1996), and Bejsebakken in North Jutland (unpublished).
5. More *ordinary settlements* with a presumed agrarian basic economy,

but with a clear element of craft activities (Jensen and Watt 1993). Examples are Stentinget in North Jutland (Nielsson 1994) and Boeslunde on Zealand (H. Nielsen 1997).

6. *Ordinary farms and villages* exclusively with crop and animal farming as the main occupation (Hvass 1993; Mikkelsen 1999).

7. *Fortified sites* with a defensive character (refuge forts) or with a definite garrison character (such as Trelleborg, Aggersborg and Fyrkat).

Among the seven settlement types there are great differences in the material culture, and types 1–5 can all be termed as 'metal-rich' or 'productive' sites. Aristocratic sites with a very large number of high-quality finds are in a class by themselves, while the decidedly primary producers, the agrarian settlements, are at the bottom of the scale in the quantity and quality of finds. Of crucial importance in the identification of this settlement hierarchy is the content of material culture in combination with settlement structure from individual sites. The finds testify to the occupants' status, resource consumption, activities and economy. Since 1980 many of the Danish settlement areas have been regularly searched with metal-detectors, and this has resulted in a large body of finds which, via local museums, has been registered at the National Museum of Denmark.

Because there has been no tradition for such widespread use of metal-detectors in Norway, Sweden and Germany, Denmark holds a prominent position in the collection, registration and partly the interpretation of finds from such 'productive' sites. Indeed, only within the last few years have detector surveys been carried out at a few Swedish and Norwegian sites, and then often with the aid of Danish detector users (for example at Uppåkra in Scania and Kaupang in South Norway). Finally, and of importance, the Danish sites have been given a high priority in rescue excavations. The number of excavated 'productive' sites is therefore higher in Denmark than in the neighbouring countries.

The first generation of 'productive' sites

The great central site at Gudme, along with the related trading place at Lundeborg are among the earliest aristocratic trading and production centres in southern Scandinavia (Jørgensen 1994; Sørensen 1994a and b; Thomsen 1994) (Fig. 15.1). The settlement at Gudme covered one sq. km. and in the period 200–600 consisted of up to fifty farms. Some 7,000 metal objects have been found in the large settlement area dating to the period 200–1100 and among the many finds are six

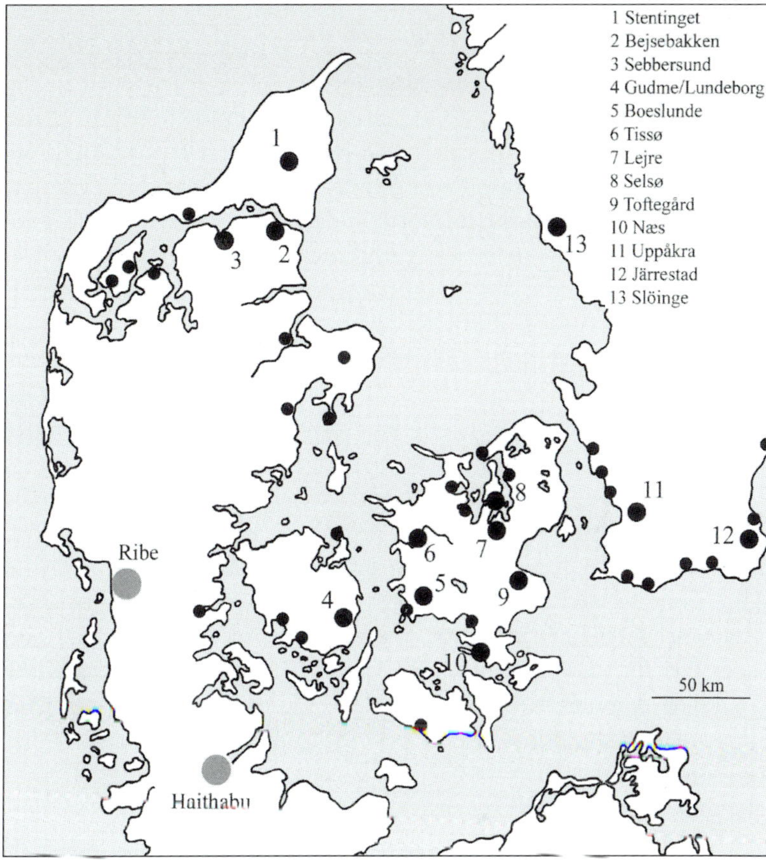

FIGURE 15.1.
The distribution of major 'productive' sites in Denmark and southern Sweden. Sites mentioned in the text are numbered.

gold hoards and five silver hoards from the fourth to sixth century period. A special feature of Gudme is that a large number of the farms belonged to craftsmen, on which goldsmiths and silversmiths worked and at which bronze casting was carried out. Elsewhere in the settlement, a presumed aristocratic residence of the fourth to fifth century has been demonstrated (Sørensen 1994b). The main building was an imposing hall of almost 500 sq. m., the largest so far found from this period in Scandinavia. Between the third and sixth centuries Gudme was divided into craftworking and elite areas, and while there was a decline from the close of the sixth century, importantly the trading and workshop activities continued up to and including the Viking Age. The picture from Gudme, showing a very long continuity of trading and production activities, can be seen at several other early centres such as Sorte Muld on Bornholm in the Baltic (Watt 1991), Boeslunde in Zealand (H. Nielsen 1997) and Uppåkra in Scania (Hårdh 2000).

The second generation of 'productive' sites

In southern Scandinavia, something appears to have happened in the sixth/seventh century to the Gudme-type site. Finds testify to a rise in the number of what we call 'metal-rich sites' and at the same time the differentiation increases as the sites begin to show specialization. As an example, Stentinget in North Jutland was a relatively ordinary settlement consisting of farms, with clear traces of craft production in the period from the sixth century up to and including the eleventh century (Nielsson 1994). However, while excavations have shown that the farm units are relatively unexceptional, the number of metal objects is far higher than at ordinary agrarian sites, including many brooches, fine Carolingian belt mounts of gilded silver, weights, ingots of bronze and lead.

On the Zealand site at Boeslunde there is a fairly large complex of smaller settlement areas, more or less all of which have metalwork finds testifying to occupation between the sixth and eleventh centuries (H. Nielsen 1997). Finds include brooches, smelted lead, weights, silver fragments, fragments of scales, a lead model for ring brooches and patrix dies for stamping sheet gold figures. Previous excavations of the Boeslunde complex have demonstrated only ordinary farm units but other finds, in the form of rich Viking Age cavalry graves, show that an aristocracy had then settled in the area.

A quite different type of settlement consists of *specialized production sites* which have only been recognised within the past few years. As an example an extensive site has just been excavated near the city of

FIGURE 15.2. Plan of the specialized production site at Næs on Zealand (after Møller-Hansen and Høier 2000, redrawn).

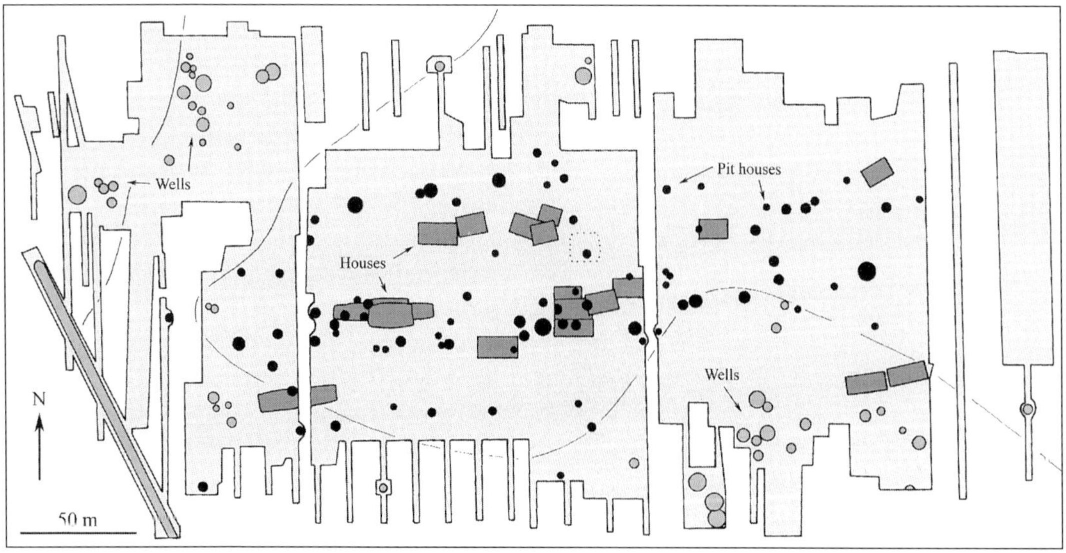

Ålborg, called Bejsebakken in North Jutland (unpublished). Although only a few large houses were found, there were no fewer than 350 pit-houses, the finds reflecting the presence of many people in the period AD 500/600–1000. It is clear, however, that this was not an actual residential settlement. Instead, the finds – including many loom-weights and spindle-whorls from the pit-houses – suggest extensive textile production, an activity normally associated with those types of structure.

A similar site investigated recently at Næs in Zealand is smaller but nevertheless very interesting (Møller-Hansen and Høier 2000) (Fig. 15.2). About twenty buildings have been found, four of them longhouses, dating to the period from the late seventh to early ninth century. In the same area seventy pit-houses of contemporary date were excavated, almost all containing loom weights and spindle whorls, showing that they probably functioned as weaving huts. The site has however yielded a new, exciting type of feature. In the lowest-lying areas of the site fifty-seven wickerwork wells were found, used primarily for retting flax (i.e. soaking it to loosen it from the woody tissue), in several of which were found bunches of flax stems. The retting of flax required frequent changes of water, and to facilitate this a 150m long channel had been laid out. By blocking this canal the wells could be flooded and the water changed. The manufacture of linen was, however, not the only type of production at the site although it clearly played a major role. In several wells antlers were also found, which had been soaked with a view to being further worked into, among other things, combs. The site at Næs also exhibits traces of a little metalworking and/or trade, in the form of weights and a scale pan.

The aristocratic sites of the sixth to eleventh century

Aristocratic sites make up the last group with trading and production activities. On Zealand there are Tissø, Lejre and Toftegård while in southern Sweden there is the new, unpublished, site of Järrestad on the east coast of Scania and Slöinge on the west coast of Halland (Lundqvist 1997). Curiously, no sites of this type can be demonstrated in West Denmark.

Toftegård

The residential complex at Toftegård on Zealand was identified in 1995, and since then *c.* 30,000 sq. m. have been excavated and about ninety buildings identified (Tornbjerg 1998). The complex was established at the beginning of the seventh century and was abandoned in the tenth century. It can be divided into a magnate's central residence covering *c.* 10,000 sq. m., with five large hall buildings (*c.* 10 × 37–40m) (Fig. 15.3) adjacent to which is an enclosed special area containing a sequence of three smaller houses. Outside the hall area a more scattered, ordinary farm complex was found, consisting of two to three contemporary farms with small farmhouses, outhouses and pit-houses. About 3,000 finds were recovered, including many gilded silver and bronze mountings and jewellery, in addition to

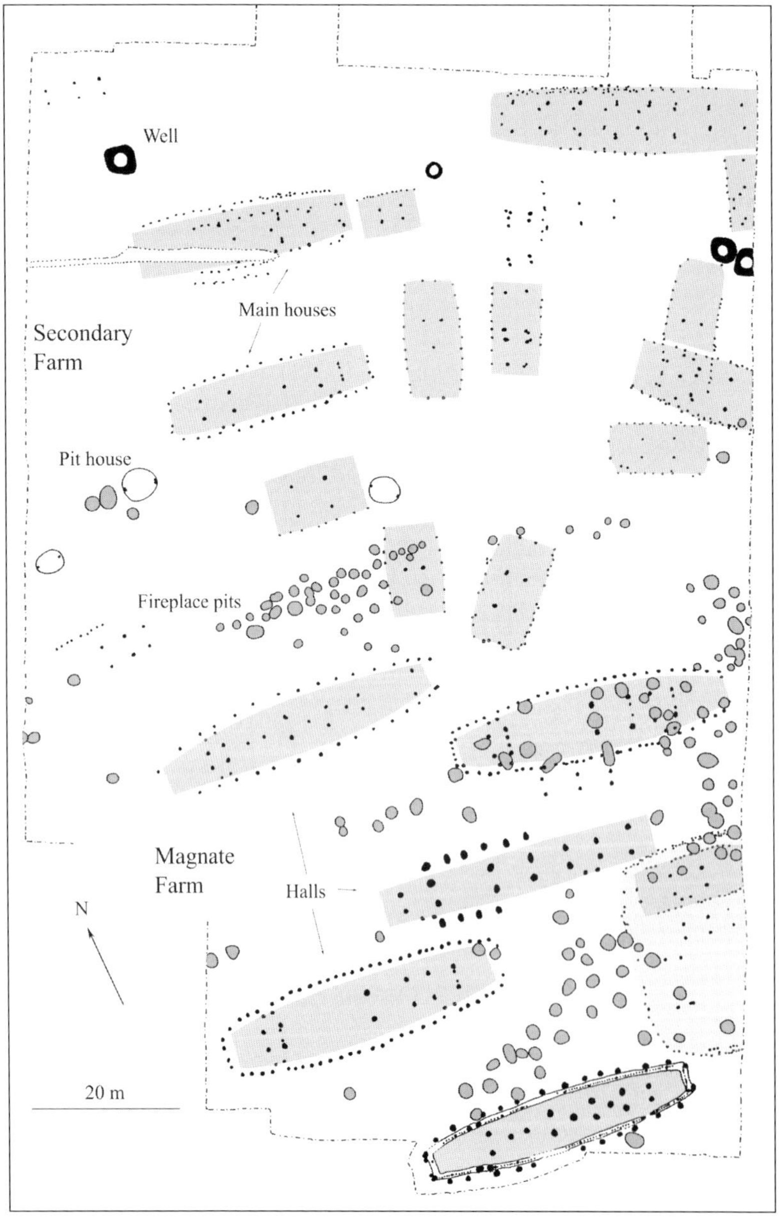

FIGURE 15.3.
Plan of the Toftegård complex near Køge. In the southern part is the central manor area with five halls from the seventh to tenth centuries and many fireplace pits. In the eastern part of this area is a fenced-in special area with a small building. The few finds in this area show that it was kept clean, unlike the rest of the complex. The picture here recalls the contemporary manor complex at Tissø. North of the halls and fireplace pits is situated one of the more ordinary farms with minor main houses, economy buildings and pit houses (after Tornbjerg 1998, redrawn).

coins, weights, bars of silver and bronze, moulds, riding equipment, imported jewellery, mountings and glass of Carolingian and Anglo-Saxon origin.

The distribution of finds at Toftegård is striking because all the high-status objects were concentrated in the hall area of the main residence, for instance all the gold-foil figures, Frankish drinking glasses, weapons and riding equipment. At Toftegård one can thus observe clear differences in status between the features and finds at the large residence, and the ordinary farm features of the site. Just as the internal hierarchy is clear at Toftegård, a similar distinction can be observed at the other two aristocratic sites, Tissø and Lejre. In contrast to the other two sites, workshop activities (bronze casting and forging) have been demonstrated in the Toftegård hall area, a difference which might indicate stratification at the aristocratic level.

Lejre

The excavated building complex in Lejre near Roskilde in Zealand must clearly be regarded as one of our largest manors (Christensen 1991 and 1997). The complex has not yet been fully excavated, but it is still possible to get some impression of its structure (Fig. 15.4). The farm complex appears to have covered an enclosed area of about 40,000 sq. m., and at present traces of about fifty houses have been excavated, which date between the seventh to tenth centuries. One of Denmark's finest Viking Age silver hoards, including four silver bowls, was found in the mid nineteenth century in the area just west of the settlement.

The settlement extends over *c.* 200,000 sq. m., of which *c.* 15,000 sq. m. have been excavated, and can be divided up into two functional areas, one for workshops, the other residential. Among the houses are four large halls of 48 × 11.5m (Fig. 15.5), and four smaller ones of 42 × 6m. Approximately 4,000 smallfinds have been recovered, including high quality objects which were clearly reserved for the elite, such as gilt jewellery, casket fittings, coins, weights, bars of silver and bronze, moulds, riding equipment, imported jewellery, mountings and glass of Carolingian and Anglo-Saxon origin. To these prestige items can be added many tools and implements.

Excavations in the residential area have led to surprising results, since it has been possible to locate several large halls, and from the seventh century until the tenth century the settlement remained at the same place. This presumed royal seat also had a successor from the late tenth/early eleventh century in the area immediately to the north (Fig. 15.4), trial trenches revealing a very large, fenced-in complex of *c.* 200 × 200m in this area. This area promises information about settlement in the important transitional phase, primarily the eleventh century, when Lejre changed its status from a heathen royal complex with great halls, burial mounds and ship settings, to a Medieval magnate's seat.

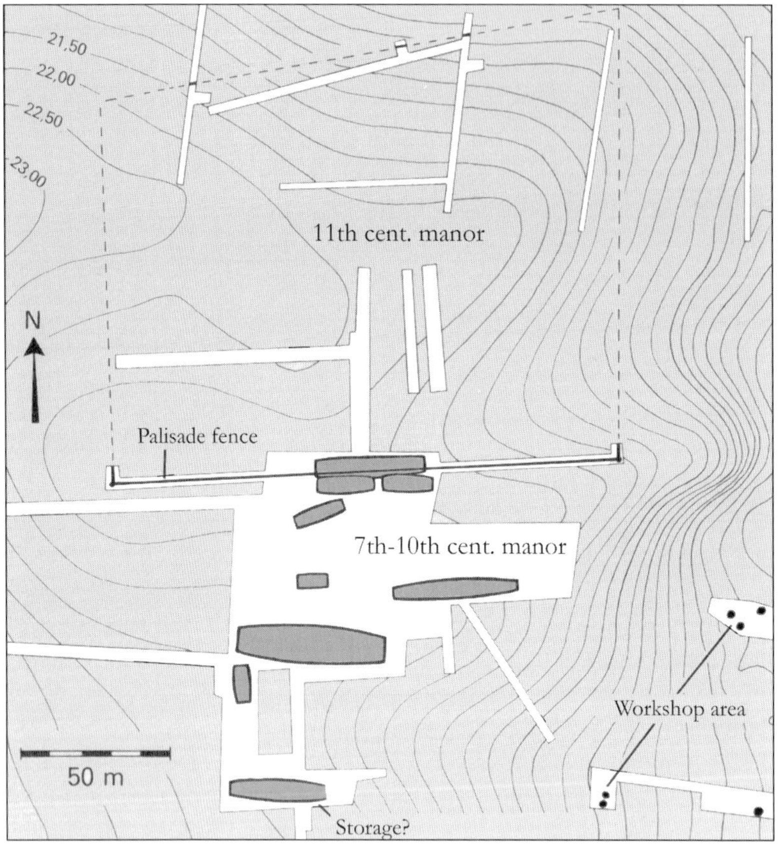

FIGURE 15.4.
The manor complex from the seventh to tenth centuries at Lejre with the residential area and workshop area to the east. North of this earlier residence an impressive complex from the eleventh century has been found, covering an area of about 40,000 square metres.

FIGURE 15.5.
Plan of one of the great halls in Lejre. The floor area is *c.*500 sq. m., the monumental architecture of the hall an active signal of power and status (after Christensen 1997, redrawn).

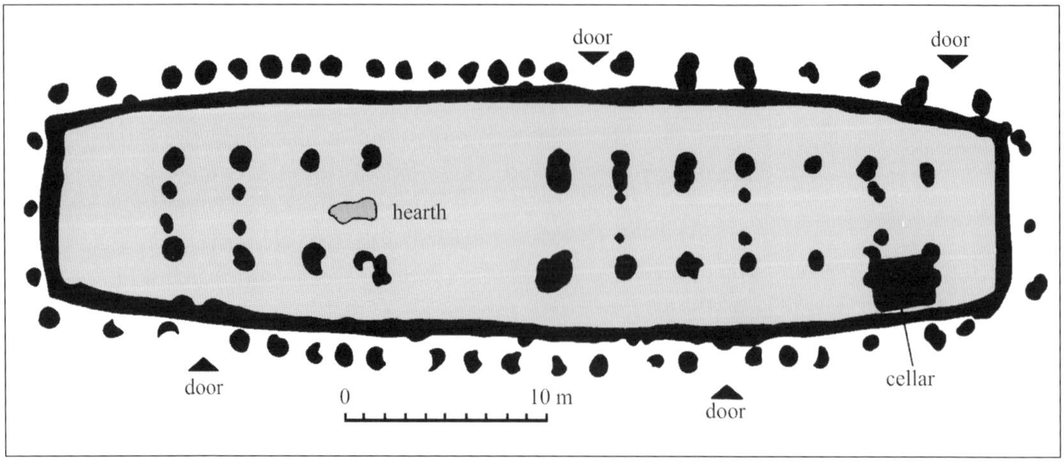

Manor and market at Lake Tissø

The best elucidated of the magnates' complexes is a new site on the west bank of Lake Tissø in West Zealand, situated some seven kilometres from the coast. Via the River Halleby Å, it would have been possible to sail even fairly large ships from the sea into the lake. Several other waterways run into the lake and the settlement had a highly strategic position with much of the population in the West Zealand area being able to sail to Tissø. The settlement extended along the whole west bank of the lake over a distance of about one and a half kilometres and a width of 200–300m, covering an area of about 500,000 sq. m. (Fig. 15.6).

The site has long yielded fine archaeological finds. In the nineteenth century weapons and other objects were found in the lakebed off the settlement when the lake was lowered to counteract flooding of the low-lying areas and subsequent drainage of the former bank zone has regularly revealed tools, dress ornaments and especially weapons. Today we have some fifty objects from the lake itself – swords, axes and lances – the great majority of which are from the Viking Age. In this connection we should dwell a little on the name of the lake, *Tissø*, which actually means 'Tir' or 'Tyr's lake'. Tir/Tyr was one of the Viking war gods, and it is tempting to interpret these lake finds as offerings to the god. The objects found so far show that this votive tradition goes back at least to around 600, close to the time of the foundation of the settlement. However, the most spectacular find from the site was made in 1977, when a local farmer found a tenth-century gold neck ring weighing 1.8 kilos. The field in which the ring was found was investigated in an excavation in 1996, demonstrating the presence of extensive workshop activities in the form of forging and bronze casting.

In 1979, the graves of two executed men were found at the crossing over the River Halleby Å, which have been radiocarbon-dated to *c.* 1030–40 – a date very close to the end of the whole settlement. In the same excavation, remains were found of a fifty metre long wooden bridge over Halleby Å, also datable to the Viking Age.

The finds

Archaeological research at Tissø began in 1975 when the National Museum started the first metal-detector surveys, metal smallfinds confirming the existence of a large settlement area. Around 1993, three local amateur archaeologists began a systematic metal-detectors survey along the lakeshore. Cooperation was quickly established and from the start they have marked their finds on a map at a scale of 1:1000.

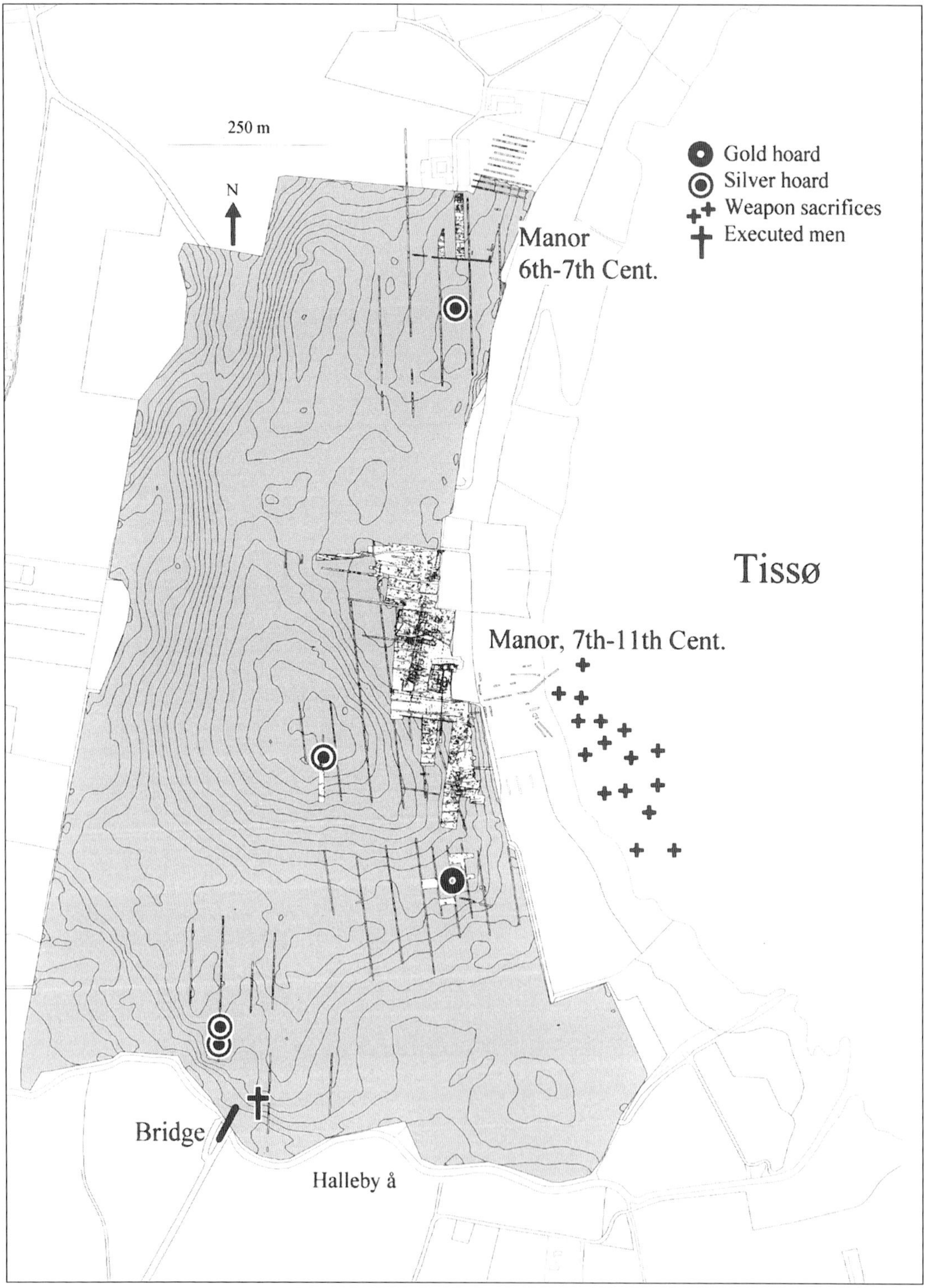
250 m
N
Gold hoard
Silver hoard
Weapon sacrifices
Executed men
Manor
6th-7th Cent.
Tissø
Manor, 7th-11th Cent.
Bridge
Halleby å

Fig. 15.7 shows the distribution of all the *c.* 10,000 mapped metal finds recovered by both the local detectorists and by the National Museum in connection with the excavations which have been conducted at Tissø every year since 1995. Their distribution appears to reflect the actual extent of settlement quite accurately and comprises a wide variety of material. About 75 percent of the objects are iron, including nails and rivets, but among the other finds are about 400 costume brooches, which show the functional lifetime of the site. The oldest are small equal-armed brooches from the mid sixth century while the numerous fibulae show that the settlement gradually began

FIGURE 15.6 (*opposite*). Map showing the archaeological status of the Tissø area in the Viking Period. Just north of the bridge, extensive traces of craft activities have been found. The workshop area stretched along the whole coast to the manor in use between the seventh and the eleventh centuries, a distance of about 700m, covering an area of about 150,000 sq. m. To the north of the manor, a market area continued some 600m further north along the coast. Here too there are clear traces of workshop activities, albeit not to the same extent as south of the manor. In the north the first manor, dating from the sixth to seventh centuries, was excavated in autumn 2002. (see Postscript).

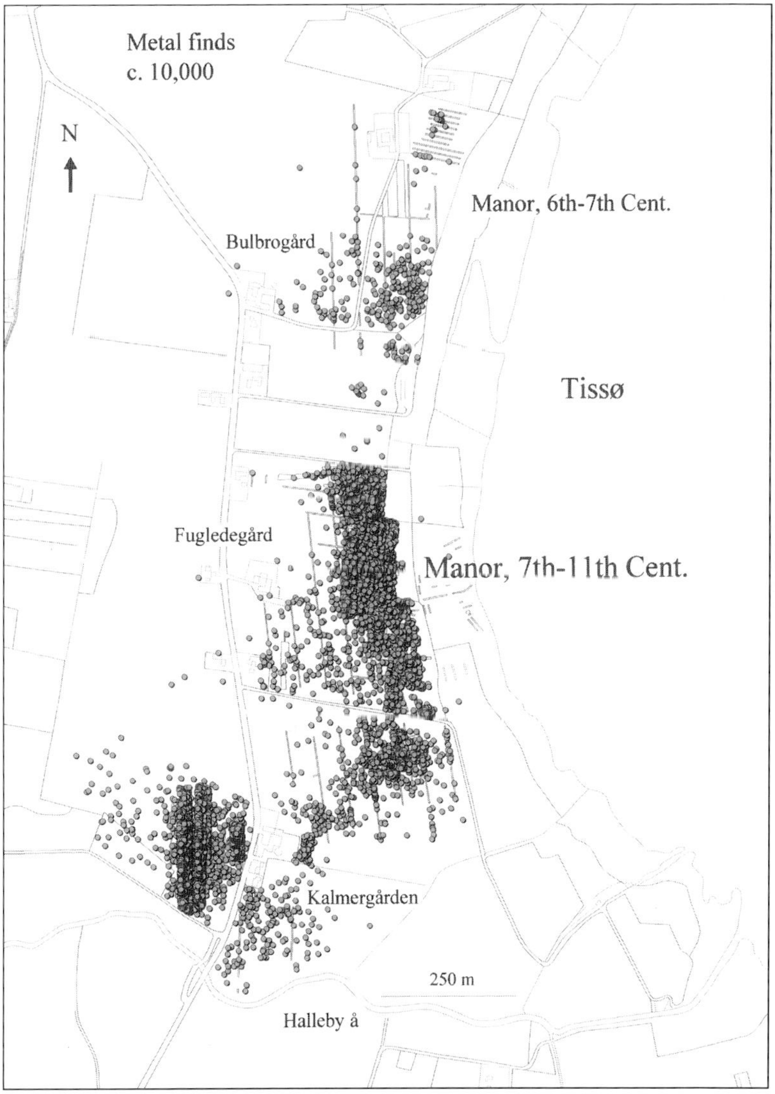

FIGURE 15.7. The distribution of *c.*10,000 finds made at Tissø in the metal-detector surveys and archaeological excavations.

at some time in the sixth century before ending sometime in the first half of the eleventh century.

The distribution of small sixth century equal-armed brooches shows a clear concentration just south of the manor in use in the sixth and seventh centuries which, with its limited distribution, suggests that activity originally began in this area (Fig. 15.8, crosses). The distribution of the so-called 'beaked' brooches dating from around 600 is quite different, these brooches being found across the whole site, indicating that the full settlement area was in operation from the beginning of

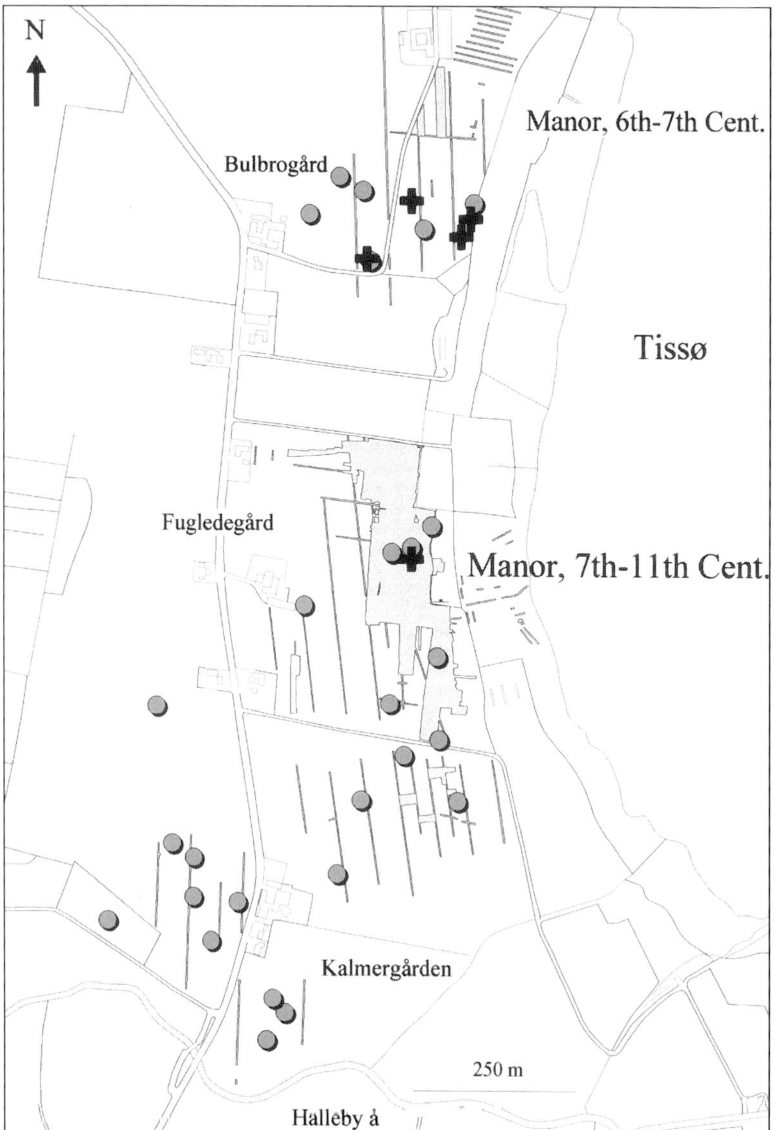

FIGURE 15.8 (*left*). Distribution map showing the equal-armed brooches from the middle of the sixth century (cross) and beaked brooches (circle) from *c.* 600.

FIGURE 15.9 (*opposite*). Tissø: the excavated area with the manor, dating from the seventh to eleventh centuries, and adjacent market. Horizontal grey strips are the traces of a medieval ridge-and-furrow field system, laid out after the abandonment of the settlement. The scattered small round features are pit-houses, of which there are about seventy. In the middle is the fenced croft area, the large manor and its central area with the large halls and smaller, separate, enclosures.

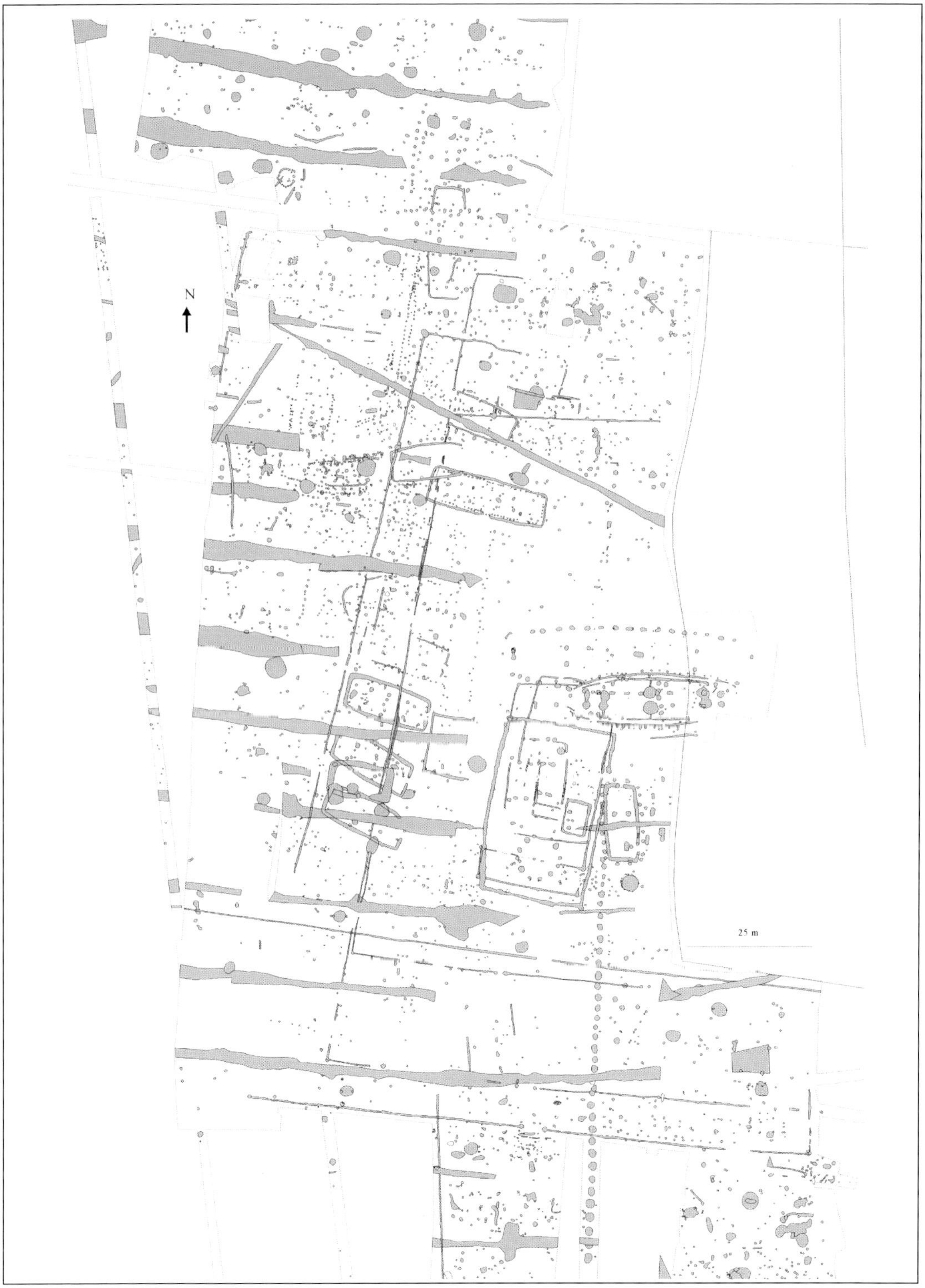
N
25 m

the seventh century (Fig. 15.8, dots). Subsequent periods show the same pattern, and for the next 400 years the active settlement area covered the maximum possible extent, only becoming abandoned some time in the first half of the eleventh century. The latest find from the settlement area is a coin of King Harthacanute, *c.* 1035.

After five years of excavation, we are now more able to understand the structure and chronological development of the settlement from its establishment in the sixth century to its abandonment in the eleventh century. For obvious reasons, the large later manor by the lakeshore has been the principal focus of excavations, from which have come the richest finds. Fig. 15.9 shows the central part of the excavation area with the whole manor complex and parts of the adjacent field areas. There are several phases within the complex, discernable through the clear horizontal stratigraphy. Four main phases have been identified, giving a unique insight into the development of a manor over 400 years. In general, the manor has a very high percentage of

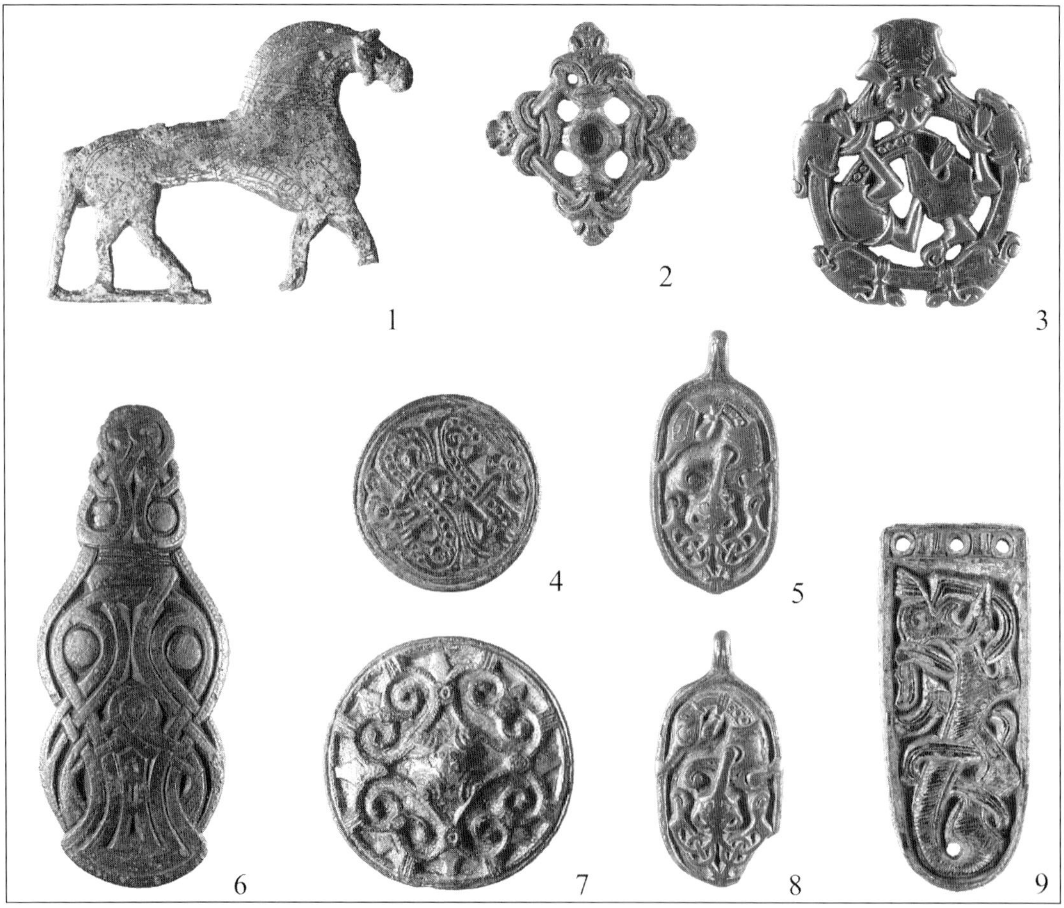

FIGURE 15.10. A selection of the fine pendants, brooches and strap-mounts of gilded silver and tin-plated bronze from the later manor at Tissø. (1) and (6) are of eighth-century date, the others are ninth to tenth century. Jewellery of this high quality is found in a clearly higher concentration within the area of the manor. Scale 1:1. (*Photographs: Pia Brejnholt*)

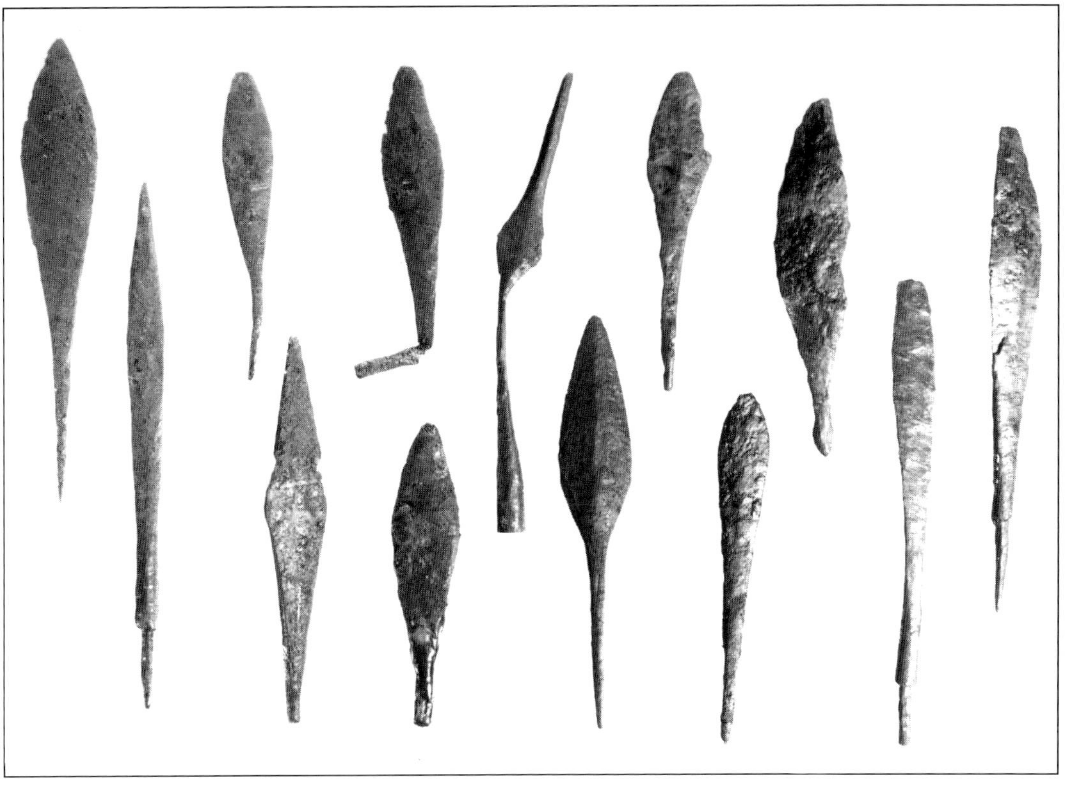

FIGURE 15.11.
A selection of arrowheads from the later manor at Tissø. (*Photograph: Danish National Museum*)

tin-plated and gilded bronze and silver objects, compared with other contemporary Danish metal-rich sites (Fig. 15.10), making it clear that aristocratic individuals lived at the site. A highly characteristic element in the finds inventory from the manor is weaponry, for example military arrowheads (Fig. 15.11). Sword hilts, pommels and other fittings have also been found, typically with inlays of silver and bronze, and the distribution of the one hundred or so weapons and weapon parts shows a clear concentration at the manor (Fig. 15.12). The aristocratic setting of the complex is stressed by cavalry equipment, in the form of bridles and spurs, which accords well with what we know of heavy cavalry graves from the Danish Viking Age.

More general comparisons of material from the manor with the finds from the market and workshop areas make it clear that prestigious objects appear far more frequently at the manor. Sherds of Frankish and Carolingian drinking glasses are restricted still further, appearing only in the hall area: there is not a single glass sherd from the workshops of the manor or the large market areas. Another striking element is the presence of contemporary Insular and Carolingian objects. Among the latter are sword-belt fittings, cross-shaped and equal-armed brooches, and about ten coins minted under Charlemagne and Louis

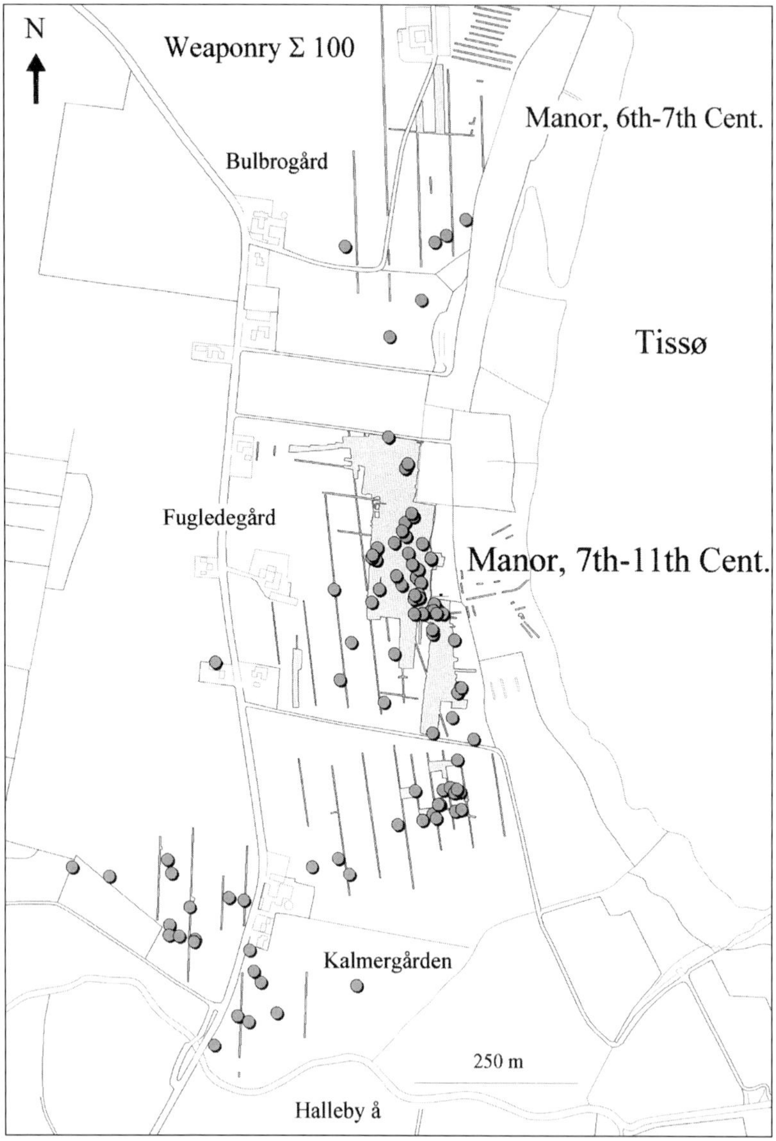

FIGURE 15.12.
Distribution map showing the weapons and weapon parts at the Tissø complex. Note the accumulation within the later manor.

the Pious. This material seems to be characteristically of late eighth- and ninth-century date.

Following the excavations in 2000, Tissø has now produced over one hundred coins, the oldest of which is a late seventh-century sceatta – incidentally the first from eastern Denmark (Fig. 15.13:1). To this may be added a small group of early Norse coins from the first half of the eighth century, with Viking house and a ship motif (Fig. 15.13:2–3). Again, it is characteristic that the early coin types – sceattas, and Carolingian and Hedeby types – come mainly from the large

FIGURE 15.13. Coins from Tissø. (1) Sceatta of Continental runic type. (2) and (3) Early Nordic or 'Hedeby-coins' from the early ninth century. Scale 3:2. (*Photographs: Pia Brejnholt*).

manor (Fig. 15.14), the dominant coin type being ninth- and tenth-century Arab issues. These are often cut to varying sizes according to weight, and their distribution across the site shows that they were used in connection with trading and probably also workshop activities.

The development of the manor

Phase One of the second manor was probably established late in the seventh century. The manor area covers about 10,000 sq. m., and in its fencing were several entrances (Fig. 15.15). At the centre lay the hall building, which was about 36 × 11.2m – a total of about 350 sq. m. under the roof. A special fenced area was built together with the walls of the hall, and in this lay a small building of 6 × 5m with an odd west-facing entrance construction. On the eastern side of the fence there was an entrance to the area. A forge appears to have been by the fence at the northern edge of the manor. Although the eastern side of the manorial enclosure was destroyed by gravel digging, remarkably we can demonstrate there were no other large buildings in the complex. The layout is highly atypical for a Danish farm, and the available material has nothing to suggest agricultural production or permanent livestock – in short, the buildings do not represent a production unit. Only leaf-cutters and sickles testify to the feeding of animals, and in this case it seems most reasonable to think of stabled horses. It is not only the structure of the house that is odd. The pits dug for the roof-bearing posts in the hall were no less than up to

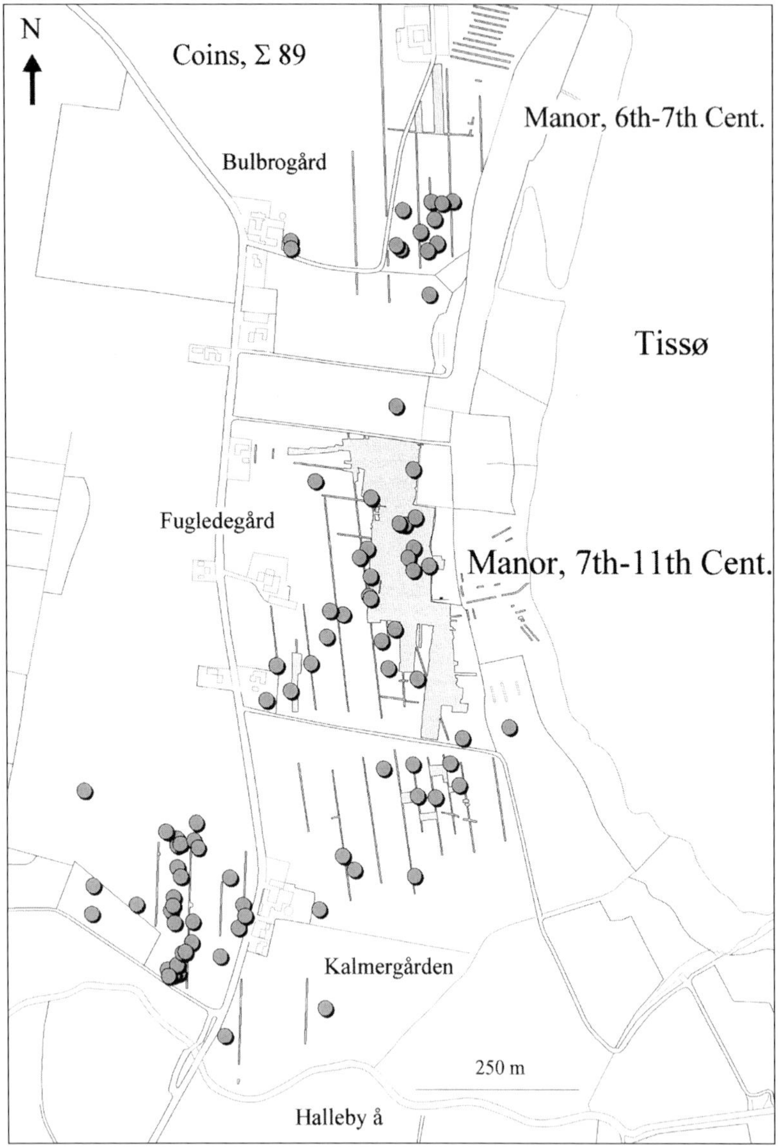

FIGURE 15.14. Distribution map of the coins at Tissø.

three metres deep. This has not been seen before on a Danish prehistoric site, and the hall was clearly an exceptional structure. The very deeply dug posts, which were about 0.6m in diameter, might indicate high wind pressure on the building – perhaps because it had two floors.

The picture of an atypical structure continued in Phase Two, from the eight and ninth centuries (Fig. 15.16). The manor's area was extended to some 15,000 sq. m. and in the south fence a wide gate was built for wagons. The hall was also rebuilt, measuring 36 × 10m,

FIGURE 15.15 (opposite). The layout of the later manor at Tissø in Phase One, preliminarily dated to the seventh to eighth centuries. Gravel extraction has destroyed the eastern part of the manor but despite this uncertainty there was a very limited number of buildings.

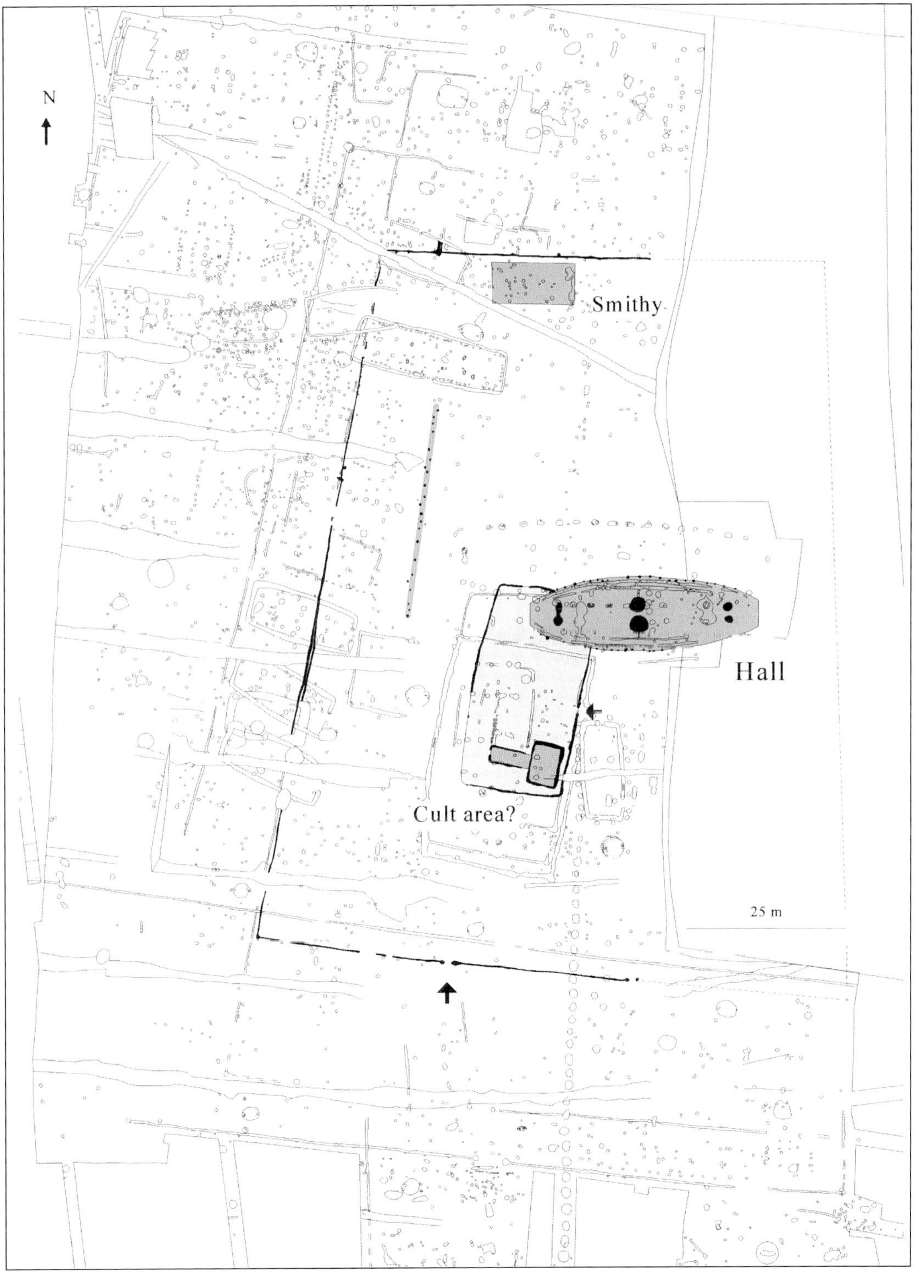
N
Smithy
Hall
Cult area?
25 m

FIGURE 15.16.
Tissø: the layout of the manor in Phase Two, preliminarily dated to the eighth to ninth centuries.

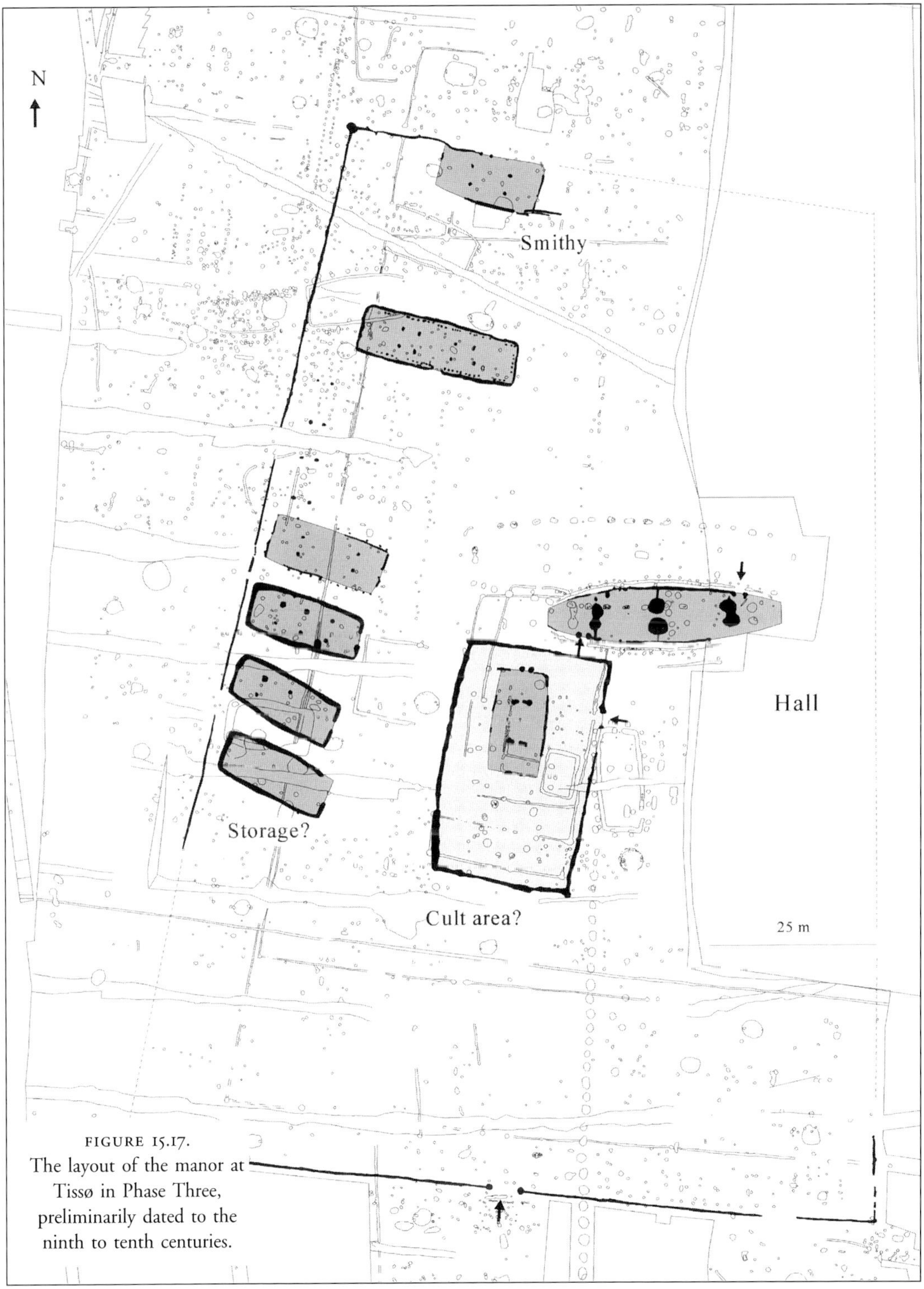

FIGURE 15.17.
The layout of the manor at Tissø in Phase Three, preliminarily dated to the ninth to tenth centuries.

and the separate fenced area was enlarged, although still being built together with the walls of the hall, and retaining the old entrance on the eastern side. The small house from Phase One disappeared and was replaced by a larger building of 20 × 6m. In the southern part of the fenced area a smallish block was separated with a transverse fence. As in Phase One, a forge remained at the northern end of the complex.

With Phase Three from the ninth to tenth century, apparently striking changes were made in the structure of the complex (Fig. 15.17). An increasing quantity of finds from the settlement suggests that this coincided with a rise in the level of activity at the site in the course of the ninth century. The area of the manor was now extended to about 18,000 sq. m., while its core structure was retained. The hall was simply rebuilt, as were the fenced separate area and related building. The separate area was, however, now detached from the hall although its original eastern entrance was retained. The forge was still placed by the north fence of the house complex but along the western fence new

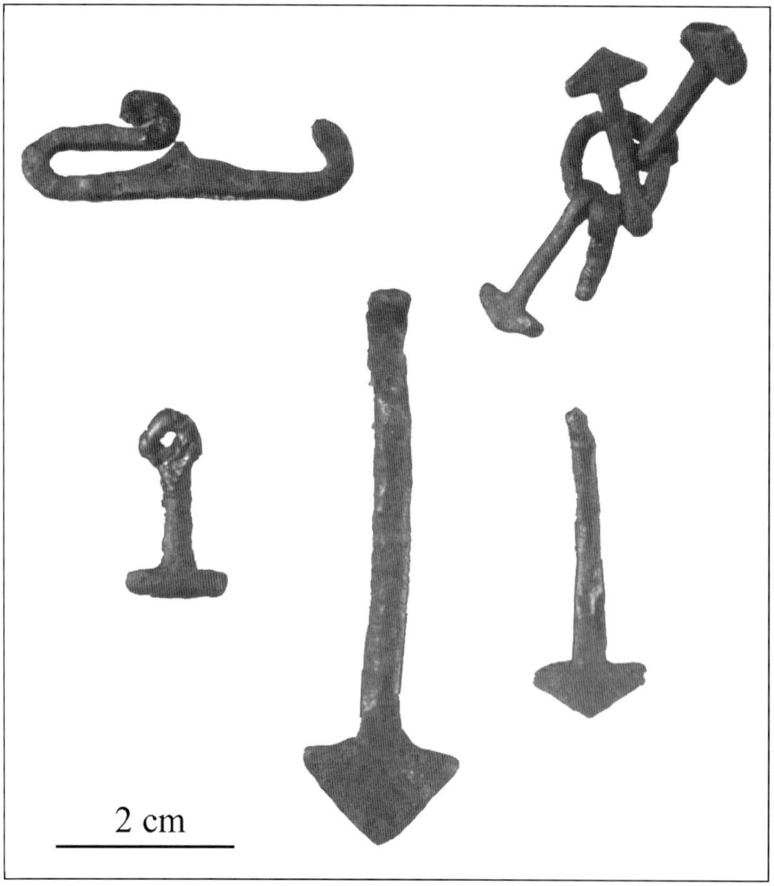

FIGURE 15.18
A selection of the Thor's hammers and a miniature strike-a-light from the later manor area at Tissø.

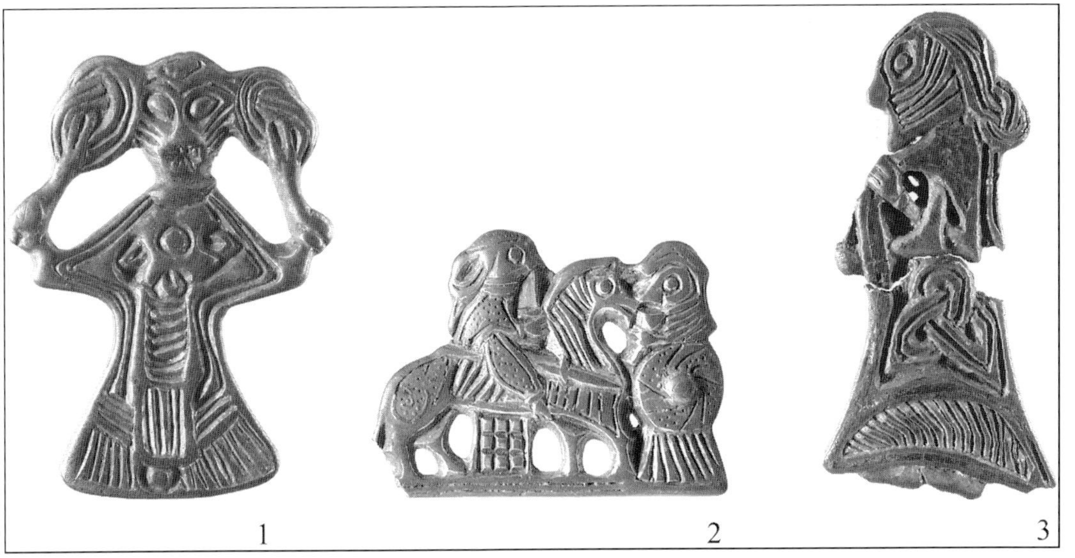

1 2 3

FIGURE 15.19. Pendants depicting the valkyries of Norse mythology, in gilded silver with niello inlays. (1) Valkyrie, or perhaps the goddess Freya, with the famous jewel Brisingamen. (2) Pendant in the form of a rider being met by a shield-bearer. The rider carries a sword and on the horse the lance is attached to the harness. The rider has braids, and the standing person wears a dress. (3) Standing Valkyrie. Scale 1:1. (*Photographs: Pia Brejnholt*)

buildings were erected. By the end of Phase Three identical structures stood along this western fence and to the north lay a large barrack.

Perhaps most striking about the development from Phase One to Phase Three is the decided conservatism; over a period of almost 350 years the combination of hall, separate area and smaller building was maintained, as was the smithy. In the same period there was an ongoing development in ordinary Danish farms and while the hall may be interpreted as the prestigious main building, the separate area and the small building are clearly something special. It is therefore perhaps worth noting that there is an unusually high frequency within the manor of finds of heathen amulets and jewellery, with motifs taken from Norse mythology (Figs. 15.18–19). Together with the weapon offerings from the lake and the mention of Tyr in the lake's name, it may be that cult activities were associated with the manor. In particular, the special fenced area of the manor was perhaps a heathen cult area – the *hov* of the sagas. The fact that a forge was a permanent fixture in the hall area could underline this supposition, because in Norse mythology the forge enjoyed a special position. In this connection we may refer to an interesting Swedish site at Borg in Östergötland with substantial evidence for pagan cult rituals in a late Viking Age manor (A.-L. Nielsen 1997; Nielsen and Lindeblad 1999).

The concluding Phase Four embraces the last half of the tenth century and the beginning of the eleventh century. In this period the complex reached its maximum area and volume, at least 25,000 sq. m., with the large carriage gate still in the southern fence and a spectacular large hall with 550 sq. m. under the roof (Fig. 15.20). Phase Four also

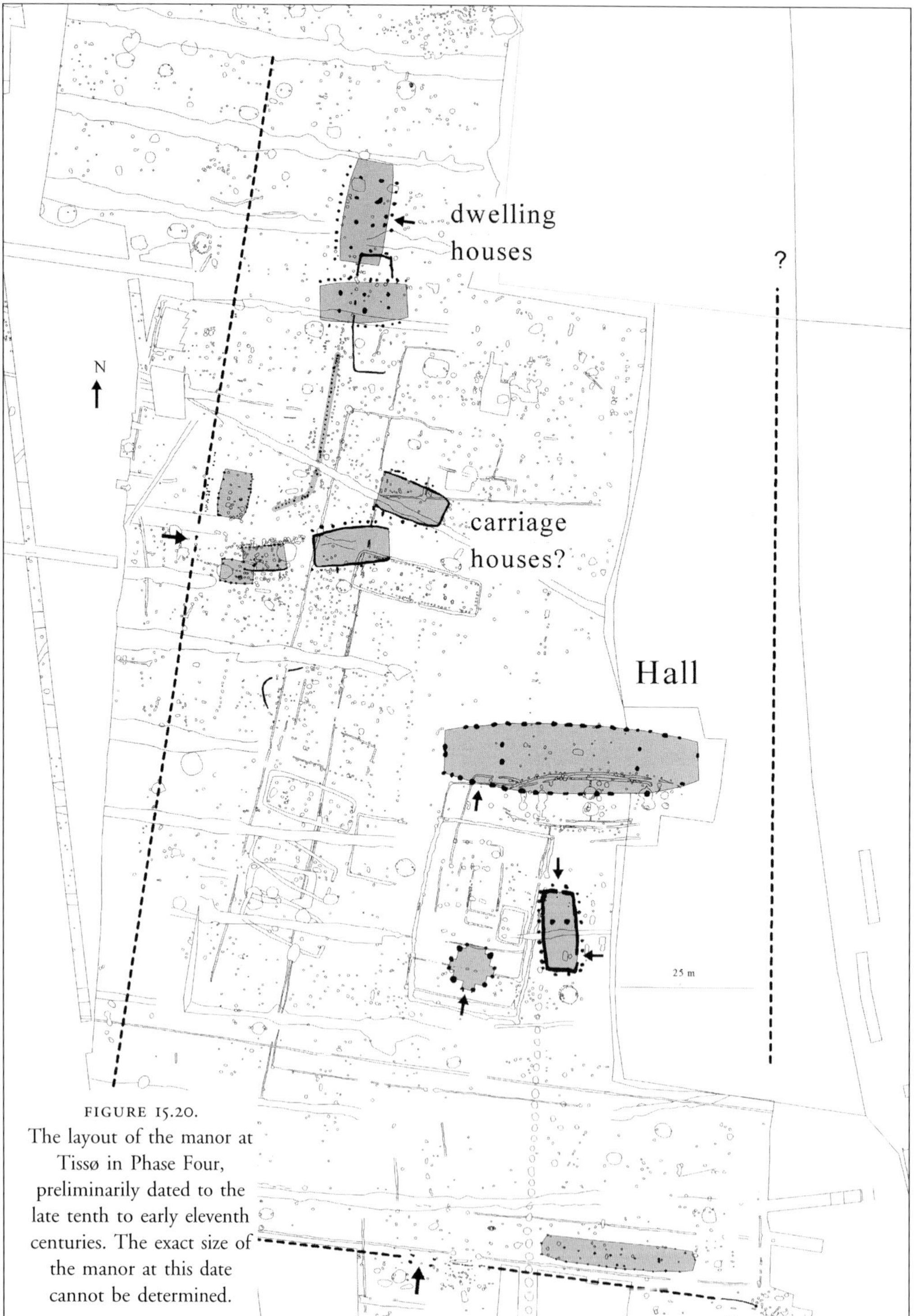

FIGURE 15.20.
The layout of the manor at Tissø in Phase Four, preliminarily dated to the late tenth to early eleventh centuries. The exact size of the manor at this date cannot be determined.

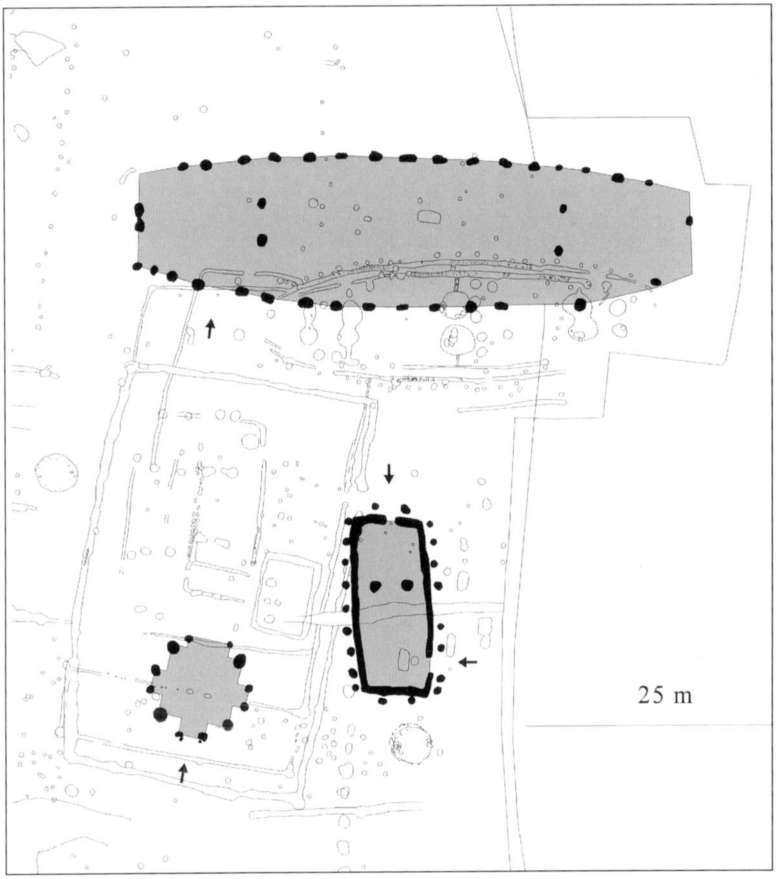

FIGURE 15.21.
Plan of the hall area with the three main buildings in Phase Four. The hall measures 48 × 12.5m. The outlines of the curved walls of the older halls, the holes for the roof-bearing posts and the related fence sections around the separate area can also be seen. It is clear that the large hall differs strikingly in construction from the older halls.

saw radical change. The hall building was of a new type, the fenced 'special' area disappeared and the other house types were replaced, mainly by houses with external raking support posts. On the site of the 'special' area, a larger house was built, at right angles to the hall, with a small cross-shaped building (Fig. 15.21). The latter is very distinctive and, judging from its location, seems to be one of the most important buildings of the complex. To the north-west of the large hall were a collection of smaller buildings, all with an open gable (perhaps carriage sheds) and at the northern end of the complex were possible dwelling houses. Several other buildings belong to this phase, and adjacent to the southern fence was a thirty-five metre longhouse of uncertain function. The total built-up area of the complex was about 2000 sq. m., but not all the buildings were standing at the same time.

Although great changes can be noted in the structure of the house complex over its 400-year history, there is one thing that never altered – it was never a production unit. Almost all the buildings in the various phases must be described as special, and many have never been seen before in Danish farm complexes. Furthermore, the halls are of a decidedly monumental type, and do not seem to be residential buildings of the type known from Lejre just seventy kilometres east of Tissø; while the halls at Lejre have many divisions into rooms (Fig. 15.5), those at Tissø have very few. They do not seem to have been permanent dwellings, and the whole central complex with hall and fencing was remarkably poor in finds. Clearly, it was kept clean compared to the other parts of the complex.

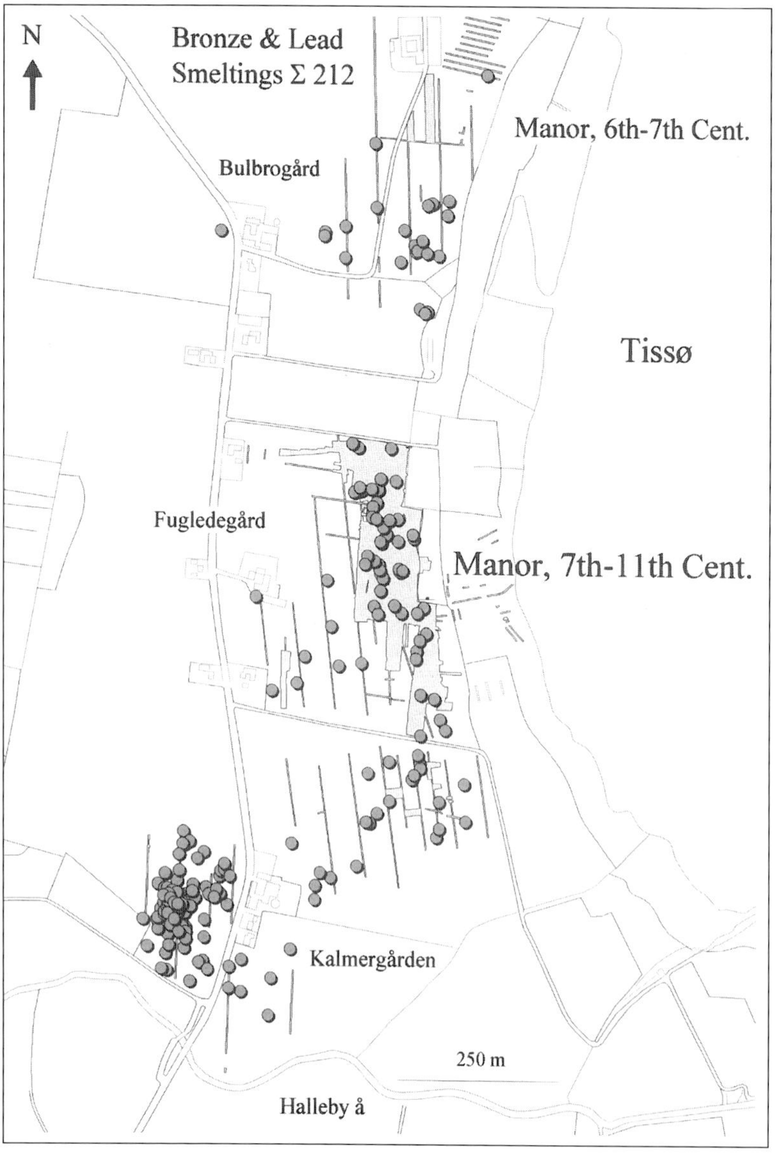

FIGURE 15.22. Distribution map of the molten bronze and lead from workshop activities at Tissø.

The workshops and the market place

Both south and north of the later manorial complex area there were extensive workshop and market areas, of relatively uniform structure. While thousands of post-holes have been excavated, it is extremely difficult to find any system, mainly because the site has been plough-damaged, leading to the truncation of post-holes and other features. This is true for all the forge furnaces, for example, and the only traces of these now are their characteristic slag in the ploughsoil or dumped in redundant pit-houses and wells. One safely identified building type in the market areas is the pit-house, of the type known from many other sites of the same character in southern Scandinavia and northern Germany. To date, about seventy pit-houses have been excavated, but the whole area must originally have had several hundred. Another building type in these workshop areas consisted of small houses or booths and, judging from the number of post-holes, there had been many of these. A large quantity of rivets and nails, mainly from the workshop areas where these small buildings predominated, testifies to their frequent repair and renewal. In other parts of the site there are signs that circular or angled fences were simply erected to create shelter for a small working area. Excavation has shown that there are no traces of permanent dwellings in these market and workshop areas; the pit-houses and small buildings may of course have been reused several times, but apparently not for long periods of residence.

FIGURE 15.23.
(1)–(4) Three bronze and one lead model for the manufacture of moulds for plate brooches and a cross-shaped brooch. (5) Bronze patrix die for stamping sheet gold for dress ornaments. All tenth century, scale 1:1. (*Photographs: Pia Brejnholt*)

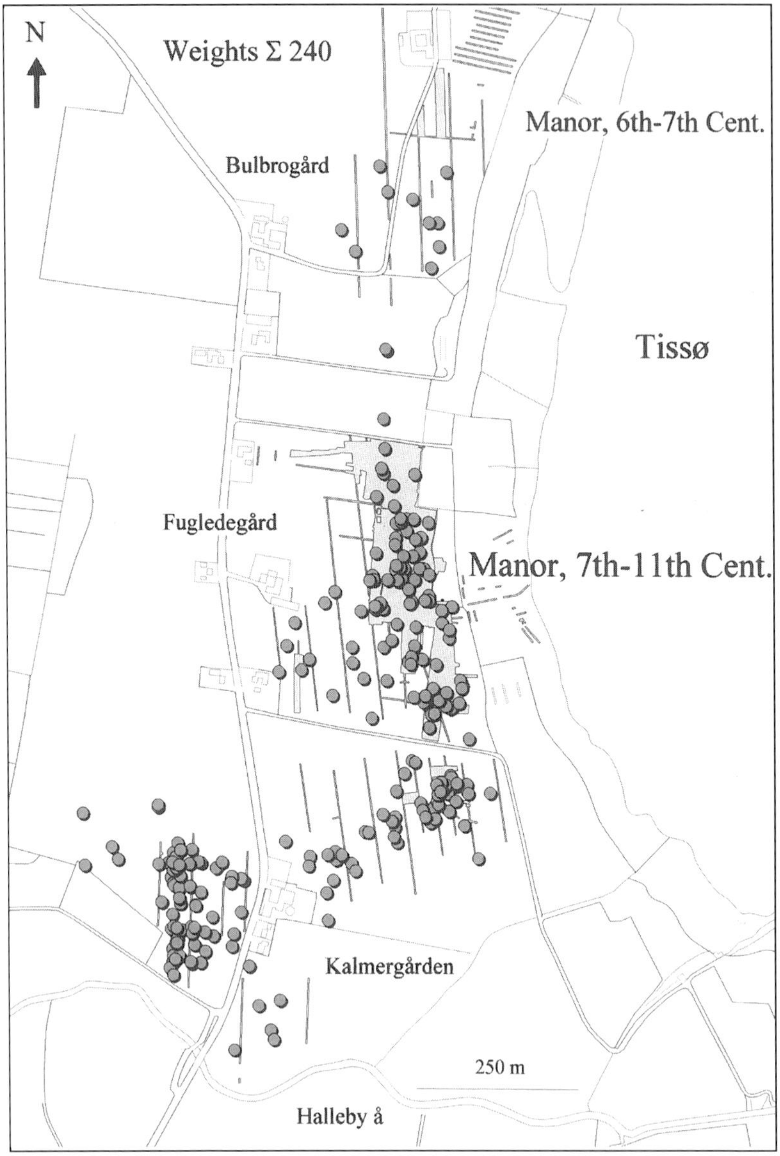

FIGURE 15.24.
Distribution map showing the weights at Tissø.

In the southern workshop area iron forging and bronze casting seems to have been the dominant activity. In the forging areas many characteristic slags from the refining of iron have been found, while semi-finished material for strike-a-lights, shears, knives and arrowheads are also common. Bronze casters worked in the same areas, and among other objects casting-moulds for bow-shaped brooches have been found, as well as miscast keys, brooches and Thor's hammers. The distribution of bronze and lead melt shows, however, that jewellery was produced over most of the site (Fig. 15.22). The jewellers appear also to have worked at the large hall itself, where several models for making moulds have been found (Fig. 15.23). Tools in the form of burins and small chisels for metalwork have often appeared in the southern workshop area and, especially here, there are indications among the finds that the same craft types were practised year after year, probably by the same craftsmen.

Trading activity is evident from the many weights, and fragments of silver and Arab coins that have been found across the site, indicating a very large part of the overall market area was functioning at the same time (Fig. 15.24). However, in contrast to town-like *emporia* such as Ribe, Hedeby, Kaupang and Birka, the quantity of finds is much smaller at Tissø, suggesting probably short, intense, periods of activity. Since such large areas were used in connection with these activities, it might suggest large numbers of people gathering at the site seasonally.

One new find makes an important contribution to place Tissø in an international context. In the southern workshop area a mid-ninth century Byzantine lead seal was found (Fig. 15.25), bearing the name of Theodosius and his titles of office. Theodosius was the head of the Byzantine armoury and military recruiting office (Laurent 1978) and from Continental sources we know that he visited Mainz in 840–1. Identical seals have been found at Hedeby and Ribe and it seems hardly coincidental that a seal has now also been found at Tissø. It has been suggested that this Byzantine official may have been in northern Europe to recruit mercenaries, or to buy up iron for the Byzantine army, which had suffered great defeats in the Near East shortly before this. It would have been natural for Byzantine officials or representatives of Theodosius to have visited places like Hedeby and Ribe on this business as

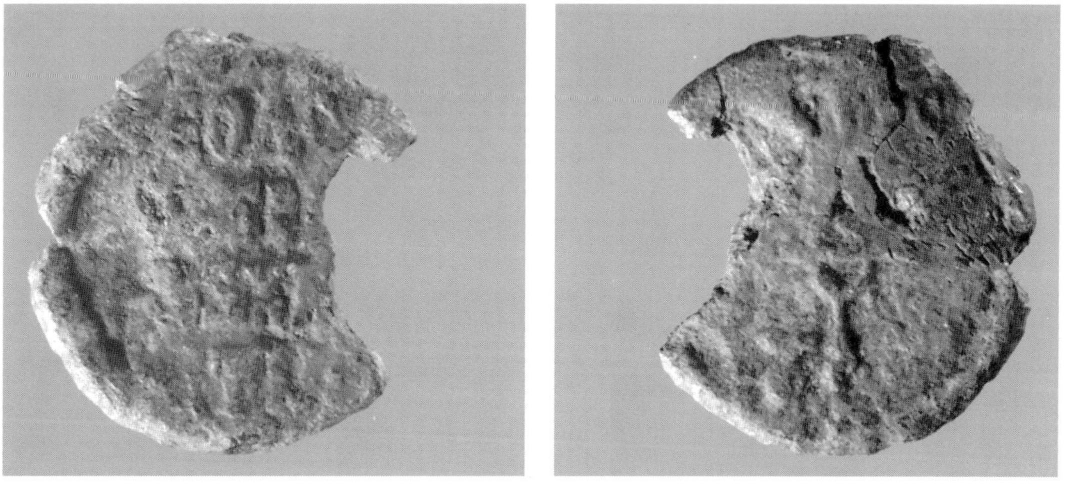

FIGURE 15.25. A lead seal of the high-ranking Byzantine official Theodosius, mid ninth century. Similar seals have also been found in the early towns of Hedeby and Ribe, and its presence at Tissø testifies to the importance of the site. Scale 2:1. *(Photograph: Danish National Museum)*

there were plenty of people there, and connections and high-level agreements could be established. The archaeological finds show that similar contacts could have been established at Tissø, which was undoubtedly the central site in West Zealand.

Royal palace? – cult site – market

I shall end by attempting an overall interpretation of the Tissø complex. From the first signs of activity at Tissø in the sixth century, by the turn of the seventh century a magnate residence had been established. At the same time, activity in the large market and workshop areas began, as well as the first weapon sacrifices in the lake. The peculiar building structure that can be seen at the second manor, particularly in Phases One and Two, might mean that Tissø was not a permanent aristocratic residence, because it quite simply lacks many of the buildings one would normally associate with such a complex. Those buildings that can be identified are, on the one hand, the sequence of single structure halls in the special enclosed area, and on the other those housing the forge at the northern end of the site. To these may be added a modest number of pit-houses that were probably only used periodically. Large quantities of bone refuse in the pit-house fills inside the manorial complex, and at the eastern end of the halls, show that during some periods there must have been many people present, a feature also reflected in the generally large volume of finds. Many artefacts show the occupants belonged to an elite and the discovery of weapon parts and horse equipment indicate that heavily-armed cavalry were also quartered in the place. Interestingly, preliminary bone analyses show that the horses from Tissø were generally larger than those known from ordinary Danish farm complexes, which might suggest trained warhorses. The aristocratic aspect is reiterated by the presence of large, slender dogs in the bone material – probably hunting hounds.

If the finds show an elite occupied the Tissø complex throughout its life, the distinctive arrangement of the buildings suggests that they did not use it as a permanent residence. We should perhaps move up a level in considering its ownership. It might have been a royal complex – not a primary residence, but an establishment belonging to the royal estate system of a peripatetic monarchy. In this connection it is interesting to draw a parallel between the structure and documented functions of the Tissø complex and those of a contemporary Carolingian imperial *Pfalz.* Around 800 Charlemagne's palatine complex at Aachen consisted of two central stone buildings: the *Aula Regia* and the *Pfalzkirche* or Palatine Chapel, which were connected by a passage

(Fig. 15.26). To enter the chapel, one first had to go through an *atrium*. In addition to the central building complex, there were dwellings and workshops, probably built not in stone, but in wood (Hugot 1965, 545). Listed below (Table 15.1) are some of the archaeological characteristics of the Tissø complex with their interpretation, and an attempt

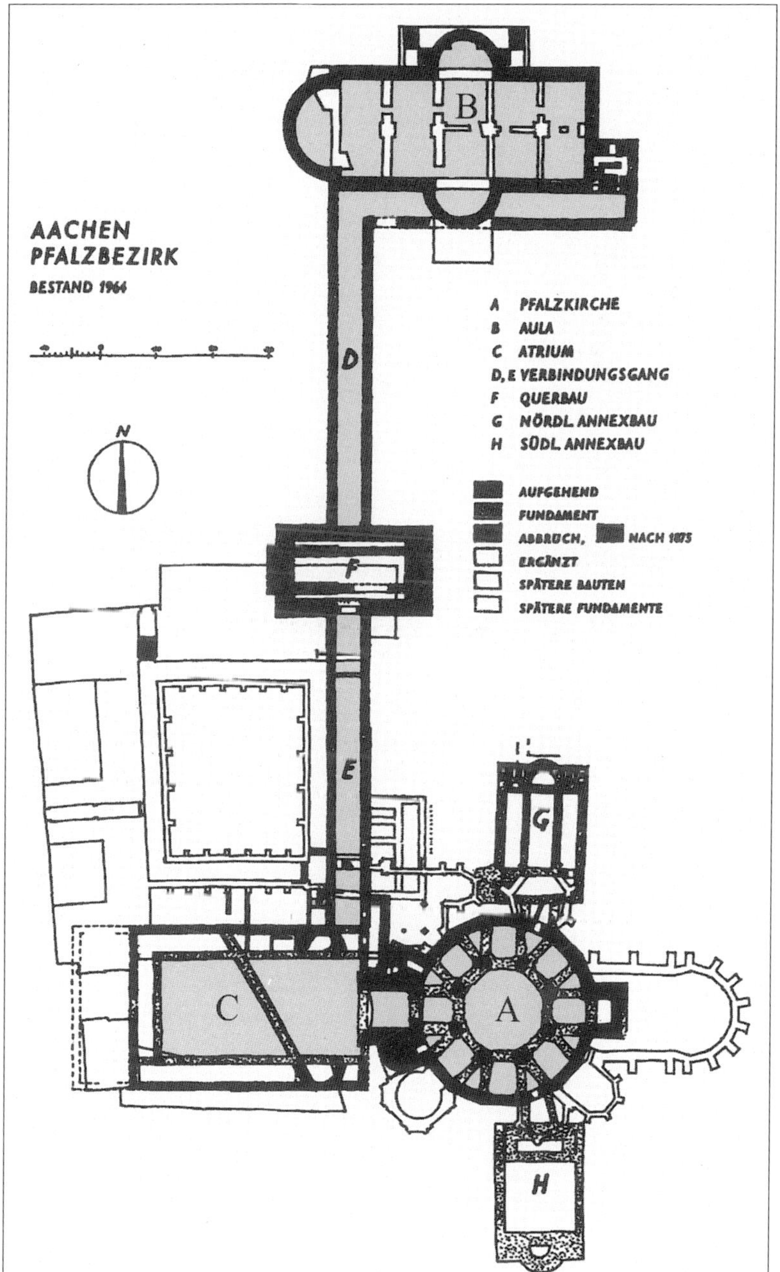

FIGURE 15.26.
Plan of the central representative area of Charlemagne's *Pfalz* in Aix, Germany (after Hugot 1965, with additions by the author).

to recognize these elements in the structure and functions described by the sources in connection with a Carolingian *Pfalz*.

Table 15.1. Features appearing at both Tissø and a contemporary Carolingian *Pfalz*.

Tissø complex	*Interpretation*	*Carolingian Pfalz*
Monumental halls	Representation	*Aula Regia*
Special fenced area and building	Cult area	Atrium and Pfalz church
Lake sacrifices	Cult activities	Church ceremonies
Weapons and horses	Retinue	*Gefolgschaft*
Executed men	Jurisdiction/trials	Jurisdiction/trials
Pit-houses/workshops	Markets	Markets

The Tissø hall can be compared to the Carolingian *Aula Regia*, and the enclosed special area with the single building corresponds to the *atrium* and Palatine Chapel. The types of activity witnessed at a Carolingian *Pfalz* during an extended stay by a ruler and his retinue are very like those we can picture at Tissø. The level of activity in the area naturally increased, the population gathering around the palace and important ecclesiastical ceremonies taking place. The latter can be compared to the celebration of possible cultic rituals in the special area of the magnate complex and the weapon sacrifices in the lake. Around the Carolingian *Pfalz* complex, market and workshop areas mushroomed, corresponding to the large, but clearly only temporarily used market areas at Tissø. When the ruler left the palace the level of activity dropped. The somewhat later palace of Tilleda, which was built in Thuringia in the tenth century, also shares certain structural parallels with the Tissø complex (Grimm 1968). Tilleda consisted of a lightly fortified castle area with the central buildings matching the Aachen complex. Tilleda also had a large forecourt area where excavations have identified pit-houses and extensive workshop activity (Grimm 1968, Abb. 7, 89f). These workshop and market functions can be seen, at both Tissø and Tilleda, immediately outside the actual residential area.

The possible function of the Tissø complex as a royal palace, but not a main residence, might also be indicated by the fact that no graves have yet been found in connection with the site. Much effort has been devoted to the search for them, and in view of the very rich finds from the complex, one might expect very rich aristocratic graves nearby. None have yet been found, nor are there antiquarian accounts of possible rich grave finds. If this absence of graves proves to be real, it provides support for the idea that the complex was not the magnate's primary residence, but only one of several; rich, dynastic graves should instead be anticipated in connection with the main residence. As to where such a main residence might have been, there now seems little doubt this was at Lejre, where the residential complex is at least as large as at Tissø, but has the character of a more permanent residence. Given the traditional view of the Danish monarchy and its development, it is extremely thought provoking that both Tissø and Lejre were established around 550–600 and only abandoned around 1000 – but that is quite another story.

Postscript

In the northernmost part of the settlement area, a small trial excavation in 1995 revealed a building/farm complex. From the size of the occupation area and certain details of the roof-bearing posts of the main building, the features were presumed to represent a late Viking Age farm. Extensive excavations of the complex in the autumn of 2002 revealed, however, that the oldest manor of the complex, dated from the 6th–7th century. From its foundation some time in the mid sixth century until its end in the early eleventh century, Tissø comprised just one manor with related market and craft areas.

Provisional results indicate that it comprised an enclosed area of 10–12,000 sq. m., which is three to five times the size of ordinary Danish farms from the 6th–7th century. At present (March 2003), with about two-thirds of the area investigated, it consists of a large hall building, two large houses and a few smaller buildings and pit-houses. The two largest houses flank an inner enclosure from the later manor 600 m. to the south. The large hall building has slightly curving long sides, six pairs of roof-bearing posts, a length of 38 metres and a maximum width of 7 metres. A radiocarbon date places the hall around AD 600. The building was unusually well constructed from large timbers and had white-plastered internal walls. The hall, and probably the whole complex, burned down in the middle of the seventh century. On the basis of the metal finds the occupation period can be set provisionally at *c.* 550–650. The relatively few finds from the excavation include several brooches, a sword pommel, a spiral bead of gold and a pair of gold pendants with inlaid garnets in cloisonné.

Acknowledgements

This chapter is a result of work within the Danish National Museum's 'War, Defence and Aristocracy' research project, supported by grants from the Danish National Research Council for the Humanities. I also wish to thank Tom Christensen of Roskilde Museum and Svend Åge Tornbjerg of Køge Museum for the latest updates on Lejre and Toftegård.

CHAPTER 16

Groß Strömkendorf: a Market Site of the Eighth Century on the Baltic Sea Coast

Astrid Tummuscheit

> Prior to his return, Godfred gave the order to destroy the coastal market place of the Danish name of *Reric* which gave his realm great benefit by the collection of taxes. He took the merchants with him and went with his entire army by sea to the port which is called Sliesthorp [Hedeby]. (Buchner 1955, 89; author's translation)

This entry, quoted from the *Royal Frankish Annals*, mentions the devastation of a trading place known by the Danish name of *Reric* in 808, an incident occurring at the end of a military campaign conducted by the Danish king Godfred against the Slavonic Obodrites. Although the passage does not contain detailed information about the geographical position of the place, it has long encouraged archaeologists to search for a site that could be connected with the historical *Reric* (Herrmann 1980 and 1988). In the course of these efforts, during the 1980s evidence grew stronger that there had been a large settlement of the Early Slavonic period (that is, of the eighth and early ninth centuries) near the village of Groß Strömkendorf (Fig. 16.1). Since the 1930s, collections of surface finds and trial excavations there had produced Early Slavonic pottery, pieces of amber and glass, fragments of quernstones made of basalt, pottery from the Rhine area and bronze objects. The location of the site, and the range of material connected with trade and production thus suggested that the settlement at Groß Strömkendorf could be identifiable with the historical *emporium* of *Reric* (Wietrzichowski 1993, 44–5; Jöns *et al.* 1997, 200; Jöns 1998a, 131; Jöns 2000).

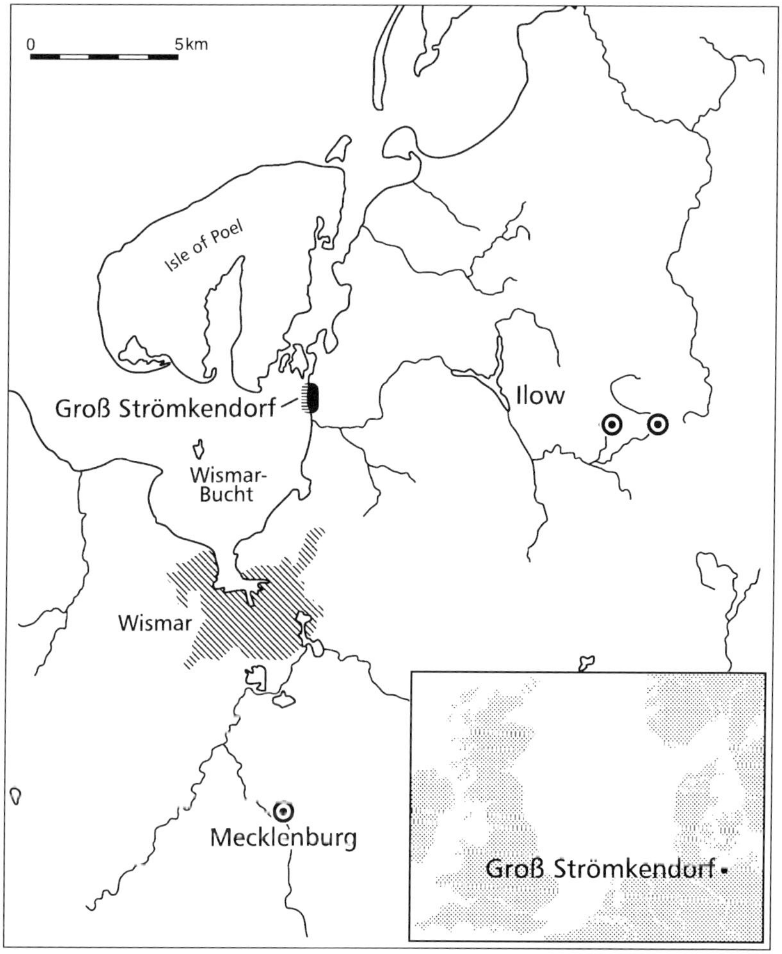

FIGURE 16.1. Location of Groß Strömkendorf and other sites mentioned in the text in relation to local topography.

The supposed importance of Groß Strömkendorf led, for the first time, to more detailed investigations between 1989–91 (Wietrzichowski 1993) and again in 1992. Small-scale excavations confirmed and consolidated the view that there had been a major settlement of the Early Slavonic period with evidence of relations with Francia, the Saxon-Frisian region and Scandinavia. Apart from a large quantity of finds, the excavations revealed a number of physical remains and allowed the first insight into the settlement's layout, for instance, pit-houses aligned in rows indicated a certain degree of planning. A sample of wood taken from one of the wells' casings could be dated to 729. Finally, in 1993 an associated cemetery of the eighth century was discovered in the immediate vicinity of the settlement site.

Within the framework of an interdisciplinary project funded by the *Deutsche Forschungsgemeinschaft*, systematic and intensive investigations of the burial ground and of the settlement site at Groß Strömkendorf

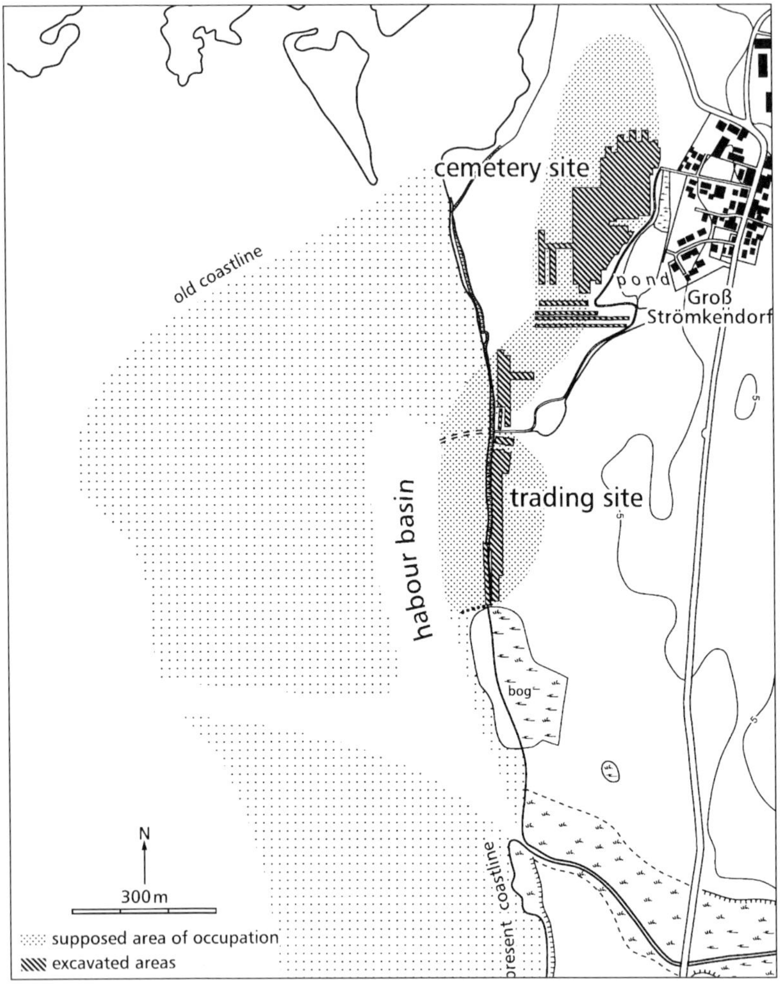

FIGURE 16.2.
Overall plan of excavated areas with reconstruction of the landscape to the west of the site. (*Archäologisches Landesmuseum Mecklenburg-Vorpommern, Schloß Wiligrad, 19069 Lübstorf*)

were carried out between 1995 and 1999 (Fig. 16.2). Analysis of the finds and structures of the 1992 and 1995–9 excavations is currently underway and this paper must be understood to be a preliminary outline (for interim reports see Wietrzichowski 1993; Jöns *et al.* 1997; Jöns 1998a and b).

As only a very few graves of the Early Slavonic period have been discovered in north-east Germany so far, investigations have focused mainly on the excavation of the cemetery site, which was completed in 1998. There is evidence for a great variety of burial customs, with different types of cremations, inhumations in unlined graves or graves with wooden coffins, and with bodies placed in supine or crouched positions. There are animal burials of dogs and horses and, finally, there are six burials with or within boats. All the boats were typical clinker-built Scandinavian vessels with iron rivets fastening

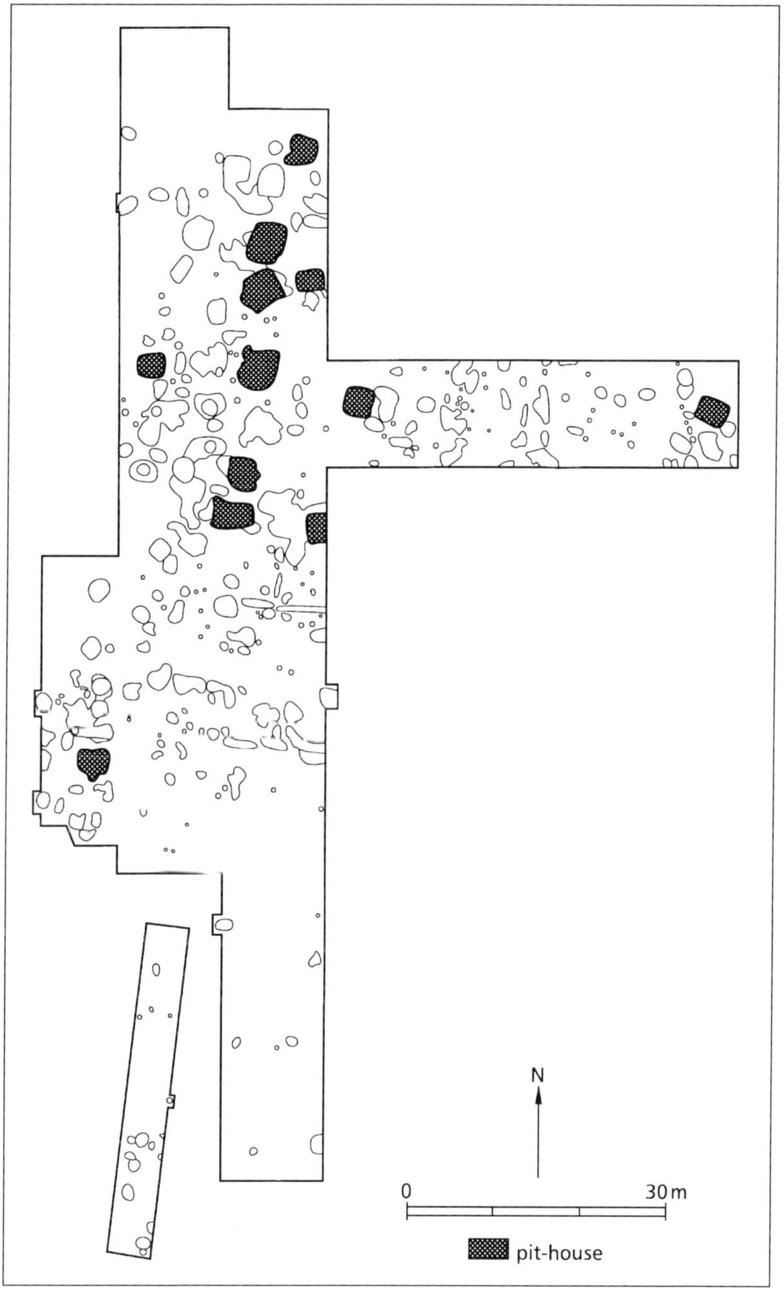

FIGURE 16.3. One part of the central area of the trading site showing the careful alignment of pit-houses (shaded).

the overlapping planks together (Jöns *et al.* 1997, 207–14; Jöns 1998a, 133–4). These different burial customs seem to represent various cultural traditions, which indicate the presence of people from Scandinavia in the North, from the Frankish kingdom and from the Saxon and Frisian regions in the West.

Another important discovery on the site was made during the summer of 1999, when aerial photographs revealed some kind of underwater 'cropmark' about 100m offshore. The filling of a roughly rectangular depression, 750m long and 150m wide, had enhanced the growth of water plants which showed as a dark anomaly. Until further research is carried out, there cannot be any certainty about its interpretation, but at present the feature is generally considered to be the remains of the harbour basin of the Early Medieval settlement.

The site

The settlement site of Groß Strömkendorf is situated on the shores of the Baltic Sea, on the eastern side of the Wismar Bay, south-east of the Isle of Poel. The morainic ground rises slightly north-eastwards from a low coastal cliff towards the burial ground at a height of three to five metres above sea level (Figs. 16.1 and 16.2).

A systematic survey of the site employing methods such as aerial photography, fieldwalking and geophysical prospection has shown that the area of occupation had covered a total of about twenty hectares. Considering the rise of sea-level and the effects of coastal erosion, it seems likely that a considerable tract of land has been destroyed by flooding since the Early Medieval period. Accordingly, the excavation concentrated on a twenty-five metre wide strip of land that stretches *c.* 550m along the coast, interrupted only by a small stream flowing into the sea. In addition, a number of trial trenches were dug to gain information about the area between the coastal settlement and the cemetery site. Finally, several traces of settlement activity have been recorded in the course of the cemetery excavations.

The finds assemblages

Groß Strömkendorf has produced a finds assemblage which can easily be paralleled with other trading sites of Early Medieval date in the Baltic Sea region. Apart from the enormous quantity of animal bone, a substantial pottery assemblage has been found. Most of it is of the Sukow-type, which was the characteristic eighth-century Slavonic fabric in the region, but there are also sherds of imported vessels such as Badorf, Tating and shell-tempered wares (*muschelgrusware*).

A significant proportion of the finds are imported, most of which can be assigned to two main areas of origin. First, there are finds from the Carolingian and the Saxon-Frisian areas. Apart from the pottery, lava quern-stones from the Eiffel region, sherds of glass funnel-beakers, metal dress-fittings and weapons have also been found. Second, a large amount of objects are of Scandinavian origin, for example whetstones of Norwegian schist and metal dress-fittings. A few coins, including sceattas, *dirhams* and *deniers*, have been recorded during the excavation and by metal-detecting.

Apart from the imported goods, there is massive evidence of on-site manufacturing which sheds light on a wide range of crafts. Among these are antler- and bone-working, with the debris hinting especially at comb-making. Glass-working waste provides evidence for the production of common blue annular beads, and working debris and unfinished objects, mainly of beads and pendants, show that amber was also being worked at Groß Strömkendorf. The site has produced a sizeable number of loomweights and spindle-whorls suggesting the manufacturing of textiles. Finally, iron and bronze slags, as well as fragments of moulds, indicate that working of iron and non-ferrous metals took place, although there is no evidence for iron production itself.

Settlement layout

In general, the excavated structural features comprise pit-houses, wells, pits, hearths and ditches. To date, about one hundred pit-houses and about eighty-five wells, thirty of which contained waterlogged wood, have been recorded. Single or double rows of houses, running parallel to the coastline and at right angles to it, are characteristic of the southern and central parts of the site (Fig. 16.3). Houses, pits and wells form groups separated by open space and lack substantial traces of physical boundaries. In some cases there are regularly aligned rows of pits which could indicate that they were used as boundaries or that they ran along pathways or fences which have not left any traces in the archaeological record. The settlement plan shows a remarkably dense occupation and although it is obvious that not all of the settlement had been planned in the same regular manner, similar rows of houses or wells occur identically aligned all over the site (Fig. 16.4).

When we turn northwards and look at the remains of dwellings excavated in the immediate surroundings of, and within, the area of the burial ground, a different picture emerges (Fig. 16.5). In this area of the site, the same types of structure such as pit-houses, pits and wells had been sited less closely together with irregular spacings of between twenty to thirty metres, a scattered distribution without any signs of an underlying system. In all cases in which there were intersections of burials with features belonging to the settlement site, the burials proved to be later on stratigraphical grounds.

Although intersecting features indicate a multi-period settlement it is difficult to distinguish different phases clearly. In discussing the settlement's layout, there is therefore the reservation that the structures

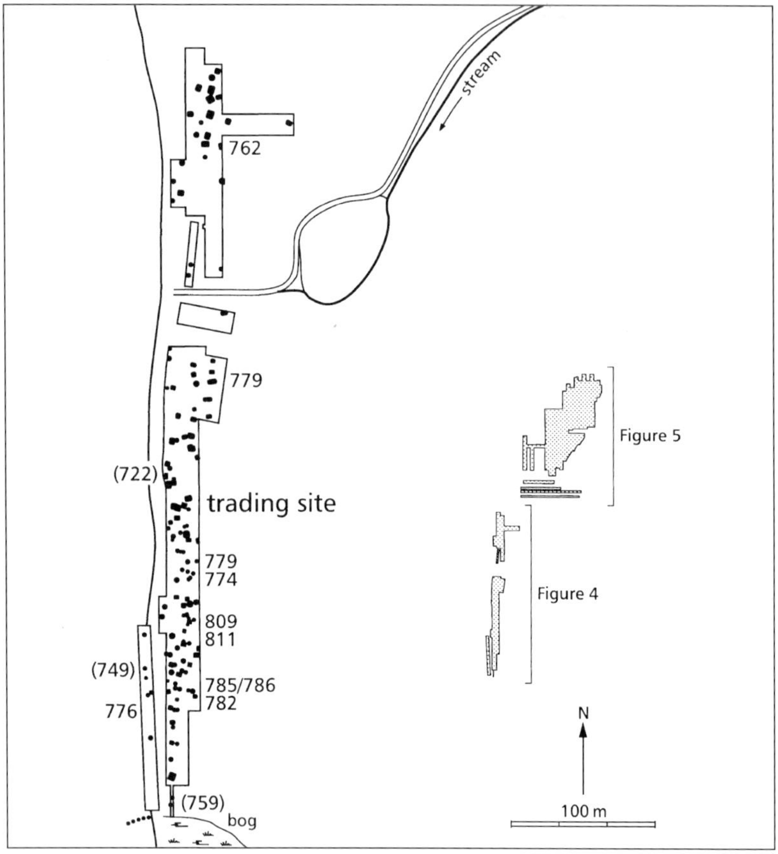

FIGURE 16.4.
Plan of the excavated area in the southern and central parts of the site showing the dense occupation and selected dendrochronological dates.

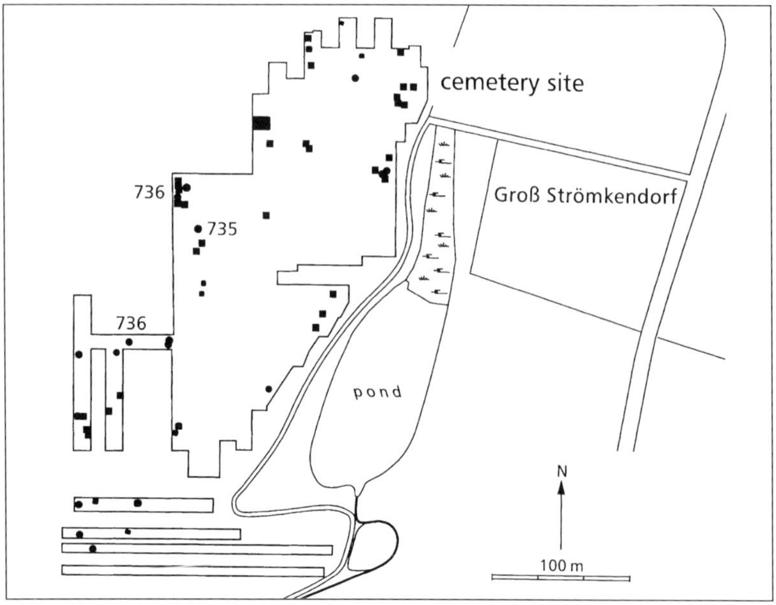

FIGURE 16.5.
Plan of the settlement structures within the area of the cemetery and dendrochronological dates.

did not all exist at the same time. It has been mentioned that a large number of wells have been excavated at Groß Strömkendorf. Thirty of these contained the waterlogged remains of wooden structures which could be dated by dendrochronology. Ninety-five samples from the thirty wells have produced dates, which provide a framework for the site's chronology, at present covering the period 722 to 811.

Considering the samples that could be dated to the exact felling year of the tree, the mapping shows a differentiation between the northern group of structures in the sphere of the cemetery site, which dates to 735/6 and the coastal settlement, that has produced mainly late eighth and early ninth centuries dates (compare Figs. 16.4 and 16.5). Although structures of the northern settlement have only been uncovered on a small scale, and the number of absolute dates is small, the evidence nevertheless indicates an early phase of occupation here in the first half of the eighth century. While the extent of the early site is difficult to assess, it seems clear that the settlement layout differed widely from the carefully aligned houses of the coastal site. In summary, the analysis of a range of dates suggests that at least two phases of activity are detectable during the eighth century. Accordingly, the recorded differences regarding the layout of the site indicate a marked change of the settlement's internal organisation during this period.

Buildings

Excavation has allowed the examination of about one hundred pit-houses (*Grubenhäuser*). Apart from a few questionable traces of post-built structures, pit-houses are the predominant house-type in Groß Strömkendorf, a prominent features of which is the limited floor space. The average pit-house was seven and a half square metres in size with the general range of floor areas being between three and a half to fourteen square metres; there is a concentration on dimensions of five to eight square metres. At least 70 percent of all houses contained the remains of a hearth, which had always been positioned in one corner of the pit. In most cases nothing but a concentration of stones and charcoal indicates the former position of the fireplace, whereas some of the buildings possessed remains of elaborate dome-shaped ovens or, in one case, a square-shaped oven built of stone slabs.

There was a great diversity in the types of pit-house structure. Most were of simple design, with a single ridge-post at each end of the building. In some cases there was evidence of raked ridge-posts, while in others there was an additional post in the middle of one of the long sides. There is also evidence for more sophisticated buildings, with six or eight posts, and there are houses without any post-holes at all which could represent the remains of log cabins. Additionally, there was a substantial number of individual constructions which could not be incorporated in the common system of structural types. In summary, the buildings of the trading place at Groß Strömkendorf show a marked variation of constructional design, yet with a noticeably narrow range of sizes and no indication of a pronounced hierarchy or functional differentiation.

The large number of finds from Groß Strömkendorf indicate that craft and manufacturing activities were important during the lifetime of the settlement. However, the primary function of pit-houses is difficult to assess, because after the demolition of a building the pits were used for rubbish disposal or to discard material excavated from a new house. It is therefore certain that most of the finds from any one *Grubenhaus* do not relate to its original function. Despite the fact that it is impossible to relate certain crafts to individual houses, it seems reasonable to assume that the huts were used as workshops. As for their use as dwellings, it is far more difficult to imagine people actually living in houses smaller than ten square metres. Even if a single person could use a small pit-house as a dwelling, it would have been impossible for extended social groups of people. From the perspective of housing, it is difficult at present to explain how marketing and production worked in Groß Strömkendorf. The heating facilities of most *Grubenhäuser*, and the evidence of the cemetery, suggest some scale of permanence and probably reflect an established community. It therefore seems probable that other houses existed outside the area of excavation.

Groß Strömkendorf is situated in the historic settlement area of the Slavonic tribe of the Obodrites. As few settlements have been excavated on a large scale and perhaps because of the difficulties in detecting certain types of houses, our knowledge about the building traditions of these peoples is still limited. It seems, however, that pit-houses were *not* the typical dwelling-type of the Slavs in northern Germany (Donat 1970 and 1998, 189). From what we know at present, the northern boundary of the distribution of Slavonic *Grubenhäuser* concentrates on an area in central Germany between the Rivers Saale and Elbe (Donat 1980, map 4). In the most north-westerly part of the Slavonic settlement area, that is, in the area surrounding Groß Strömkendorf, no pit-houses of the eighth century have been uncovered so far. One of the central questions regarding the buildings of Groß Strömkendorf is therefore what kind of building tradition the pit-houses reflect and where its origins lie.

From the Roman Iron Age onwards, pit-houses occurred frequently in northern Europe as minor outbuildings of farms associated with longhouses. As one of the typical features of these constructions is the lack of a hearth, they are never interpreted as dwellings but instead as workshops or storage buildings. In contrast to this pattern, settlements connected with trade and exchange, comprising predominantly or exclusively pit-houses, do appear in northern Germany, Denmark and Sweden from the Migration period onwards (Weinmann 1994, 165). Especially in the surroundings of Hedeby and in the settlement area of the Saxons north and south of the River Elbe, pit-houses furnished with a hearth occur from the eighth century. The origins of the new tradition to build sunken huts regularly with a hearth in one corner of the pit have been widely regarded as being influenced by Slavonic traditions known from central Germany (Donat 1980, 68; Meier 1994, 74). At Groß Strömkendorf, it is difficult at present to establish certain links to any known building tradition. It is, however, clear that there are strong connections to similar settlements and house types in modern Lower Saxony, in the surroundings of Hedeby in modern Denmark, and in southern Sweden.

In summary, evidence from the cemetery and settlement site at Groß Strömkendorf indicates the presence of people from various regions of Early Medieval northern Europe. Whereas an earlier phase of occupation showed an extensive layout characterised by houses, pits and wells grouped together in an irregular manner, the later settlement phase displayed distinct signs of planning, providing evidence for the 'urban' character of the site. The eighth- and early ninth-century date, the settlement layout, the evidence of the buildings, the rich material connected with trade and manufacturing activities, the location on the shores of the Wismar Bay, and the size of the settled area, all indicate that the site at Groß Strömkendorf is most probably to be identified with the *emporium* of *Reric* mentioned in the *Royal Frankish Annals*. It follows that examination of the hinterland of Groß Strömkendorf/*Reric* can be approached through written evidence in addition to the archaeological data.

Archaeological and historical context

Archaeological research on the hinterland of Groß Strömkendorf has so far been carried out on a limited scale (for a summary see Schmitz 1999), because archaeologists have usually focused upon investigating the many remains of Slavonic fortresses. At present, a distribution map of Early Slavonic finds and archaeological sites is based exclusively on surface finds, giving a rough impression of the settlement pattern in the environs of the trading centre (Fig. 16.6). Although there is no information about the character of those settlements or their exact dates, the concentration of occupation within a radius of approximately

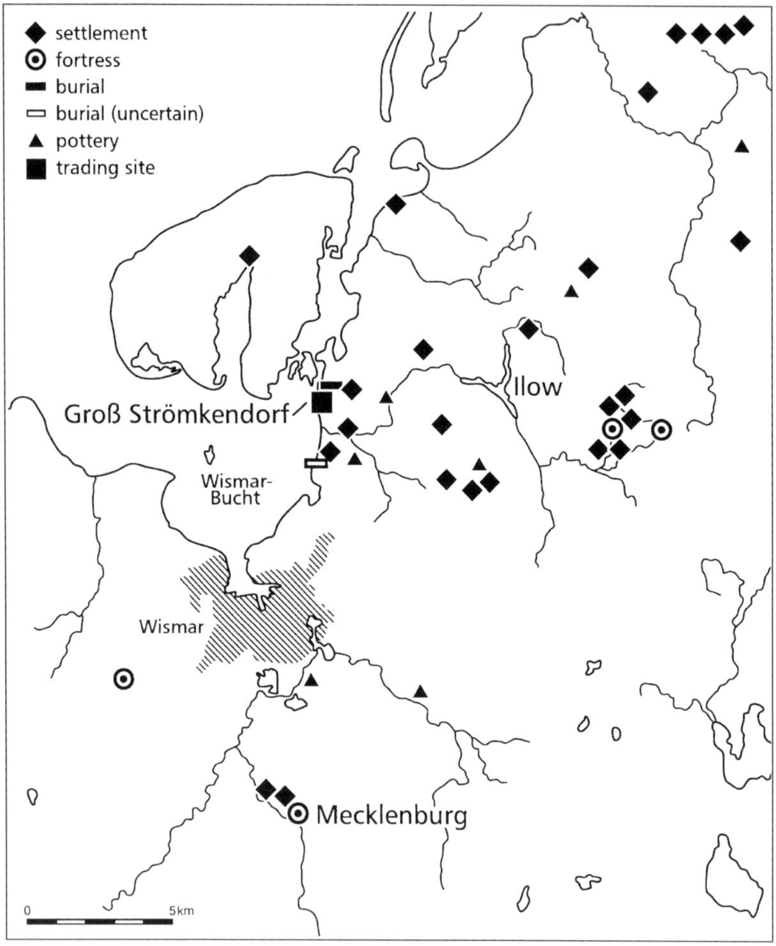

FIGURE 16.6. Map showing the distribution of finds and archaeological sites in the hinterland of Groß Strömkendorf (after Schmitz 1999, Abb. 27).

twelve kilometres around Groß Strömkendorf is noticeable and possibly reflects the close interdependence of centre and hinterland. Apart from the settlement sites three fortresses have been recorded in the immediate vicinity of Groß Strömkendorf. They are situated at Ilow (two fortresses) and at Mecklenburg. Regarding their proximity to the trading settlement, all three fortresses could be considered to be associated political centres but direct links are difficult to establish as their dates are all uncertain. Thus, Ilow site II has produced radiocarbon dates covering a period from 660 to 780 (Schmitz 1999, 85). As the trial excavations at site I did not reach the natural subsoil, the earliest absolute date of 840 (*ibid.*, 65), gained from a wood sample, must be treated with caution because there is no clear evidence for the beginning of the fortification.

The origins of the seat of the Obodrite overlord at Mecklenburg has also been the subject of discussions. While the earliest reliable tree-ring dates of the tenth century come from the third phase of construction, radiocarbon dates support the suggestion that the earliest fortress had been built around the middle of the eighth century (Gabriel 1986; Herrmann and Heußner 1991, 269; Brather 1996a, 148; Schmitz 1999, 90).

A closer inspection of the historical evidence offers the opportunity to shed light on the wider political context in which Groß Strömkendorf/*Reric* must be seen. The account of the *Royal Frankish Annals* shows that at the beginning of the ninth century *Reric* was the focus of military confrontations between the Danish king Godfred and Draško, the overlord of the Slavonic Obodrites. Apart from the description of the events at the trading site itself, the annals contain references to Slavonic overlords and to the devastation of fortresses, indicating the existence of well-established political units in the vicinity of *Reric*.

More generally, this was a period of political and military rivalry between the Frankish kingdom (allied to the Obodrites) and the Danes. It is obvious from the written sources that Danish and Slavonic interests collided at the *emporium* of *Reric*. Although the *Royal Frankish Annals* provide evidence for the raid on the Slavonic coast, there is no doubt that the Danes did not act merely as pirates, but had the ability to raise taxes at the market place called *Reric*. Even so, the origins of Danish claims on the settlement are obscure and a dependent relationship between the Danish ruler and the merchants of *Reric* appears to have existed. As a result of the opposing ambitions of Slavs and Danes, Godfred destroyed the *emporium* and moved the merchants to another trading site which was probably under closer control – Hedeby.

While we are able to draw a coherent picture of the situation at the beginning of the ninth century, it is uncertain whether the described conditions can be transferred back to the eighth century. A number of absolute dates from Groß Strömkendorf prove that the settlement already existed by about 730. Given the early beginnings of the site, questions concerning the Slavonic colonisation of modern north-east Germany are brought into focus. Until recently, Germanic peoples were thought to have left the region during the fifth and sixth centuries, with Slavonic settlement starting not later than the sixth century. These datings have had to be adjusted according to new results from dendrochronology (Herrmann and Heußner 1991; Biermann *et al.* 1999). At present, archaeologists assume that the Slavonic colonisation of the area commenced around 700 (Brather 1996a, 14–17; Leube 1996, 269, Biermann *et al.* 1999, 236–42). It is therefore possible that the first traces of occupation at Groß Strömkendorf can be considered to be among the earliest evidence of Slavonic settlement in the region. At present, the character of the earliest settlement is uncertain, as is whether it was based on an agrarian economy or whether it represents a direct predecessor of the trading site. The situation in the area surrounding Groß Strömkendorf is equally obscure. As the discussion of the dates of the fortresses in the vicinity of the settlement has shown, it would appear unlikely that around 730 there was a well-defined political unit comparable to that of the early ninth century (compare Brather 1996b, 188–93).

During the course of the eighth century there is evidence at Groß Strömkendorf for a marked change of settlement layout, which shows strong influences of an authority in control. A considerable number of absolute dates shows increased building activity during the 760s and especially during the decades from 770 to 790, which could be connected with a general extension of the settlement. Although there is no clear evidence to date the changed internal organisation of the site, it is tempting to relate the increased building activities of the late eighth century with the development of a settlement of early urban character.

The events at Groß Strömkendorf/*Reric* coincide with the beginning of the autocracy of Charlemagne (771) and, in subsequent years, with the submission of the Saxons (772–804) and the first recorded contacts between the Franks and Obodrites (in 789). There is certainly archaeological evidence for Frankish influences on the material culture of the Slavs, as well as on the design of fortifications (Brather 1996b, 189–92). Because there is some evidence for the origins of the fortresses in the vicinity of Groß Strömkendorf around the middle of the eighth century, a connection with the developments at the trading site can be deduced. It seems likely that at Groß Strömkendorf the marked changes of internal organisation around the second half of the eighth century are linked to the formation of political structures in the immediate surroundings of the site, and to the frequent contacts of the Obodrites with the Frankish kingdom. Consequently, the Danish claims to *Reric* might date back to a period prior to the consolidation of Slavonic power in the region.

Acknowledgements

The author is deeply grateful to Holger Dieterich, Kiel who was the principal illustrator and who prepared all the figures for publication. My thanks go to Alexander Pöche, Lübstorf for constructive criticism on an earlier draft. Thanks are also due to the Archäologisches Landesmuseum Mecklenburg-Vorpommern, Schloß Wiligrad, Lübstorf and Regina Schmitz, Lübstorf for permission to reproduce illustrations.

CHAPTER 17

Tjitsma, Wijnaldum: An Early Medieval Production Site in the Netherlands

Caroline Tulp

Wijnaldum

Tjitsma is a *terp* or dwelling mound near the village of Wijnaldum in the coastal area of Friesland province, in the north-west of the Netherlands (Fig. 17.1). It is one of several *terpen* still visible in the landscape which, in the provinces of Friesland and Groningen, are frequently searched by metal-detectorists and which yield a lot of metal finds.

Between 1991 and 1993 part of Tjitsma *terp* was excavated, for four principal reasons. First, an increasing number of metal-detector finds indicated that the top of the *terp* was eroding. Secondly, excavation allowed the erosion caused by agricultural activities like ploughing and deep-ploughing to be studied and raised the prospect of yielding more information on how to improve the protection of this type of monument. Third, in the 1950s a large gold and garnet brooch had been found (front cover), which suggested that Tjitsma represented the remains of an Early Medieval trading place of some importance. Finally, excavation offered the opportunity to establish an improved regional pottery chronology for the Early Middle Ages and to learn more about the *terp* region in general.

The excavation was undertaken by students and staff from the Universities of Groningen and Amsterdam. The number of excavated levels varied in each trench, a mechanical digger removing soil in layers of five centimetres or less, so that all the metal finds could be located by use of a metal-detector and plotted three-dimensionally. Additionally, the soil from features was wet-sieved through a 4 × 4mm mesh. As a result, the excavation yielded many small finds like beads, and environmental evidence such as charcoal and small fish and bird bones. Several different occupation periods were defined by

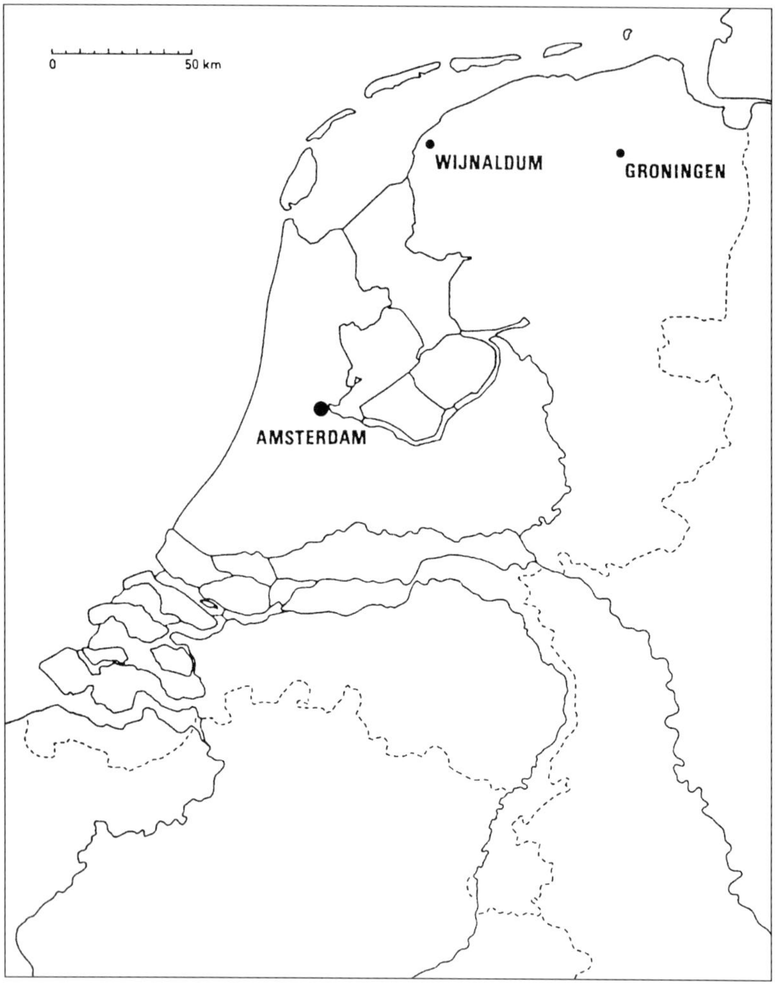

FIGURE 17.1.
The location of Tjitsma *terp*, Wijnaldum (after Besteman, Bos and Heidinga 1993).

pottery finds and in post-excavation eight different phases have been identified (all AD): I, 175–250; II, 250–300/325; III, 425–550; IV, 550–650; V, 650–750; VI, 750–800; VII, 800–850; VIII, 850–950 (Gerrets and de Koning 1999). There was a small gap in occupation between 325–425.

Craftworking evidence was found, for instance half-manufactured combs and unworked blanks are evidence for bone- and antler-working, although the small scale of production suggests the items were for local consumption instead of wider trade. Textile production is indicated by the finds of pottery loomweights, bone needles and spindle-whorls of different materials inside some small buildings. Amber had been worked on site in the fifth and sixth centuries while melted glass paste and many beads indicate local glass production (especially of beads) in the sixth century (Sablerolles 1999). None of these crafts provide evidence for mass production. There is, however, much evidence for the working of various metals, which seems to have taken place on a somewhat larger scale.

The working of precious metals

No evidence was found for the refining of gold and silver at Tjitsma, but there were traces of both the melting and working of precious metals in different periods of occupation. Evidence for the working of gold and silver was relatively common, the finds dating from the beginning of the fifth century through to the ninth century and including droplets of gold and silver, ingots, bars and rods, a die, a small hammer and a crucible fragment with tiny gold droplets. Other evidence is more indirect, coming from fragments of silver and gold objects, gold wire and touchstones.

The oldest indications of silverworking on the site came from the fifth century, from an ingot, a bar, a rod, and a droplet. A small iron hammer (Fig. 17.2a), of a type usually interpreted as used for working precious metals, was also found. Although no direct evidence for goldworking was found from this period, a gold sword mount containing eight gold nails was found with some pieces of lead, which was clearly meant for remelting or reuse (Fig. 17.2b).

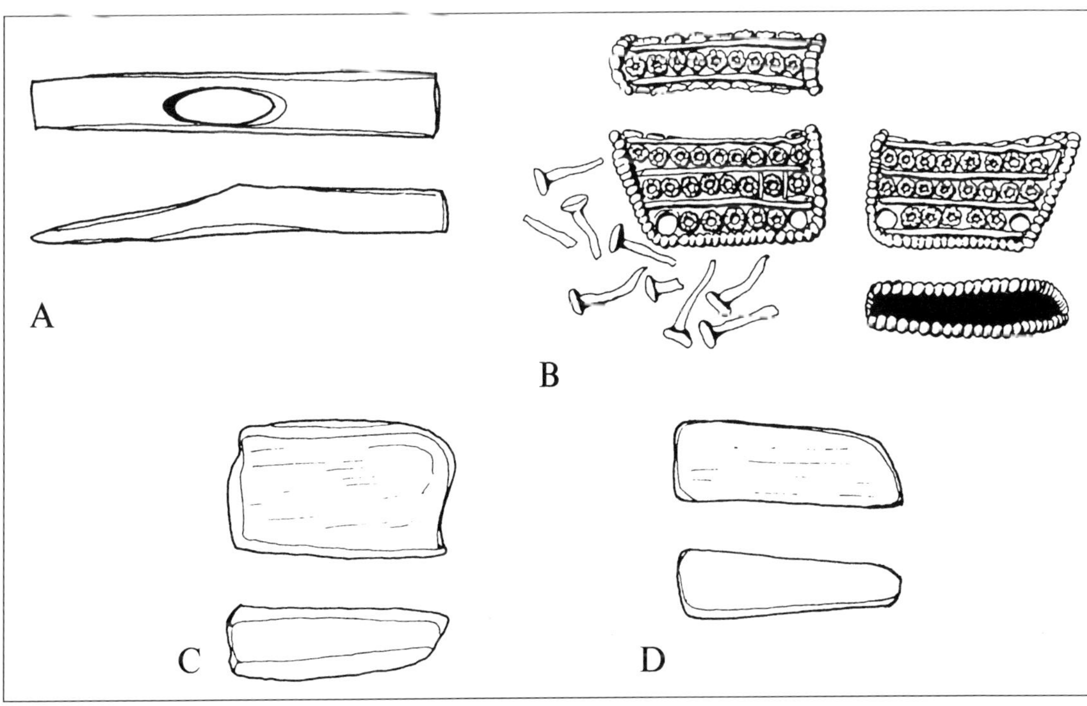

FIGURE 17.2. Finds associated with precious metalworking. (a) Small hammer. (b) Gold ?scabbard mount with nails. (c) and (d) Touchstones (*all J de Koning*). Scale 1:1.

the site (IV, or 550–650) was provided by a touchstone with traces of gold (Fig. 17.2c). These stones, used to test the quality of metals by the marks they leave on them, provide only indirect evidence for goldworking because they were also used in trade. This particular touchstone is rectangular, black (like lydite) with flat sides and slightly rounded edges and corners, its very regular and smooth surface having traces of gold on the front as well as on the back. The same period also yielded a fragment of rough garnet, retrieved from a well. Garnet, a semi-precious stone, was much used in the Early Medieval period in precious gold jewellery like the large golden cloisonné disc-on-bow brooch found at Tjitsma (front cover) (Mazo Karras 1985, 168–71; Nijboer and van Reekum 1999).

More finds date from 650–750, for example a crucible rim sherd fragment with a greyish-green glaze on the outside and also on the inside near the rim. The glaze contains many gold droplets, which vary from 0.1–0.5mm in diameter. A more spectacular find is a die for making cross-hatched patterns on gold foil (Fig. 17.3). Cross-hatched foil was commonly used in cloisonné jewellery of the period, being mounted in cells behind plates of translucent garnet. The

FIGURE 17.3. Copper-alloy die stamp with cross-hatched decoration. Size of object 17.4 × 16.1mm. (*Photograph: Colin Slack, English Heritage*)

Tjitsma pattern consists of squares of about one square millimetre, each divided into sixteen or twenty smaller squares. The die itself is of about thirty square millimetres, is made from copper-alloy (Tulp and Meeks 2000), and was found near to the brooch fragments and other traces of goldworking. No evidence for silverworking was found in this period.

Another touchstone was found in layers dating from the next period (750–800), again of oblong shape with flat sides and slightly rounded edges, and bearing traces of gold on one side (Fig. 17.2d). From the end of this period or the beginning of the next derives a thin gold rod which under the microscope shows stress marks caused by hammering. From Period VIII (850–950) one gold and two silver droplets were found which means that this is the only period in which it is certain that there was contemporaneous silver as well as goldworking.

Some other precious metal finds were found both before and after the excavation by amateur archaeologists, including a thick golden rod, a silver and a gold bar, a silver drop, a piece of melted silver and two gold melt pieces. These, and the finds from the excavation, are not concentrated in one specific part of the *terp,* with the exception of those from 650–750 which were found in the eastern part of the excavation. In the final period the finds seem to be from the southern area. Gold or silver working evidence does not occur in every occupation period but this does not necessarily mean that precious metals were not being worked; simply, excavation has not provided any positive evidence for the practice. The caveat must be added that not all the finds can be dated and this may have influenced the overall picture of precious metalworking.

It seems likely that at least in those periods for which there is evidence of gold or silver working, an itinerant smith went to the *terp* for commissions, because there is no direct evidence for a precious metalworker living at Tjitsma. What is clear from the above-average number of finds of precious metalworking, like bars, ingots and rods, is that between the fifth and ninth centuries there were times when there was much gold or silver in circulation.

Ironworking

Not only were many iron objects found at Tjitsma, there was much evidence for ironworking, including slags, fragments of hearth lining, hammerscale and bars. Two kinds of iron ore exist in the Netherlands: iron ore from rattlestones, which are found at the Veluwe, Nijmegen and Montferland; and bog ore found in the north of the Netherlands in peaty areas. At Tjitsma however, no traces were found of the production of iron from either bog ore or rattlestones. Instead, bars were probably imported from the south of Sweden.

Some early iron slags date from the period 250–300 and a feature was found which could be interpreted as the floor of a smithy, containing many corroded iron objects. The floor surface consisted of a rusty coloured loamy layer that contained a lot of charcoal and hammerscale. Unfortunately, the objects within were too corroded to distinguish between scrap metal, parts of objects, semi-manufactured objects or even tools.

By Period III (425–550), the concentration of ironworking finds had moved from the north to the west of the *terp* and a small amount of slags were also found dating to 475–550. From the beginning of the sixth century the evidence for ironworking began to increase. From Period IV (550–650) there is a large concentration of slags, hearth linings and bases. Because the slags formed on the bottom of a hearth, the form of the hearth itself can be deduced. All those from Tjitsma are more or less round and plano-convex in shape, the majority of which are datable belonging to the period 550–650. In many cases cinder was also found in relation to metalworking finds like hearth material or slags.

After 650 the number of ironworking finds diminishes quickly, but this picture is tempered by many of the iron finds and bars dating

FIGURE 17.4.
Iron bars from Tjitsma.
(a) Long bar.
(b) 'Ploughshare' (after J de Koning). (c) 'Spindle-shape'.
Scale 1:2.

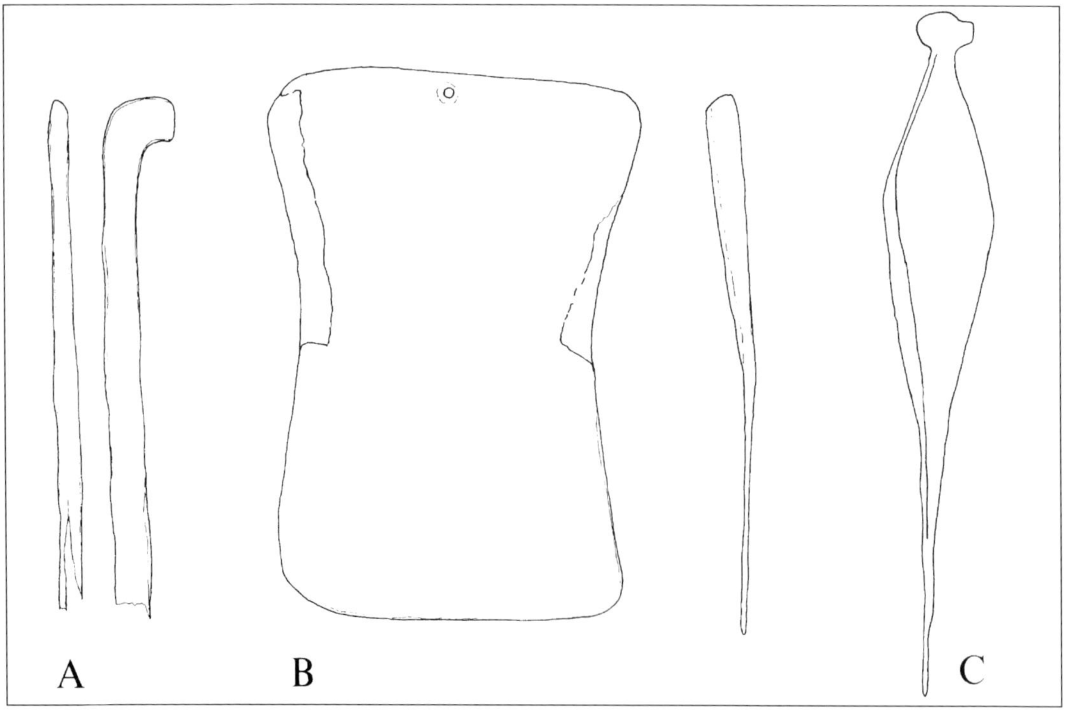

from this period. Most probably, ironworking continued elsewhere, perhaps to the south of the site which was not excavated. Different types of iron bar seem to have circulated during the eighth and ninth centuries, and can be divided into four groups. The first type, represented by two bars, is long, thin and flat (Fig. 17.4a) while another group are 'ploughshare' bars; Tjitsma has two which are quite flat with partially folded sides (Fig. 17.4b). The third type, identified by Schmutzhart (1997, ii, 64), is a spindle-shaped bar with a knob on one side and a long sharp point on the other (Fig. 17.4c). The fourth group consists of iron rods, but it is unclear whether these objects are bars, semi-manufactured objects or smithing refuse. Among the tools used in manufacturing iron objects were two large iron punches of long, rectangular shape, tapering at one end. Only one can be dated, to 775–850 (*ibid.*, ii, 73).

A total of 37.6kg of slag was found at Tjitsma, most of it from the western part of the excavation. The slag all derived from wells and middens rather than a smithy or workshop area and it is possible that the work area of the smith was situated slightly further to the west of the concentration.

Copper alloys

During the excavation much copper-alloy was found, in the form of objects including coins, ingots, bars and sheeting, as well as scrap metal, drops, melt and casting pieces. Many of the sheet fragments are folded and some have clear cutting marks. Evidence for bronzeworking comes from lead fragments, which could have been used for alloying, found in the same contexts as pieces of copper-alloy and the fragments of crucibles, often from the same scrap metal contexts. Further evidence consists of moulds and several semi-manufactured objects.

From 250–350 bronzeworking was concentrated in the northern part of the excavated area. Four hearths were excavated, and open moulds for casting ingots, crucible fragments, copper and lead scrap metal, a copper ingot and three bars were all found in the vicinity. The smithy floor also dates from this period, hammerscale, iron objects, copper-alloy and lead all being found in the floor, indicating these different metals to have been worked in the same place. Unfortunately, it is unknown whether one smith was working both metals, or whether different metalworkers were working alongside each other. It is also unclear whether there is a difference in the dates, with a smith working iron and later the same area being used by another smith, for bronzeworking, yet all within the same archaeological period.

In Period III (425–550) the focus of the bronzeworking appears to have shifted from the north to the west of the *terp*. No actual workshop was found, but all the metalworking finds were concentrated here, including two bars and several hearths. Many Roman bronze coins, both cut and uncut were also found in dated features, while to the east of the *terp* a coin was found together with a melted copper-alloy

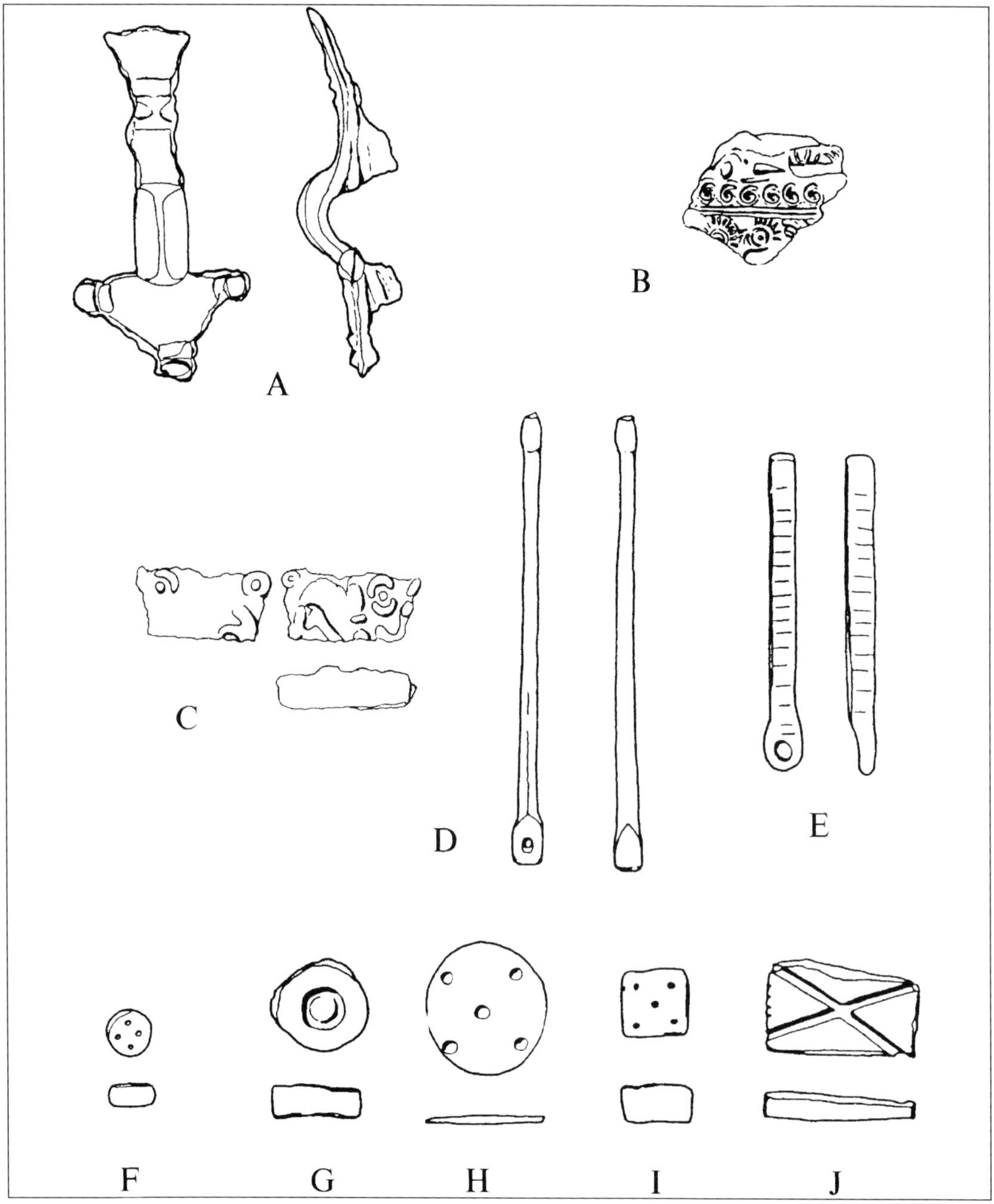

fragment; four other coins within a metalworking context were located near each other, some cut into quarters. Only four of the metalworking crucibles from Tjitsma contain copper-alloy droplets. All the fragments of crucible walling (except for two almost complete examples) are small, making it difficult to say anything about their original size or shape, but most date from the fifth to the beginning of the seventh century and appeared in the metalworking concentration, often in the same features as lead, copper-alloy, or moulds. Within this, the bulk of the copper-alloy finds recovered date from 550–650 and were concentrated to the west of Tjitsma. After 650 the number of bronzeworking finds diminishes rapidly with no concentration, although the stray finds tend to be from the eastern part of the *terp* and by Periods VI–VII (750–850) some copper-alloy finds were found in the south part of the *terp* but again no longer forming any concentrations.

Among the metalworking debris was much hearth material, weighing 21.8kg and characterised by being mostly glazed on the inside, often with some slag remains attached. The hearth walls sometimes consisted of a more or less powdery, thick loamy layer in several colours, varying from yellow to pink/purple. No real tuyères (which protect the bellows from the fire) were found at the *terp*, only holes in the linings of hearths, through which the tuyères passed. These pieces of hearth lining had a very glazed and slag-like front, the earliest dating from 475–550 and the latest to 750–850. The tuyères were all found in contexts containing iron slags and fragments of hearth material.

Three semi-manufactured copper-alloy objects of interest were also found in the metalworking areas. The first is a cruciform brooch with its casting flash lines still visible and the perforations for the hinge yet to be made (Fig. 17.5a). The other two are semi-manufactured keys. One was found together with two fragments of lead sheet and while neither keys have flash lines, they remain rough and unfinished, with their bits yet to be added. Production is also indicated by open moulds, some dated to the sixth century, which were found principally in the metalwork concentration. They include the fragment of a mould for a brooch which could have been part of either a closed mould or one consisting of several parts. The brooch was probably of square-headed form and the mould preserves much fine detail (Fig. 17.5b).

FIGURE 17.5 (*opposite*). Assorted finds from Tjitsma. (a) Unfinished copper-alloy cruciform brooch. (b) Fragment of a mould for a brooch, probably of square-headed form. (c) Lead object with an animal, possibly a model for mould-making. (d) and (e) Copper-alloy balance arms. (f)–(j) Copper-alloy weights (*all J de Koning*). Scale: all at 1:1.

Lead

Much lead was found in the excavations, probably having been used in bronzeworking; almost without exception, pieces of lead were found together with copper-alloy scraps and sometimes with pieces of moulds or crucible sherds.

The first period of the site's use revealed lead finds only in the smithy floor and near some hearths in the northern part of the *terp*, but from the end of the following period (425–550) onwards, more lead finds were found across the site. Noteworthy among these is one object decorated on both sides (Fig. 17.5c). The find looks like an animal figure but is unlikely to be a trial casting because it has no flash lines and the fact that both sides are decorated make it doubtful that it is a brooch or a brooch trial piece. It may instead have been a model used for making a two-piece mould.

Other small finds

There are a number of finds that cannot be associated with only metalworking. For instance, several weights and scales have been recovered at Tjitsma, as have two fragments of copper-alloy beam balances, all of which may have been used in trade. One balance fragment is long and rectangular with a hole at one end, while the other has the same shape, but is shorter, having lines upon it, presumably for measurement although they are not equally spaced (Fig. 17.5d and e). Among the many weights from the *terp*, a selection of which are shown in Fig. 17.5f-j, most were retrieved from the area of metalworking although not apparently deriving from these manufacturing contexts. All the copper-alloy weights are flat and have marks, for instance four or five dots or a cross, but there seems to be no relation between the weight and the marks. Most appear to date from the seventh century and help to suggest a date for the balances.

More immediately appealing is the large golden cloisonné disc-on-bow brooch found at Tjitsma in the 1950s (front cover). Although it is known to have been found in a ditch, the exact findspot is unclear. Over the years other fragments of the brooch have been discovered by metal-detectorists and during the excavation several more fragments were retrieved. The brooch dates from the late sixth to early seventh century and consists of pieces of silver and gold alloys (Nijboer and van Reekum 1999). Its back has evidence for cutting, suggesting two possible interpretations: that it was in the possession of a smith for reuse, or for repair. Of these, the cut-marks and the absence of any fragments of the disc suggests the imminent reuse of the brooch. In this scenario, the disc could have been reused for making another piece of jewellery. Evidence supporting its need for repair could be the wear evident on the brooch (Nijboer and van Reekum 1999). The pattern of the foil die found in excavation on the *terp* (Fig. 17.3) does not fit that on the gold foil of this brooch, making it uncertain whether the brooch was produced locally. The die and the rough piece of garnet are, however, evidence that a smith working at Tjitsma had the knowledge to make these kind of brooches.

Among other precious finds from the site was the gold scabbard mount, dating from the early sixth century, excavated in a layer of turves (Fig. 17.2b). Only one side is decorated, with rows of small circles consisting of granules carelessly melted together, the rows separated from each other by thin, uneven, strips of gold wire. The edges of the mount are bordered by a row of granules and the corners are pierced with small holes. The object had been folded double and then used to contain eight small gold nails which would fit through the mount's holes – the nails therefore appear to be associated with the mount, especially had the mount been one of a matching pair, positioned either side of a scabbard. When taken off, the eight nails had evidently been kept in one of the mounts. It is uncertain whether the mount and the nails were going to be reused on another scabbard or whether they were all intended for remelting.

Among other gold or gilded objects were a pendant, a bird brooch, the decorated knob of a brooch and a pendant using a forged coin. Few silver objects were found and where datable, belong to the eighth and ninth centuries. The objects consist of two brooches, an Arab *dirhem*, a pendant and two bracelets. A silver nail which was recovered may have been used to attach a shield boss (Huisman 1997).

Among the many copper-alloy objects recovered are mounts, buckles, brooches, needles, jewellery, weights, keys, knives, nails, tweezers and military objects (Huisman 1997). The lead and lead/tin alloyed objects appear to date from around the eighth and ninth centuries and include three mounts, a lead sieve, a weight, four spindle whorls, a pendant, a pseudo-coin fibula and a Maltese cross-shaped fibula (Huisman 1997). 145 iron objects were studied out of a total of about 2,500. Of these 145, about half were tools for working metal, wood, bone and antler, and possibly leather. The rest of the objects were used in hunting, personal grooming, and in a domestic context. No tools for agriculture or cattle were found (Schmutzhart 1997).

Wijnaldum in context

The problem with interpreting the results of the excavation is the representativity of the site. Tjitsma is only one in a row of *terpen* and remains only partially excavated, making it difficult to say something about social and economic differentiation between these settlements. Indeed, few examples have been excavated in the *terp* region more generally. In Oosterbeintum an Early Medieval cemetery was excavated in 1987 (Knol *et al.* 1995–6), while Ezinge and Godlinze were excavated at the beginning of the twentieth century (Waterbolk 1991; van Giffen 1919). In 1997 the lower levels of the partly-disturbed *terp* of Winsum in Friesland were excavated, but the finds remain only partly published in a small Dutch university publication. It is, consequently, difficult to compare Wijnaldum to other sites in the region. More recently, there have been many metal objects recovered from the *terpen*, but as metal-detector finds, they have no context. A familiar associated problem is the uncertainty over how many finds are being made but left unreported to the provincial archaeological authorities and museums. Such a loss of information is not new: in the first half of the last century much of the fertile soil of the *terpen* was sold and moved, destroying the sites in the process. Finally, there is an unevenness in the quality of research into these Early Medieval sites. In contrast to earlier excavations, wet sieving was undertaken during the Wijnaldum excavation, resulting, for instance, in the discovery of many beads and small bird and fish bone fragments. This level of information cannot be compared easily with the results from other sites.

With these reservations in mind, some comment may be offered. The importation of both metal, such as iron ore, and pottery at Tjitsma indicates the site's participation in wider trade networks, despite the evidence for only small-scale craft production within the *terp*. Its location may have much to do with this. Tjitsma is located close to the sea, and to the important trade routes from Dorestad to England, north Germany and Scandinavia, and to the river systems heading inland. Interestingly, despite this, Wijnaldum appears never to have grown into a major trade centre. Within the wider context of the *terpen*, the discovery of metal objects appear to say something about the importance of some sites despite a lack of excavation.

Many gold finds are known from sixth- and seventh-century Friesland and among the metal-detector finds from *terpen*, some appear to be richer in finds than others. For example, Dongjum *terp* is quite rich, while a large gold deposit was found in Wiewerd. Wijnaldum similarly appears to be among the richer *terpen*, although not on the same scale as Scandinavian production centres like Birke or Helgö. Nevertheless, its imported goods and rich metalwork assemblage indicates that it constituted a small production centre engaged in trade and presumably controlled by a local chief. The principal difficulty remains the need for qualitative data from other *terpen* with which to compare Wijnaldum – and this provides the challenge for future archaeological investigation.

Acknowledgements

I would like to thank the following people and institutions: the Laboratory of Conservation and Material Sciences of the Groningen Institute of Archaeology (GIA), University of Groningen (RUG); Jurjen Bos and Danny Gerrets for their cooperation; Justine Bayley and Nigel Meeks for helping me with the analyses of several finds; English Heritage Ancient Monuments Laboratory and the Department of Scientific Research of the British Museum for the use of their facilities; and the Netherlands Organisation for Scientific Research (NWO) for funding my internship at English Heritage.

CHAPTER 18

The Fate of the Ports of the Lower Seine Valley at the End of the Ninth Century

Jacques Le Maho (translated by Joy Southam)

This chapter investigates the consequences of the Scandinavian raids on the ports of the Lower Seine valley in the second half of the ninth century. It examines: the impact of these raids during the period from the first Viking incursion in 841 to the lifting of the siege of Paris in 886; the consequences of transforming the city of Rouen into a fortified town in 889–90; the population movements that textual and toponymic sources suggest in the Lower Seine area between the end of the 880s and the end of the ninth century; and the circumstances of the establishment of the first Viking colonies.*

The peopling of the Lower Seine before the end of the 880s

In Rouen, a distinction needs to be made between the area surrounded by city walls, and the suburban area. The seat of Notre Dame cathedral and its chapter, of several monasteries, of the count's palace and doubtless many residences of the local leading citizens, Rouen was a centre of administrative and religious power. The intramural area, which covered close on 18 hectares, was probably quite sparsely populated. Around the houses of the clergy and the monastic cloisters extended courtyards, gardens and vast orchards, and the city almost certainly contained a number of open spaces. The likely presence of quite a number of private courtyards, with their buildings scattered randomly, only reinforces the impression of a semi-rural landscape,

* This chapter represents the summary of a study set out in more detail in a work in preparation on *Rouen et les Vikings – De la Cite Carolingienne à la Ville Normande.* One may find there all the references and arguments which it has not been possible to include in this present paper.

similar to the appearance of Winchester and London during the first centuries of the Anglo-Saxon period.

Outside the walls, the settlement pattern differed. Though numerous spaces were not built up, and vast cemeteries extended around the funerary churches, the artisan quarters were located in this *suburbium.* Different *portus* assured the provisioning of the town. We may recall two well-known texts from the eighth and ninth centuries, the *Life of St Winnebald* where a market 'near to the city of Rouen' is mentioned, and the account in Nithard's *History of the Sons of Louis the Pious*, of the arrival in 841 of a convoy of twenty-eight merchant ships, to a harbour site on the left bank of the Seine and therefore opposite the city (Scholz and Rogers 1972, 147). The main population of craftsmen and tradesmen therefore resided in an area outside the walls, doubtless scattered in quite a large district around the city. Finally, on the eve of the first Viking raid, a considerable part of the revenues of the *portus* of Rouen, exactly half according to a confirmation charter of 876, went to the Rouen abbey of Saint-Ouen, the remainder of the taxes probably entering fiscal coffers (Le Maho 1995); this point is of importance as we will see later.

If the presence of an important royal mint in Rouen tends to focus the attention of Carolingian economic historians on this town, it should not be forgotten that the Lower Seine region sheltered numerous other ports up to the end of the ninth century. Most of these were monastic properties. The abbeys situated in immediate proximity to the river, such as Jumièges, Fontenelle (Saint-Wandrille-Rançon), and *Logium* (Caudebec-en-Caux) on the north bank, *Pentale* (Saint-Samson-de-la-Roque) and *Pennante* (Saint-Pierre-du-val) on the south bank, made use of their own ports on the Seine, to which were occasionally added annexed sites like those of Jumièges at Duclair, at Vieux-Port and at Quillebeuf. The abbeys a little further from the Seine also had access to the river. It is quite probable that the monks of Montivilliers, for example, had berths for their ships at Harfleur in the pre-Viking period. Other *vici* harbour installations belonged to establishments such as Sanvic at the entrance to the bay of the Seine, probable site of the *portus* of the abbey of Saint-Denis, through which passed a cargo of lead from Quentovic in 810; *Moriniacus*, an unidentified river port local to Rouen, which a text of 860 mentions as the property of Corbion Abbey (Saint-Lhômer) in the Perche; or even Pont-de-l'Arche above Rouen, perhaps a possession of the monastery of Saint-Vigor de Bayeux.

Fishing must have represented an important activity to these monastic ports, but they also ensured the passage of men and goods, whether over short distances – it seems that most of these crossing points had been under the control of the abbeys – or, for more important journeys. It was by boat that the principal monasteries of the Seine like Fontenelle and Jumièges maintained communication with their estates of the Parisis, Cotentin, Bessin or Boulonnais regions. The involvement of these abbeys in Channel trade is also well known. Documentary sources, however, give us little information on the importance of settlements associated with these ports. Most often one has to be content with vague hints, like the prosperity which trade with England brought to the Jumièges region in the lifetime of St Philibert (eighth to ninth century). We have only two indications of figures in our sources: the taking of sixty-eight hostages by the Vikings from the port of the abbey of Saint-Denis (without doubt Sanvic); and the mention of the twenty-eight smallholdings in the port of Fontenelle belonging to the monastic estate. These references suggests the existence of settlements, extensive in the second case, indicating that the port ought to be distinct from the monastic *vicus* closer to the abbey, where metals, leathers and textiles delivered in large quantities to the monastery were processed. The impression which emerges from this brief outline of the Lower Seine landscape before the first Viking raids is that of an active and populated countryside, but in which economic activities were scattered in a nebula of harbour-sites or of craft and merchant *vici*, without a real preponderance appearing around Rouen.

In spite of repeated incursions by Scandinavian war bands from 841, this system held together without much modification until the end of the 880s. The abbeys were, however, nearly all evacuated before this date. The monks from Saint-Ouen, Rouen, found refuge at Gasny (Eure) towards the beginning of the 860s, then, after the Viking raid of 876, to Condé-sur-Aisne (Aisne), near Soissons. The move must have been followed by other Rouen communities, like those caring for the relics of St Mellon and St Filleul, while the body of St Austreberthe, foundress of the monastery of Pavilly, was taken to Saint-Valéry-sur-Somme and then to Ponthieu. The monks of Fontenelle left as early as 858 on a long exodus which took them as far as Montreuil-sur-Mer and to Boulogne-sur-Mer. As for those at Jumièges, after a number of episodes, their wandering ended at Haspres (Nord) in the Cambrai area. At the start of the 880s it is likely that not a single monastery operated in the Lower Seine area.

Despite this, the activity of the ports had not ceased. From their coastal refuges of Boulogne and Ponthieu, the monks of Fontenelle had kept in contact with their lands on the Seine, and a text from the abbey of Centule suggests that the abbot of Jumièges, who had withdrawn to Saint-Riquier in the 860s, was doing the same. Even at

Rouen, the royal mint continued to strike coinage in abundance after 864, demonstrating the maintenance of economic activity and survival of commercial links between the city of the Lower Seine and Quentovic. Saint-Ouen's possession of half the revenues from the town *portus* was confirmed in 876, and there is no reason to think that these rights fell into disuse. In 885, the Vikings arriving at Rouen from the interior of the country found enough merchant boats on site to get their whole army across the river. From all this, it seems that a large part of the active population had stayed in the area, in other words that the *vici* of the Seine were still inhabited. Even in Rouen, there is no indication of a withdrawal by the inhabitants from the city's suburbs. Like the example of Nantes, it presents all the characteristics of an 'open town' and it is apparently into the almost deserted Roman *castrum* of Rouen that the Vikings entered on at least two occasions, first in 851, and again in 885. Revealingly, Archbishop Venilon had a refuge fitted out at Andely in the Vexin from the beginning of the 860s while in 876 Archbishop John finally had to leave the province and retreated to his residence at Braine in the Soissons area, where he was joined by his canons. Nothing indicates that the archbishop returned to Rouen before the end of the 880s.

Rouen: a city of refuge from 888 to 890

During the winter of 889–890, the Vikings who had just been repelled from the Parisian region by Odo, made their way towards the Cotentin and laid siege to the town of Saint-Lô. A large number of inhabitants took refuge in this stronghold, including Lista, bishop of Coutances. The town was taken and all the population was killed, including the bishop. The Vikings continued their progress into the interior of the country without meeting much resistance. They were only driven away in the autumn of 890, by a coalition of Breton forces commanded by Alan the Great. Meanwhile, the Viking attacks had provoked a massive exodus of clerics and religious communities from the Cotentin and from the extreme west of the Bessin area.

In dealing with these multiple movements, thirteen groups can be identified who moved to the east of the province with their relics. Several of them settled in Rouen itself. Bishop Ragenard, Lista's successor to Coutances, settled with his canons in the city's church of Saint-Saveur. The probable site of an ancient monastery, this church and its adjoining lands, was granted to them by King Odo (the alleged gift by Rollo to Bishop Thierry in 913 is, to all appearances, only a confirmation). Soon rechristened with the title of Saint-Lô, Saint-Saveur's church was to remain the see for the bishops of Coutances until the beginning of the eleventh century. The monks of the abbey of *Nantus* (Saint-Marcouf, Manche) settled opposite the city at the port of Emendreville, while another group occupied a chapel near the high south defensive wall with the relics of St Candide, an obscure individual venerated at Picauville (Manche). We should also mention the probable journey to Rouen of a fourth group with the relics of St Leon of Coutances, a fifth with the body of St Germain the Scot and a sixth with that of St Jean originally from Deux-Jumeaux (Calvados) in the diocese of Bayeux. All left the Cotentin or the western borders of the Bessin, probably at the end of 889 or at the beginning of 890 (Le Maho 1999).

The fact that these monks in exile chose the city of Rouen to fall back to, with the obvious intention of settling there, shows the situation in the town had changed radically. In fact, archaeology bears witness to major transformations in the city district. Part of the high north defensive wall of the *castrum* was reconstructed at the end of the ninth century, as was the Beauvais gate at the northern entrance to the ancient *cardo maximus*. In the interior of the city itself, the road system was the subject of a complete reconstruction. Numerous north-south axes, inherited from the Gallo-Roman system were abandoned and new roads developed, spreading out to east and west at a right angle to a central north-south road (Gauthiez 1998, 81–3). At the same time, archaeological finds witness a rapid and considerable increase in the density of settlement inside the walled city. Close to the cathedral, excavations from 1980–90 brought to light remains of two small blocks of dwellings established at the end of the ninth century on the edge of the Rue Saint-Romain and the Rue du Change, on ground previously occupied by the canonical cloister and buildings of the archbishop's palace. Their construction coincides with the establishment of the new road system and it was probably the same for numerous other settlement sites located inside the city, but which have so far only been revealed as courtyard floors and clusters of domestic pits; the *terminus post quem* of these are invariably the end of the ninth or beginning of the tenth centuries. The houses brought to light next to the cathedral were regular in plan, constituting enclosures in strips perpendicular to the road with a constant width of six metres.

Thus, when the religious groups chased from the Cotentin came to settle in Rouen, it seems that the town's fortifications were repaired and that the intramural zone was the subject of an important urban redevelopment, accompanied by a general restructuring of the land register and a parcelling out of the land plots. This raises a series of questions, one of them being to whom the initiative for this operation can be attributed. The archbishop might be considered first, on the assumption that he had returned to Rouen in 889–90, which is not certain; on the other hand it is clear that his long absence had enabled the extension of secular power in a large part of the town to his cost. Originally, large areas of the city belonged to the monasteries and to notable families. But, when it had become obvious that the religious communities in their distant refuges were no longer in a position to administer their estates in Rouen, these monastic properties had been united into the charge of the royal fisc. This is known for the monastery of Saint-Saveur, in the king's hands in 889–90, and it is very probably the case for Saint-Amand, which was in Rollo's hands after 911. As for the properties of the great Rouen families, they were also destined to rejoin the public domain once the city was declared *loca deserta*; one can assume that the flight of the urban elite, because of the Viking danger, had considerably increased the number of properties in escheat. At the end of the ninth century, therefore, the king had almost complete control over the whole city, reserving the estate of the archbishop and chapter. It follows that the reorganisation of this urban space resulted from an initiative by King Odo (888–98).

The election of Odo by the elders of the kingdom had been the political reward for his brilliant victory over the Vikings at the siege of Paris (885–6). The first major success achieved over the Scandinavian invaders, this victory restored confidence to the Frankish authorities and encouraged the establishment of a complete defensive infrastructure in Francia. *Castella* were built just about everywhere by counts and abbots, and a number of cities were transformed into refuge-towns. The case of Rouen is therefore not isolated. However, in comparison to Chartres, Angers and Rheims, for example, the city was almost empty of inhabitants when it was subject to this urban reconstruction. The question is therefore to determine the origins of the civilian population which then came to repopulate the city, established in a space designed and refitted for the circumstances.

We might first consider the refugees coming from the surrounding countryside. But contrary to this hypothesis, toponymic data, as early as the documentary and archaeological evidence, indicates a great continuity in the occupation of peasant villages in the Seine valley throughout the period under consideration. On the other hand, there are numerous signs of a strong concentration of artisans and merchants in the city. In a passage doubtless inspired by a tradition from Jumièges – to which we will return – Dudo of Saint-Quentin (writing 1015×1026) alluded to merchant refugees in Rouen. A famous document from the abbey of Saint-Denis, the pseudo-gift of Dagobert (621–37) but dated variously to the end of the ninth or beginning of the tenth century, also mentions the 'merchants of Rouen'. Finally, if the archaeological data is quite sparse on the subject, it remains significant that the only two areas of intramural settlement dating from the beginning of the tenth century to have been the subject of extensive excavations, the cathedral quarter and the Lycée Camille-Saint-Saëns, have yielded, in the former, traces of metal-working activity and in the latter, waste from bone-working. It is a small step to imagine that at the end of the ninth century refugees made up the core of the large population residing in the city into the middle ages, whose professions came to provide several street names in this part of the city, including those of exchange, ironworkers and hosiers.

These observations lead us to suppose that at least a part of the population within the city at the end of the ninth century came from the ancient harbour and mercantile districts of the Rouen suburbs. Their transfer into the walled zone by Odo might be compared with the operation carried out by Alfred the Great for the transfer of the merchant suburb of *Lundenwic* into the city of London. But the transferred population seems much too large to have come only from the immediate area. Since the departure of the monks, the ports and monastic *vici* of the Lower Seine had maintained their activity to a creditable level, but there came a point at which the religious communities in exile were no longer in a state to administer them. One after another, most of these *vici* ended by falling into the royal fisc, with the exception, perhaps, of some riverside settlements still in the possession of powerful lay abbots who themselves owed their benefices to royal favour. We may therefore suggest that at the end of the 880s, the vast majority of the harbour *vici* of the Seine were in the hands of the king. Consequently, there are good reasons for thinking that the inhabitants of these *vici*, craftsmen and merchants, constituted the largest part of the population settled in the city of Rouen. This parallels other well-known cases, for instance the transferral to Montreuil-sur-Mer of the *portus* of the Lower Canche valley, and of the inhabitants of *Hamwic* and the *vici* of the Southampton region, into the city of Winchester. By relocating the main merchant population of the countryside in the same urban site, the organisers of the operation clearly aimed to control these human resources better and to draw from them the maximum profit. We must not, therefore, misjudge the real character of these population movements; far from being spontaneous, they were planned, organised and even accomplished under constraints. Indeed, we may recall a famous precedent, the transfer to Hedeby in 808 by the Danish king Godfred, of the whole population of the port of *Reric*, identified as Groß Strömkendorf, in the bay of Wismar at Mecklenburg (Tummuscheit, this vol.). Here, the deportees – they cannot be called anything else – had to complete a crossing of almost 130km.

The ports of the Seine: from abandonment to reoccupation by the Vikings

Transferring a large part of the population of the Seine *vici* to Rouen around 888–90, led to a massive desertion of these ports. Correlating numerous sources makes us realise the extent of this phenomenon, and the sites concerned may be divided into two categories: those ports which were permanently abandoned or for a long time, and those that were reoccupied by the Scandinavians.

During the exodus of the clergy from the Cotentin to the Rouen region in 889/890, several groups came to settle in the villages on the banks of the Seine vacated by the inhabitants. The best documented case is of the three ports in the Jumièges region, all ancient dependencies of the abbey. According to a late twelfth-century account inserted in a collection, the *Miracula Sancti Pauli*, the place called Saint-Paul, on the north bank (localité de Saint-Paul, commune Duclair), had been abandoned some time during the 880s. A group of monks reoccupied the houses surrounding the church and placed in the latter the body of St Clair which the clerics had carried with them on leaving the Cotentin. We are less well informed about the conditions prevailing with the setting up of two other groups, one with the body of St Hameltrude at the port of Saint-Vaast, on the south bank opposite Jumièges (loc. de Saint-Vaast, comm. Heurtcauville), the other with the body of St Pèlerin in a port on the north bank (loc. de Le Passage, comm. Jumièges). The new occupants only lived there a few years; after their departure, the three sites were abandoned again, leaving only the churches, of which two fell into ruins (loc. de Le Passage and Saint-Paul) (Le Maho 1999, 150–60). The other monastic ports of the Seine shared a similar fate. Those of Fontenelle Abbey, in the Caude-becquet region, were abandoned for good; when in 960 this settlement was restored, the monks' port was transferred to Caudebec. A tradition of 'deserted village' was also attached to the hamlet of Grestain in the Seine bay, probable site of the abbey of Pennante (comm. Saint-Pierre-du-Val, Eure), mentioned for the second time in 833. At the beginning of the eleventh century, only the ruins of the ancient chapel of Notre Dame remained on the site.

It would seem that the cases of prolonged abandonment were in a minority. Indeed, if we examine the map of Scandinavian place-names in the Lower Seine, the evidence is striking, although the density of these place-names is no more significant in this region than elsewhere.

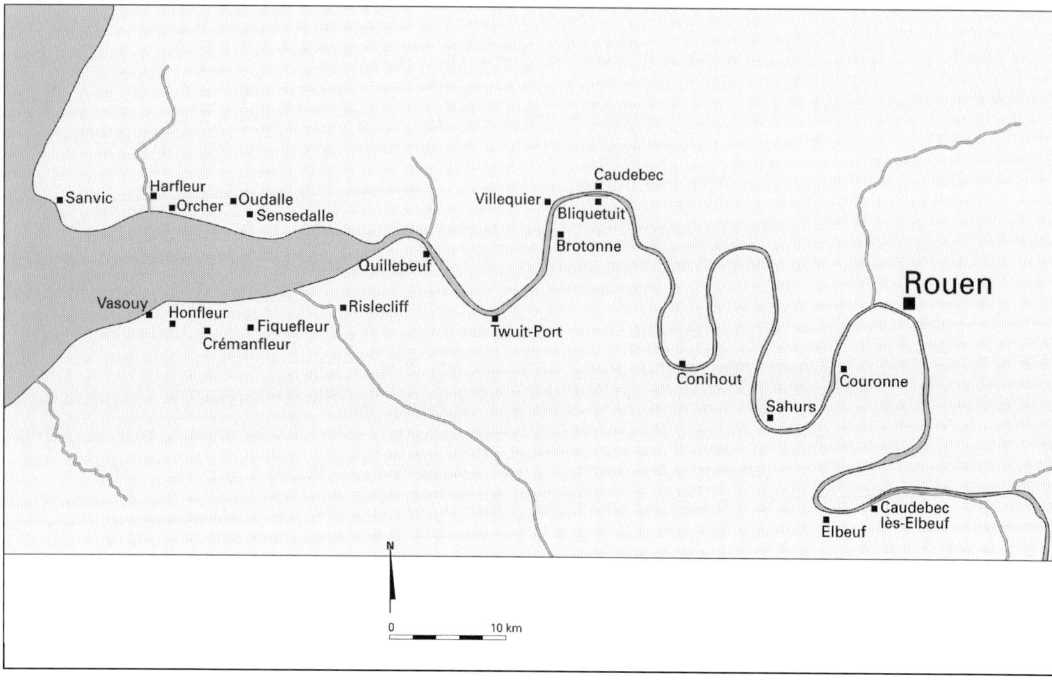

FIGURE 18.1.
The ports of the Lower Seine in the ninth and tenth centuries.

But, in all cases, the sites are closely linked to the river economy, as mercantile and harbour villages, and fishing or sail-making hamlets. Moreover, there are numerous signs of occupation on these sites from the pre-Viking period.

We may begin our inventory on the north bank, progressing upstream (Fig. 18.1). At the entrance of the bay, near the point of Chef-de-Caux, is Sanvic, which seems to correspond to the anonymous *portus* of Saint-Denis Abbey, mentioned in a charter of 810. Next is Harfleur at the mouth of the Lézarde, a port which was perhaps part of the possessions of Montivilliers Abbey in the pre-Viking era, and which would appear to be the ancient *Caracotinum* of the *Antonine Itinerary*. Then there are Orcher, Oudalle and Sensedalle, where three small valleys overlook a vast expanse of salt marshes; and Villequier, a possession of Fontenelle Abbey since the seventh century and probably one of the 'Mesnils' on the banks of the Seine mentioned in a diploma of Charles the Bald of 854; and Caudebec-en-Caux, once a river port, and crossing point on the Rouen route to Lower Normandy and site of the nunnery of *Logium*, last mentioned in 833. Continuing upstream there is Conihout, a hamlet six kilometres upstream from the Carolingian port of Jumièges Abbey; and to finish on the north bank, there is Sahurs, attested as a possession of the church of Bayeux in the eleventh century and a possible pre-Viking dependency of this church.

The Fate of the Ports of the Lower Seine Valley at the End of the Ninth Century

On the south bank, there is the same procession of Scandinavian place-names and the same relationship with the harbour sites. The series begins at the entrance of the bay with Honfleur, Crémanfleur and Fiquefleur, all three at the mouth of inshore streams. Next is Rislecliff at the mouth of the Risle, a port frequented in the pre-Viking period by ships from the abbeys of Pental and Saint-Germain-des-Prés. At Quillebeuf was a major *portus*, returned to Jumièges Abbey at the time of its restoration *c.* 942; further upstream were two ancient river crossings also part of the estates restored to Jumièges, the first at Vieux-Port, formerly Twuit-Port, on the old route from Lillebonne to Brionne, the second at Bliquetuit opposite Caudebec-en-Caux, on the route from Rouen to Brionne. Between the two was Brotonne, a replacement of the primitive place-name *Arelaunum* which indicates a royal Merovingian estate with its forest, palace and port on the Seine, last mentioned in its old form in a Jumièges diploma of 849. On the outskirts of Rouen and in the area of the town's harbour dependencies, we find Couronne (comm. of Grande-Couronne and Petit-Couronne), whose pre-Viking name may be ignored, but where the archaeology and church dedications witness Merovingian antecedents; upstream from the town, one finds Elbeuf and Caudebec-lès-Elbeuf, site of the large ancient *vicus* of *Uggade*. In total, therefore, there are some twenty hamlets or localities, of which a large majority are ancient monastic ports, which received a new Scandinavian name in the tenth century.

To get a more exact idea of the importance of this wave of toponymic change, it remains to outline the list of ports surviving under their ancient or later Medieval names. Leaving aside three recently alleged cases of continuity which are far from secure,* we can only see in this series the names of Quenneport (comm. Val-de-la-Haye), generally identified as *Quenzicoportus* in a charter of 875; La Fontaine (comm. of Hénouville); Duclair, witnessed about 860 under the form *Duroclarum*; Le Trait, site of a very old river crossing (*trajectus*); Aizier (canton of Quillebeuf) which derived from the ancient *Aysiacus*; and perhaps Jobles (comm. of Fatouville-Grestain), if its eleventh-century name *Joninis* can be equated with the *Jovitinos*/*Jovitinis* of a Fontenelle

* The ancient port of Leure, today part of Le Havre, is called *Lodorum* in the charters of Longueville Priory at the end of the twelfth century (Cacheux 1916; 21, 26 and 29) from whence comes the hypothesis of a name composed with the ancient suffix *–durum* (Beaurepaire 1969, 35). However, the most ancient attestation, under the form *Lure c.*1060 makes this interpretation problematic (Beaurepaire 1984, 557). There is little at Croisset (commune Canteleu) and at La Bouille (commune of Crand-Couronne) to identify the *Crisciago* and *Botilo* of Bishop Bertrand of Mans' will as has been suggested recently (Weidemann 1986, 17 No. 15).

Abbey charter of 854. Even if no exact correlation is possible with these examples, the numbers are eloquent: only five or six names were maintained compared to about twenty cases of name changes.

How can this wave of toponymic change be interpreted? It is difficult to use the same argument as that advanced for estates renamed with a Scandinavian name in rural surroundings, for example in the Caux region; that interpretation ascribes changes to a minority Scandinavian presence with the local chiefs having received these places in freehold after 911. For the ports, the greater number of the centres concerned were taken into the public domain in the tenth and eleventh centuries. On the other hand, with the exception of a few dependencies like 'the clearing of *Belingethuyth*' or the small islands of the Seine exploited for their pasture like the *Torholm* islands (Oiseel) and *Engohomme* (by Martot), there is sparse evidence here for Scandinavian place-names based on an anthroponym; the vast majority of Scandinavian place-names in the Lower Seine are of a descriptive nature and allied to the Viking nomenclature of the Cotentin seaboard studied by René Lepelley. Here, as noticed by David Bates, the toponymic groupings of this type imply a mass peopling occurred in a relatively short time (Bates 1982, 18). In these circumstances the toponymic changes, with the renaming of old settlements, would be linked to a renewal of population density, that is, to the substitution of the indigenous population by Viking groups.

The circumstances of Viking settlement in the Lower Seine

From the foregoing, it follows that a good number of secondary settlements on the Seine, abandoned because of the transfer of their inhabitants to Rouen, were repopulated by groups of Scandinavian or Anglo-Scandinavian origin. It remains to be determined when this episode took place and under what conditions this installation of newcomers took place.

In all likelihood, the Vikings were unable to settle in these places before their evacuation by the Frankish population, and therefore not before the years 888–90, as it was only then that the transfer of inhabitants to Rouen took place. Neither can it have taken place in 890 because the Vikings, chased from Francia by King Odo, were then operating in the Cotentin. Moreover, it is precisely because they had been cleared from the Lower Seine region that it became a place of refuge for the clergy fleeing the Cotentin. When, at the end of 890 the Vikings were expelled from Brittany by Alan the Great, they re-entered the Seine but did not stop, proceeding directly to Noyon where they established their winter quarters. In 892 the last groups still operating in northern France and the Escaut region departed to raid in England. Only in 896 did a Viking fleet again enter the Seine estuary. Under the command of a chief to whom Frankish sources give the name Hundeus, this group was probably one of those mentioned by the *Anglo-Saxon Chronicle, s.a.* 896, in reporting Viking war bands returning to the Continent because they had been unable to settle in England and found themselves without resources.

Arriving in Francia, it seems that Hundeus had the intention of negotiating with the Carolingian authorities. He could not hope for any gesture from King Odo, hostile as always to any sort of arrangement with the Vikings. He therefore sought out Charles the Simple, whom Odo had driven out to Lotharingia; Charles proposed baptism for Hundeus, provoking the fury of Archbishop Fulk of Rheims. The acceptance of baptism by a Viking chief normally required some form of remuneration in land and silver but it is not known what was granted or promised to Hundeus. In any case, Charles was at that time hardly in a position to cede any land to the Viking chief in the west of the kingdom, then under Odo's control. But, on the death of the latter in 898, Charles regained his crown, the entirety of his territories and the possibility of negotiating as he pleased with the Vikings. In these circumstances, it seems difficult to place the arrival of Rollo in Francia before 898. Supporting an early date is a passage by Adhemar of Chabannes, writing in the 1020s, calling to mind the shaky friendly terms between Rollo and Rannulf II of Poitiers, who died in 890 (Bauduin 1999, 12; Chavanon 1897). However, this late source is a feeble authority, especially as in the same sentence Adelmar describes the marriage of Ebalus Manzer, count of Poitiers with Rollo's daughter Adèle, which is a flagrant error: Adèle's husband was, more probably, William 'Towhead', son of Ebalus (Searle 1988, 54 and n. 74).

In his famous account of Rollo's first entry into the Lower Seine, Dudo of Saint-Quentin reports that the Viking chief took his fleet as far as the Jumièges port of Saint-Vaast. There, according to Dudo, he received emissaries from the archbishop who asked him to spare the city of Rouen, which was only inhabited by a defenceless civil population and merchants without resources; Rollo promised not to attack (Lair 1865, 152–3). In spite of the serious reservations usually provoked by Dudo's accounts (Yver 1969), in particular those concerning Rollo, this passage deserves the greatest attention. The place of the meeting is not known to have been invented and more than just the archbishop's mediating role and the situation of Rouen's population, all this tallies with the context at the end of the ninth century. On the other hand, it is clear that an old Jumièges tradition existed, remembering the ruin of the abbey in the ninth century and its reconstruction by William Longsword *c.* 942 (Lemarignier 1955). Today this source is lost, but fragments are preserved in William of Jumièges' *Gesta Normannorum ducorum* (completed *c.* 1070: van Houts 1992, xxxviii); Dudo borrowed heavily from it, in particular to write the passage which he devotes to Jumièges and the work of William Longsword. On this basis, except in the details – the date of 876 assigned to this episode is evidently wrong – the accuracy of the Jumièges agreement is plausible.

It is a small step from this to the suggestion that Viking settlement in the Lower Seine was a direct consequence of this agreement. Property of the royal fisc, including these deserted ports, would have been ceded to the Vikings by the Carolingian authorities in exchange for a promise of non-aggression against the city of Rouen. This scenario of a 'legal' settlement seems the more likely. Indeed, there had been at least one precedent. In 877 Charles the Bald had surrendered the island of Bièce near Nantes, with the right to trade, to a group of Vikings who had escaped from the siege of Angers, in exchange for the promise that they would accept baptism. Thus, the Seine valley must have seen the establishment of a kind of cohabitation between the indigenous population, urban and peasant, and the Scandinavian or Anglo-Scandinavian groups settled in the harbour *vici*.

The situation was undoubtedly difficult for the religious communities of the Cotentin who had found refuge in the river area in 890: most of them left the region. The group occupying the port of Saint-Paul near Jumièges left with the body of St Clair to settle in a place in the Vexin which took the name Saint-Clair-sur-Epte; the monks of Saint-Marcouf left the port of Emendreville to reach Senlis, then Corbény; the Graville group fled to Conflans with the body of St Honorine, a translation which one source dates to the reign of Charles the Simple, therefore after 898. On the other hand, it seems that the Vikings gave sufficient guarantees to the people of Rouen for them to feel secure inside the city walls. As far as is known, the clergy from the church in Coutances, settled since 890 at Saint-Sauveur, did not leave the town, and it is highly probable that the count mentioned in a charter granted in 906 by Charles the Simple to his chancellor Ernustus had been the count of Rouen. Conforming to the Jumièges agreement, the city of the Lower Seine therefore remained a protected haven where there remained not only a large Frankish population, but also a religious and administrative framework. Knowing whether the mercantile suburb was part of the harbour *vici* ceded to the Vikings by the Jumièges agreement, is a complex problem, about which we can only spare a few words. It is not out of the question that some Vikings soon settled outside the walls, as happened at York. But, supposing this was the case, the occupation was not prominent: the Rouen suburbs have not preserved any place-name of Scandinavian origin. This fact is certainly not new. However, this perhaps gives insufficient prominence to Flodoard's mention of the numerous departures that were provoked at Rouen among the Scandinavian population upon the entry into the town of the French after the death of William Longsword in 942.

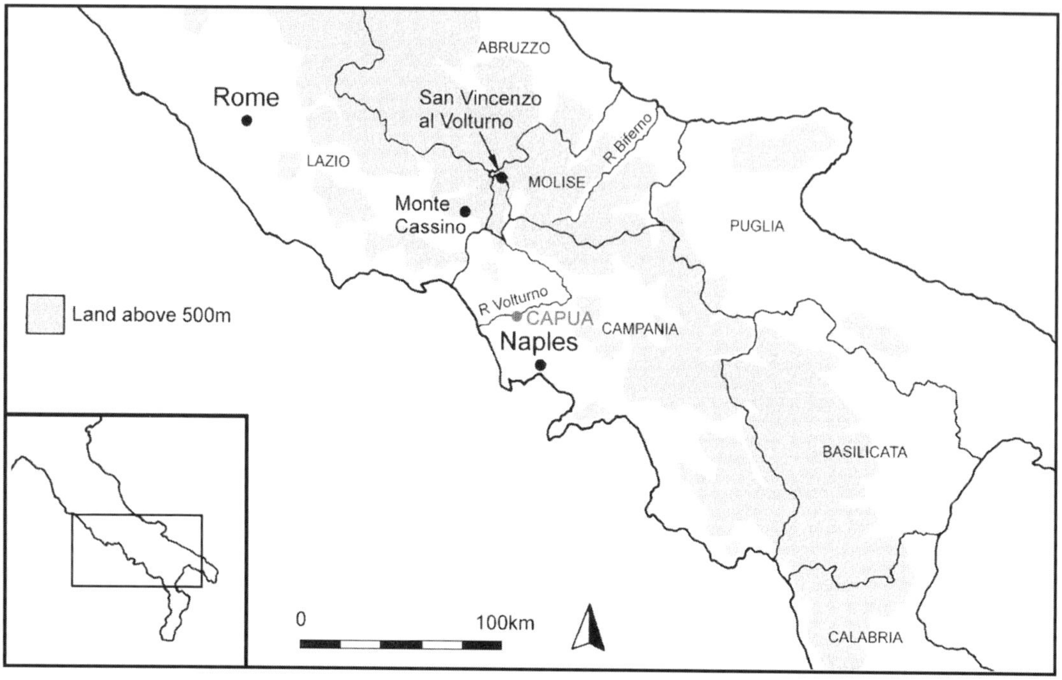

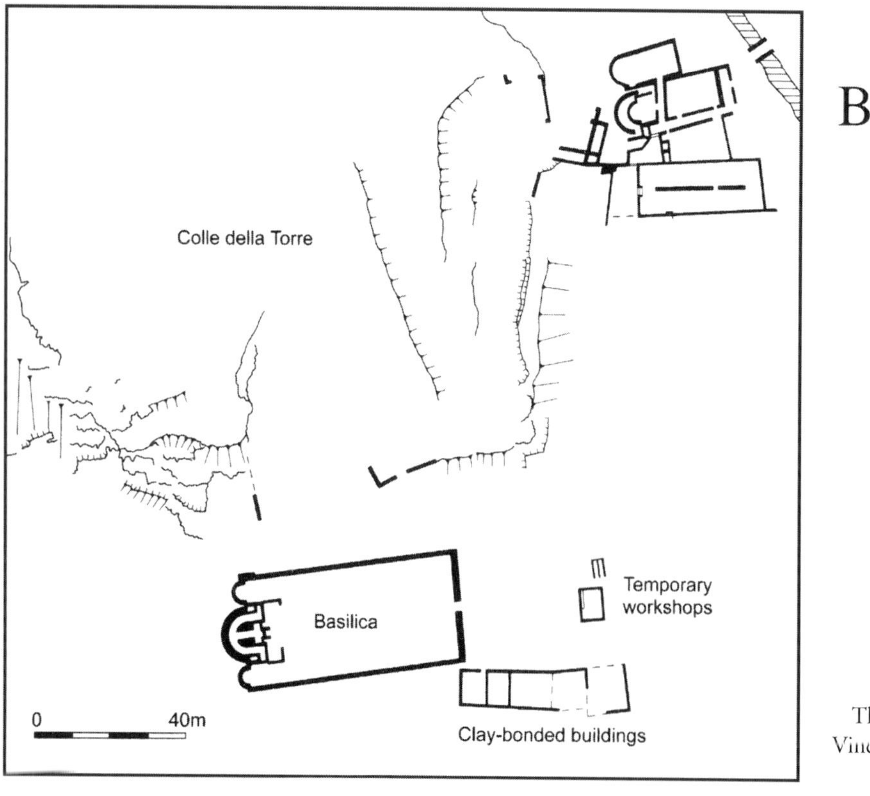

FIGURE 19.1.
The location of San Vincenzo (a) and a plan of the site (b).

CHAPTER 19

San Vincenzo in the Making: The Discovery of an Early Medieval Production Site on the East Bank of the Volturno

Matthew Moran

Introduction

Much is now known of the archaeology of inland production and trading sites in Early Medieval northern Europe, and their economic context. The same may not be said of Italy, however, where our knowledge of commodity production and exchange is limited to sites on the seaboard, and exceptional inland contexts such as Rome. Away from the coasts, in city and countryside alike, commerce and patronage were based above all on land ownership and largesse. Thus the making of San Vincenzo al Volturno coincided with a period, *c.* 800–50, in which the monastery received from private donors gifts of land in all parts of Beneventan territory. This paper considers how the monastery translated its immense agricultural revenues into prestige artefacts and buildings. Particular attention is given to newly excavated evidence of a production site established *c.* 820 alongside the monastery, on the opposite bank of the River Volturno.

San Vincenzo al Volturno

San Vincenzo al Volturno stands high in the upper Volturno valley, in the modern region of Molise, approximately 170km south-east of Rome, and about 30km north-east of Monte Cassino (Fig. 19.1a). The site is approximately 530m above sea level, in the lower Mainarde, the foothills of the Apennines (Fig. 19.1b). San Vincenzo is almost equidistant from the east and west coasts of the Italian peninsula – or as far inland as it is possible to get. British-led excavations at San

Vincenzo al Volturno began in 1980, with two principle objectives – first, to identify the location and aspect of the Early Medieval monastery; and, second, to examine the monastery's relationship to settlement in the landscape (Hodges 1993, 6).

Prior to *c.* 780, and despite the institution's growing political and cultural significance (Wickham 1995, 138–52), San Vincenzo was a materially unprepossessing place. The monastery's founders evidently restored parts of a fifth-century villa using pre-existing building stone and tiles, mortared with clay, but otherwise, there is practically no evidence of material culture production in the monastery (Hodges 1993, 128–34). By contrast, a structured reconfiguration occurred in the period *c.* 790–840, which was made possible by the presence and production of people skilled in tile-making, bronze-casting, and iron- and glass-working (Hodges and Mitchell 1996; Mitchell 1994b; Mitchell and Hansen 2001). The nucleus of this production was the monumental abbey-church, San Vincenzo Maggiore, beneath which a sequence of temporary tile, bronze and glass workshops was excavated (Mitchell 1996; Francis and Moran 1997).

To judge from the material culture of the eighth-century monastery and other sites within the *Terra Sancti Vincentii* (Hodges 1984; Wickham 1985), the makers of San Vincenzo were not native to the territory ceded to the monastery at its foundation *c.* 700 by Gisulf I, duke of Benevento. The author of the abbey's twelfth-century chronicle, the *Chronicon Vulturnense* (i, 221), describes how the monastic community co-operated with lay workers during the construction of San Vincenzo Maggiore. In pursuing the makers of San Vincenzo, the importance of other sites of different kinds became apparent (Hodges 1997a, 199) – particularly the settlements of the monastery's lay *familia* referred to in documents contained in the *Chronicon Vulturnense.* This awareness was among a number of factors that prompted two short seasons of survey and excavation on the east bank of the River Volturno, opposite the site of the Early Medieval monastery, in 1996 and 1997.

A production site in the making

Survey of the east bank of the River Volturno was carried out in 1980 and 1986, and again in the period 1989–97 (Hodges and Mitchell 1985). Geophysical survey was undertaken in 1993 (Fig. 19.2). Surface collection survey identified a broad scatter of *Vernice Nera* pottery dating between the third to first centuries BC, in fields immediately to the east of a Late Roman bridge on the Volturno, the Ponte della Zingara, and in an arc extending approximately 300m to the south.

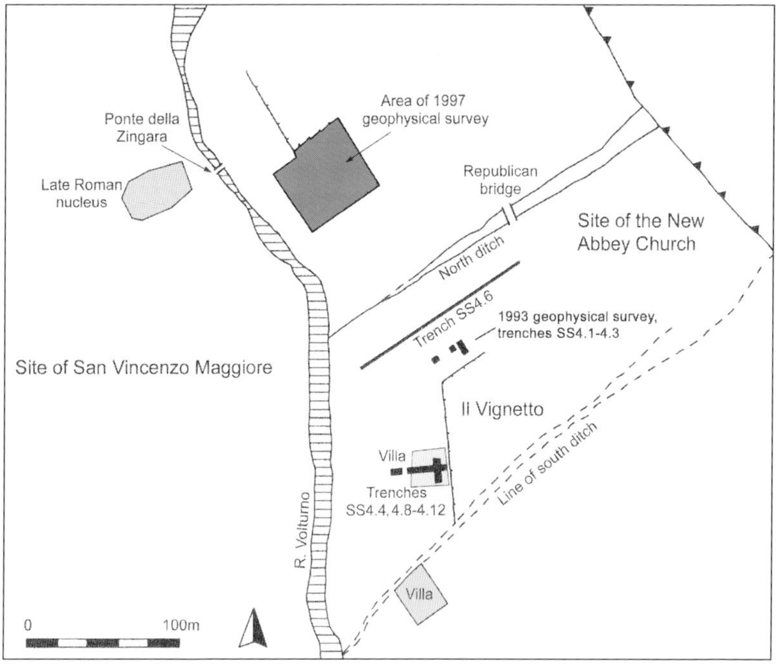

FIGURE 19.2. Site plan, showing the surveyed and excavated areas, and prominent archaeological features, on the east bank of the Volturno.

Together with a number of fragmentary inscriptions, marbles, sculptures and roofing tiles, this material was associated with an Iron Age (Samnite) and Republican *vicus* (Hodges 1993, 7).

Furthermore, two widespread scatters of Imperial period material were located, one in the area south of the medieval abbey's twelfth-century enclosure ditch, the other in a field to the north, beneath an ancient terraced olive grove known locally as 'il vignetto'. This material from both areas, dating between the first to fourth centuries AD, is interpreted as evidence of a high-status villa associated with one of the *Decuriones* of Isernia (J Patterson 1985). In addition, fragments of glass-working crucible were picked up over a large area to the north of the excavated area, opposite the Ponte della Zingara. Similar material was identified in soil disturbed by the digging of a service trench along the access road to the south of the excavated area. Analysis of this material pointed to the presence of an extensive production site in this area in the eighth and ninth centuries.

Geophysical survey identified structural remains in a low-lying area to the west of the New Abbey, immediately north of 'il vignetto'. Excavations in the summer seasons of 1996 and 1997 (Fig. 19.3) identified a multi-period site with a discontinuous settlement sequence from the sixth century BC to the end of the ninth century AD (Gilkes and Moran 2001; Gilkes, Moran and Tremlett forthcoming). The latest occupation deposits were associated with an eighth- to ninth-

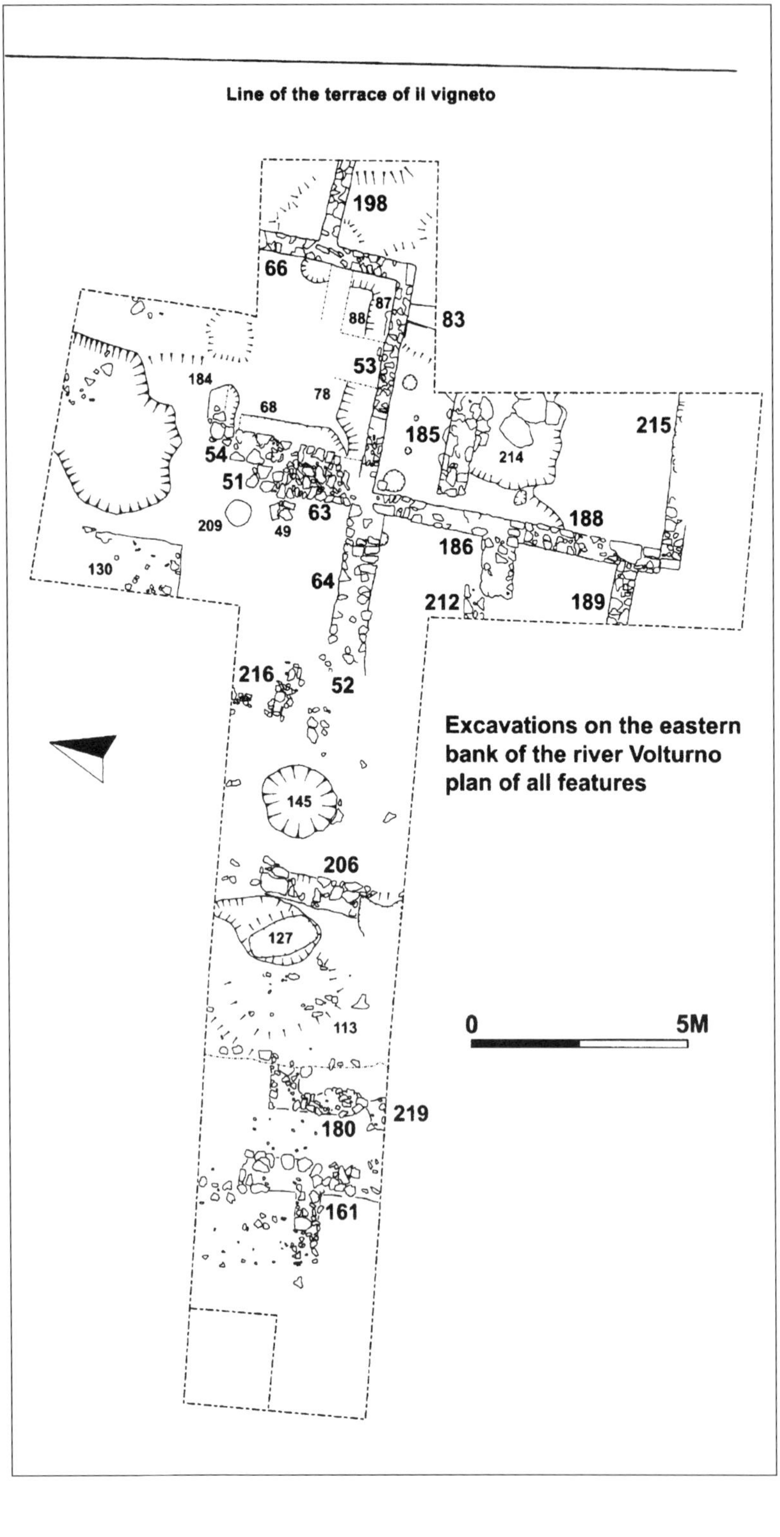

FIGURE 19.3.
Plan of the 1996–7 excavations.

century production site, which partly occupied the levelled remains of a Samnite-Roman *vicus.* Together, the evidence of survey and excavation suggests that productive activity once occupied a large area of the east bank of the Volturno, opposite the Early Medieval monastery.

A single (hypothetical) Early Medieval structure, of timbered or *pisé* construction, was identified during the excavations. The building had a mortar floor which was separated from an external cobbled yard by a beam slot or eaves-drip gully. While the building was in use, the floor of a room in the adjacent Roman complex was cut by a rubbish pit, subsequently filled with sherds of glass-working crucibles. Contemporaneously, a well was used for dumping waste from a ninth-century pottery kiln. The cobbled area adjacent to the Early Medieval structure was covered by a trample layer, incorporating

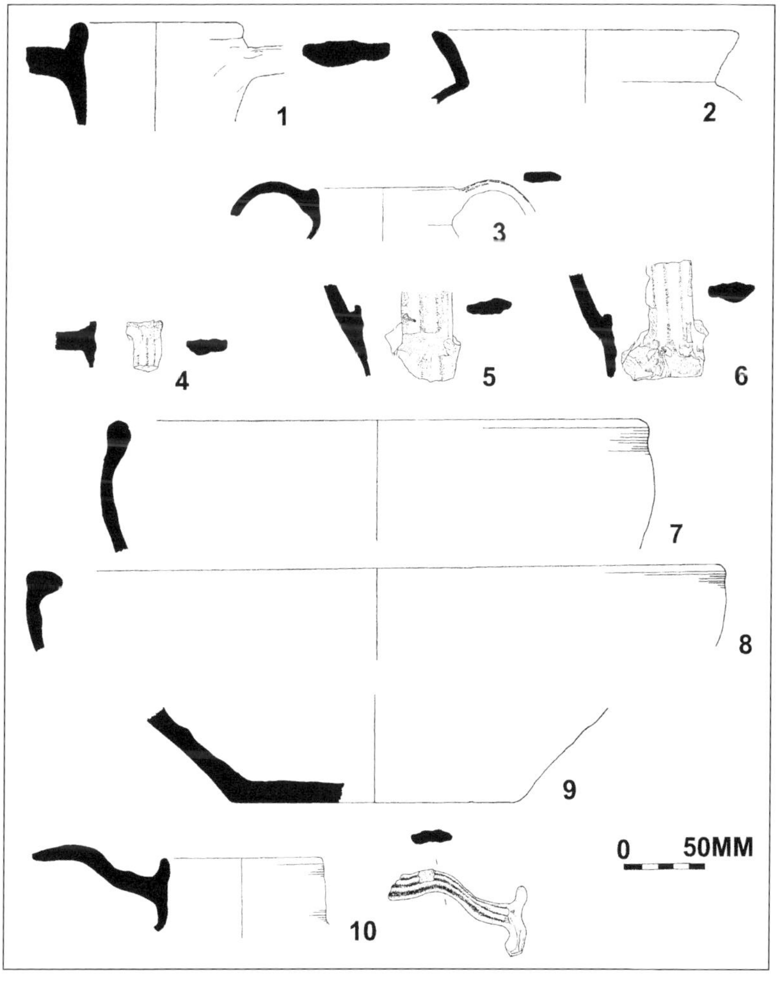

FIGURE 19.4.
Early Medieval red-painted pottery from the excavations.

iron-working waste, fragments of burnt tile and travertine, and glass-working crucibles. The quantity and homogeneity of the artefactual evidence strongly suggest that the material originated in the immediate vicinity of the excavated area, in workshops active on the east bank of the Volturno during the late eighth and ninth centuries.

The ceramic sequence from the site mirrors that of the Early Medieval monastery, comprising a large assemblage of red-painted wares of San Vincenzo fabric 4.5 (H Patterson 1985; Arthur and Patterson 1994) (Fig. 19.4). The presence of pottery wasters, and misshapen sherds of imperfectly fired vessels, strongly suggests that a pottery kiln was active in this area in the ninth century. Given the homogeneity of the assemblage, it seems likely that this material was redeposited from a nearby production site, either when the kiln, or kilns, was periodically swept out, or during demolition. A small quantity of possible kiln debris (burnt travertine fragments, and burnt and vitrified tile) was identified in Early Medieval deposits on the site.

In addition, forty-three sherds of glass-working crucible were recovered from Early Medieval occupation levels, of a wheel-thrown ware belonging to San Vincenzo fabric 4.3, which is attributed to a clay source at Colli al Volturno (Hodges 1991; Patterson 2001) (Fig. 19.5). The material compares closely with the diagnostic forms of glass-working crucibles recovered from tips and fills associated with an early ninth-century glass workshop excavated beneath the atrium of San Vincenzo Maggiore (*ibid.*; Stevenson 1997) (San Vincenzo crucible forms C2 and C8) (Fig. 19.5:8). Most of the crucible sherds retained thick glassy residues, a deep deposit of dark green glass adhering to one sherd of a broad-based glass crucible (form C10d), of a kind

FIGURE 19.5. Early Medieval glass-working crucibles from the excavations.

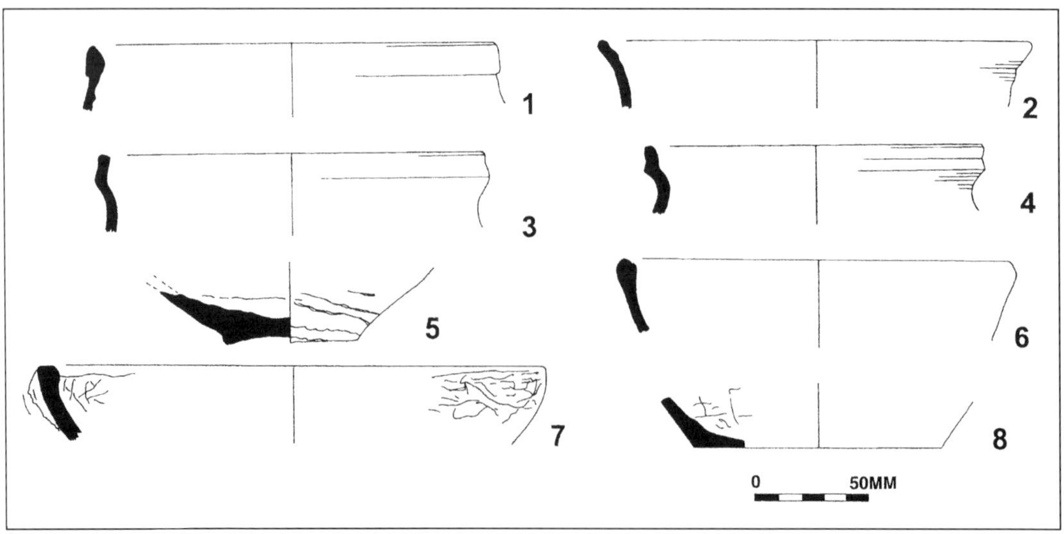

associated with the working of window glass (Dell'Acqua 1997). Some evidence of iron-working was also recovered, superficial examination identifying a number of ferrous objects as bloom and slag. Carpentry nails excepted, no finished glass or iron artefacts were recognized during excavation.

The identification of this extensive production site on the east bank of the Volturno raises a number of questions. How were these structures related to the workshops identified within the monastic precinct west of the river, alongside the Carolingian-era abbey-church, San Vincenzo Maggiore? How do these discoveries affect our understanding of the topography of the Early Medieval monastery? What were the economic and socio-political contexts of the production site east of the Volturno? And what was the relation of the technologies (and technologists) located within and without the monastery?

The structure identified with the production site on the east bank belongs to a vernacular tradition of service and storage buildings, such as those set up alongside temporary workshops ahead of construction of San Vincenzo Maggiore, *c.* 790 (Fig. 19.6). Between 1986 and 1998, excavation on the west bank of the Volturno revealed that prior to the construction of the church atrium, a complex of partly timbered, clay-bonded or *pisé* buildings with mortar floors and adjacent cobbled yards stood to the south of a sequence of temporary structures for tile-making, bronze-casting and glass-working (Francis and Moran 1997, 377; Moran 2000, 171–5). The complex comprised two large spaces (7 × 9m and 11 × 19m), possibly unroofed yards, with two smaller structures in the west. No evidence of productive activity was found, and the building was interpreted as storage space for fuel, tools, raw materials and finished products, and possibly as shelter or living quarters for artisans or builders. Subsequently, part of the clay-bonded artisanal complex was used for glass production (Moreland 1985). Use of the building ceased with that of the temporary workshops, when the atrium of San Vincenzo Maggiore was built, in the second or third decade of the ninth century.

Of necessity, temporary workshops of this kind were located on or alongside the building site. However, neither survey nor excavation suggests that prestige monastic buildings occupied the east bank of the Volturno in the eighth and ninth centuries. Rather, it seems the extramural production site already described was established on the east bank of the Volturno once construction of San Vincenzo Maggiore was close to completion. Numismatic evidence from the latter building suggests this happened no sooner than the 830s, while the ceramic series from the site east of the river can be attributed to the period *c.* 830–80 (Gilkes, Moran and Tremlett forthcoming).

In inland Early Medieval Italy, commerce and patronage depended upon largesse and the wealth of landownership (Wickham 1981, 84–6; Albertoni 1997). San Vincenzo's expansion coincided with numerous gifts of lands from private Beneventan donors (Wickham 1995, 138–52). Between 800–19, nineteen private charters of gift are recorded from followers of the Beneventan princes, involving nearly sixty estates and a dozen lesser properties and marginal lands, from Venafro to Apulia

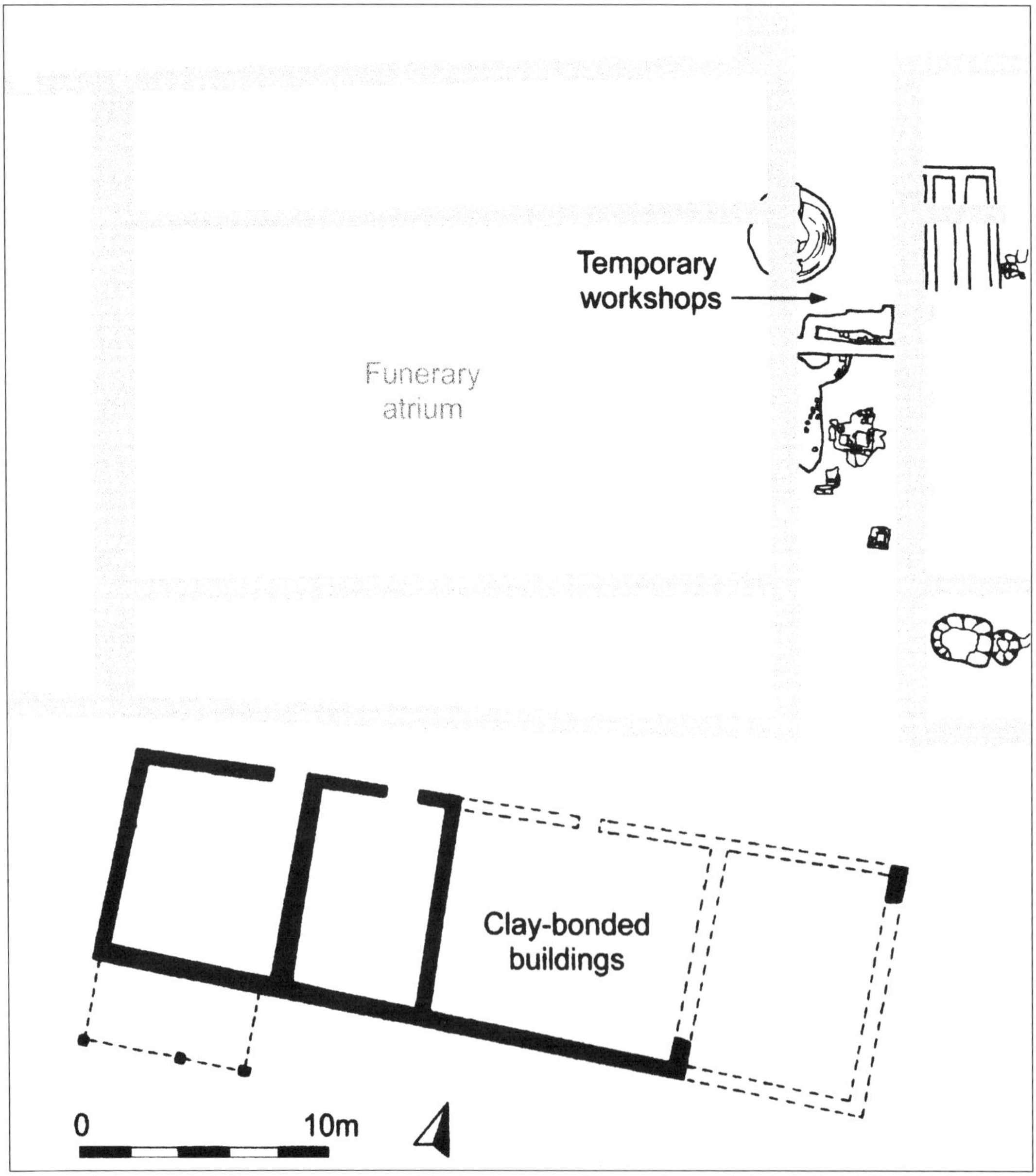

(*Chronicon Vulturnense* 34–51 and i, 275). There were fourteen donations of property in the immediate vicinity of the monastery, especially around Venafro and at Vairano and Isernia; others in the countryside around Alife, Benevento, Telese and Salerno; four or five in the plain of Capua; one in the Salernitano; and a string of thirteen properties in Apulia (Lesina, Siponto, Lucera, Canosa, Acerenza, Taranto and Oria) (Wickham 1985, 19–22; 1995, 144). Many of these properties were in or close by the political centres of the Lombard south, and thus were subject to the control of powerful *gastalds* (at Capua, Venafro, Telese, and Acerenza) (Marazzi 1996). Others were close to production and trading centres in Apulia (Arthur and Patterson 1998).

There has been much debate about precisely how the monastery translated its immense agricultural revenues into prestige artefacts and buildings (Wickham 1995; Marazzi 1996). Some information is given in the laws of Liutprand (*Leges*, i, col. 177 No. 4), which stipulates prices that could be charged by the builders' federation, the *magistri commacini*. Under the terms of the code, the patron was to provide artisans and labourers with food and wages in coin. However, given the function of coin in late eighth- and ninth-century Italy, builders may not always have demanded payment in cash, even when their patrons were able to provide it (Arslan 1994 and 2000; Rovelli 1994). Thus, during the rebuilding of the walls of Rome under Gregory III (731–41), the workers received materials and their rations from the pope himself, and no mention is made of payment in coin (Davis 1992, 27).

In ninth-century Italy, ecclesiastical institutions ceded lands to specialist artisans in return for materials for the building of monasteries and churches. On 31 May 841, Rampert, bishop of Brescia, granted land outside the city to some tile-makers, in return for material for the construction of the suburban church, San Faustino (*CDL*, 140 No. 247). The tile-makers were licensed to dig for clay on the site, and to build kilns and other structures there for the storage of raw materials, fuel, tools and the finished product.

By coincidence, the first phase of productive activity at San Vincenzo after *c.* 790 was tile-making, centred upon a large, vaulted tile kiln with twin firing chambers, similar in form to Roman brick kilns known from Varazze and elsewhere (Moran 2000). The vast numbers of tiles produced are entirely unlike the Early Medieval roofing tiles known from sites in the *terra*, such as Colle Sant'Angelo (Hodges 1997a, 186–8). Evidently, the tile makers of San Vincenzo were not native to the territory ceded to the monastery at its foundation *c.* 700, the *Terra Sancti Vincentii*, although it is possible they hailed from estates granted to the monastery during the first quarter of the ninth

FIGURE 19.6.
Plan of Early Medieval clay-bonded structures, showing their relation to the temporary workshops, prior to construction of the atrium of San Vincenzo Maggiore.

century. In antiquity, the region's tile-makers had enjoyed the praises of Cato, who recommended Venafro as a good place to buy bricks and tiles (*De Agri Cultura* 135, 1). Could it be that specialist tile-makers were still to be found at or around Venafro in the early ninth century?

The patronage of the Beneventan nobility gave San Vincenzo the seigneurial and judicial powers to mobilize the human and material resources needed for the monastery's spectacular rebuilding. In a number of cases, grants of *curtes* and *terrae* were accompanied by families of *servi*; meanwhile, the monastery received a sharp increase in food renders from aristocratic donors (Wickham 1995). During the Carolingian-era reconstruction of the monastery (*c.* 790–830), the makers of San Vincenzo inhabited a complex of clay-bonded (part-timbered?) buildings and cobbled yards, perhaps while cultivating lands on low-lying ground to the south of San Vincenzo Maggiore. *Condumae*, family groups of servile persons, occupied Casa Lorenzo, a broad terrace on the edge of the Rocchetta plain, less than two kilometres from the site (Hodges 1997a, 184).

From production site to monastic workshop

As the construction of San Vincenzo Maggiore came to completion *c.* 820, artisans in certain trades established the production site on the east bank of the Volturno (Fig. 19.2), while within the monastery, the *pisé* building associated with the temporary workshops was partially dismantled and rebuilt in mortar-bonded masonry (Fig. 19.7a). Shortly thereafter, three lateral mortar-bonded walls were inserted, creating four square or rectangular rooms – the so-called 'collective workshop' (Fig. 19.7b) (Hodges 1991, 70–4; Mitchell 1996, 148–55; Hodges and Mitchell 1996, 51–3). This probably took place no earlier than the 830s, to judge from the presence of two silver *deniers* of Sico of Benevento (817–32). Later, following an earthquake in 848, further alterations were made – Room A was given a rubble-built bench and a tiled floor; and Room C was lavishly remodelled as living quarters. Inside, wattle partitions and screens subdivided the space, and the walls were plastered and painted; outside, the eaves were adorned with a row of decorated terracotta corbels. This elaborate architecture replaced the clay-bonded vernacular of the original structure. The room seems to have been used as a tool store in the second half of the ninth century, and was thus interpreted as the office of the monastic superintendent of works, the chamberlain (Mitchell 1996, 150–3).

At different times in the period 830–81, the adjoining rooms of the so called 'collective workshop' were used by artisans engaged in fine

FIGURE 19.7.
Fig. 19.7. Plans of (a) the Early Medieval clay-bonded structures and adjoining yards and (b) the so-called 'collective workshop'.

metal-working, bone- and ivory-carving, and possibly textile manufacture (*ibid.*, 148–55). During this period, Room A was used for the composition and finishing of items of fine metalwork and enamels. Finds from the latest occupation deposits included bronze sheet, strips of gilded- and silvered-bronze beaded wire, tacks, hooks and fittings, and two trays of coloured glass cloisonné enamel. In a space to the north of the room, small crucibles were used to heat the tiny quantities of glass needed by the enamellers. It was here that copper-alloy trays

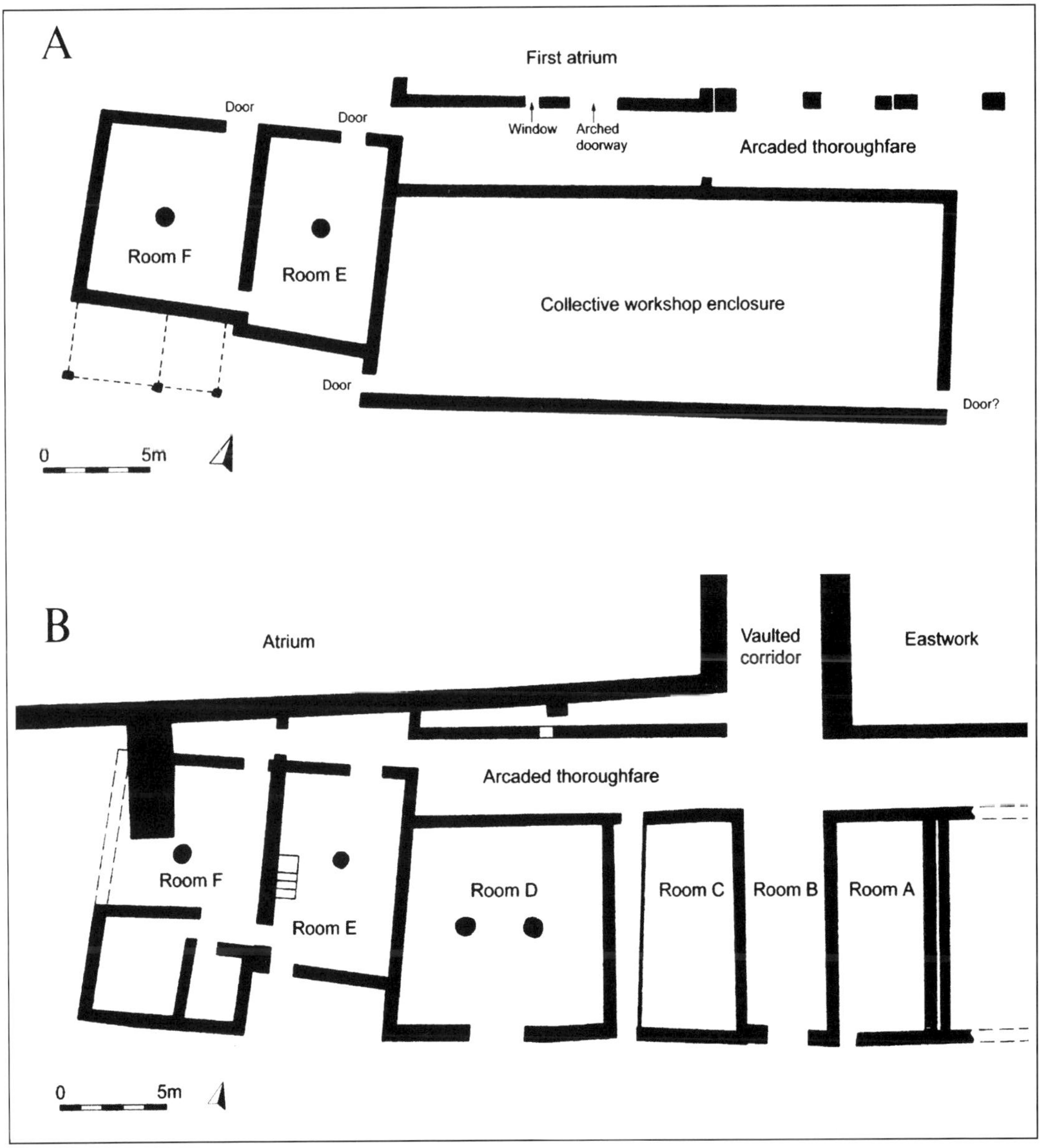

were fashioned and fused with coloured glass to create cloisonné enamels, and it was here that the finished objects were gilded or silvered. Otherwise, Room A had been used for the cold assembly and finishing of elaborate liturgical objects such as book covers, reliquaries and processional crucifixes.

During the ninth century, silvered-iron objects of personal adornment, such as belt buckles and strap-ends, mounts and fittings – as well as bridle furniture – were produced at San Vincenzo. A spectacular set of sword-belt mounts, and associated bridle fittings, has been discovered in late ninth-century contexts in the monastery, including two distinctive D-shaped buckles (Mitchell 1994b and 2001). A third, unsilvered iron buckle of this kind was found during excavation in Room B, although no evidence of smithing has been found there or elsewhere in the monastery. Instead, the buckle may have been manufactured elsewhere, and imported to the workshops for silvering. The two Beneventan *deniers* referred to above were probably intended as a source of silver for this purpose, and, similarly, the silver inlay had been extracted from the incised recto of a three-ounce Byzantine weight found in the excavation of Room A. Thus it seems the production of the monastery's internal workshops was limited to the assembly and finishing of luxury objects fashioned from materials originated elsewhere, with prestige items brought to the internal workshops for gilding or silvering. The presence of the extramural production site suggests that it was from these less pretentious buildings east of the Volturno that materials for the monastery's luxury artisans were supplied in prepared form by another order of (lay?) artisans.

The monastery's production of luxury arts in the ninth century may be divided into two categories: liturgical objects (reliquaries, book-covers and crosses) incorporating *cloissoné* enamels and carved bone and ivory, for display within the monastery (Mitchell 1985 and 1992; Mitchell and Hansen 2001); and items of personal adornment (sword-belt and bridal furniture), in iron inlaid with silver (Mitchell 1994b and 2001). Objects in the latter category were possibly distributed by the monastic community as gifts to distinguished patrons; the set of sword-belt mounts and associated bridle furniture referred to above was recovered from Early Medieval deposits associated with a furnished grave within the monastery, in an area associated with the reception of distinguished guests.

The extramural production site and the monastic workshop were the last links in an operational chain of sites engaged in sourcing, collecting, and distributing materials on the monastery's behalf. Further fieldwork is needed to identify the location and nature of these sites, while the volume of production, and the extent of its distribution, remains largely unknown. Given the paucity of traded commodities (except pottery) identified by survey and excavation at sites in the *terra*, it may be that production was limited to the local demand of the monastic community and their elite supporters.

From workshop to market

By the time its impressive buildings were complete *c.* 830, San Vincenzo was in decline. This recession was brought on by the Beneventan civil war (839–49) and its consequences, and subsequent Arab attacks (Wickham 1995, 147–51). It is therefore significant that private patronage continued to favour lay dependencies in the *terra* into the 850s, enhancing their form and status, even as the monastery itself dwindled (Hodges 1997a, 184). From the mid-ninth century, we find groups of families patronizing local churches (*plebes*) in San Vincenzo's inner *terra*, such as San Pietro *ad Itrias*, a chapel founded in the 840s, and San Eleuterio, built in the 850s near the later village of Filignano.

In ninth-century Italy, approximately half of the documented markets were promoted by the monasteries, the rest by secular powers (Settia 1991). In particular, markets were sponsored by powerful families, on the occasion of the feasts of popular local saints. Were the churches of San Pietro *ad Itrias* and San Eleuterio the locations for markets in the second half of the ninth century? Moreover, did the production site identified on the east bank of the Volturno, have its own church, in common with *Eulogimenopolis*, the contemporary artisanal *borgo* beneath Monte Cassino (Hoffman 1980, 54), just thirty kilometres away?

In 1994–6, excavations within the atrium of the Romanesque abbey-church and the cloister of the New Abbey, east of the river (Fig. 19.2), revealed a large number of post-holes in the travertine bedrock (Bowden forthcoming). Similar features were identified during restorations beneath the nave floor of the present church. There is limited, as yet unpublished, evidence that these features belong to an Early Medieval settlement, possibly one clustered about a small ninth-century church, as at *Eulogimenopolis* (Bowden *et al* 1996, 475; Wickham 1985). Was this church incorporated by the builders of the Romanesque abbey-church, when the monastery was moved to the east bank of the Volturno, at the end of the eleventh century? And was a market held alongside the church and settlement in the later ninth century, where a regional sheep fair was held in meadows east of the Volturno in the first half of the nineteenth century? (Hodges 1993, 1–4)

From countryside to city

Both the archaeological and documentary records testify to San Vincenzo's failure to exploit its vast economic potential beyond the demands of the Carolingian-era building programme. This appears to be reflected in the changing use of buildings within the precinct, alterations being made to the monastery's internal workshops following an earthquake in 848 – Room D was converted into a granary, while Room E became an olive press. At the same time, the monastery may have tried to control the production of high-status metalwork in its internal workshops, where sword-belt fittings and other items of personal adornment were produced, possibly for market. A small number of penannular brooches in copper-alloy were found in the latest abandonment horizons within the so-called 'collective workshop'; a similar object was found during excavation at Vacchereccia, a dependent site in the *terra* (Hodges 1984, fig. 7.6).

In the aftermath of the Beneventan civil war, Italy's mountainous and thinly populated interior would scarcely have been an appropriate venue for the transaction of regional trade. Ninth-century sources make clear that the upper orders of Lombard society adamantly refused to pay double tithes to diocesan bishops, preferring instead to make over their wealth to private churches (Stutz 1909, 191–2; Loyn and Percival 1975, 47–9). In the second half of the ninth century, southern Lombard donors reserved their wealth to local churches, which were the venues for markets; and by this time, the foremost markets of central and southern Italy were to be found on the coasts, at Gaeta, Naples, Amalfi and Salerno to the west, and Pescara, Trani, Otranto and Taranto to the east. Most of these were political centres under *gastalds*; others were seats of the Lombard court. In this way, the drift in patronage had the effect of leaching production sites and markets, and their communities, from Italy's mountainous interior, to the plain and the sea.

Early Medieval activity on the east bank of the Volturno evidently came to an end in the last quarter of the ninth century, probably in 881 when Saracen mercenaries despatched by the bishop-duke of Naples raided and torched the monastery (Hodges 1997b). The *Chronicon Vulturnense* makes clear that the monks were betrayed by lay brothers, who showed the Saracens into the cloister through the internal workshops (*Chronicon Vulturnense* i, 362–70). In the wake of the devastation, the surviving monks sheltered in the *vicus* of the lay *familia*, a place known in the twelfth century as *Castellum Samnie*, before heading south to the Lombard capital at Capua, at the mouth of the River Volturno. Was *Castellum Samnie* situated on the east bank of the Volturno, around the ruins of the Samnite and Roman *vici* and cemetery, in the area of the excavated production site? (Bowden *et al.* 1996).

San Vincenzo's uprooted and impoverished monastic elite had much to gain from the move to Capua, where it quickly sought and was granted the patronage of the Capuan court. The monastery's *familia* likewise stood to benefit from the journey to Capua, a busy commercial entrepôt. From this perspective, the Capuan diaspora may be interpreted as a monastic strategy in response to changing economic circumstances. Alternatively, it would not be a misrepresentation of the written sources to suggest that the success of the Saracen sack and San Vincenzo's subsequent move to Capua came about on the initiative of the monastery's artisans. Within forty years the monks were back, rebuilding the monastery where the lay artisans' settlement, and possibly church, had once stood (Valente 1995, 57–62; Hodges and Mitchell 1996, 133–8), while the descendants of the last generation of San Vincenzo's makers became the first generation of the artisanate of an emergent Medieval southern city.

Acknowledgements

Thanks to Tim Pestell and Katharina Ulmschneider for inviting me to participate in the conference and its publication, and to Paul Blinkhorn, Karen Francis, Oliver Gilkes, Richard Hodges, Pippa Humphreys and John Mitchell.

Bibliography

Published primary sources

Anglo-Saxon Chronicle, Garmonsway, G. N. ed. and trans. (1972) *The Anglo-Saxon Chronicle*, Dent, London.

Blake, E. O. ed. (1962) *Liber Eliensis* Camden Society Third Series 92, Royal Historical Society, London.

Cacheux, P. Le (1916) *Chartes de l'abbaye de Jumièges*, Société de l'Histoire de la Normandie, Caen.

CDL, Troya, C. ed. (1852–6) *Codice diplomatico Longobardo dal DLXVIII al DCCLXXIV* 4 vols, Stamperia reale, Naples.

Chavanon, J. ed. (1897) *Adhémar de Chabannes, Chronique*, Paris.

Chronicon Vulturnense, Federici, V. ed. (1925) *Chronicon Vulturnense del Monaco Giovanni* 3 vols, Istituto storico italiano, Rome.

Davis, R. ed. and trans. (1992) *The Lives of the Eighth-Century Popes (Liber Pontificalis)*, Liverpool University Press, Liverpool.

DB Cambridgeshire, Rumble, A. ed. (1981) *Domesday Book: Cambridgeshire*, Phillimore, Chichester.

DB Hampshire, Munby, J. ed. (1982) *Domesday Book: Hampshire*, Phillimore, Chichester.

DB Lincolnshire, Morgan, P. and Thorn, C. eds (1986) *Domesday Book: Lincolnshire*, Phillimore, Chichester.

DB Norfolk, Brown, P. ed. (1984) *Domesday Book, Norfolk* 2 vols, Phillimore, Chichester.

DB Suffolk, Rumble, A. ed. (1986) *Domesday Book, Suffolk* 2 vols, Phillimore, Chichester.

De Agri Cultura, Ash, H. B. and Hooper, W. D. eds (1935) Cato *De Agri Cultura*, Harvard University Press, Cambridge, Mass. and Heinemann, London.

Dumville, D. N. and Lapidge, M. eds (1984) *The Annals of St Neot's with Vita Primo Sancti Neoti* The Anglo-Saxon Chronicle: A Collaborative Edition 17, Boydell and Brewer, Woodbridge.

Finberg, H. P. R. ed. (1964) *The Early Charters of Wessex*, Leicester University Press, Leicester.

Harper-Bill, C. ed. (1990) *English Episcopal Acta VI: Norwich 1070–1214*, British Academy and Oxford University Press, Oxford.

Hart, C. R. ed. (1966) *The Early Charters of Eastern England*, Leicester University Press, Leicester.

Historia Ecclesiastica, Colgrave, B. and Mynors, R. A. B. eds (1969) *Bede's Ecclesiastical History of the English People* Oxford Medieval Texts, Oxford University Press, Oxford.

Hoffman, H. ed. (1980) *Die Chronik von Montecassino* Monumenta Germaniae Historica Scriptores 34, Hahnsche Buchhandlung, Hannover.

Illingworth, W. ed. (1812–18) *Rotuli Hundredorum temp. Hen. III et Edw. I* 2 vols, Royal Commission, London.

Jessopp, A. and James, M. R. eds (1896) *The Life and Miracles of St William of Norwich*, Cambridge University Press, Cambridge.

Kemble, J. M. (1839–48) *Codex Diplomaticus Ævi Saxonici* 8 vols, English Historical Society, London.

Keynes, S. D. and Kennedy, A. (forthcoming) *The Book of Bishop Æthelwold* ASNC Guides, Texts and Studies 4, Cambridge University Department of Anglo-Saxon Norse and Celtic, Cambridge.

Lair, J. ed. (1865) *Dudo of St Quentin De Moribus et Actis Primorum Normanniae Ducum*, Société des Antiquaires de Normandie, Caen.

Leges, (1904–6) *Leges IV* Monumenta Germaniae Historica 2 vols, Hannover.

Loyn, H. R. and Percival J. (1975) *The Reign of Charlemagne. Documents on Carolingian Government and Administration*, Edward Arnold, London.

Lund, N. (1984) *Two Voyagers at the Court of King Alfred*, Sessions, York.

Mortimer, R. ed. (1979) *Leiston Abbey Cartulary and Butley Priory Charters* Suffolk Records Society Suffolk Charters 1, Boydell and Brewer, Woodbridge.

Plummer, A. ed. (1896) *Venerabilis Baedae Opera Historica* 2 vols, Clarendon Press, Oxford.

Sawyer, P. H. (1968) *Anglo-Saxon Charters. An Annotated List and Bibliography* Royal Historical Society Guides and Handbooks 8, Royal Historical Society, London.

Scholz, B. W. and Rogers B. (1972) *Carolingian Chronicles*, Ann Arbor, Michigan.

Tangl, M. ed. (1916 reprinted 1955) *Die Briefe des heiligen Bonifatius und Lullus* Monumenta Germaniae Historica Epistolae Selectae 1, Weidmannsche Buchhandlung, Berlin.

Thorpe, L. trans. (1969) *Einhard and Notker the Stammerer. Two Lives of Charlemagne*, Penguin, Harmondsworth.

van Houts, E. (1992) *The Gesta Normannorum Ducorum of William of Jumièges, Orderic Vitalis and Robert of Torigni Vol. 1* Oxford Medieval Texts, Clarendon Press, Oxford.

Vita Anskarii, Waitz, G. ed. (1884) *Vita Anskarii* Monumenta Germaniae Historica, Scriptores Rerum Germanicarum in usum scholarum, Hannover.

Weidemann, M. (1986) *Das Testament des Bishofs Berthramn von Le Mans*, Römisch-Germanisches Zentralmuseum, Mainz.

Whitelock, D. (1930) *Anglo-Saxon Wills*, Cambridge University Press, Cambridge.

Whitelock, D. ed. (1955) *English Historical Documents: c. 500–1042*, Eyre and Spottiswoode, London.

Secondary sources

Adkins, P. (1989) 'Rook Hall', *Current Archaeology* 115, 262–4.

Ahnlund, N. (1922) 'Svinnegarns Källa', *Rig* 5, 59–76.

Albertoni, G. (1997) *L'Italia Carolingia*, La Nuova Italia Scientifica, Rome.

Allen, M. (2001) 'The volume of the English currency, 1158–1470', *Economic History Review* 54, 595–611.

Allison, K. J. (1955) 'The lost villages of Norfolk', *Norfolk Archaeology* 31, 116–62.

Andrén, A. (1998) 'En centralort utan textbelägg? – Uppåkra som ett historiskt-arkeologiskt problem' in *Centrala Platser Centrala Frågor*, eds

L. Larsson and B. Hårdh, Almqvist and Wiksell International, Stockholm, 137–46.

Andrews, P. (1992) 'Middle Saxon Norfolk: evidence for settlement 650–850', *The Norfolk Archaeological and Historical Research Group Annual* 1, 13–28.

Andrews, P. (1995) *Excavations at Redcastle Furze, Thetford, 1988–9* East Anglian Archaeology 72, Norfolk Museums Service, Gressenhall.

Andrews, P. ed. (1997) *Excavations at Hamwic Vol. 2: Excavations at Six Dials* CBA Research Report 109, Council for British Archaeology, York.

Archibald, M. (1988) 'English medieval coins as dating evidence' in *Coins and the Archaeologist*, eds J. Casey and R. Reece, 2nd edn, Seaby, London, 264–301.

Arnold, C. J. (1982a) *The Anglo-Saxon Cemeteries of the Isle of Wight*, British Museum, London.

Arnold, C. J. (1982b) 'Excavations at Eastry Court Farm, Eastry', *Archaeologia Cantiana* 98, 121–35.

Arnold, C. J. (1988) *An Archaeology of Early Anglo-Saxon Kingdoms*, Croom Helm, London.

Arslan, E. A. (1994) 'La circolazione monetaria (secoli V–VIII)' in *La storia dell'alto medioevo italiano (VI-X secolo) alla luce dell'archeologia*, eds R. Francovich and G. Noyé, All'Insegna del Giglio, Florence, 497–519.

Arslan, E. A. (2000) 'Zecche e circolazione della moneta' in *Il futuro dei Longobardi: l'Italia e la costruzione dell'Europe di Carlo Magno*, eds C. Bertelli and G. P. Brogiolo, Skira, Milan, 105–13.

Arthur, P. and Patterson, H. (1994) 'Ceramics and early medieval central and southern Italy: "a potted history"' in *La Storia dell'alto medioevo italiano (VI–X secolo) alla luce dell'archeologia*, eds R. Francovich and G. Noyé, All'Insegna del Giglio, Florence, 409–43.

Arthur, P. and Patterson, H. (1998) 'Local pottery in southern Puglia in the sixth and seventh centuries' in *Ceramica in Italia: VI–VII secolo* 2 vols, ed. L. Saguì, All'Insegna del Giglio, Florence, 511–30.

Astill, G. (1985) 'Archaeology, economics and Early Medieval Europe', *Oxford Journal of Archaeology* 4, 215–32.

Aston, M. (1986) 'Post-Roman central places in Somerset' in *Central Places, Archaeology and History*, ed. E. Grant, Sheffield University, Sheffield, 49–77.

Atkin, M. (1985) 'The Anglo-Saxon urban landscape in East Anglia', *Landscape History* 7, 27–40.

Backhouse, J. and Webster, L. (1991) *The Making of England. Anglo-Saxon Art and Culture AD 600–900*, British Museum Press, London.

Barton, K. J. (1968) 'Settlements of the Iron Age and Pagan Saxon periods at Linford, Essex', *Transactions of the Essex Archaeological Society* Third Series 1, 57–104.

Basford, H. V. ed. (1980) *The Vectis Report: A Survey of Isle of Wight Archaeology*, Isle of Wight County Council, Newport.

Bassett, S. (1989) 'In search of the origins of Anglo-Saxon kingdoms' in *The Origins of Anglo-Saxon Kingdoms* Studies in the Early History of Britain, ed. S. Bassett, Leicester University Press, London and New York, 3–27.

Bates, D. (1982) *Normandy Before 1066*, Longman, London.

Bauch, A. (1984) *Quellen zur Geschichte der Diözese Eichstätt Band 1: Biographien der Gründungszeit*, Johann Michael Sailer Verlag, Eichstätt.

Bauduin, P. (1999) 'Aux origins du duché de Normandie', *Bulletin de l'Office Universitaire d'Etudes Normandes* 7, Caen.

Beaurepaire, F. De (1969) *La Toponymie de la Normandie*, Cahiers Léopold Delisle 18, 1–2.

Beaurepaire, F. De (1984) *Dictionnaire topographique de la Seine-Martime* 2 vols, A. et J. Picard, Paris.

Besteman, J. C., Bos, J. M., Gerrets, D. A., Heidinga, H. A. and de Koning, J. eds (1999) *The Excavations at Wijnaldum. Reports on Frisia in Roman and Medieval Times*, A. A. Balkema, Rotterdam.

Besteman, J. C., Bos, J. M. and Heidinga, H. A. (1993) *Graven naar Friese Koningen. De Opgravingen in Wijnaldum*, Uitgeverij van Wijnen, Franeker.

Biddle, M. *et al.* (1990) *Artefacts from Medieval Winchester* Winchester Studies 7. ii, Clarendon Press, Oxford.

Biermann, F., Dalitz, S. and Heußner, K.-U. (1999) 'Der Brunnen von Schmerzke, Stadt Brandenburg a. d. Havel, und die absolute Chronologie der frühslawischen Besiedlung im nordostdeutschen Raum', *Prähistorische Zeitschrift* 74, 219–43.

Bird, E. (1997) *The Shaping of the Isle of Wight*, Ex Libris, Bradford on Avon.

Birkedahl, P. and Johansen, E. (1993) 'Nikolajbjerget', *Skalk* 1993:1, Højbjerg, 3–8.

Blackburn, M. A. S. (1989a) 'What factors govern the number of coins found on an archaeological site?' in *Coins and Archaeology. Medieval Archaeology Research Group Proceedings of the First Meeting at Isegran, Norway 1988* BAR Int. Ser. 556, eds H. Clarke and E. Schia, British Archaeological Reports, Oxford, 15–24.

Blackburn, M. A. S. (1989b) 'Znaleziska pojedyncze jako miara aktywnosci monetarnej we wczesnym sredniowieczu' (Single-finds as a measure of monetary activity in the Early Middle Ages), *Prace i materialy. Muzeum Archaeologicznego i Etnograficznego w Lodzi. Seria numizmatyczna i konserwatorska* 9, 67–85. [with English summary].

Blackburn, M. A. S. (1993a) 'Coin circulation in Germany during the Early Middle Ages: The evidence of single-finds' in *Fernhandel und Geldwirtschaft*, ed. B. Kluge, Jan Thorbecke Verlag, Sigmaringen, 37–54.

Blackburn, M. A. S. (1993b) 'Coin finds and coin circulation in Lindsey, *c.* 600–900' in *Pre-Viking Lindsey* Lincoln Archaeological Studies 1, ed. A. Vince, City of Lincoln Archaeological Unit, Lincoln, 80–90.

Blackburn, M. A. S. (2002) 'Finds from the Anglo-Scandinavian site of Torksey, Lincolnshire' in *Moneta Mediævalis: studia numizmatyczne i historyczne ofiarowane Profesorowi Stanislawowi Suchodolskiemu w 65. rocznice urodzin* [Numismatic and historical studies presented to Professor Stanislaw Suchodolski on his 65th birthday], ed. B. Paszkiewicz, Warsaw, 89–101, pl. 5.

Blackburn, M. A. S. and Bonser, M. J. (1984a) 'Single finds of Anglo-Saxon and Norman coins 1', *British Numismatic Journal* 54, 63–73.

Blackburn, M. A. S. and Bonser, M. J. (1984b) 'Sceattas, a styca, and other coin finds from a site in north-east Lincolnshire' in *Sceattas in England and on the Continent* BAR Brit. Ser. 128, eds D. Hill and D. M. Metcalf, British Archaeological Reports, Oxford, 233–7.

Blackburn, M. A. S. and Bonser, M. J. (1985) 'Single finds of Anglo-Saxon and Norman coins 2', *British Numismatic Journal* 55, 55–78.

Blackburn, M. A. S. and Bonser, M. J. (1986) 'Single finds of Anglo-Saxon and Norman coins 3', *British Numismatic Journal* 56, 64–101.

Blackburn, M. A. S., Colyer, C., and Dolley, M. (1983) *Early Medieval Coins from Lincoln and its Shire,* c. *700–1100* The Archaeology of Lincoln 6:1, Lincoln Archaeological Trust, London.

Blackburn, M. A. S. and Pagan, H. E. (1986) 'A revised check-list of coin hoards from the British Isles, *c.* 500–1100' in *Anglo-Saxon Monetary History*, ed. M. A. S. Blackburn, Leicester University Press, Leicester, 291–313 [an updated on-line version is available at http://www.medievalcoins.org].

Blackburn, M. A. S., Rogerson, A. and Margeson, S. (unpublished) 'A productive Middle and Late Saxon Site at Bawsey, Norfolk'.

Blackburn, M. A. S. and Sorenson, D. (1984) 'Sceattas from an unpublished site near Cambridge' in *Sceattas in England and on the Continent* BAR Brit. Ser. 128, ed. D. Hill and D. M. Metcalf, British Archaeological Reports, Oxford, 223–7.

Blair, J. (1992) 'Anglo-Saxon minsters: a topographical review' in *Pastoral Care Before the Parish* Studies in the Early History of Britain, eds J. Blair and R. Sharpe, Leicester University Press, Leicester, 226–66.

Blair, J. (1994) *Anglo-Saxon Oxfordshire*, Alan Sutton, Oxford.

Blair, J. (1996a) 'The minsters of the Thames' in *The Cloister and the World: Essays in Medieval History in Honour of Barbara Harvey*, eds J. Blair and B. Golding, Oxford University Press, Oxford, 5–28.

Blair, J. (1996b) 'Palaces or minsters? Northampton and Cheddar Reconsidered', *Anglo-Saxon England* 25, 97–121.

Blair, J. (forthcoming) *The Church in Anglo-Saxon Society*.

Blair, J. and Ramsay, N. eds (1991) *English Medieval Industries*, Hambledon Press, London and Rio Grande.

Blinkhorn, P. (1998) *Post-Roman Pottery from Lake End Road, Maidenhead, Berkshire*, Oxford Archaeological Unit, unpublished.

Blinkhorn, P. (1999) 'Of cabbages and kings: production, trade and consumption in Middle Saxon England' in *Anglo-Saxon Trading Centres: Beyond the Emporia*, ed. M. Anderton, Cruithne Press, Glasgow, 4–23.

Bonser, M. J. (1997) 'Fifteen years of coin finds from productive sites', *Yorkshire Numismatist* 3, 39–45.

Bonser, M. J. (1998) 'Single finds of ninth-century coins from Southern England: a listing' in *Kings, Currency, and Alliances*, eds M. A. S. Blackburn and D. M. Dumville, Boydell Press, Woodbridge, 199–240.

Boon, G. C. (1991) 'Byzantine and other exotic ancient bronze coins from Exeter' in *Roman Finds from Exeter* Exeter Archaeological Reports 4, eds N. Holbrook and P. T. Bidwell, Exeter City Council/University of Exeter, Exeter, 38–45.

Booth, J. (1997) 'Northumbrian coinage and the productive site at South Newbald', *Yorkshire Numismatist* 3, 15–38.

Booth, J. and Blowers, I. (1983) 'Finds of sceattas and stycas from Sancton', *Numismatic Chronicle* 143, 139–45.

Bowden, W. (forthcoming) 'Excavations in the new abbey' in *San Vincenzo al Volturno 4*, eds W. Bowden and R. Hodges.

Bowden, W., Coutts, C. M., Hodges, R. and Marazzi, F. (1996) 'Excavations and survey at San Vincenzo al Volturno 1995', *Archeologia Medievale* 23, 467–76.

Brather, S. (1996a) *Feldberger Keramik und frühe Slawen. Studien zur nordwestslawischen Keramik der Karolingerzeit*, Rudolf Habelt, Bonn.

Brather, S. (1996b) '"Germanische", "slawische" und "deutsche" Sachkultur des Mittelalters – Probleme ethnischer Interpretation', *Ethnographisch-Archäologische Zeitschrift* 37, 177–216.

Brewster, T. C. M. and Hayfield, C. (1988) 'Cowlam deserted village: a case study of post-medieval village desertion', *Post-Medieval Archaeology* 22, 21–109.

Bridbury, A. R. (1955) *England and the Salt Trade in the Later Middle Ages*, Clarendon Press, Oxford

Brookes, S. J. (1998) *Dark Age Economics Reconsidered: Evidence for Trade and*

Emporia in Early- to Mid-Saxon Kent, Unpublished MA Thesis, University College London.

Brookes, S. J. (forthcoming) *Landscapes, Communities and Exchange: a Reassessment of Anglo-Saxon Economics and Social Change AD 400–900 with Special Reference to Kent*, PhD Thesis, University College London.

Bruce-Mitford, R. (1978) *The Sutton Hoo Ship Burial Vol. 2, Arms, Armour and Regalia*, British Museum, London.

Buchner, R. ed. (1955) *Quellen zur karolingischen Reichsgeschichte 1. Ausgewählte Quellen zur deutschen Geschichte des Mittelalters*, Wissenschaftliche Buchgesellschaft, Darmstadt.

Bu'Lock, J. D. (1960) 'The Celtic, Saxon and Scandinavian settlement of Meols in Wirral' *Transactions of the Historic Society of Lancashire and Cheshire* 112, 1–28.

Bushe-Fox, J. P. (1928) *Second Report on the Excavation of the Roman Fort at Richborough, Kent*, Oxford University Press, Oxford.

Callander, J. G. (1933) 'A collection of prehistoric relics from the Stevenston Sands, Ayrshire and other objects in the National Museum', *Proceedings of the Society of Antiquaries of Scotland* 67, 26–34.

Cameron, K. (1998) *A Dictionary of Lincolnshire Place Names*, English Place Name Society, Nottingham.

Campbell, B. M. S. (1986) 'The complexity of manorial structure in medieval Norfolk: a case study', *Norfolk Archaeology* 39, 225–61.

Campbell, E. (1996) 'The archaeological evidence for external contacts, imports, trade and economy in Celtic Britain AD 400–800' in *External Contacts and the Economy of Late Roman and Post Roman Britain*, ed. K. R. Dark, Boydell, Woodbridge, 83–96.

Campbell, E. and Lane, A. (1993) 'Excavations at Longbury Bank, Dyfed and Early Medieval settlement in south Wales', *Medieval Archaeology* 37, 15–77.

Campbell, J. (2000) *The Anglo-Saxon State*, Hambledon, London and New York.

Carlsson, D. (1991) 'Harbours and trading places on Gotland AD 600–1000' in *Aspects of Maritime Scandinavia AD 200–1200*, ed. O. Crumlin Pedersen, Viking Ship Museum, Roskilde, 145–58.

Carr, R. D. (1985) 'Brandon, Staunch Meadow 1979–84', *Fenland Research* 2, 35–41.

Carr, R. D., Tester, A. and Murphy, P. (1988) 'The Middle Saxon settlement at Staunch Meadow, Brandon', *Antiquity* 62, 371–7.

Carver, M. O. H. (1989) 'Kingship and material culture in Early Anglo-Saxon East Anglia' in *The Origins of Anglo-Saxon Kingdoms*, ed. S. Bassett, Leicester University Press, Leicester, 141–58.

Carver, M. O. H. (1993) *Arguments in Stone* Oxbow Monograph 29, Oxbow Books, Oxford.

Carver, M. O. H. (1998) *Sutton Hoo, Burial Ground of Kings?*, British Museum, London.

Christensen, A. E. (1933) 'Dansk Torve – og Markedsväsen i Middelalderen' in *Handel och Samfärdsel*, eds J. Brøndsted and A. Schück, Nordisk Kultur 16, Bonniers, Stockholm, 181–90.

Christensen, P. B. and Johansen, E. (1992) 'En handelsplads fra yngre jernalder og vikingetid fra Sebbersund', *Aarbøger for Nordisk Oldkyndighed og Historie* 1991, 199–229.

Christensen, T. (1991) *Lejre – syn og sagn*, Roskilde Museums Forlag, Roskilde.

Christensen, T. (1997) 'Hallen i Lejre' in ... *Gick Grendel att söka det höga huset ... Arkeologiska källor till aristokratiska miljöer i Skandinavien under yngre*

järnålder, eds J. Callmer and E. Rosengren, Halland länsmuseer, Halmstad, 47–54.
Clarke, H. and Ambrosiani, B. (1991) *Towns in the Viking Age*, Leicester University Press, Leicester.
Clarke, H. and Carter, A. (1977) *Excavations in King's Lynn 1963–70*, Society for Medieval Archaeology Monograph 7, Society for Medieval Archaeology, London.
Coin Register, published annually in *British Numismatic Journal* since 1987.
Corbett, W. and Dent, D. (1993) '4. The soil landscapes' in *An Historical Atlas of Norfolk*, ed. P. Wade-Martins, Norfolk Museums Service, Norwich, 18–19.
Cormack, W. F. (1965) 'Northumbrian coins from Luce Sands, Wigtownshire', *Transactions of the Dumfries and Galloway Natural History and Antiquarian Society* 52, 149–50.
Coutts, C. (1991) *Pottery and the Emporia: Imported Pottery in Middle-Saxon England with Special Reference to Ipswich*, Unpublished PhD Thesis, University of Sheffield.
Cox, B. (1994) 'The pattern of Old English *burh* in early Lindsey', *Anglo-Saxon England* 23, 35–56.
Cox, B. (1996) 'The Yarboroughs in Lindsey', *English Place Name Society Journal* 28, 50–60.
Crabtree, P. J. (1996) 'Production and consumption in an early complex society: animal use in Middle Saxon East Anglia', *World Archaeology* 28 (1), 58–76.
Cramp, R. (1976) 'Monkwearmouth and Jarrow: the archaeological evidence' in *Famulus Christi: Essays in Commemoration of the Thirteenth Centenary of the Birth of the Venerable Bede*, ed. G. Bonner, SPCK, London, 5–18.
Crowson, A., Lane, T. and Reeve, J. eds (2000) *Fenland Management Project Excavations 1991–1995*, Lincolnshire Archaeology and Heritage Reports 3, Heritage Lincolnshire, Heckington.
Cubitt, C. (1995) *Anglo-Saxon Church Councils* c. *650*-c. *850*, Leicester University Press, London and New York.
Cunliffe, B. W. (2001) *Facing the Ocean. The Atlantic and its Peoples*, Oxford University Press, Oxford.
Dalberg, V. and Sørensen, J. K. (1979) *Stednavneforskning 2*, Akademisk forlag, København.
Darby, H. C. (1977) *Domesday England*, Cambridge University Press, Cambridge.
Dark, K. (2000) *Britain and the End of the Roman Empire*, Tempus, Stroud.
Darling, M. J. (1993) *Caister on Sea Excavations by Charles Green, 1951–55* East Anglian Archaeology 60, Norfolk Archaeological Unit, Gressenhall.
Davies, J. A. (1996) 'The Iron Age and Roman periods' in *A Festival of Norfolk Archaeology*, eds S. Margeson, B. Ayers and S. Heywood, Norfolk and Norwich Archaeological Society, Norwich, 21–9.
Davies, W. and Vierck, H. (1974) 'The contexts of Tribal Hidage: social aggregates and settlement patterns', *Frühmittelalterliche Studien* 8, 223–93.
De Jersey, P. (1997) 'Cast away riches: estimating the volume of Celtic coinage found in Britain', *Yorkshire Numismatist* 3, 1–13.
Dell'Acqua, F. (1997) 'Ninth-century window glass from the monastery of San Vincenzo al Volturno (Molise, Italy)', *Journal of Glass Studies* 39, 33–41.
Detsicas, A. (1983) *The Cantiaci*, Alan Sutton, Gloucester.
Didsbury, P. (1990) 'Fieldwork in Cottam and Cowlam parish', *Yorkshire Archaeological Journal* 62, 63–7.
Dolley, R. H. M. (1961) 'The Anglo-Saxon coins from Meols Sands', *Transactions of the Historic Society of Lancashire and Cheshire* 113, 197–202.

Donat, P. (1970) 'Zur Nordausbreitung der slawischen Grubenhäuser', *Zeitschrift für Archäologie* 4, 250–69.
Donat, P. (1980) *Haus, Hof und Dorf in Mitteleuropa vom 7. bis 12. Jahrhundert*, Akademie Verlag, Berlin.
Donat, P. (1998) 'Aktuelle Fragen der Erforschung westslawischer Dorfsiedlungen' in *Slavonic Countries in the Middle Ages. Profanum and Sacrum,* eds H. Kócka-Krenz and W. Losinski, Publishing House of the Poznan Society for the Advancement of the Arts and Sciences, Poznan, 187–99.
Duby, G. (1978) *Guerriers et Paysans*, Presses Universitaires de France, Paris.
Dumville, D. N. (1992) 'Ecclesiastical lands and the defence of Wessex in the First Viking Age' in *Wessex and England From Alfred to Edgar* Studies in Anglo-Saxon History 3, ed. D. N. Dumville, Boydell Press, Woodbridge, 29–54.
Dunger, G. T. (1997) 'A new moneyer for a Portrait/Dorob C penny of Ecgberht', *Spink Numismatic Circular* 105.9, 322.
Dunning, G. C. (1947) 'Chillerton Down Camp, Gatcombe, Isle of Wight', *Proceedings of the Isle of Wight Natural History and Archaeological Society* 4, 51–3.
Dunning, G. C. (1956) 'Trade relations between England and the Continent in the Late Anglo-Saxon Period' in *Dark Age Britain*, ed. D. B. Harden, Methuen, London, 218–313.
Dyer, C. (1985) 'Towns and cottages in eleventh-century England' in *Studies in Medieval History Presented to R. H. C. Davies*, eds H. Mayr-Harting and R. I. Moore, Hambledon, London, 91–106.
Dyson, T. (1980) 'London and Southwark in the seventh century and later: a neglected reference', *Transactions of the London Archaeological Society* 31, 83–95.
Edwards, N. and Lane, A. (1988) *Early Medieval Settlements in Wales, AD 400 – 1100*, Early Medieval Wales Archaeological Research Group, Cardiff and Bangor.
Ekwall, E. (1960) *The Concise Oxford Dictionary of English Place-Names* 4th edn, Oxford University Press, Oxford.
Ekwall, E. (1964) *Old English Wic in Place-Names*, A.-B. Lundequista Bokhandeln, Uppsala and Copenhagen.
EMC – *Early Medieval Corpus of Single Finds of Coins in the British Isles, 410–1180*, http://www.medievalcoins.org
van Es, W. A. and Hessing, W. A. M. eds (1994) *Romeinen, Friezen en Franken in Het Hart van Nederland*, Matrijs, Utrecht.
Esmonde Cleary, A. S. (1989) *The Ending of Roman Britain*, Batsford, London.
Everitt, A. (1979) 'Place-names and *pays*: the Kentish evidence', *Nomina* 3, 95–112.
Everitt, A. (1986) *Continuity and Colonization: the Evolution of Kentish Settlement*, Leicester University Press, Leicester.
Everson, P. (1993) 'Pre-Viking settlement in Lindsey' in *Pre-Viking Lindsey* Lincoln Archaeological Studies 1, ed. A. Vince, City of Lincoln Archaeological Unit, Lincoln, 91–100.
Fenwick, V. (1984) 'Insula de Burgh: excavations at Burrow Hill, Butley, Suffolk, 1978–81', *Anglo-Saxon Studies in Archaeology and History* 3, 35–54.
Fenwick, V. (1985) 'Butley', *Current Archaeology* 97, 53–4.
Finberg, H. P. R. (1957) 'Some early Gloucestershire estates' in *Gloucestershire Studies*, ed. H. P. R. Finberg, Leicester University Press, Leicester, 1–16.
Fisher, J. L. (1968) *A Medieval Farming Glossary ... from Essex Records*, Essex Record Office, Chelmsford.
Fleming, R. (1985) 'Monastic lands and England's defence in the Viking Age', *English Historical Review* 395, 247–65.
Foot, S. (1993) 'The kingdom of Lindsey' in *Pre-Viking Lindsey* Lincoln

Archaeological Studies 1, ed. A. Vince, City of Lincoln Archaeological Unit, Lincoln, 128–40.

Francis, K. and Moran, M. (1997) 'Planning and technology in the Early Middle Ages: the temporary workshops at San Vincenzo al Volturno' in *I Congresso Nazionale di Archeologia Medievale*, ed. S. Gelichi, All'Insegna del Giglio, Florence, 373–8.

Freshwater, T. (1996) 'A lava quern workshop in Late Saxon London', *The London Archaeologist* 8 (2), 39–45.

Fulford, M. (1989) 'Byzantium and Britain: a Mediterranean perspective on post-Roman Mediterranean imports in western Britain and Ireland', *Medieval Archaeology* 33, 1–6.

Gabriel, I. (1986) Review of *Die Mecklenburg – eine Hauptburg der Obodriten*, P. Donat, Akademie Verlag, Berlin, *Offa* 43, 385–6.

Gauthiez, B. (1998) 'The planning of the town of Bury St Edmunds: a probable Norman origin' in *Bury St Edmunds: Medieval Art, Architecture, Archaeology and Economy* BAA Conference Transactions 20, ed. A. Gransden, British Archaeological Association, London, 81–97.

Gem, R. (1995) 'Anglo-Saxon minsters of the Thames Estuary' in *Thames Gateway: Reading Historic Buildings and Landscapes on the Thames Estuary*, RCHME, Swindon.

Geological Survey of Great Britain (England and Wales), 1:50000, Drift Sheet 330.

Gerrets, D. A. and de Koning, J. (1999) 'Settlement development on the Wijnaldum-Tjitsma terp' in *The Excavations at Wijnaldum. Reports on Frisia in Roman and Medieval Times*, eds J. C. Besteman, J. M. Bos, D. A. Gerrets, H. A. Heidinga and J. de Koning, A. A. Balkema, Rotterdam, 73–123.

Gibben, J. B. (1902) 'Roman burial', *Archaeologia Cantiana* 25, lxvi.

van Giffen, A. E. (1919) 'Een Karolingisch grafveld bij Godlinze', *Derde Jaarverslag van de Vereniging voor Terpenonderzoek* 3, 39–96.

Gilkes, O. and Moran, M. (2001) 'San Vincenzo without the walls – excavations 1996–7', *Papers of the British School at Rome* 69, 385–92.

Gilkes, O., Moran, M. and Tremlett, S. (forthcoming 2002) 'Without walls at San Vincenzo: excavations on the east bank of the Volturno, 1996–7', *Papers of the British School at Rome.*

Golding, B. J. (1989) 'An introduction to the Hampshire Domesday' in *The Hampshire Domesday*, gen. ed. A. Williams, Alecto Historical Editions, London, 1–27.

Gough, R. ed. (1789) *Camden's Britannia* [annotated and edited by G. J. Copley (1977) Hutchinson, London].

Green C., Green, I. and Dallas, C. (1987) 'Excavations at Castor, Cambridgeshire in 1957–8 and 1973', *Northamptonshire Archaeology* 21, 109–48.

Grierson, P. (1975) *Numismatics*, Oxford University Press, Oxford.

Grierson, P. and Blackburn, M. (1986) *Medieval European Coinage 1. The Early Middle Ages (5th–10th Centuries)*, Cambridge University Press, Cambridge.

Griffiths, D. (1994) 'Trade and production centres in the Post-Roman north, the Irish Sea perspective' in *The Archaeology of Gudme and Lundeborg* Arkeologiske Studier 10, eds P. O. Nielsen, K. Randsborg and H. Thrane, Akademisk Forlag, Copenhagen, 184–8.

Griffiths, D. (1996) 'The maritime economy of the Chester region in the Anglo-Saxon period' in *'Where Deva spreads her Wizard Stream': Trade and the port of Chester. Papers from a seminar held at Chester, November 1995* Chester

Archaeology Occasional Paper 3, ed. P. Carrington, Chester City Council, Chester, 49–60.

Griffiths, D. and Philpott, R. A. (in prep.) *Meols: The Archaeology of the North Wirral Coast*, National Museums and Galleries on Merseyside, Liverpool.

Grimm, P. (1968) *Tilleda. Eine Königspfalz am Kyffhäuser. Teil 1: Die Hauptburg*, Deutsche Akademie der Wissenschaften zu Berlin, Schriften der Sektion für Vor- und Frühgeschichte Band 24, Akademie Verlag, Berlin.

Gurney, D. (1993) 'The Roman period' in *An Historical Atlas of Norfolk*, ed. P. Wade-Martins, Norfolk Museums Service, Norwich, 34–5.

Gurney, D. (1996) 'The "Saxon Shore" in Norfolk' in *A Festival of Norfolk Archaeology*, eds S. Margeson, B. Ayers and S. Heywood, Norfolk and Norwich Archaeological Society, Norwich, 30–9.

Gurney, D. (1997) 'A note on the distribution of metal-detecting in Norfolk', *Norfolk Archaeology* 42, 528–32.

Hadley, D. M. (2000) *The Northern Danelaw: Its Social Structure c. 800–1100* Studies in the Early History of Britain, Leicester University Press, Leicester.

Hald, K. (1963) 'The cult of Odin in Danish place-names' in *Early English and Norse Studies Presented to Hugh Smith*, eds A. Brown and P. Foote, Methuen, London, 99–109.

Haldenby, D. (1990) 'An Anglian site on the Yorkshire Wolds', *Yorkshire Archaeological Journal* 62, 51–63.

Haldenby, D. (1992) 'An Anglian site on the Yorkshire Wolds', *Yorkshire Archaeological Journal* 64, 25–39.

Haldenby, D. (1994) 'An Anglian site on the Yorkshire Wolds – part III', *Yorkshire Archaeological Journal* 66, 51–6.

Haldenby, D. (1997) 'A study of ninth-century Anglo-Saxon strap-ends. Part one', *Treasure Hunting*, December 1997, 23–9.

Haldenby, D. (1998a) 'A study of ninth-century Anglo-Saxon strap-ends. Part two', *Treasure Hunting*, February 1998, 38–43.

Haldenby, D. (1998b) 'A study of ninth-century Anglo-Saxon strap-ends. Part three, *Treasure Hunting*, April 1998, 38–41.

Hansen, I. L. and Wickham, C. eds (2000) *The Long Eighth Century: Production, Distribution and Demand* The Transformation of the Roman World 11, Brill, Leiden.

Hårdh, B. (2000) 'Uppåkra – a centre in South Sweden in the first millennium AD', *Antiquity* 74, 640–8.

Harmer, F. E. (1950) '*Chipping* and *Market*. A lexicographical investigation' in *Early Cultures of North-West Europe*, eds C. Fox and B. Dickens, Cambridge University Press, Cambridge, 335–57.

Hart, C. R. (1992) *The Danelaw*, Hambledon Press, London.

Hase, P. H. (1975) *The Development of the Parish in Hampshire*, Unpublished PhD Thesis, University of Cambridge.

Hase, P. H. (1988) 'The mother churches of Hampshire' in *Minsters and Parish Churches: The Local Church in Transition 950–1200*, ed. J. Blair, Oxford University Committee for Archaeology, Oxford, 45–66.

Haslam, J. (1980) 'A Middle Saxon iron smelting site at Ramsbury, Wiltshire', *Medieval Archaeology* 24, 1–68.

Hasted, E. (1778–99) *The History and Topographical Survey of the County of Kent* 4 vols, Simmons and Kirkby, Canterbury.

Hawkes, S. C. (1970) 'Early Anglo-Saxon Kent', *Archaeological Journal* 126, 186–92.

Hawkes, S. C. (1974) 'Notes and news: air reconnaissance', *Antiquity* 48, 213–15.

Hawkes, S. C. (1976) 'Investigations and excavations during the year: interim report by Mrs. S. C. Hawkes, M. A., F. S. A., on the excavations at Eastry', *Archaeologia Cantiana* 92, 247–8.
Hawkes, S. C. (1979) 'Eastry in Anglo-Saxon Kent: its importance, and a newly-found grave' in *Anglo-Saxon Studies in Archaeology and History* 1 BAR Brit. Ser. 72, eds S. C. Hawkes, D. Brown and J. Campbell, British Archaeological Reports, Oxford, 81–113.
Hawkes, S. C. (1982) 'Anglo-Saxon Kent *c*. 425–725' in *Archaeology in Kent to AD 1500* CBA Research Report 48, ed. P. Leach, Council for British Archaeology, London, 64–83.
Helle, K. (1985) 'Bergen blir by' in *Middelalderbyen*, ed. I. Øye, Bryggens Museum, Bergen, 5–23.
Herrmann, J. (1980) 'Über das historische und siedlungsgeschichtliche Umfeld des Seehandelsplatzes Reric zu Beginn des 9. Jahrhunderts', *Offa* 37, 201–7.
Herrmann, J. (1988) 'Zur Struktur von Handel und Handelsplätzen im südwestlichen Ostseegebiet vom 8. –10. Jahrhundert', *Bericht der Römisch-Germanischen Kommission* 69, 720–39.
Herrmann, J. and Heußner, K. -U. (1991) 'Dendrochronologie, Archäologie und Frühgeschichte vom 6. bis 12. Jh. in den Gebieten zwischen Saale, Elbe und Oder', *Ausgrabungen und Funde* 36, 255–90.
Herschend, F. (1989) 'Vikings follow Gresham's Law' in *Approaches to Swedish Prehistory* BAR Int. Ser. 500, eds T. B. Larsson and H. Lundmark, British Archaeological Reports, Oxford, 373–93.
Hill, D. and Cowie, R. (2001) *Wics: The Early Medieval Trading Centres of Northern Europe*, Sheffield Academic Press, Sheffield.
Hill, P. (1997) *Whithorn and St Ninian, The Excavation of a Monastic Town 1984–91*, Sutton, Stroud.
Hines, J. (2000) 'Welsh and English: mutual origins in Post-Roman Britain?' *Studia Celtica* 24, 81–103.
Hinman, M. (1999) *Buildings and Floods: A Sequence of Deeply Stratified Medieval and Post-Medieval Deposits at Market Mews, Wisbech* Cambridge Archaeological Field Unit Report 156, unpublished.
Hirth, K. G. (1998) 'The distributional approach: a new way to identify marketplace exchange in the archaeological record', *Current Anthropology* 39 (4), 451–76.
Hobbs, R. (2001) 'Finding our past: The Portable Antiquities Scheme in England and Wales' in *Indulgence or Necessity? Research in Museum Archaeology* The Museum Archaeologist 26 Conference Proceedings Stoke-on-Trent 1999, ed. P. J. Wise, Society of Museum Archaeologists, Colchester.
Hockey, S. F. (1970) *Quarr Abbey and its Lands 1132–1631*, Leicester University Press, Leicester.
Hockey, S. F. (1982) *Insula Vecta: The Isle of Wight in the Middle Ages*, Phillimore, Chichester.
Hodges, R. (1978) 'Ports of trade in Early Medieval Europe', *Norwegian Archaeology Review* 11 (2), 97–117.
Hodges, R. (1984) 'Excavations at Vacchereccia (Rocchetta Nuova): a later Roman and Early Medieval settlement in the Volturno valley, Molise', *Papers of the British School at Rome* 52, 148–94.
Hodges, R. (1988) 'The rebirth of towns in the Early Middle Ages' in *The Rebirth of Towns in the West AD 700–1050* CBA Research Report 68, eds R. Hodges and B. Hobley, Council for British Archaeology, London, 1–7.

Hodges, R. (1989a) *Dark Age Economics. The Origins of Towns and Trade, AD 600–1000* 2nd edn, Duckworth, London.

Hodges, R. (1989b) *The Anglo-Saxon Achievement*, Duckworth, London.

Hodges, R. (1991) 'A fetishism for commodities: ninth-century glass-making at San Vincenzo al Volturno' in *Archeologia e storia della produzione del vetro preindustriale*, ed. M. Mendera, All'Insegna del Giglio, Florence, 67–90.

Hodges, R. ed. (1993) *San Vincenzo al Volturno 1: The 1980–86 Excavations Part I* Archaeological Monographs of the British School at Rome 7, British School at Rome, London.

Hodges, R. ed. (1995) *San Vincenzo al Volturno 2: The 1980–86 Excavations Part II* Archaeological Monographs of the British School at Rome 9, British School at Rome, London.

Hodges, R. (1997a) *Light in the Dark Ages: The Rise and Fall of San Vincenzo al Volturno*, Duckworth, London.

Hodges, R. (1997b) '10 October 881. The sack of San Vincenzo al Volturno' in *Vltra Terminvm Vagari: Papers in honour of Carl Nylander*, eds B. Magnusson, S. Renzetti, P. Vian and J. Voicu, Associazione Internazionale di Archeologia Classica-Edizioni Quasar, Rome, 129–41.

Hodges, R. and Hobley, B. (1988) *The Rebirth of Towns in the West AD 700–1050* CBA Research Report 68, Council for British Archaeology, London.

Hodges, R. and Mitchell, J. eds (1985) *San Vincenzo al Volturno: The Archaeology, Art and Territory of an Early Medieval Monastery* BAR Int. Ser. 252, British Archaeological Reports, Oxford.

Hodges, R. and Mitchell, J. eds (1996) *The Basilica of Abbot Joshua at San Vincenzo al Volturno* Miscellanea Vulturnense 2, Abbazia di Montecassino, Monte Cassino and Monteroduni.

Hodges, R. and Whitehouse, D. (1983) *Mohammed, Charlemagne and the Origins of Europe: Archaeology and the Origins of the Pirenne Thesis*, Duckworth, London.

Hogarth, A. C. (1973) 'Structural features in Anglo-Saxon graves', *Archaeological Journal* 130, 104–19.

Hooke, D. (1985) *The Anglo-Saxon Landscape: The Kingdom of the Hwicce*, Manchester University Press, Manchester.

Huggett, J. (1988) 'Imported grave goods and the Early Anglo-Saxon economy', *Medieval Archaeology* 32, 63–96.

Hugot, L. (1965) 'Die Pfalz Karls des Grossen in Aachen' in *Karl der Grosse. Lebenswerk und Nachleben. Karolingische Kunst* Band 3, Düsseldorf, 534–72.

Huisman, M. (1997) *Non-ferro metaalvondsten van de opgraving Wijnaldum-Tjitsma. De vroeg-middeleeuwse periode (300–1000 n. Chr)* 3 vols, Unpublished BA Thesis, University of Groningen.

Hume, A. (1863) *Ancient Meols, or Some Account of the Antiquities Found on the Sea Coast of Cheshire*, John Russell Smith, London.

Hurst J. D. ed. (1998) *A Multi-Period Salt Production Site at Droitwich: Excavations at Upwich* CBA Research Report 107, Council for British Archaeology, York.

Hvass, S. (1993) 'The settlement' in *Digging into the Past. 25 Years of Archaeology in Denmark*, eds S. Hvass and B. Storgaard, The Royal Society of Northern Antiquaries/Jutland Archaeological Society, Copenhagen and Højbjerg, 187–94.

Isle of Wight County Council (1992) *Romans on the Wight*, Isle of Wight County Council, Newport.

Jankuhn, H. *et al.* eds. (1973) *Vor-und Frühformen der Europäischen Stadt im Mittelalter, Vanderhoeck and Ruprecht*, Göttingen.

Jensen S. (1991) *The Vikings of Ribe*, Den Antikvariske samling, Ribe.

Jensen, S. (1993) 'Early towns' in *Digging into the Past. 25 Years of Archaeology in Denmark,* eds S. Hvass and B. Storgaard, The Royal Society of Northern Antiquaries/Jutland Archaeological Society, Copenhagen and Højbjerg, 202–5.

Jensen, S. and Watt, M. (1993) 'Trading sites and central places' in *Digging into the Past. 25 Years of Archaeology in Denmark,* eds S. Hvass and B. Storgaard, The Royal Society of Northern Antiquaries/Jutland Archaeological Society, Copenhagen and Højbjerg, 195–201.

Jessup, R. (1970) *South-East England,* Thames and Hudson, London.

Johanek, P. (1985) 'Der "Außenhandel" des Frankenreiches der Merowingerzeit nach Norden und Osten im Spiegel der Schriftquellen' in *Untersuchungen zu Handel und Verkehr der Vor-und Frühgeschichtlichen Zeit in Mittel- und Nordeuropa, Teil III: Der Handel des frühen Mittelalters,* eds K. Düwel *et al.*, Vandenhoeck and Ruprecht, Göttingen, 214–54.

Johanek, P. (1987) 'Der fränkische Handel der Karolingerzeit im Spiegel der Schriftquellen', in *Untersuchungen zu Handel und Verkehr der Vor- und Frühgeschichtlichen Zeit in Mittel- und Nordeuropa Teil IV: Der Handel der Karolinger und Wikingerzeit,* eds K. Düwel *et al.*, Vandenhoeck and Ruprecht, Göttingen, 7–68.

Johnson, S. (1983) *Burgh Castle, Excavations by Charles Green 1958–61* East Anglian Archaeology 20, Norfolk Museums Service, Gressenhall.

Jolliffe, J. E. A. (1933) *Pre-Feudal England: The Jutes,* Oxford University Press, London.

Jones, J. D. (1959) 'A penny of Æthelræd II from the Isle of Wight', *Proceedings of the Isle of Wight Natural History and Archaeological Society for 1959* 5.4, 157–9.

Jöns, H. (1998a) 'Der frühgeschichtliche Seehandelsplatz von Groß Strömkendorf' in *Struktur und Wandel im Früh- und Hochmittelalter. Eine Bestandsaufnahme aktueller Forschungen zur Germania Slavica,* ed. C. Lübke, Franz Steiner, Stuttgart, 127–43.

Jöns, H. (1998b) 'Groß Strömkendorf – handelspladsen ved Wismar – et exempel på urbaniseringens tidlige fase i det vestslaviske område' in *Beretning fra syttende tværfaglige vikingesymposium,* ed. D. Meier, Forlaget Hikuin og Afdeling for Midelalder-arkæologi, Højbjerg, 31–54.

Jöns, H. (2000) 'Reric – Vorläufer Haithabus?', *Archäologie in Schleswig/ Arkæologi i Slesvig* 6, 90–102.

Jöns, H., Lüth, F. and Müller-Wille, M. (1997) 'Ausgrabungen auf dem frühgeschichtlichen Seehandelsplatz von Groß Strömkendorf, Kr. Nordwestmecklenburg', *Germania* 75, 193–221.

Jope, E. M. (1966) *An Archaeological Survey of County Down,* HMSO, Belfast.

Jørgensen, B. (1982) *Dansk Stednavneleksikon: Jylland – nordlige del,* Gyldendal, Copenhagen.

Jørgensen, L. (1994) 'The find material from the settlement of Gudme II – composition and interpretation' in *The Archaeology of Gudme and Lundeborg. Papers Presented at a Conference at Svendborg, October 1991* Arkæologiske Studier 10, eds P. O. Nielsen, K. Randsborg and H. Thrane, Akademisk Forlag, Copenhagen, 53–63.

Jørgensen, L. (1998) 'En storgård fra vikingetid ved Tissø, Sjælland – en foreløbig præsentation' in *Centrala Platser. Centrala Frågor. Samhällsstrukturen under Järnåldern,* Acta Archaeologica Lundensia, Series in 8° 28, eds L. Larsson and B. Hårdh, Almquist and Wiksell, Lund, 233–48.

Kelly, D. B. (1962) 'Researches and discoveries in Kent: Lyminge', *Archaeologia Cantiana* 77, 205.

Kelly, D. B. (1978) 'Researches and discoveries: Sittingbourne', *Archaeologia Cantiana* 94, 267.

Kelly, S. (1992) 'Trading privileges from eighth-century England', *Early Medieval Europe* 1, 3–28.

Klackenberg, H. (1992) *Moneta nostra. Monetarisering i medeltidens Sverige*, Almqvist and Wiksell International, Stockholm.

Knol, E. (1993) *De Noord-Nederlandse Kustlanden in de Vroege Middeleeuwen*, Unpublished PhD Thesis, Vrije Universiteit Amsterdam.

Knol, E., Prummel, W., Uytterschaut, H. T. *et al.* (1995–6) 'The Early Medieval cemetery of Oosterbeintum (Friesland)', *Palaeohistoria* 37/38, 245–426.

Knowles, D. and Hadcock, N. (1971) *Religious Houses of England and Wales* 2nd ed, Longmans, London.

Knox, C. (1941) 'St. Margaret's Bay, and the Roman roads from Richborough to Dover and Canterbury', *Archaeologia Cantiana* 54, 34–40.

Koht, H. (1921) *Innhogg og Utsyn i Norsk Historie*, Aschehoug, Kristiana.

Kreusch, F. (1965) 'Kirche, Atrium und Portikus der Aachener Pfalz' in *Karl der Grosse. Lebenswerk und Nachleben. Karolingische Kunst* Band 3, Düsseldorf, 463–533.

Kulturhistorisk Leksikon, Danstrup, J., Kerkkonen, G., Már Lárusson, M., Hødnebø, F. and Granlund, J. eds (1956–78) *Kulturhistorisk Leksikon for nordisk middelalder fra vikingetid til reformationstid* 22 vols, Roskilde and Bagger, Copenhagen.

Lafaurie, J. (1961) 'Les routes commerciales indiquées par les trésors et trouvailles monétaires mérovingiens' in *Moneta e scambi nell'alto medioevo* Settimane di studio del Centro italiano di studi sull'alto medioevo 8, CISAM, Spoleto, 231–78.

Lane, A. and Campbell, E. (2000) *Dunadd, An Early Dalriadic Capital*, Oxbow Books, Oxford.

Lane, T. (1993) *The Fenland Project 8: The Northern Fen Edge* East Anglian Archaeology 66, Scole Archaeological Committee, Sleaford.

Langford, K.-J. (2002) Letter to the Editor, *Rescue News* Spring 2002, 5.

Larsen, J. H. (1980) 'Vikingtids handelsplass i Valle, Setesdal', *Universitets Oldsaksamling Skrifter*, ny rekke 3, 143–8.

Larsen, J. H. (1985) 'En mulig handelsplass i Grimstadområdet i vikingetiden', *Universitets Oldsaksamlings Årbok for 1984–5*, 111–20.

Latham, R. E. (1965) *A Revised Medieval Latin Word-List*, British Academy, London.

Laurent, V. (1978) 'Ein byzantinisches Bleisiegel aus Haithabu', *Berichte über die Ausgrabungen in Haithabu* 12, 36–40.

Leah, M. (1992) 'The Fenland Management Project: excavations at three Middle Saxon marshland sites at West Walton, Walpole St Andrew and Hay Green', *Fenland Research* 7, 49–59.

Leahy, K. A. (1993) 'The Anglo-Saxon settlement of Lindsey' in *Pre-Viking Lindsey* Lincoln Archaeological Studies 1, ed. A. Vince, City of Lincoln Archaeological Unit, Lincoln, 29–44.

Leahy, K. A. (2000) 'Middle Saxon metalwork and coins from South Newbald and the 'productive site' phenomenon in Yorkshire' in *Early Deira, Archaeological Studies of the East Riding in the fourth to ninth centuries AD*, eds H. Geake and J. Kenny, Oxbow Books, Oxford, 51–82.

Leahy, K. A. and Patterson, C. (2001) 'New light on the Viking presence in Lincolnshire; the artefactual evidence' in *Vikings and the Danelaw. Select Papers from the Proceedings of the Thirteenth Viking Congress*, eds J. Graham-Campbell, R. Hall, J. Jensen and D. N. Pasons, Oxbow Books, Oxford, 181–202.

Le Maho, J. (1995) 'Rouen à l'époque des incursions Vikings (841–911)', *Bulletin de la Commission des Antiquités de la Seine Maritime* 43, 143–202.

Le Maho, J. (1999) 'Un exode de reliques dans les pays de la basse Seine à la fin du IXe siècle', *Bulletin de la Commission des Antiquités de la Seine Maritime* 46 (for 1998), 136–88.

Lemarignier, J. F. (1955) 'Jumièges et le Monachisme Occidental' in *Jumièges: Congrès Scientifique du XIIIe Centenaire* 2 vols, Lecerf, Rouen, ii 752–64.

Leube, A. (1996) 'Germanische Völkerwanderungen und ihr archäologischer Fundniederschlag. Slawisch-Germanische Kontakte im nördlichen Elb-Oder-Gebiet. Das 5. und 6. Jahrhundert östlich der Elbe. Ein Forschungsbericht (II)', *Ethnographisch-Archäologische Zeitschrift* 36, 259–98.

Lewis, M. (2002) 'The Portable Antiquities (Voluntary Recording) Scheme: its impact in Kent and the future for London', *London Archaeologist* 9 (12), 330–7.

Liddiard, R. (2000) *'Landscapes of Lordship' Norman Castles and the Countryside in Medieval Norfolk 1066–1200* BAR Brit. Ser. 309, Archaeopress, Oxford.

Lidén, H.-E. (1970) 'Utgravningen av Mære kirke', *Nord-Trøndelag Historielag Årbok for 1969*, 18–58.

Liversage, G. D. (1967) 'Excavations at Dalkey Island, Co. Dublin, 1956–9', *Proceedings of the Royal Irish Academy* 66 C, 53–234.

Losco-Bradley, S. and Wheeler, H. M. (1984) 'Anglo-Saxon settlement in the Trent Valley: some aspects' in *Studies in Late Anglo-Saxon Settlement*, ed. M. Faull, Oxford University Committee for Archaeology, Oxford, 101–14.

Loveluck, C. P. (1994) *Exchange and Society in Early Medieval England 400–700 AD*, Unpublished PhD Thesis, University of Durham.

Loveluck, C. P. (1996) 'The development of the Anglo-Saxon landscape: economy and society "On Driffield", East Yorkshire, 400–750 AD', *Anglo-Saxon Studies in Archaeology and History* 9, Oxbow Books, Oxford, 25–48.

Loveluck, C. P. (1998) 'A high-status Anglo-Saxon settlement at Flixborough, Lincolnshire', *Antiquity* 72, 146–61.

Loveluck, C. P. (2001) 'Wealth, Waste and Conspicuous Consumption. Flixborough and its importance for Mid and Late Saxon settlement studies' in *Image and Power in the Archaeology of Early Medieval Britain*, eds H. Hamerow and A. MacGregor, Oxbow Books, Oxford, 78–130.

Lundqvist, L. (1997) 'Slöinge: om et pågående project' in ... *Gick Grendel att söka det höga huset ... Arkeologiska källor till aristokratiska miljöer i Skandinavien under yngre järnålder*, eds J. Callmer and E. Rosengren, Halland länsmuseer, Halmstad, 89–98.

Mackinder, H. (1902) *Britain and the British Seas*, Heinemann, London.

Maddicott, J. R. (1997) 'Plague in seventh-century England', *Past and Present* 156, 7–54.

Malmer, B. (1981) 'Monetary circulation in south-eastern Sweden *c.* 1350–1500 in the light of three major church-finds', *Nordisk Numismatisk Årsskrift*, 147–59.

Manby, T. G. (1986) *Thwing, Excavation and Field Archaeology in East Yorkshire 1986: the Anglo-Saxon Cemetery*, Yorkshire Archaeological Society Prehistoric Research Section, Leeds.

Manby, T. G. (1988) 'Excavation and field archaeology in East Yorkshire: the Thwing project 1973–87' in *Council for British Archaeology Group 4 Forum 1988*, Yorkshire Archaeological Society, Leeds, 16–18.

Marazzi, F. (1996) 'San Vincenzo al Volturno tra VIII e IX secolo: il percorso della grande crescita' in *San Vincenzo al Volturno: Cultura, Istituzioni, Economia*

Miscellanea Vulturnense 2, ed. F. Marazzi, Abbazia di Montecassino, Monte Cassinoa and Monteroduni, 41–92.

Margary, I. D. (1946) 'Roman roads in West Kent', *Archaeologia Cantiana* 59, 29–63.

Margary, I. D. (1948) 'Notes on Roman roads in East Kent', *Archaeologia Cantiana* 61, 126–32.

Margary, I. D. (1973) *Roman Roads in Britain*, 3rd edn, John Baker, London.

Margham, J. (1992) 'Carisbrooke: a study in settlement morphology', *Southern History* 14, 1–28.

Matthews, K. (1999) 'The Iron Age of north-west England and Irish Sea trade' in *Northern Exposure: Interpretative Devolution and the Iron Ages in Britain* Leicester Archaeological Monographs 4, ed. B. Bevan, Leicester University Archaeological Research Centre, Leicester, 173–95.

Mawer, A. (1924 reprinted 1980) *The Chief Elements Used in English Place-Names* (pt ii of Stenton, F. M. and Mawer, A. *Introduction to the Study of English Place-Names*) English Place-Name Society, Cambridge University Press, Cambridge.

Mawer, A. and Stenton, F. M. with Houghton, F. T. S. (1927 reprinted 1969) *The Place-Names of Worcestershire* English Place-Name Society 4, Cambridge University Press, Cambridge.

Mazo Karras, R. (1985) 'Seventh-century jewellery from Frisia, a re-examination', *Anglo-Saxon Studies in Archaeology and History* 4, 159–77.

McCormick, M. (2001) *Origins of the European Economy: Communications and Commerce AD 300–900*, Cambridge University Press, Cambridge.

McKitterick, R. ed. (1995) *The New Cambridge Medieval History Vol. 2 c. 700–900*, Cambridge University Press, Cambridge.

Meaney, A. (1964) *A Gazetteer of Early Anglo-Saxon Burial Sites*, George Allen and Unwin, London.

Meier, D. (1994) *Die wikingerzeitliche Siedlung von Kosel (Kosel-West), Kreis Rendsburg-Eckernförde*, Wachholtz, Neumünster.

Menuge, N. J. (2000) 'The foundation myth: some Yorkshire monasteries and the landscape agenda', *Landscapes* 1:1, 22–37.

Metcalf, D. M. (1974) 'Sceattas found at the Iron Age hill fort of Walbury Camp, Berkshire', *British Numismatic Journal* 44, 1–12.

Metcalf, D. M. (1976) 'Twelve notes on sceatta finds' *British Numismatic Journal* 46, 1–18.

Metcalf, D. M. (1980) 'Continuity and change in English monetary history c.973–1086, part 1', *British Numismatic Journal* 50, 20–49.

Metcalf, D. M. (1984a) 'Monetary circulation in southern England in the first half of the eighth century' in *Sceattas in England and on the Continent* BAR Brit. Ser. 128, eds D. Hill and D. M. Metcalf, British Archaeological Reports, Oxford, 27–71.

Metcalf, D. M. (1984b) 'Twenty-five notes on sceatta finds' in *Sceattas in England and on the Continent* BAR Brit. Ser. 128, eds D. Hill and D. M. Metcalf, British Archaeological Reports, Oxford, 193–205.

Metcalf, D. M. (1987) 'A topographical commentary on the coin finds from ninth-century Northumbria *c.* 780-*c.* 870' in *Coinage in Ninth-Century Northumbria* BAR Brit. Ser. 180, ed. D. M. Metcalf, British Archaeological Reports, Oxford, 361–82.

Metcalf, D. M. (1988a) 'The coins' in *Southampton Finds, Volume 1: The Coins and*

Pottery from Hamwic Southampton Archaeology Monographs 4, ed. P. Andrews, Southampton City Museums, Southampton, 17–59.

Metcalf, D. M. (1988b) 'Monetary expansion and recession: interpreting the distribution-patterns of seventh- and eighth-century coins' in *Coins and the Archaeologist*, ed. J. Casey and R. Reece, 2nd edn, Seaby, London, 230–53.

Metcalf, D. M. (1988c) 'A plate of Anglo-Saxon coins found at Reculver, Kent, in the eighteenth century', *British Numismatic Journal* 58, 126–9.

Metcalf, D. M. (1989) 'The availability and uses of gold coinage in England *c.* 580–670: Kentish primacy reconsidered' in *Festskrift till Lars O. Lagerqvist* Numismatiska meddelanden 37, eds U. Ehrensvärd *et al.*, Svenska Numismatiska Föreningen, Stockholm, 267–74.

Metcalf D. M. (1993–4) *Thrymsas and Sceattas in the Ashmolean Museum Oxford* 3 vols, Royal Numismatic Society/Ashmolean Museum, London.

Metcalf, D. M. (1998a) *An Atlas of Anglo-Saxon and Norman Coin Finds, 973–1086*, Royal Numismatic Society/Ashmolean Museum, London.

Metcalf, D. M. (1998b) 'The monetary economy of ninth-century England south of the Humber: a topographical analysis' in *Kings, Currency, and Alliances*, eds M. A. S. Blackburn and D. M. Dumville, Boydell Press, Woodbridge, 167–97.

Metcalf D. M. (2001) 'Determining the mint-attribution of East Anglian sceattas through regression analysis', *British Numismatic Journal* 70, 1–11.

Metcalf, D. M. and Northover, P. (1985) 'Debasement of the coinage in southern England in the age of king Alfred', *Numismatic Chronicle* 145, 150–76.

Metcalf, D. M. and Northover, P. (1989) 'Coinage and alloys from the time of Offa and Charlemagne to *c.* 864', *Numismatic Chronicle* 149, 101–20.

Metcalf, D. M. and Walker, D. R. (1967) 'The "wolf" sceattas', *British Numismatic Journal* 36, 11–28.

Mikkelsen, D. K. (1999) 'Single farm or village? Reflections on the settlement structure of the Iron Age and the Viking Period' in *Settlement and Landscape, Proceedings of a Conference in Aarhus, Denmark, May 4–7 1998,* eds C. Fabech and J. Ringtved, Jutland Archaeological Society/Aarhus University Press, Højbjerg, 177–93.

Miller, E. (1951) *The Abbey and Bishopric of Ely* Cambridge Studies in Medieval Life and Thought New Series 1, Cambridge University Press, Cambridge.

Mills, A. (1991) *A Dictionary of English Place-Names*, Oxford University Press, Oxford.

Milne, G. and Richards, J. D. (1992) *Wharram: A Study of Settlement on the Yorkshire Wolds, VII. Two Anglo-Saxon Buildings and Associated Finds* York University Archaeological Publications 9, York University, York.

Mitchell, J. (1985) 'An early medieval enamel from San Vincenzo al Volturno' in *San Vincenzo al Volturno: The Archaeology, Art and Territory of an Early Medieval Monastery* BAR Int. Ser. 252, eds R. Hodges and J. Mitchell, British Archaeological Reports, Oxford, 177–84.

Mitchell, J. (1992) 'A carved ivory head from San Vincenzo al Volturno', *Journal of the British Archaeological Association* 45, 66–76.

Mitchell, J. (1994a) 'The display of script and the uses of painting in Longobard Italy' in *Testo e immagine nell'alto medioevo: XLI Settimana di Studio del Centro Italiano di Studi sull'Alto Medioevo. Spoleto 15–21 aprile 1993*, CISAM, Spoleto, 887–954.

Mitchell, J. (1994b) 'Fashion in metal; a set of sword-belt mounts and bridal furniture from San Vincenzo al Volturno' in *Studies in Medieval Art and*

Architecture Presented to Peter Lasko, eds D. Buckton and T. A. Heslop, Alan Sutton, London, 127–56.

Mitchell, J. (1996) 'Monastic guest quarters and workshops: the example of San Vincenzo al Volturno' in *Wohn- und Wirtschaftsbauten frühmittelalterlicher Klöster*, ed. H. -R. Sennhauser, Hochschulverlag an der ETH Zürich, Zürich, 127–55.

Mitchell, J. (2001) 'A set of sword-belt mounts of iron inlaid with silver and associated bridle furniture' in *San Vincenzo al Volturno 3: The 1980–86 Excavations Part III: The Finds*, eds J. Mitchell and I. L. Hansen, CISAM, Spoleto, 393–410.

Mitchell, J. and Hansen, I. L. eds (2001) *San Vincenzo al Volturno 3: The 1980–86 Excavations Part III: The Finds*, CISAM, Spoleto.

Møller-Hansen, K. and Høier, H. (2000) 'Næs – en vikingebebyggelse med hørproduktion', *KUML* 2000: Årbog for Jysk Arkæologisk Selskab, 59–89.

Monneret De Villard, U. (1920) 'Note sul memoratorio dei maestri commacini', *Archivio Storico Lombardo* 4, 1–16.

Moore, I. E. (1988) *The Archaeology of Roman Suffolk*, Suffolk County Council, Ipswich.

Moran, M. (2000) 'Produzione di laterizi in un monastero meridionale in epoca carolingia: San Vincenzo al Volturno (Isernia)' in *I laterizi nell'alto medioevo italiano*, eds S. Gelichi and P. Novara, Società di studi ravennati, Ravenna, 169–84.

Moreland, J. (1985) 'A monastic workshop and glass production at San Vincenzo al Volturno, Molise' in *San Vincenzo al Volturno: The Archaeology, Art and Territory of an Early Medieval Monastery* BAR Int. Ser. 252, eds R. Hodges and J. Mitchell, British Archaeological Reports, Oxford, 37–59.

Morris, E. L. and Dickinson, T. (2000) 'Early Saxon graves and grave-goods' in *Excavations at Carisbrooke Castle, Isle of Wight, 1921–1996*, ed. C. J. Young, Wessex Archaeology, Salisbury, 86–97.

Morris, J. (1973) *The Age of Arthur*, Weidenfeld and Nicholson, London.

Morris, R. (1989) *Churches in the Landscape*, Dent, London.

Morton, A. D. ed. (1992) *Excavations at Hamwic Vol. 1: Excavations 1946–83, Excluding Six Dials and Melbourne Street* CBA Research Report 84, Council for British Archaeology, London.

Myres J. N. L. and Southern W. H. (1973) *The Anglo-Saxon Cemetery at Sancton, East Yorkshire* Hull Museum Publication 218, Hull Museum, Hull.

Nash-Williams, V. E. (1950) *The Early Christian Monuments of Wales*, University of Wales Press, Cardiff.

Naylor, J. (2001) 'York and its region in the eighth and ninth centuries AD: an archaeological study', *Oxford Journal of Archaeology* 20 (1), 79–105.

Nenk, B. S. *et al.* (1991) 'Medieval Britain and Ireland in 1990', *Medieval Archaeology* 35, 126–238.

Nenk, B. S. *et al.* (1992) 'Medieval Britain and Ireland in 1991', *Medieval Archaeology* 36, 184–308.

Newman, J. (1989) 'East Anglian Kingdom Survey – final interim report on the south-east Suffolk survey', *Bulletin of the Sutton Hoo Research Committee* 6, 17–20.

Newman, J. (1992) 'The Late Roman and Anglo-Saxon settlement pattern in the Sandlings of Suffolk' in *The Age of Sutton Hoo*, ed. M. O. H. Carver, Boydell and Brewer, Woodbridge, 25–38.

Newman, J. (1996) 'The true provenance of the Woodbridge sceatta hoard', *The British Numismatic Journal* 65, 217–18.

Newman, J. (1999) '*Wics*, trade and hinterlands: the Ipswich region' in *Anglo-Saxon Trading Centres: Beyond the Emporia*, ed. M. Anderton, Cruithne Press, Glasgow, 32–48.

Nielsen, A. -L. (1997) 'Pagan cultic and votive acts at Borg. An expression of the central significance of the farmstead in the Late Iron Age' in *Visions of the Past. Trends and Traditions in Swedish Medieval Archaeology* Lund Studies in Medieval Archaeology 19, eds H. Andersson, P. Carelli and L. Ersgård, Riksantikvarieämbetet, Stockholm, 373–92.

Nielsen, A. -L. and Lindeblad, K. (1999) 'The king's manor at Borg. Changes in space and time 700–1500 AD' in *Settlement and Landscape. Proceedings of a Conference in Aarhus, Denmark, May 4–7 1998*, eds C. Fabech and J. Ringtved, Jutland Archaeological Society/Aarhus University Press, Højbjerg, 478–9.

Nielsen, H. (1997) 'Et regionalt rigdomscenter i Sydvestsjælland' in ... *Gick Grendel att söka det höga huset ... Arkeologiska källor till aristokratiska miljöer i Skandinavien under yngre järnålder*, eds J. Callmer and E. Rosengren, Halland länsmuseer, Halmstad, 55–70.

Nielsson, T. (1994) 'Stentinget – en boplads med handel og håndværk fra germansk jernalder og vikingetid', *Vendsyssel nu & da* 14, 64–77.

Nijboer, A. J. and van Reekum, J. E. (1999) 'An examination of the golden disc-on-bow brooch from Wijnaldum' in *The Excavations at Wijnaldum. Reports on Frisia in Roman and Medieval Times*, eds J. C. Besteman, J. M. Bos, D. A. Gerrets, H. A. Heidinga and J. de Koning, A. A. Balkema, Rotterdam, 203–17.

O'Grady, M. M. (1979) 'Hedgerows and tracks', *Archaeologia Cantiana* 94, 111–26.

Palmer, J. B. (1997) *The Siting of Late Saxon Towns: An Investigation of Their Origins*, Unpublished MSt Thesis, University of Oxford.

Palmer, J. B. (1998) *The Hinterland of Wics: An Investigative Study*, Unpublished MPhil Thesis, University of Oxford.

Parfitt, K. (1999) 'Anglo-Saxon Eastry: some recent discoveries and excavations', *Archaeologia Cantiana* 118, 45–53.

Parkhouse, J. (1997) 'The distribution and exchange of Mayen lava quernstones in Early Medieval north-western Europe' in *Trade in Medieval Europe* Papers of the Medieval Europe Brugge 1997 Conference 3, eds G. de Boe and F. Verhaeghe, Instituut voor het Archaeologische Patrimonium, Zellik, 97–105.

Patterson, H. (1985) 'The late Roman and early medieval pottery from Molise' in *San Vincenzo al Volturno: the Archaeology, Art and Territory of an Early Medieval Monastery* BAR Int. Ser. 252, eds R. Hodges and J. Mitchell, British Archaeological Reports, Oxford, 83–110.

Patterson, H. (2001) 'The pottery' in *San Vincenzo al Volturno 3: The 1980–86 Excavations Part III: The Finds*, eds J. Mitchell and I. L. Hansen, CISAM, Spoleto, 69–128.

Patterson J. (1985) 'A city called Samnium?' in *San Vincenzo al Volturno: the Archaeology, Art and Territory of an Early Medieval Monastery* BAR Int. Ser. 252, eds R. Hodges and J. Mitchell, British Archaeological Reports, Oxford, 185–99.

Pelteret, D. A. E. (1995) *Slavery in Early Medieval England*, Boydell Press, Woodbridge.

Pestell, T. J. (2001a) 'Monastic foundation strategies in the Early Norman diocese of Norwich' in *Proceedings of the Battle Conference Anglo-Norman Studies* 24, ed. J. Gillingham, Boydell and Brewer, Woodbridge, 199–229.

Pestell, T. J. (2001b) 'New surveys at Bromholm Priory', *Church Archaeology* 4, 52–4.

Pestell, T. J. (forthcoming) *Monasteries and Landscapes. Foundation Strategies in East Anglia* c. *650–1200* Studies in Anglo-Saxon History, Boydell Press, Woodbridge.

Philp, B. (1965) 'Report, 1965: Faversham', *Archaeologia Cantiana* 80, li–lii.

Philpott, R. A. (1998) 'Three Byzantine coins found near the north Wirral coast in Merseyside', *Transactions of the Historic Society of Lancashire and Cheshire* 148, 197–202.

Philpott, R. A. (1999) 'Recent archaeological finds from Merseyside and their archaeological significance', *Medieval Archaeology* 43, 194–202.

Pirie, E. J. E. (1986a) *Post-Roman Coins from York Excavations 1971–81* The Archaeology of York 18.1, York Archaeological Trust, London, 59–68.

Pirie, E. J. E. (1986b) 'Finds of "sceattas" and "stycas" of Northumbria', in *Anglo-Saxon Monetary History*, ed. M. A. S. Blackburn, Leicester University Press, Leicester, 67–90.

Pirie, E. J. E. (1997) 'The Early Medieval coins' in P. Hill, *Whithorn and St Ninian: the Excavations of a Monastic Town 1984–91*, Sutton, Stroud, 332–45.

Pirie, E. J. E. (2000) *Thrymsas, Sceattas and Stycas of Northumbria. An Inventory of Finds Recorded to 1997*, Galata Print, Llanfyllin.

Plattner, S. M. (1976) 'Periodic trade in developing areas without markets' in *Regional Analysis Vol. 1: Economic Systems*, ed. C. Smith, Academic Press, London, 69–90.

Platts, G. (1985) *Land and People in Medieval Lincolnshire* A History of Lincolnshire 4, The Society for Lincolnshire History and Archaeology, Lincoln.

Plunkett, S. J. (1999) 'The Anglo-Saxon loom from Pakenham, Suffolk', *Proceedings of the Suffolk Institute of Archaeology* 30, 277–98.

Raby, F. J. E. (1934) *A History of Secular Latin Poetry in the Middle Ages* 2 vols, Clarendon Press, Oxford.

Redknap, M. (1991) 'The Saxon pottery from Barking Abbey, London. Part 1: local wares', *The London Archaeologist* 6 (13), 353–9.

Redknap, M. (1992) 'The Saxon pottery from Barking Abbey, London. Part 2: the continental imports', *The London Archaeologist* 6 (14), 378–88.

Redknap, M. (2000) *Vikings in Wales: An Archaeological Quest*, National Museums and Galleries of Wales, Cardiff.

Renfrew, C. (1975) 'Trade as action at a distance' in *Ancient Civilizations and Trade*, eds J. Sabloff and C. C. Lamberg-Karlovsky, University of New Mexico Press, Albuquerque, 3–59.

Renfrew, C. (1977) 'Alternative models for exchange and spatial distribution' in *Exchange Systems in Prehistory*, eds T. K. Earle and J. E. Ericson, Academic Press, New York, 71–90.

Resi, H. G. (1987) 'Reflections on Viking Age local trade in stone products' in *Proceedings of the Tenth Viking Congress: Larkollen, Norway, 1985*, ed. J. E. Knirk, *Universitets Oldsaksamlings Skrifter* New Series 9, 95–102.

Reynolds, A. J. (1998a) *Anglo-Saxon Law and the Landscape*, Unpublished PhD Thesis, University College London.

Reynolds, A. (1998b) 'Executions and hard Anglo-Saxon justice', *British Archaeology* 31, 8–9.

Richards, J. D. (1995) 'An inscribed chalk weight from Cottam', *Medieval Archaeology* 38, 167–9.

Richards, J. D. (1999a) 'Cottam: An Anglian and Anglo-Scandinavian settlement on the Yorkshire Wolds', *Archaeological Journal* 156, 1–110.

Richards, J. D. (1999b) 'What's so special about 'productive sites'? Middle Saxon settlements in Northumbria' in *The Making of Kingdoms,* eds T. Dickinson and D. Griffiths, *Anglo-Saxon Studies in Archaeology and History* 10, 71–80.

Richards, J. D. (1999c) 'Anglo-Saxon Settlements of the Golden Age' in *Northumbria's Golden Age,* ed. J. Hawkes and S. Mills, Sutton Publishing Limited, Stroud, 44–54.

Richards, J. D. (2000) 'The Anglo-Saxon and Anglo-Scandinavian evidence' in *Wharram: A Study of Settlement in the Yorkshire Wolds VIII: The South Manor Area* York University Archaeological Publications 10, eds P. A. Stamper and R. A. Croft, York University, York, 195–200.

Richards, J. D. (in prep.) 'A Romano-British farmstead at Cottam, East Yorkshire'.

Rigold, S. E. (1961) 'The supposed see of Dunwich', *Journal of the British Archaeological Association* 24, 55–9.

Rigold, S. E. (1969) 'Recent investigations into the earliest defences of Carisbrooke Castle', *Chateau Gaillard* 3, 128–38.

Rigold, S. E. (1972) 'Sturry from 500 AD to Domesday' in *Sturry – the Changing Scene,* ed. K. H. McIntosh, K. H. McIntosh, Ramsgate.

Rigold, S. E. (1975) 'The Sutton Hoo coins in the light of the contemporary background of coinage in England' in *The Sutton Hoo Ship-Burial I,* ed. R. L. S. Bruce-Mitford, British Museum Press, London, 653–77.

Rigold, S. E. (1977) 'Small change in the light of medieval site-finds' in *Edwardian Monetary Affairs (1279–1344)* BAR Brit. Ser. 36, ed. N. J. Mayhew, British Archaeological Reports, Oxford, 59–80.

Rigold, S. E. and Metcalf, D. M. (1977) 'A check-list of English finds of sceattas', *British Numismatic Journal* 47, 31–52.

Rigold, S. E. and Metcalf, D. M. (1984) 'A revised check-list of English finds of sceattas' in *Sceattas in England and on the Continent* BAR Brit Ser 128, eds D. Hill and D. M. Metcalf, British Archaeological Reports, Oxford, 245–68.

Roesdahl, E. (1982) *Viking Age Denmark,* British Museum, London.

Rogerson, A. (1995) *A Late Neolithic, Saxon and Medieval Site at Middle Harling, Norfolk* East Anglian Archaeology 74, Norfolk Museums Service, Gressenhall.

Rogerson, A. and Silvester, R. J. (1986) 'Middle Saxon occupation at Hay Green, Terrington St Clement', *Norfolk Archaeology* 39, 320–2.

Ross, S. (1991) *Dress Pins from Anglo-Saxon England: Their Production and Typo-Chronological Development,* Unpublished DPhil Thesis, University of Oxford.

Rovelli, A. (1992) 'Circolazione monetaria e formulari notarili nell'Italia altomedievale', *Bullettino Istituto Storico Italiano per il Medio Evo* 98, 109–44.

Rovelli, A. (1994) 'La funzione della moneta tra l'VIII e il X secolo. Un'analisi della documentazione archeologica' in *La storia dell'alto medioevo italiano (VI-X secolo) alla luce dell'archeologia,* eds R. Francovich and G. Noyé, All'Insegna del Giglio, Florence, 521–37.

Russo, D. G. (1998) *Town Origins and Development in Early England,* c. *900–950 AD,* Greenwood Press, London.

Sablerolles, Y. (1999) 'Beads of glass, faience, amber, baked clay and metal, including production waste from glass and amber bead making' in *The Excavations at Wijnaldum. Reports on Frisia in Roman and Medieval Times,* eds J. C. Besteman, J. M. Bos, D. A. Gerrets, H. A. Heidinga and J. de Koning, A. A. Balkema, Rotterdam, 253–86.

Sandnes, J. and Stemshaug, O. (1980) *Norsk Stadnamnleksikon,* 2nd edn, Det Norske Samlaget, Oslo.

Sawyer, B. and Sawyer, P. H. (1993) *Medieval Scandinavia. From Conversion to Reformation c. 800–1500*, University of Minnesota Press, Minneapolis.
Sawyer, P. H. (1965) 'The wealth of England in the eleventh century', *Transactions of the Royal Historical Society* Fifth Series 15, 145–64.
Sawyer, P. H. (1986) 'Early fairs and markets in England and Scandinavia' in *The Market in History*, eds B. L. Anderson and A. J. H. Latham, Croom Helm, London, 59–77.
Sawyer P. H. (1998) *Anglo-Saxon Lincolnshire* A History of Lincolnshire 3, The Society for Lincolnshire History and Archaeology, Lincoln.
Scarfe, N. (1999) 'Domesday churches' in *An Historical Atlas of Suffolk,* eds D. Dymond and E. Martin, 3rd edn, Suffolk County Council, Ipswich, 52–3.
Schmidt, T. (2000) 'Marked, torg og kaupang – språklige vitnemål om handel i middelalderen', *Collegium Medievale* 13, 79–102.
Schmitz, R. (1999) *Das Umfeld von Groß Strömkendorf, Ldkr. Nordwestmecklenburg, in frühslawischer Zeit und die Grabung am Burgwall Ilow, Ldkr. Nordwestmecklenburg, Fdpl. 2*, Unpublished MA Thesis, University of Kiel.
Schmutzhart, D. (1997) *De Terp Tjitsma: Een Studie Naar Ijzeren Voorwerpen uit de Vroege Middeleeuwen*, Unpublished BA Thesis, University of Amsterdam.
Scott, I. R. (1993) *The Evidence From Excavations for Late Iron Age, Roman and Saxon Occupation at Romsey* Test Valley Archaeological Trust Report 28/92 (unpublished).
Scott, I. R. (1996) *Romsey Abbey. Report on the Excavations 1973–91* Hampshire Field Club Monograph 8, Test Valley Archaeological Trust, Winchester.
Scull, C. J. (1990) 'Scales and weights in Early Anglo-Saxon England', *Archaeological Journal* 147, 183–215.
Scull, C. J. (1992) 'Before Sutton Hoo: structures of power and society in early East Anglia' in *The Age of Sutton Hoo*, ed. M. O. H. Carver, Boydell Press, Woodbridge, 3–24.
Scull, C. J. (1993) 'Archaeology, early Anglo-Saxon society and the origins of Anglo-Saxon kingdoms', *Anglo-Saxon Studies in Archaeology and History* 6, 65–82.
Scull, C. (1997) 'Urban centres in pre-Viking England?' in *The Anglo-Saxons from the Migration Period to the Eighth Century: An Ethnographic Perspective*, ed. J. Hines, Boydell Press, Woodbridge, 269–310.
Searle, E. (1988) *Predatory Kinship and the Creation of Norman Power, 840–1066*, University of California Press, Berkeley and London.
Settia, A. A. (1991) *Chiese, strade e fortezze nell'Italia medievale* Italia Sacra, Studi e Documenti di Storia Ecclesiastica 46, Herder Editrice e Libreria, Rome.
Shephard, J. (1979) *Anglo-Saxon Barrows of the Later Sixth and Seventh Centuries AD*, Unpublished PhD Thesis, University of Cambridge
Sherlock, D. (1984) 'The Coins' in V. Fenwick 'Insula de Burgh: Excavations at Burrow Hill, Butley, Suffolk 1978–81', *Anglo-Saxon Studies in Archaeology and History* 3, 44–52.
Sherratt, A. (1996) 'Why Wessex? The Avon river route and river transport in later British prehistory', *Oxford Journal of Archaeology* 15 (2), 211–34.
Silvester, R. J. (1988) *The Fenland Project Number 3: Marshland and the Nar Valley, Norfolk* East Anglian Archaeology 45, Norfolk Museums Service, Gressenhall.
Smith, C. (1976) 'Regional economic systems: linking geographical models and socioeconomic problems' in *Regional Analysis Vol. 1: Economic Systems*, ed. C. Smith, Academic Press, New York, 3–63.
Sørensen, P. Ø. (1994a) 'Houses, farmsteads and settlement pattern in the Gudme area' in *The Archaeology of Gudme and Lundeborg. Papers Presented at a*

Conference at Svendborg, October 1991 Arkæologiske Studier 10, eds P. O. Nielsen, K. Randsborg and H. Thrane, Akademisk Forlag, Copenhagen, 41–7.

Sørensen, P. Ø. (1994b) 'Gudmehallerne. Kongeligt byggeri fra jernalderen', *Nationalmuseets Arbejdsmark* 1994, 25–39.

Sørensen, S. A. and Ulriksen, J. (1996) *Selsø-Vestby. Vikingernes Anløbsplads ved Selsø*, Museet Færgagården, Roskilde.

Spufford, P. (1988) *Money and its Use in Medieval Europe,* Cambridge University Press, Cambridge.

Staf, N. (1933) 'Marknader och marknadsterminer i Sverige' in *Handel och Samfärdsel* Nordisk Kultur 16, eds J. Brøndsted and A. Schück, 191–99.

Stedman, M. (1998) 'Three Early Saxon metalwork finds from the Isle of Wight', *Proceedings of the Hampshire Field Club and Archaeological Society* 53, 109–19.

Steedman, K. (1994) 'The excavation of an Anglo-Saxon site at Riby Cross Roads, Lincolnshire', *Archaeological Journal* 151, 212–306.

Stevenson, J. (1997) 'Ninth century glassware production at San Vincenzo al Volturno, Italy: some new evidence from recent excavations' in *Material Culture in Medieval Europe* Papers of Medieval Europe Brugge 1997 Conference 7, eds G. de Boe and F. Verhaeghe, Instituut voor het Archaeologische Patrimonium, Zellik, 125–36.

Stine, J. H. (1962) 'Temporal aspects of tertiary production elements in Korea' in *Urban Systems and Economic Development*, ed. F. R. Pitts, University of Oregon, Eugene, 68–88.

Stoertz, C. (1997) *Ancient Landscapes of the Yorkshire Wolds, Aerial Photographic Transcription and Analysis*, Royal Commission on Historic Monuments of England, Swindon.

Stott, P. E. F. (1991) 'Saxon and Norman Coins from London' in *Aspects of Saxo-Norman London 2: Finds and Environmental Evidence* LaMAS Special Paper 12, ed. A. G. Vince, London and Middlesex Archaeological Society, London, 279–325.

Stubbs, W. (1862) 'The cathedral diocese and monasteries of Worcester in the eighth century', *Archaeological Journal* 19, 236–52.

Stukelely, W. (1776) *Itinerarium Curiosum*, 2nd edn, Baker and Leigh, London.

Stutz, U. (1909) 'Das karolingische Zehntgebot', *Zeitschrift der Savigny-Stiftung für Rechtsgeschichte* 29, 191–2.

Suchodolski, S. (1996) 'Absence of mind or magic? A few remarks on the so-called small or single coin finds', *Quaderni Ticinesi Numismatica e Antichità Classiche* 25, 317–27

Taayke, E. *et al.* eds (1996) *Het Vroeg-Middeleeuwse Grafveld van Oosterbeintum*, Vereniging voor Terpenonderzoek Jaarverslagen 73–4 (for 1989–90), Groningen.

Tatton-Brown, T. (1984) 'The towns of Kent' in *Anglo-Saxon Towns of Southern England*, ed. J. Haslam, Camelot Press, Chichester, 1–36.

Tatton-Brown, T. (1988) 'The churches of Canterbury diocese in the 11th century' in *Minster and Parish Churches: The Local Church in Transition, 950–1200* Oxford University Committee for Archaeology Monograph 17, ed. J. Blair, Oxford University Committee for Archaeology, Oxford, 105–18.

Taylor, H. M. and Taylor, J. (1980) *Anglo-Saxon Architecture* 2 vols, Cambridge University Press, Cambridge.

Thomas, C. (1988) 'The context of Tintagel; a new model for the diffusion of post-Roman Mediterranean imports', *Cornish Archaeology* 27, 7–25.

Thomas, C. (1990) 'Gallici Nautae de Galliarum Provinciis, a sixth/seventh century trade with Gaul reconsidered', *Medieval Archaeology* 34, 1–26.

Thomas, G. (1996) 'Silver wire strap-ends from East Anglia', *Anglo-Saxon Studies in Archaeology and History* 9, 81–100.

Thomsen, P. O. (1994) 'Lundeborg – an early port of trade in south-east Fünen' in *The Archaeology of Gudme and Lundeborg. Papers Presented at a Conference at Svendborg, October 1991* Arkæologiske Studier 10, eds P. O. Nielsen, K. Randsborg and H. Thrane, Akademisk Forlag, Copenhagen, 23–9.

Tomalin, D. (1977) *Newport Roman Villa*, Isle of Wight County Council, Newport.

Tomalin, D. (1987) *Roman Wight: a Guide Catalogue*, Isle of Wight County Council, Newport.

Tornbjerg, S. Å. (1998) 'Toftegård – en fundrig gård fra sen jernalder og vikingetid' in *Centrala Platser. Centrala Frågor. Samhällsstrukturen under Järnåldern* Acta Archaeologica Lundensia, Series in 8° 28, eds L. Larsson and B. Hårdh, Almquist and Wiksell, Lund, 217–32.

Tulp, C. and Meeks, N. (2000) 'The Tjitsma (Wijnaldum) die: a 7th century tool for making a cross-hatched pattern on gold foil, or a master template?', *Historical Metallurgy* 34 (1), 13–24.

Ulmschneider, K. (1999) 'History, archaeology, and the Isle of Wight in the Middle Saxon period', *Medieval Archaeology* 43, 19–44.

Ulmschneider, K. (2000a) *Markets, Minsters, and Metal-Detectors: The Archaeology of Middle Saxon Lincolnshire and Hampshire Compared* BAR Brit. Ser. 307, Archaeopress, Oxford.

Ulmschneider, K. (2000b) 'Settlement, economy and the 'productive' site in Anglo-Saxon Lincolnshire, AD 650–780', *Medieval Archaeology* 44, 53–79.

Ulriksen, J. (1994) 'Danish sites and settlements with a maritime context, AD 200–1200', *Antiquity* 68, 797–811.

Ulriksen, J. (1998) *Anløbspladser. Besejling og Bebyggelse i Danmark Mellem 200 og 1100 e. Kr.*, Vikingeskibshallen i Roskilde, Roskilde.

Valente, F. (1995) *San Vincenzo al Volturno: architettura ed arte* Miscellanea Vulturnense 1, Abbazia di Montecassino, Monte Cassino and Monteroduni.

Vince, A. and Young, J. (1990–1) 'The East Midlands Anglo-Saxon Pottery Project', *Lincoln Archaeology* 3, 38–9.

Vincent, N. (1999) 'The Foundation of Wormegay Priory', *Norfolk Archaeology* 43, 307–12.

Wade, K. (1980) 'The Anglo Saxon settlement at Bonhunt Farm, Wicken Bonhunt, Essex' in *Archaeology in Essex to AD 1500* CBA Research Report 34, ed. D. Buckley, Council for British Archaeology, London, 96–103.

Wade, K. (1993) 'The urbanisation of East Anglia: – the Ipswich perspective' in *Flatlands and Wetlands: Current Themes in East Anglian Archaeology* East Anglian Archaeology 50, ed. J. Gardiner, Scole Archaeological Committee, Gressenhall, 144–151.

Wade, K. and West, S. E. (1983) 'The origin and development of the Kingdom of East Anglia Project' in *Bulletin of the Sutton Hoo Research Committee* 1, ed. M. O. H. Carver, 18–20.

Wade-Martins, P. (1980) *Excavations in North Elmham Park, 1967–1972* East Anglian Archaeology 9, 2 vols, Norfolk Archaeological Unit, Gressenhall.

Wade-Martins, P. ed. (1997) *An Historical Atlas of Norfolk*, Norfolk Museums Service, Norwich.

Waterbolk, H. T. (1991) 'Ezinge' in *Reallexikon der Germanischen Altertumskunde* 8/1–2, ed. V. Grasshoff, Walter de Gruyter, Berlin and New York, 60–76.

Watt, M. (1991) 'Sorte Muld. Høvdingesæde og kultcentrum fra Bornholms yngre jernalder' in *Fra Stamme til Stat i Danmark 2: Høvdingesamfund og Kongemagt,* eds P. Mortensen and B. M. Rasmussen, Aarhus Universitetsforlag, Aarhus, 189–97.

Webster, L. and Backhouse, J. eds (1991) *The Making of England: Anglo-Saxon Art and Culture, AD 600–900*, British Museum Press, London.

Webster, L. E. and Cherry, J. (1972) 'Medieval Britain in 1971', *Medieval Archaeology* 16, 147–212.

Weinmann, C. (1994) *Der Hausbau in Skandinavien vom Neolithikum bis zum Mittelalter*, Walter de Gruyter, Berlin.

Welch, M. (1991) 'Contacts across the Channel between the fifth and seventh centuries: a review of the archaeological evidence' in *Studien zur Sachsenforschung* 7, ed. H. -J. Hß ler, Lax, Hildesheim, 261–9.

Welldon-Finn, R. (1962) 'Hampshire' in *The Domesday Geography of South-East England*, eds H. C. Darby and E. M. J. Campbell, Cambridge University Press, Cambridge, 287–363.

West S. E. (1985) *West Stow: The Anglo-Saxon Village* East Anglian Archaeology 24, 2 vols, Suffolk Archaeological Unit, Bury St Edmunds.

West, S. E. (1998) *A Corpus of Anglo-Saxon Material from Suffolk*, East Anglian Archaeology 84, Suffolk County Council Archaeology Service, Bury St Edmunds.

West, S. E., Scarfe, N. and Cramp, R. (1984) 'Iken, St Botolph and the coming of East Anglian Christianity', *Proceedings of the Suffolk Institute of Archaeology and History* 35, 279–301.

White, R. *et al.* (in prep.) Report on the Excavations at Cefn Cwmwd, Anglesey by Birmingham University Field Archaeology Unit.

Whitelock, D. (1972) 'The pre-Viking age Church in East Anglia', *Anglo-Saxon England* 1, 1–22.

Wickham, C. (1981) *Early Medieval Italy. Central Power and Local Society 400–1000*, Macmillan, London.

Wickham, C. J. (1985) 'The *terra* of San Vincenzo al Volturno in the eighth to twelfth centuries: the historical framework' in *San Vincenzo al Volturno: the Archaeology, Art and Territory of an Early Medieval Monastery* BAR Int. Ser. 252, eds R. Hodges and J. Mitchell, British Archaeological Reports, Oxford, 227–58.

Wickham, C. (1995) 'Monastic lands and monastic patrons' in *San Vincenzo al Volturno 2: The 1980–86 Excavations Part II* Archaeological Monographs of the British School at Rome 9, ed. R. Hodges, British School at Rome, London, 138–52.

Wietrzichowski, F. (1993) 'Untersuchungen zu den Anfängen des frühmittelalterlichen Seehandels im südlichen Ostseeraum unter besonderer Berücksichtigung der Grabungsergebnisse von Groß Strömkendorf', *Wismarer Studien zur Archäologie und Geschichte* 3, 1–112.

Williams, A. (1992) 'A bell-house and a burh-geat: lordly residences in England before the Norman Conquest' in *Medieval Knighthood IV: Papers from the fifth Strawberry Hill Conference 1990*, ed. C. Harper-Bill and R. Harvey, Boydell Press, Woodbridge, 221–40.

Williams, R. J. (1993) *Pennylands and Hartigans. Two Iron Age and Saxon Sites in Milton Keynes* Buckinghamshire Archaeological Society Monograph 4, Buckinghamshire Archaeological Society, Aylesbury.

Williamson, T. (1993) *The Origins of Norfolk*, Manchester University Press, Manchester.

Wilson, D. M. (1958) 'Medieval Britain in 1957', *Medieval Archaeology* 2, 183–9.

Wilson, D. M. (1964) *Anglo-Saxon Ornamental Metalwork 700–1100 in the British Museum*, British Museum, London.

Wilson, D. M. (1984) *Anglo-Saxon Art from the Seventh Century to the Norman Conquest*, Thames and Hudson, London.
Wise, P. J. and Seaby, W. A. (1995) 'Finds from a new "productive site" at Bidford-on-Avon, Warwickshire', *Birmingham and Warwickshire Archaeological Society Transactions* 99, 57–64.
Witney, K. P. (1976) *The Jutish Forest*, Athlone Press, London.
Witney, K. P. (1982) *The Kingdom of Kent*, Phillimore, Chichester.
Wood, I. (1983) *The Merovingian North Sea* Occasional Papers on Medieval Topics 1, Viktoria Bokförlag, Alingsås.
Yorke, B. (1989) 'The Jutes of Hampshire and Wight and the origins of Wessex' in *The Origins of the Anglo-Saxon Kingdoms* Studies in the Early History of Britain, ed. S. Bassett, Leicester University Press, London, 84–96.
Young, A. (1813 facsimile reprint 1969) *General View of the Agriculture of the County of Suffolk*, Sherwood, Neely and Jones, London.
Young, C. J. (1983) 'Carisbrooke Castle to 1100', *Chateau Gaillard* 11, 281–8.
Young, C. J. (2000) *Excavations at Carisbrooke Castle, Isle of Wight, 1921–1996*, Wessex Archaeology, Salisbury.
Youngs, S. (1999) 'A Northumbrian plaque from Asby Winderwath, Cumbria' in *Northumbria's Golden Age*, eds J. Hawkes and S. Mills, Stroud, Sutton, 281–95.
Youngs, S. M. *et al.* (1984) 'Medieval Britain and Ireland in 1983', *Medieval Archaeology* 28, 203–65.
Youngs, S. M. *et al.* (1986) 'Medieval Britain and Ireland in 1985', *Medieval Archaeology* 30, 114–98.
Youngs, S. M. *et al.* (1988) 'Medieval Britain and Ireland in 1987', *Medieval Archaeology* 32, 225–314.
Yver, J. (1969) 'Les Premières Institutions du Duché de Normandie', *Settimane di Centro Italiano di Studi sull'Alto Medioevo* 16, CISAM, Spoleto, 299–366.

Index